Listening to Reason

CULTURE, SUBJECTIVITY, AND NINETEENTH-CENTURY MUSIC

Michael P. Steinberg

PRINCETON UNIVERSITY PRESS

PRINCETON AND OXFORD

Copyright © 2004 by Princeton University Press
Published by Princeton University Press, 41 William Street,
Princeton, New Jersey 08540
In the United Kingdom: Princeton University Press, 3 Market Place,
Woodstock, Oxfordshire OX20 1SY

Library of Congress Cataloging-in-Publication Data

Steinberg, Michael P.
Listening to reason : culture, subjectivity, and nineteenth-century
music / Michael P. Steinberg.
p.   cm.
Includes bibliographical references (p.) and index.

Contents: Staging subjectivity in the Mozart/Da Ponte operas. Staging subjectivity ;
Don Giovanni and the scene of patricide ; Le nozze di Figaro and the scene of
emancipation; Così fan tutte and the scene of instruction — Beethoven: heroism and
abstraction. Heroism and abstraction ; Heroism and anxiety ; Fidelio ; The symphony
no. 9 — Canny and uncanny histories in Biedermeier music. Biedermeier music ;
Mendelssohn's canny histories ; Schumann's uncanny histories; Back to Schubert —
The family romances of music drama. The family romances of music drama ; Siegmund's
death ; Subjectivity and identity — The voice of the people at the moment of the nation.
People and nations ; Brahms, 1868 ; Verdi, 1874 ; Dvořák, 1890 — Minor modernisms.
Music trauma, or, is there life after Wagner? ; Three fins de siècle ; The road into the
open — The musical unconscious.

ISBN: 0-691-11685-7 (alk. paper)
1. Music—19th century—History and criticism. 2. Subjectivity in music.
3. Cultural awareness. I. Title.

ML196.S74 2004
780'.9'034—dc21   2003053592

British Library Cataloging-in-Publication Data is available

This book has been composed in Goudy
Printed on acid-free paper. ∞
www.pupress.princeton.edu
Printed in the United States of America

10 9 8 7 6 5 4 3 2 1

For Carl Schorske and Leon Botstein

Contents

Illustrations

Preface

"The origins of this book," a colleague of mine once wrote, "are obscure even to myself, but the occasion of its conception I remember quite vividly."[1] In my own case, the occasion that launched this book is indeed clear to me, though at the time I had no clue of the eventual project's shape. In August 1990 I gave a short preconcert lecture on Brahms at the first Bard Music Festival. To an audience awaiting a performance of the D minor piano concerto, I argued that the urgency and debate in Brahms's musical texture engaged cultural issues and differences as well as musical ones, that Brahms's late nineteenth-century musical discourse had incorporated music's capacity to think, to argue, and to develop the position of a thinking, feeling subject in juxtaposition with a multiple and challenging cultural and political world. "Absolute" music, I argued, lived in the world and spoke to it. Here was the first kernel of this book's argument of the importance of nineteenth-century music as a language of subjectivity. I gave that lecture and ultimately wrote this book as a cultural historian committed to music not only as an object of study (or a vehicle of pleasure) but as a mode of cultural experience and understanding and, itself, as a potential language of cultural analysis.

What we colloquially refer to as "classical" European music (a category looser than and distinct from that of the classical style or period) accrues through the nineteenth century as a mutually referential world of unusual coherence. The composers and works I engage in this book are generally well known to their peers and successors. In a process itself reflective of that coherence, this book's argument has evolved incrementally. Through the 1990s, the project was nurtured consistently by my lecture and essay assignments at the Bard Festival and its annual reconsideration of a single composer: Mendelssohn in 1991, Strauss in 1992, Dvořák in 1993, Schumann in 1994, Bartók in 1995. A volume of essays and documents on each year's composer "and his world" has appeared annually since 1990 from Princeton University Press; this book's chapter 4, on Mendelssohn and Schumann, contains arguments initially explored in essays I wrote for these collections. In the early 1990s I introduced aspects of the project into my cultural history courses at Cornell, and by the time of a sabbatical year in 1995–96 I had developed the conviction that there should be a book here, though there certainly wasn't one yet. A first draft was complete in 1998; its revisions continued to benefit from the

---

[1] David Warren Sabean, *Power in the Blood: Popular Culture and Village Discourse in Early Modern Germany* (Cambridge: Cambridge University Press, 1984), p. ix.

Bard Festival, specifically from my editorial work on *Beethoven and His World* with Scott Burnham in 2000 and from symposia held in conjunction with the Beethoven, Debussy, and Mahler festivals of 2000 through 2002.

There were other venues as well. Since 1992 I have worked as a coeditor of the *Musical Quarterly*, responsible for the section called "Music and Culture." Ongoing discussions with fellow editors and contributors have guided my sense of the purview and potential of that rubric. My initial sustained attention to Mozart was occasioned by the Mozart year of 1991 and my work with the bicentennial Mozart symposium sponsored by the Woodrow Wilson Center in Washington, D.C. The Amsterdam School for Cultural Analysis (ASCA) and the Internationales Forschungszentrum Kulturwissenschaften (IFK) in Vienna have become intellectual homes even more than scholarly venues; their work and style have shown how to connect the international with the interdisciplinary, aesthetic analysis with cultural and political analysis. I think especially of the symposium on the cultural analysis of the senses, which I coconvened with Mieke Bal in Amsterdam in 1998, and the one on opera and cultural analysis that took place in Vienna in 1999. (The papers from the latter appeared in the *Musical Quarterly* [vol. 85, no. 1].)

The chapters that follow here on Beethoven and Wagner began to take shape in 1995–96—the year, it seemed, of the roving Wagner conference; the year also of a most creative and refreshing *Ring* cycle at the Lyric Opera of Chicago. Visiting appointments at the University of Chicago and Princeton that year offered generous venues for idea-testing with colleagues and students; it is a pleasure to record my gratitude simultaneously and so relevantly to my three universities: Princeton, Chicago, and Cornell. At Cornell, our weekly European history and music colloquia and the seminars of the Society for the Humanities have been especially generous sources of exchange and critique.

"From Mozart to Mahler" might thus have appeared in my subtitle; these two composers indeed frame my discussion in multiple ways—temporal, spatial, and cultural. First, they mark in musical as well as historical terms what we can almost conventionally refer to as the "long nineteenth century," a period that commences with the crises of old regimes in Europe and ends in 1914–18 with the debacle of modern warfare, the collapse of empires, and a new era of the machine. The "age of revolution," in the felicitous phrase E. J. Hobsbawm used to juxtapose the industrial revolution in England with the French Revolutions of 1789 and 1848, ushers in a period that another historian has called "classical modernity."[2] Modernity's scope includes society as

---

[2] E. J. Hobsbawm, *The Age of Revolution, 1789-1848* (New York: Mentor Books, 1962); Detlev J. K. Peukert, *The Weimar Republic: The Crisis of Classical Modernity* (New York: Hill and Wang, 1992).

well as its imaginations and its arts; its "classical" aspect relates, I would suggest, to its anthropomorphisms, including the nineteenth-century focus on the human being who can still believe that some form of emancipation is possible and who orients work and imagination toward that goal. New modes of subjectivity are defined, debated, and defended, and music plays a key role in that process. After 1918, European (as indeed American) society changes decisively again, as mass politics and mass culture infuse and redefine its terrain, both in essential cooperation with technology. Subjectivities are decentered, and their correlative soundscapes alter too, forgoing psychological coherence for new abstractions and multiplicities and forgoing anthropomorphic argument for a soundscape more reflective of the expanding technological referential world. To Walter Benjamin's observation that the period of the Great War of 1914–18 bequeathed the machine gun and the movie camera to the world, we must add the recognition of sound recording technology. If, from a central European vantage point, the nineteenth century ends with Gustav Mahler and the twentieth begins with Arnold Schoenberg, that shift remains undercontextualized and underinterpreted a century later, especially with regard to musical technology. Schoenberg's project, and one reason for its persistent underexposure, involves the difficult conjunction of his ethical, epistemological project and his deanthropomorphized soundscape.

"From Mozart to Mahler" implies also a location in space as well as in time, a reference to central Europe and to the city of Vienna. Although this book offers no sustained focus on nor analysis of Vienna, its repeated referential and circumstantial attention to Vienna does say something about the way Viennese history, like the musical history it closely partners, incorporates key European debates, conflicts, and ambiguities. These include the cultural and political dialectics of "north" and "south," "west" and "east," Protestant and Catholic, Jewish and Catholic/Protestant, German and Italian, German and French, German and Slavic, the symphonic and the operatic, and—to flag the dialectic I shall introduce with some explanation in the introduction— the baroque and the modern.

The paragraphs above as well as the pages that follow would seem to mark this book as preternaturally dedicated to Carl Schorske and Leon Botstein. The project would have been inconceivable without them; the dedication is all the same a fully willed expression of gratitude and friendship within and beyond the bounds of the present book. Thinking history and music in the company of these two scholars is a lifetime honor and lesson. I am fundamentally grateful as well to friends and scholars from various disciplines whose readings of drafts proved consistently incisive and instructive, especially Mieke Bal, Scott Burnham, Daniel Herwitz, Isabel Hull, David Levin, Martha Nussbaum, Emanuele Senici, and David Yearsley. I want to thank Walter Lippincott, Elizabeth Powers, and Fred Appel at Princeton University Press, as well as two anonymous readers (a cultural historian and a musicologist) whose input has been most helpful.

My most indispensable and most critical reader is Suzanne Stewart Steinberg, who here as everywhere in our life together has captured the elusive harmony of truth and love.

Listening to Reason

INTRODUCTION

Musical form and cultural life have begun to recognize and speak to each other in recent years, owing in part to the initiatives of performing arts organizations and universities. Opera, especially regional opera, is booming. "Opera studies" is a growing and exciting field. Concert halls have had more difficulty rejuvenating their audiences and have responded with creative (and sometimes desperate) programming. The preconcert lecture, a rarity only a decade ago, is now more the norm than the exception. To be sure, the *ur*-preconcert lecture tended to offer a kind of pop-analysis, recalling in its economy and focus the opening monologue of a flight attendant: "Three minutes into the exposition you will hear a noise; this is normal." But as programming has become more context oriented, so have these verbal introductions to the music. Similarly, in the university, the academic discussion of music has begun, belatedly, to blur disciplinary boundaries. Literary scholars write about music; musicologists are concerned with culture, politics, and society.

This book is an essay in the cultural history of music. It attempts to make good on a practice I have been increasing—in both extent and conviction—in my courses in European cultural history in recent years (as well as in a good number of preconcert lectures and symposia). This is the discussion of music as a key genre in the history of cultural and aesthetic form, and equally as a significant existential component in the history of cultural life. The case for music as a dimension of history, and therefore as a concern of professional historians, seems still to require special pleading. Cultural and intellectual historians have become comfortable in engaging linguistic and visual texts—primary sources, so to speak—from the fields of philosophy, literature, painting, and film. Cultural history's engagement with music, however, seems inhabited and inhibited by two taboos.

First, music is routinely judged a genre too formal to admit discussion by "nonspecialists"—synonymous with nonmusicologists. Technical aspects of musical structure and notation discipline (in both senses of the word) discussion and combine with the substantial problem of music's unreproducibility, in print, by means other than musical notation. Readers may recall director Milos Forman's depiction, in the film *Amadeus*, of Antonio Salieri's technical ability to hear, quasi-literally, Mozart's music and be moved to tears by glancing momentarily at a score. Such ability—residing as it does at the height of musical literacy—becomes dubious in itself if it obviates the actual hearing that embraces music's contingency on performance. Performance involves both physicality and otherness—the otherness of someone else's rendering.

Famously, the only version of *Don Giovanni* that Johannes Brahms was interested in "hearing" was the version that traveled from the score through his head; we can be grateful that he grudgingly consented to hear, literally, Gustav Mahler's performance in Budapest in December 1890, a conjunction that arguably changed music history.

In recent institutional memory, musicologists have kept the technical bar high and have thus borne substantial responsibility for their own closed shop. Their reason was more profound than the existence or authority of music's technical aspects alone. The ascent of abstract formalism in musicology follows a historical curve, which might be worth comparing to the rise of analytical (as distinct from and often opposed to continental) philosophy, especially the mode known as logical positivism, which formed in 1920s Vienna and made its way to England and the United States. Logical and musicological positivism both reacted strongly—perhaps too strongly—to the historically evident (but not historically necessary) tendencies of culturally based arguments to evolve into blueprints of cultural exceptionalism and ideology. Nineteenth-century German philosophy, music, and musicology helped build national and ultimately fascist ideology. Thus, the wish to isolate aesthetic and logical discourses from ideology (and ultimately from fascism) helped determine the intellectual and political values of philosophy and music departments in American universities during and after the Nazi period, at a time when their faculties were enriched and reoriented by numerous distinguished émigré scholars. On the music side, the understanding of music as a mode of cultural discourse was largely banished. Music as a mode of mathematics seemed ideologically safer. In the case of nineteenth-century music, the association of music and nationalism combined to exclude even the music itself from the academic canon. Nineteenth-century music returned slowly, first declared safe by and for formalists, and then engaged by contextualists as well.

Ironically, the irredentist contextualists tended to look for a scholarly example to an émigré thinker who had always defended, indeed insisted on, cultural analysis: Theodor Adorno. As a pianist, theorist, and onetime student of Alban Berg in Vienna, Adorno's formal credentials were impeccable. As a philosopher and first-generation scion of the so-called Frankfurt School of critical and social theory, Adorno helped articulate the school's founding principle that a social science cannot be nonreflexive, in other words, that social and cultural analysis always takes the form of a dialogue between a culturally embedded analyst and the object-world of his or her analysis. No human subject resides outside of culture, nor does any object not found in nature. Music's cultural context becomes the source of its critical potential.

The hegemony of postwar formalist musicology may be now in question, and a "new musicology," perhaps no longer so new, is committed to cultural analysis. Adorno remains partly responsible for this turn. But in a situation rich with multiple and painful ironies, Adorno's mode of analysis claimed a foothold in American musicology in the 1980s through the prolific work of the German musicologist Carl Dahlhaus. Dahlhaus rigorously retrod the nineteenth-century musical and cultural ground that Adorno had marked out. Dahlhaus's imprimatur seemed to render Adorno respectable. Subsequently, when the second wave of contextual critical models entered musicological discourse in the 1980s and 1990s, importing concerns of political, gender, and feminist analysis while at the same time interrogating the boundaries between art music and popular music, the discursive and professional barriers they faced turned out to be more malleable.

But this conundrum remains largely restricted to music departments. More likely than not, my history students and colleagues are not aware of these histories, debates, and trends in the relevant scholarship. And my historian colleagues, aware of them or not, have not been as receptive to the musical dimensions of history as the musicologists have increasingly been to historical contexts.

Thus, the second problem facing the integration of music into history and the humanities, and emotionally intertwined with the first reason for music's relative absence, is the perception that nineteenth-century bourgeois music—the music engaged in this book—traverses and survives the twentieth century as an increasingly elite and socially marginal form. Here, Adorno has been of little help. If Adorno increased the cultural and critical capital of modern music and of musical analysis, he lost just as much ground with his infamous opposition of progressive and regressive music, and their implied associations with progressive and regressive listeners. Adorno confused regressive listening with regressive music. Though he by no means spared some members of the modernist canon from the side of the regressive (Wagner and Stravinsky are the key examples here), he reserved the hell-circle of the regressive mostly for "popular" music—most specifically, jazz. So "classical music" has endured a double exile: from other genres of cultural and aesthetic production, and from the democratic legitimacy of the "popular." Bizet's *Carmen* may be analogous in both accessibility and mystery to Manet's *Olympia*; it does cost more to attend an opera than to go to a museum. It does not cost more to go to *Carmen* than it does to hear the Dave Matthews Band live (to draw an example from my own family discussions). Moreover, material economies may be independent of the mental economies of regressive and progressive listening. Nietzsche and Don Jose's opinions notwithstanding, a routine performance of *Carmen* can be a pretty regressive affair.

When I ask students to listen, often for the first time, to any one of the works under discussion in this book, they often approach it with a benign but generous curiosity. Many will have had no exposure to such music at all. This estrangement results in part from the removal of "classical music" from the vocabulary of basic bourgeois taste and cultural legitimacy (no great intellectual loss, if perhaps a significant financial loss for musical institutions) and in part from the disappearance of "music appreciation" curricula from secondary schools (a far greater loss). At the same time, increasingly large numbers of students who have no inherited or otherwise assumed cultural connections with this music are heartened to discover and engage the cultural embeddedness of the music. The discovery is especially rewarding for those who play instruments themselves and who have achieved significant technical and interpretive competence. Their curiosity often evolves into a series of questions: why is this music so intense (Why is it so self-important)? What is it trying to do? Increasingly, these questions seem to me instinctively and uncannily precise. They coax toward articulation a sense of historical specificity and difference that young players and listeners sense instinctively through the music. They sense, on the one hand, that the music remains discursively and emotionally relevant to listeners today; on the other, that the music and its implied habits of listening do the cultural, historical work of another era.

This book attempts to explore such questions historically. What *was* this music "trying to do"? What was it trying to do aesthetically, culturally, politically? So to interrogate the cultural history of music implies as well the importance of music to cultural history. At the same time, I want to take seriously the fact that the question is most often asked in the present tense: what *is* the music trying to do? The present tense suggests two things. We hear the musical works as occurring in the present with a present (in both senses of the word) agenda. When we then reinsert them into their historical contexts, they still retain a trace of contemporaneity, and through that trace we can follow our own ways of linking past and present. There is a key difference between the transhistorical and the ahistorical. The sequence of reception may be described as follows: a musical work is heard to be trying to accomplish something; we question what it was trying to accomplish at a given time, or we question the extent to which we understand, share, or indeed wish to recuperate that agenda.

This agenda involves the making of subjectivity. The music engaged in this book gains formal and cultural importance for its capacity to organize subjectivity. Moreover, insofar as music can be understood to possess a quality of simulated agency, it would appear to achieve a condition of subjective experience for itself. Thus, a language of subjectivity becomes hard to distinguish from an experience of subjectivity, a convergence that historians after Foucault have marked with the term "discourse." Discourse can be defined as the exchange of meaning. It adds action and materiality to thought and language. Music becomes possible and, indeed, privileged as a discourse of subjectivity when both music and subjectivity become understandable and understood as modes of cultural exchange, debate, and understanding.

What is "subjectivity"? I would like to account briefly for my reliance on this term by arguing for its distinction—historical and theoretical—from two other, related terms of discourse: on the one side, the discourse of "the self," selfhood, and the individual; on the other side, the discourse of "the subject" itself. In my usage of the term "subjectivity" as both a theoretical and historical category, subjectivity does not denote a *property* of the subject, in either sense of the word property—that of quality and that of ownership. Rather, I want the term to denote the *life* of the subject, conceived in such a way as potentially to produce an internal critique of the category of "the subject," a category that I also believe often to be inadequately interpreted against its historical contingencies and existential realities. Subjectivity thus marks, in my usage, the subject in motion, the subject in experience and analysis of itself and the world. This is a predicament at once redolent of contingency yet inherently critical of self-understanding in terms of a fixed position.

The modern idea of the subject has an intellectual history that distinguishes itself from the history of the idea of the self, selfhood, or the individual. I understand these latter articulations to posit the rights and the body and physical life, as argued in the classical liberal discourse of individual integrity and freedom, from John Locke to John Stuart Mill. Selfhood is thus understood as a property of the body, which at the same time is entitled to own physical property. In Locke's optimistic view, the body with rights houses a potentially open and infinite mind. In Mill's melancholic inheritance of the liberal tradition, the body with rights must indeed be protected—not only from harm but from any intervention it may deem coercive. Thus individualism—the political and economic autonomy of the possessive body—comes to impede what Mill calls individuality.

The "subject" and its genealogy posit a more ambiguous relationship between the world and the self, and consequently between power and freedom, authority and autonomy. It proceeds via the Cartesian argument of the subject as the cogito, the thinking agent, who thinks about him/herself in relation to the world. The history of philosophy can be understood to move this understanding of the subject, along with the privileging of epistemology over ontology, from Descartes, Spinoza, Leibniz, and Hume, to Rousseau, Kant, and Hegel, to modern phenomenology (in particular Husserl) and then to post-Freudian psychoanalytic theory, especially that of Jacques Lacan. (Freud offers a nodal exception here, as he depends both on this continental tradition and on Mill's liberal one. On the one hand, the charting of the unconscious and the id augments and, indeed, explodes the contingency of the subject on culture and ideology. On the other hand, the normativity of the functioning ego posits political responsibility as the equivalent of mental health.)

Kant's so-called Copernican revolution in philosophy involves his repositioning of the subject from a state of contingency to a state of autonomy; thus, the "transcendental subject" of the *Critique of Pure Reason*, which produces the possibility of knowledge of the world. As Ernst Cassirer stressed, however, Kant's transcendental subjectivity is immediately distinguished from the ever popular notion of subjectivity and of the subjective as synonyms for the individual and the arbitrary. In Cassirer's summary, Kant's "concept of the subjective expresses a foundation in a necessary procedure and a universal law of reason." Subjectivity means the capacity to reason, universal across the human species and thus built on an ethical as well as epistemological foundation.[1] This universal foundation can therefore be understood as a displacement of the dynamic of contingency on which baroque subjectivity rested. Early Romantic thinkers such as Herder and Humboldt strove to redefine the Kantian universal in terms of culture; in doing so they reemphasized the contingency of subjective formation and thus the "subjected" quality of subjectivity.

Post-Kantian philosophies of the subject continue to rearticulate this assumption of contingency, whereby the autonomy of the subject becomes increasingly an epistemological and cultural fiction, as the subject as thinking agent is contingent on culture. This tradition's seventeenth-century *démarche* provides its location in a baroque contradiction, in which the subject's autonomy remains at odds with its subjection to a power outside of itself. The word itself incorporates the ambiguity, deriving from the Latin *subjectum* (and the Greek *hupokeimenon*) or "lying under." In this context, the subject fuses with the subjected, as in the category of the monarch's subject. The constant element in the varied meanings of the "baroque" (of which more below) is the inability to resolve this contradiction. The emancipation of the subject is thus equivalent to the desire of modernity. Modern claims of emancipation from the baroque contradiction involve the subject becoming transparent to itself, enclosed within itself, and hence divided into subject and object. The subject creates visible and analyzable objects out of the world.

Through the claim of transparence, Enlightenment epistemology privileges the observing subject, thus repeating and reinforcing the privileged subject that the baroque had defined in terms of power. Politically, this claim of transparency risks the transformation of pure subjects into pure objects, objects of surveillance and / or objects of control. Freedom becomes the power to subvert: this is the problem of both the Lockean and the Hegelian state.

The critique of transparence constitutes perhaps the main complication, the main subversion, in the history of Western philosophy. It is possibly as old as Plato. It complicates the production of the subject at the same time as it impedes the subject's investiture with power and ideology. As a critique of baroque power, of Enlightenment epistemology, and of their persistent, if often unintentional alliance, the modern critique of transparence is at least as old as Jean-Jacques Rousseau. Rousseau stands as possibly the most pained and the

---

[1] Ernst Cassirer, *Kant's Life and Work*, trans. J. Haden (New Haven: Yale University Press, 1981), p. 151. Two recent anthologies that examine legacies and developments in the European philosophy of the subject are James D. Faubion, ed., *Rethinking the Subject: An Anthology of Contemporary European Social Thought* (Boulder: Westview Press, 1995), and Eduardo Cadava, Peter Connor, and Jean-Luc Nancy, eds., *Who Comes after the Subject?* (New York: Routledge, 1991).

most abiding critic of the pre-Kantian Enlightenment, an Enlightenment whose principal delusion involves its repetition of baroque claims of knowledge and power. The critique of transparence decenters the subject, whose epistemological legitimacy depends on its transparence to itself. The knowledge that calls itself postmodern questions its own authority in developing a vantage point on the world. If the analyzing agent is itself of the object-world, how can it claim analytical distance from its objects of analysis? In recent years, scholars have moved these questions onto concrete grounds in the politics of difference. In such relations of power, the empowered and the subaltern are constituted differently, but both are constituted as subjects and objects. In the epistemological organization of all these cases, the postmodern claims a position in relation to the modern that repeats the position taken earlier by the modern in relation to the claims of Enlightenment.[2]

Rousseau, the modernist critic of Enlightenment claims, was a musician, composer, and musical theorist. Put more urgently, Rousseau required and depended upon music to think subjectivity, to understand subjectivity as itself an aesthetic discourse, a mode of art. Rousseau thus attempted to formulate a modern discourse of subjectivity in reliance on music. Rousseau posited music's ability to think subjectivity in a way that would resist articulation and representation, and therefore to resist its investiture as ideology and power. In doing so, Rousseau posited music at the core of the philosophical, political, and indeed aesthetic discourse of subjectivity. The problem was that he was ahead of the music of his time (and the music he wrote himself proved inadequate to his critical agenda). So whereas Rousseau has survived at the foundation of the modern discourse of subjectivity, with the cultivation of subjectivity the goal of his educational as well as political theory, the presence and urgency of the musical correlative have tended to drop out of discussion.

I understand subjectivity as a mode of first-person experience resistant to the articulation or representation implied by the category of the subject. As the experience rather than the position of the "I," subjectivity displaces the paradigm of an autonomous subject facing an outside world in favor of a lived experience that is inherently contingent on culture. Subjectivity is thus a mode of experience where self and world are difficult to distinguish. Subjectivity resides at the borders of autonomy and integration, and must be allowed culturally, politically, and discursively to live there. The endless work of subjectivity involves the constant renegotiations of the boundaries between self and world, with the world and history continuously reappearing in the texture of the self in the form of language, other cultural practices, and received ideas and ideologies. Subjectivity is a matter not only of and for philosophy, but of

---

[2] For a compelling intellectual history of the critique of Enlightenment thinking as a critique of visual ideology, see Martin Jay, *Downcast Eyes: The Denigration of Vision in Twentieth-Century French Thought* (Berkeley and Los Angeles: University of California Press, 1993).

politics, psychology, and art. In fact it makes the most sense to me to think of subjectivity as an art, and therefore as a mode of being most knowable through art.

To my own thinking, the most valuable contemporary account of that middle ground between self and culture that I am calling subjectivity was adumbrated by the British psychoanalyst D. W. Winnicott. Winnicott's 1971 book *Playing and Reality* offers an account of the development of early childhood subjectivity through play, conceived as a dialogue between the developing self and the world. The book itself developed from an earlier essay on the phenomenon of the "transitional object," the random object such as a blanket or toy through which the child negotiates his or her place in the object-world. Winnicott's argument rests throughout on what he calls the paradox in the infant's use of the object. According to that paradox, neither the baby nor the analyst will (or should) think to ask the question "Did you conceive of this or was it presented to you from without?" "The important point," Winnicott asserts, "is that no decision on this point is expected. The question is not to be formulated." "The location of cultural experience," to cite one of Winnicott's chapter titles, "is in the *potential space* between the individual and the environment." Culture and subjectivity cannot be understood to originate inside, outside, or anywhere, or indeed to originate at all.[3]

The theory of subjectivity that Winnicott places, literally, in the protected sphere of the nursery has analogous importance in the history and theory of modern subjectivity as a discursive phenomenon. A subjectivity that is culturally contingent must also be allowed by that very cultural context to develop. Thus, liberal theory, the theory of the autonomous subject that possesses an attribute of subjectivity—is unconvincing for its assumption that subjectivity is, precisely, under the protection of a preexisting subject. The individual's capacity for subjectivity must indeed be understood to be contingent on the integrity and safety of the body; in this respect Winnicott's nursery is indeed valid as a metonym for society at large. But the safe body, the body with rights, does not produce subjectivity. This is precisely the insight that produced the melancholy of Mill's rethinking of liberal politics in his 1859 essay *On Liberty*: the individual construed and protected by the liberal state as a body with rights will not necessarily produce individuality, will not easily experience a rich mental life.

The articulation of subjectivity occupies much of modern philosophy and intellectual history and does so, clearly, in ways more extensive and more intricate than I can outline here. But philosophy holds no monopoly on the question of subjectivity. "Everywhere I go, " Freud said, "I find that the poet has been there before me." The contingency of philosophy and intellectual

---

[3] D. W. Winnicott, *Playing and Reality* (London: Routledge, 1971), pp. xi–xii, 11–12, 100, and passim.

history on culture, including aesthetic culture, constitutes a large-scale reinforcement of the subject's contingency on culture.

The modern articulation of subjectivity relied importantly on music. That is to say that modern music—form and experience, production and reception—participated in the making of subjectivity. Modern subjectivity relied concomitantly on the argument that music has the capacity to organize subjectivity. This capacity is both formal and cultural. The argument for music's formal capacity to organize subjectivity is based on two properties that I consider fundamental to the cultural production and experience of modern music. I will call them the two fictions of modern music because they ascribe capacities of consciousness and agency to music, unwarranted ascriptions from a commonsense point of view.

The first fiction holds that music can and does speak in the first person. Music is therefore heard to bear and express subjectivity. If the music itself says "I," then we have a hypothetical answer to Edward T. Cone's famous question "If music is a language, then who is speaking?"[4] But the answer is not Cone's. In question is not the subjectivity of the composer or of anyone outside the music itself. The subjectivity is of the music itself, which according to the same fundamental fiction has the capacity of memory, a sense of past and future, and a language for their articulation. Musical subjectivity cannot therefore be absorbed into the subject-positions of the composer or the listener.

Also, I intend this assertion of the fiction of music's first-person voice as an amendment to the important and now well-known assertion of the narrative capacities and tendencies of nineteenth-century music.[5] The first-person voice I am interested in operates in the present tense; it negotiates with the world in real time. Rather than narrating, therefore, it shares with its listeners a discovery and presentation of the self as a performative act . Presentation in the sense of becoming present runs parallel to production and distinct from "representation," in the same way that production remains distinct from "reproduction." Music's self-consciousness resides in the fiction that the music listens—to itself, its past, its desires.

This is the second and related fiction: that music listens. The fiction of music as a listening subjectivity implies that the subjectivity inscribed in musical utterance is immediately a mode of intersubjectivity. I stress intersubjectivity rather than intertextuality to conform to my argument that the music is understood to listen, think, and therefore also to remember and to refer. As a result, there is a mutuality between the aesthetic viability of a music's subjectivity and the cultural, political, and indeed aesthetic possibility of subjectivity

---

[4] Edward T. Cone, *The Composer's Voice* (Berkeley and Los Angeles: University of California Press, 1974).

[5] Here the key recent work is Carolyn Abbate, *Unsung Voices: Opera and Musical Narrative in the Nineteenth Century* (Princeton: Princeton University Press, 1991).

and intersubjectivity in modern life. The pun in "listening to reason" grasps these mutualities: listening to music takes place at the same time as music (invested with the fiction of subjectivity) listens and reasons; listening in order to reason, to learn the (political) art of subjectivity.

The validity of reason depends on its distinction from instrumental reason. Instrumental reason, the practice whereby subjects make other subjects into objects, is Adorno's main cognitive, political, and ethical demon, occupying and defining the dark side of Enlightenment. According to this distinction, reason involves the continuous negotiation of difference, otherness and others, without reifying others into objects. Reason, construed as a necessary foil to and critique of instrumental reason, parallels precisely the construal of subjectivity as a critique of "the subject." Adorno identified his study *Philosophy of Modern Music* as "an extended appendix" to his and Max Horkheimer's *Dialectic of Enlightenment*."[6] At the same time, I would argue, Adorno failed to make the crucial distinction between subject and subjectivity. He respects and loves only those objects that speak for and from his own subject position, which includes rigorous critique to be sure but is redolent as well of the tastes and ideology of the central European bourgeoisie. As a result, his cultural and social analysis of music contextualizes from within the history of the bourgeois subject rather than the history of subjectivity, which may be just as bourgeois a phenomenon but which is also more consistently self-critical and self-questioning. Adorno thus valorized music that he identified with, excluding from his canon not only jazz and Stravinsky but also, for example, Benjamin Britten, whose opacity (to Adorno) earned him the badge of "triumphant meagerness."[7] Adorno too quickly dismissed musical subjects that were also musical "others" to himself and his identifications. It follows that my own cultural history and cultural analysis of music parts company from Adorno at the same time as it acknowledges Adorno's work as its indispensable foundation.

If music is heard and understood to feel and think, then it is understood as a mode of subjectivity more than as an object, an "art object," or indeed a "work of art." In this context it is worth invoking and insisting on the inflection of the words "art" and "work" as processes and verbs rather than fixed entities and nouns. Whether the "work of art" should be considered as an object or as an action is a key debate in modernist aesthetics. When, in a famous exchange between modernist art critics, Clement Greenberg asserted that a work of art should be understood as an act, Harold Rosenberg replied by asking how an act could be hung on a wall. The context of music would not have afforded so glib a rejoinder; a musical work is not reducible to a representative object—score, recording, or other. A musical work remains a

[6] Theodor Adorno, *Philosophy of Modern Music*, trans. A. Mitchell and W. Blomster (New York: Seabury Press, 1973), pp. xiii–xiv.

[7] Ibid., p. 7.

function of performance, with the veracity (to leave alone the "authenticity") of every performance a font of debate. But in the plastic and visual arts as well, when the aesthetic object is unquestionably present, aesthetic significance is not necessarily a function of the object. Ironically, it is in the field of modern European art history, where the status of the art object may seem least debatable, that the cultural analysis of art and the interpretation of objects as formal and contextual acts had already developed. A century ago, the historian of art, religion, and culture, and occasional anthropologist Aby Warburg initiated a style of scholarship that can be described as the cultural history of images, which provides a key model for what I want to call the cultural history of music.

Warburg understood aesthetic import as an encapsulation of desire: cultural desire, inhabited by form. In art, culture desires to work through the power of the demons of history and nature. Warburg's scholarship focuses on Renaissance and Reformation Europe, which he innovatively considered as a single field. His principal theme was "the survival of antiquity": namely, the relevance of previous cultural battles between order and chaos. In his early, student work on Botticelli's *Birth of Venus* and *Spring*, Warburg argued that "the representation of motion always reflects a search for an antique source."[8] In Botticelli's painting, motion appears in accessory forms, namely the garments and hair of the principal figures. Painterly form thus joins with cultural desire, namely the desire to produce the future by finding and wrestling with the past. The realization of that desire is aesthetic, meaning that it is articulated as feeling and as form. Warburg called it *Denkraum*: literally, the space for thought. Like Winnicott, Warburg understands subjectivity spatially. For both Winnicott and Warburg, though, spatial form presupposes cultural specificity.

Music was first anointed as a privileged discursant of subjectivity by German Romantic theorists, intellectual siblings of Herder and Humboldt, including Hoffmann, Wackenroder, Tieck, and, a generation later, Schopenhauer. Schopenhauer's central assertion that music possessed the ability to personify human will rather than merely represent it proved a decisive influence on Wagner and Nietzsche. But this philosophical continuum took as its musical correlative a specific musical and cultural moment, focused on Beethoven and on the symphony, and granted it a transcendental imprimatur and the status of an absolute. "Absolute music," as I will argue in chapter 2, is an ideology formulated by Wagner and retroimposed on the early Romantic period, its philosophers of art, its composers (principally Beethoven), and its music (prin-

[8] Gertrud Bing, editorial foreword to Aby Warburg, *The Renewal of Pagan Antiquity*, trans. David Britt (Los Angeles: Getty Research Institute, 1999), p. 81. Warburg's 1893 thesis, *Sandro Botticelli's Birth of Venus and Spring: An Examination of Concepts of Antiquity in the Italian Early Renaissance*, appears on pp. 89–156 of this volume.

cipally the symphony). The "absolute" fuses and perhaps confuses a category of autonomy with one of authority, thus reinstating the baroque contradiction. The music (together with its theorists) that argues for and as a discourse of subjectivity does so, I will argue, with specific historical and cultural contexts and contingencies in mind. It does so as well from the vantage point of a discursive practice deemed abstract rather than absolute, in other words, autonomous by reason of its distance from the world of representation. Its analytical urgency is a function at once of its inhibitions and its suspicions with regard to the world of representation and power. My analysis of musical subjectivity proceeds initially from Mozart through Mendelssohn, then attempts to locate its persistence in those aspects of Wagner that contradict his own ideological imperialism, and seeks finally to locate its survival in the post-Wagnerian recovery from musical and other ideologies.

Informing my discussion is a pair of terms that continue to be embraced and feared by historians and music historians: the baroque and the modern. These terms denote both historical periods as well as cultural, political, and aesthetic styles but remain available and relevant to later periods as elements of cultural vocabularies and ideology. Through the production of subjectivity, modernity distances itself from baroque subjection without falling into the Enlightenment trap of transparence. Here music is key. The resistance to baroque power entails an emancipation from the power of representation, and representation is associated closely with the visual world. Baroque culture involves the power of visuality, which also means the tendency of visuality to metastasize into visual ideology. The critical drive of music involves the critique of the assumed authority of the visual and visible worlds.

In his durable study of fifty years ago, Carl Friedrich assigned "the age of the baroque" a dual historical template.[9] Baroque politics, involving the establish-

---

[9] Carl Friedrich, *The Age of the Baroque* (New York: W. W. Norton and Sons, 1952). More recently, Robin Blackburn has proposed the dialectic of power and harmony to describe the baroque. His cogent summary is worth citing:

> One term for evoking the ethos and aspirations of early European colonialism is "the baroque." This word, originally referring to a misshapen pearl and then applied to tortuously elaborate demonstrations in scholastic logic, became attached to the discrepant, bizarre and exotic features of post-Renaissance culture. It was finally adopted to evoke those principles of *power and harmony* which would reconcile such discordant elements. The baroque appears in a Europe confronting Ottoman might and discovering the material culture of Asia, Africa, and America. It is first sponsored by the Jesuits, the Counter-Reformation and the Catholic monarchs and courts in an attempt to meet the challenges of the Puritans, though subsequently some Protestant monarchs also adopted aspects of the baroque. . . .
>
> Since the baroque had a special link to the Counter-Reformation, it loomed larger in Catholic than in Protestant countries, and everywhere it was associated with royal and aristocratic display, focusing on a utopia of harmony, a cornucopia of abundance and a diorama of elegance. The baroque favoured a sanitized and controlled vision of civil society. While the baroque as spectacle retained a link to the world of colonial slavery, it exhibited a public entrepreneurship,

ment of modern state power in Europe, he dated to the half-century between 1610 and 1660. Baroque culture, harder to define and to enclose, he assigned two full centuries: 1550–1750. He described both categories according to the dialectic of power and insecurity. It is, I would suggest, the very reliability of power and insecurity that continues to render unreliable any further attempts to pin down the baroque. Baroque politics strives for wholeness in an age of anxiety, becoming more reactionary as holism eludes the grasp of power and its ambitions. Insecurity produces movement and indeed violence.

Baroque culture and politics emerge from the Reformation and post-Reformation breakdown of a unified sacred cosmology provided by European Christianity. Subjection persists, but in the name of whom? Modernity, particularly modern subjectivity in its distinction from subjection, establishes legitimacy when the question is no longer asked.

The problem is that the question continues to be asked. The baroque returns, like Hamlet's father. The category of the modern usually signifies either the true or the false claim of emancipation—from nature (via industrialization), from religion (via secularization), or from unearned authority (via political reform or revolution). Religion remains present. Power remains undistributed. And that intermediary period of alleged transition between the baroque and the modern, namely, the age of enlightenment, can be understood as a crucible of their unresolved juxtaposition rather than as the procurer of an emancipatory modernity. Baroque politics and baroque style juggle absolutism with excess but tend to fold the subversive or emancipatory power of excess back into the service of absolutism. Similarly, what is modern has the capacity to reify its emancipatory potential into new forms of tyranny. This is the dialectic of enlightenment as argued by Adorno and Horkheimer.

By "modernity" I mean a sense of the present that is held to be both tied to and emancipated from the past. Modernist agendas, within and outside the arts, are often described in terms of a claimed break with the past. Both the claim (when it is actually made) and its historiographical rehearsals are largely unconvincing. Some forms of modernism have no doubt claimed radical newness, the result of which is a quick modulation into ideology. But those modernisms that have insisted on self-awareness as a fundamental criterion have considered the relationship to history as a primary dimension of that self-awareness and self-critique. These modernisms, as discourses of forward-mindedness or futurity, have also paid close attention to history. Their sense of

---

the positive face of mercantilism, which contrasted with the private enterprise that was the driving force behind the New World's civil slavery. (See Blackburn, *The Making of New World Slavery* [London: Verso 1997] pp. 20–21.)

See also my discussion in chapter 1, "The Ideology of the Baroque," in *Austria as Theater and Ideology: The Meaning of the Salzburg Festival* (Ithaca: Cornell University Press, 2000), and in "The Materiality of the Baroque," in *Intellectual Traditions in Movement* (Amsterdam: ASCA Press, 1998), pp. 179–90.

the present can be described according to the psychoanalytical principle of "repetition with difference." Difference is the hallmark of the modern: difference from the past, difference between persons and between cultures—differences, in both cases, we might hope as historians and as citizens, where dialogue is encouraged rather than foreclosed.

The modern project of subjectivity, in which music plays a key part, involves the critique of baroque power along with its dissemination through visual means and visual culture. Music offers at least a nonvisual and sometimes an antivisual discourse; its non- or antivisuality accrues a coherent critique of baroque power and baroque representation. The critique of visual ideology gained momentum as well as methods in the agendas of the Reformation. As has often been argued, the Elizabethan, or more accurately Shakespearean, theater of the word was one initiative whereby text outpaced image for an engagement with reality. This kind of critique engages the Protestant/Catholic divide and indeed adopts a Protestantizing energy but it does not necessarily take sides in a clear fashion. In late-eighteenth- and nineteenth-century Europe, the displaced authority of Catholic and Protestant ideologies continues to define geopolitical and cognitive, cultural, and political styles. Historically, subjectivity is a Protestantizing trope, even when it is pursued by Catholics. Enter Mozart.

Mozart takes on the baroque world and its regimes of power with intricate engagements of Catholic and Protestant referential worlds. At once Catholic and anti-Catholic, Mozart sets a new, aural regime of musical engagement against the visually conceived and represented worlds of the Catholic baroque. Although his project unfolds as music—or as music drama—it makes use of Protestantizing tropes and gestures that it shares with forebears and contemporaries such as Shakespeare and Rousseau. Mozart's musical discourse of subjectivity can be heard most clearly in his juxtapositions of solo instruments with orchestra and in his operatic characterizations. The parallel ways in which solo instruments and individual operatic characters engage their musical and dramatic contexts argue for a basic similarity between music with and without explicit dramatic correlatives. A character such as Figaro combines explicitly a political, emotional, and musical education into a musical and dramatic idiom capable of exploring and expressing subjectivity and intersubjectivity. With the characterization of Don Giovanni, Mozart and Da Ponte move from realism to myth in the drive to define the stakes of musical and psychological modernity with the most ambitious attention to historic and political reality. For them, and for this book, that move involves the return of the baroque. In *Così fan tutte*, Mozart and Da Ponte add to their intricate *mise-en-jeu* of subjectivity and theatricality an explicit scene of instruction, steering their cultural analysis into the orbit of Rousseau.

The case of Beethoven is still more intricate. A Catholic, like Mozart, Beethoven engenders a more structural paradox in the pursuit of a Protestantizing musical aesthetic that becomes codified as "absolute music." (As said, I will take issue with this category in chapter 2.) But Beethoven's Protestantizing aesthetic is vexed, indeed even contradicted, by his desire to share in the perks of the old regimes of aristocratic privilege and baroque representation. The conflicts and ambiguities of the baroque and the modern remain present, perhaps surprisingly so, in Beethoven's work and context. Chapter 2 is on Beethoven, his Catholic origins, his aristocratic pretensions, and his musical ethic of bourgeois emancipation. Heroic style, in the later Beethoven, may not be disentanglable from a disavowal of psychic and cultural complication.

Mendelssohn's musical subjectivity engages, through metaphors and other modes of underarticulation, the complicated Jewish-Protestant negotiations of his family history. At the same time, they combine to form a fragile symbiosis of both style and conviction, contingent on a historical moment that does not itself last. Mendelssohn's interreligious and multicultural mediations are explicitly and stylistically refined, with precisely that disavowal of the heroic gesture that reduces his stock for posterity. If Mendelssohn portrays intellectually and musically the fragile success of an intercultural subjectivity, Schumann portrays its entrapment in history. Indeed, Mendelssohn's fragile musical discourse recalls Walter Benjamin's image, after a Paul Klee drawing, of the angel of history, pausing and hovering long enough to observe the past before being blown into the future.

That future, from the standpoint of 1850, belongs to Richard Wagner. The book's central chapter focuses on ideology and ambivalence in Wagner. I consider Wagner a kind of black hole of the nineteenth century and of nineteenth-century studies, because the work is so important as an event and so fascinating and seductive as an aesthetic behemoth. Wagner moves music into an ideological space, in my terms, by transforming its idiom from one of subjectivity to one of identity. If subjectivity can be abstracted as an "a = a" equation, or more precisely an "a becomes a" equation, then identity can be described as an "a = b" equation, or more precisely an "a = b" equation disguised as an "a = a" equation. In other words, a principle of identity asserts the identity of two unequal things. When the strongest polarity of identity definition is national identity, as it is in the Wagnerian and mid-nineteenth-century German contexts, then subjectivity is held to be identical with the nation if it is to be considered viable at all. Music becomes explicitly national (that is, German) with a long list of attributes, avowals, and disavowals. At the same time, and indeed within as well as outside Wagner's oeuvre, musical subjectivity either follows into dominant ideologies of identity, such as nationalism, or strives to maintain a critical integrity as an articulation of subjectivity. The latter initiative persists within the Wagnerian oeuvre as its mark of ambivalence. There is, moreover, an analogous formal ambivalence at stake in Wagner's music. This is the tension between a music produced and heard as formally autonomous—Wagner used the term "absolute"—and a music produced as a mirror of nature, or a mimetic duplication of some extramusical world. In the case of Wagner the concern is with his systems of related leitmotivs and their possible construction of a music of pictures. For Adorno, the music of pictures flattered the regressive listener, amounting to the double insult of the claim to mythic totality at the level of the disposable commodity. In this case, the dialectic of subjectivity and identity is echoed in the stylistic tension between musical language, which attempts to address and understand a world outside of itself, and a system of musical pictures, which disavows externality. As Adorno argued, form and ideology cannot be separated in Wagner. The result is what might be called a crisis in musical integrity.

Wagner successfully engineered a mythical status for his own work; a principal function of myth, unlike history, is to foreclose on boundaries. The "Wagner effect" lies beyond the fact that he is both brute and sage, but in the fact that the boundary between these is maddeningly hard to draw. There is an overriding ambiguity in Wagner between the brute and the sage, between the founder of a viable and potent modern racism and the craftsman not only of great art but of an art that contains passionate energies of cultural and self-critique. Wagner's beauty remains perhaps always seductive and dangerous but not always cruel. As an event, the brute Wagner wins. In that light, the chapter on Wagner seeks to hold Wagner and Wagnerism accountable for the mid-century crisis of modernity and hence for the assault of ideology on subjectivity. At the same time, it holds Wagner interpretation accountable *to* the legacy of ambiguity that Wagner produces and that he demands in response.

Chapters 5 and 6, which follow the one on Wagner, ask "Is there life after Wagner?" They chart musical languages of the recovery of the modern from the Wagnerian ideologies of nationhood, cultural homogenization, and aesthetic totalization. I turn first to the genre of the requiem mass (Brahms, Verdi, Dvořák) to ask how the voice of the people is posited in contradistinction to the voice of the nation. I return to opera to investigate how gender and nation claim reconstitution in non-Wagnerian terms—in other words, without simply repeating the ideologies on other national and gendered grounds (Debussy, Bartók, Janáček). Though the material considered here stretches well into the twentieth century—as late as 1926 with *The Makropoulos Case*—the concerns and stylistic idioms both speak in terms redolent of the nineteenth century.

The concluding chapter is also posed in the form of a question, but this one goes unanswered, in any case more unanswered than the question in chapter 6. It asks how the understanding of nineteenth-century music as a language of subjectivity impacts the conceptualization of twentieth-century music. It seeks no more than to pose the contours for the discussion of how twentieth-century music engages the psychoanalytic mapping of the unconscious. I work on the assumption, which I believe can be and has been argued historically, that twentieth-century discourses of subjectivity incorporate the Freudian topographies of the unconscious. The resulting question is what this new ground of subjectivity does to and with music's position as a language of subjectivity. Wagnerian claims remain most active here: specifically the claim that music can become a language of the *articulated* unconscious, the unconscious rendered conscious. This claim contradicts Freud's definition of the unconscious as the realm that resists articulation. Freud explicitly, notoriously, disavowed any sustained engagement between psychoanalysis and music. Mahler agonized over the question of music and the unconscious. Schoenberg increasingly shut it down. If Freud was right about the unavailability of the unconscious, then Schoenberg was right, too, about its inadmissibility to musical articulation. Does Schoenberg's revolution shut down subjectivity at the same time as it seeks to shut down ideology?

As Wagner had done with *Die Meistersinger von Nürnberg*, Schoenberg wrote an autobiographical opera in *Moses und Aron*. Moses's (read Schoenberg's) opposition to Aaron recapitulates the modern musical tradition's opposition to visuality, representation, and their excesses. Moses and Aaron become allegories of the modern and the baroque. But in rejecting visuality and ideology, Moses disavows music itself and, finally, loses the faculty of language altogether. The verdict is still out on the issue of Schoenberg's similar culpability. Whether or not Schoenberg shut down a music of subjectivity is perhaps the unanswerable corollary to the more reliable proposition that Schoenberg, out of respect for the unconscious, shut down its depiction in music. But that is an issue for a book on the twentieth century.

Chapter One

STAGING SUBJECTIVITY IN THE
MOZART / DA PONTE OPERAS

Staging Subjectivity[1]

The three operas that W. A. Mozart and Lorenzo Da Ponte wrote together between 1786 and 1790 add up to a triadic *mise-en-jeu* of old-regime cultural power with a new argument, musically and dramatically conceived, for subjectivity. To argue that these operas stage subjectivity is in turn to put into play the powerful ambivalences of both these terms.

Subjectivity involves here the enactment of personal freedom. This enactment proceeds through ongoing negotiations between individuality and power. The negotiation is never-ending first because the threat of power to subjectivity persists, in the form of both external and internalized presences. Consequently, subjectivity at once resists external power and seeks nurturing from the very powers that impede it: fathers and states, cultures and economies, and interiority and the contingency of inner life on the cultural world outside it. In this way, the liberal theory of the autonomous subject is not adequate to the cultural history of subjectivity. The former provides the crucial principle of the subject as the body with rights. Subjectivity is indeed contingent on that principle. At the same time, subjectivity defined as the life of the first person cannot control the boundary between (internal) self and (external) world, experienced as it is via those phenomena that lie across that very boundary: culture, language, the unconscious, and ideology.

The momentum of "enactment" implies, moreover, a second viscous conceptual boundary: that between performance and performativity This pair forms a distinction rather than an opposition, but the distinction must be clear before it can be recomplicated. The meaning of performance begins in the conventions of theater, whereby a preexisting entity is performed according to the rules of repetition and representation. The jargon of the per-

---

[1] I owe the phrase "Staging Subjectivity" to Mieke Bal, who used it as the title of her part of a joint lecture we gave at the conference "Ästhetik der Inszenierung" at the Frankfurt Opera in March 2000. See the resulting essays: Mieke Bal, "*Mise en scène*: Zur Inszenierung von Subjektivität," followed by my essay "Blinde Oper oder Orpheus kehrt zurück," in *Ästhetik der Inszenierung*, ed. Josef Früchtle and Jörg Zimmermann (Frankfurt: Suhrkamp Verlag, 2001), pp. 198–239.

formative has its contemporary origin not in the theater but in the philosophy of language, specifically J. L. Austin's distinction between the performative and the constative as two different kinds of speech acts. In Austin, the performative enacts what it describes (as in "I promise"), whereas the constative only describes a condition outside of itself.[2] In Hamlet's parsing of the problem (which gives him profound difficulty), performance is (mere) "acting" and the performative involves acting in the sense of (real) action.

The performance/performative distinction determines the ambivalence of the stage. As a platform for the re-presentation of social order but also for the presentation of social disruption and novelty, the stage mediates between the old and the new, between the baroque and the modern, between traditional authority and break-out subjectivity. To argue that the Mozart/Da Ponte operas "stage subjectivity" is to activate precisely that charged ambiguity and boundary between these categories. It is also to assert that these works themselves do so, and in an exceptional and exceptionally self-aware manner. That self-awareness is abetted by the intricacies of music drama. The play of subjectivity thus unfolds on multiple levels: that of musical form and the musical characterization of persons, that of the persons as "real people," that of the persons as stage characters, and finally that of the persons as actors in plays-within-the-play, in disguise and dissimulation vis-à-vis fellow characters.

The staging of subjectivity is thus coeval with the subjectivization of the stage. Later in the chapter, I will have occasion in the context of the Mozart/Da Ponte operas to address some positions of two major European theorists of the stage: Shakespeare and Rousseau. I flag their names now to alert the reader's recognition of their importance to the dialectic of staging subjectivity and subjectivizing the stage. Their arguments are as different as they are crucial. Hamlet (1603) sets baroque legitimacy against modern subjectivity just as it sets the conventions of the stage ("acting") against the world of material action. Thus Hamlet the play interrogates more intensely and pushes much further than the character Hamlet is able to the dialectic of "acting" and action. Rousseau's position is less balanced and more contradictory. The would-be opera composer's antitheatrical rage, captured most succinctly in his Letter to d'Alembert of 1758, has continued to offend and perplex.[3] In both cases, the critique of baroque power is tied up with the rhetoric of religious difference, and religious difference, specifically Catholic-Protestant difference, turns out

---

[2] J. L. Austin, How To Do Things With Words (Cambridge: Harvard University Press, 1955).

[3] See for example Jonas Barish, The Anti-theatrical Prejudice, which pathologizes Rousseau's position in the chapter called "The Case of Jean-Jacques Rousseau" (Berkeley and Los Angeles: University of California Press, 1981), pp. 256–94 and passim.

to be much more central than conventionally assumed. In this respect their work prefigures and resembles that of Mozart and Da Ponte.[4]

Of the three Mozart/Da Ponte operas, the middle one, *Don Giovanni* (Prague, October 1787), takes on the heaviest historical burden in its representation of a baroque system of power. Its main character is drawn as both a social and sexual transgressor; he is neither a murderer nor a rapist, but he kills and seduces without hesitation. In other words, he preys on the world. At the same time, the opera invests Don Giovanni's energy with a modernist critical force that subverts the various surrounding incarnations of baroque authority. The world on which he preys requires intervention. If, as Kierkegaard and many successors have suggested, the operatic audience wants to be seduced by Don Giovanni, then it may be difficult to determine whether listeners place themselves in the same subject and social positions of the Don's "victims," or, rather, whether they want to participate in his modernist eros and join the attack on traditional society, perhaps even at the cost of some violence.

Le nozze di Figaro (Vienna, May 1786) takes on the sharpest contemporary political burden in its representation of power, class, and gender differences. Here, the political and emotional regimes of patriarchal domination have been displaced by structures of difference lodged within the same generation. Patriarchal domination is rationalized as class domination. The opera's political and dramatic focus is the emancipation of modern subjects and the resulting equilibration of desire and stability. The modern subject is thus defined as a subject of desire. *Le nozze di Figaro* is explicitly about the subject defined as the body with rights. The autonomous body has rights of ownership over production and reproduction, labor and pleasure. At the same time, the opera stages the passage from subject to subjectivity as a contingent relationship. Subjectivity is given a future here, as it is not in *Don Giovanni*, but that future is highly uncertain and contingent on the emancipation of the autonomous subject. The political, social, and economic subject presumes an unviolated body. Contingent on the state of the subject (the body with rights of ownership of labor and pleasure) resides the problem of subjectivity. *Figaro's* emotional and aesthetic hope resides in the potential of the newly autonomous bourgeois subject to produce a viable subjectivity. Marriage becomes the "stage" for the bourgeois founding myth: the union of subject and subjectivity.

That union, flashed in a moment of hope at the end of *Le nozze di Figaro*, is dislodged by *Così fan tutte* (Vienna, January 1790). *Così* unleashes a brave new world of subjectivity, a tabula rasa of interpersonal relations marked more

---

[4] *Hamlet* has been set most famously at the center of baroque politics and representation in Walter Benjamin's *Origin of German Tragic Drama*. Benjamin argues that the play exemplifies tragic drama (*Trauerspiel*: literally, mourning play) rather than tragedy as the character Hamlet exemplifies melancholy in his inability to develop his critique of power into political action. See Benjamin, *The Origin of German Tragic Drama*, trans. J. Osborne (London: Verso, 1977), pp. 136–42 and passim.

as negative space than as a new structural foundation. Subjectivity is marked here as an unmanageable erotic energy. Modern subjects now function, as they did not in *Don Giovanni*, relatively unfettered to old social orders, but they have little hope of reconciling modern order with modern eros, as the proposition had been staged in *Le nozze di Figaro*. The emancipation of subjectivity opens perhaps a Pandora's box, in which emotional flux must reside somewhere on the spectrum between pleasure and terror.[5]

These operas mark three steps of a revolutionary articulation of modern subjectivity. No telos is implied, as the future's uncertainty intensifies with each one's ending. Notwithstanding the temptations of convenience and affection, one should ask, Why focus on these three of Mozart's operas? Indeed, no vacuum from other Mozart operas and their themes is sustainable: *Idomeneo* (Munich, January 1781) and *Die Entführung aus dem Serail* (Vienna, July 1782) at the beginning of the operatic decade and *La Clemenza di Tito* and *Die Zauberflöte* at the end (Prague and Vienna, September 1791) all deal with patriarchal order, power, and political legitimacy. At the same time, the Da Ponte operas reach a higher level of musical-dramatic as well as cultural-political argument, and they do so in their depictions of musically produced subjectivities. As a trio they hold a unique position in the breaking away from aesthetic (operatic) as well as contextual convention. *Don Giovanni* carries the neologism *dramma giocoso*; the epigraph might be productively attached to all three operas, and only to these three. *Idomeneo* is still an *opera seria*; *Tito* quotes the form and may or may not qualify as one itself, just as it may or may not advocate the patriarchal legitimacy that it emplots. *Figaro* and *Così* both quote the forms and categories of *opera buffa*, but do so from so much distance as to be reckoned external to them.[6]

---

[5] The presence of these themes and their varying possibilities and degrees of resolution with the three operas can be argued to have informed the broad contours of their reception. This cumulative history of judgment informs Joseph Kerman's judgments in *Opera as Drama* (New York: Vintage Books, 1956). Thus, *Figaro*'s hint of social resolution may be said to have contributed to the ongoing sense of this one as the most formally perfect of the operas. In the case of *Don Giovanni*, unresolved social and erotic conflict may have informed the general judgment that no authoritative performing version of the opera is establishable. The choices demanded by the presence of the Prague and Vienna versions of the opera and their incompatibilities are significant. The point here is that similar issues exist in the case of *Figaro* (namely, the 1789 version without Susanna's aria "Deh vieni" [see below]), but the debates about competing performance versions have been suppressed in the service of the ideology of the perfect opera. The case of *Così* is the most extreme. Here, the imbalanced economy of eros and society has generated, it might be argued, the persistent split reception of "divine music" despite "nonsense text." Wagner's judgment along these lines is the best known. But a parallel argument appears in Peter Kivy's assertion that *Così* be understood as a perfect opera (defined as "drama-made-music") but as a flawed "work of art." See Kivy, *Osmin's Rage: Philosophical Reflections on Opera, Drama, Text* (Princeton: Princeton University Press, 1988), pp. 260–62.

[6] On Mozart and opera buffa, see *Opera Buffa in Mozart's Vienna* ed. Mary Hunter and James Webster (Cambridge: Cambridge University Press, 1997).

The staging of subjectivity is these operas' musical project. Mozart brings to them a sophistication of character painting and character development with a musical vocabulary that has been honed in the ostensibly nondramatic and nonrepresentational context of "music alone." Thus, the musical rhetoric that serves the psychological definition of characters reaches the operatic stage from other, ostensibly nondramatic, so-called purely musical settings. Clear examples are the run of piano concerti that Mozart composed in Vienna between 1781 and 1786, as well as chamber pieces featuring solo instruments, such as, famously, the clarinet quintet in A, composed in September 1789 and carrying the Köchel number 581, just seven numbers in advance of *Così fan tutte* (K. 588). Mozart's operatic preoccupations may be responsible for the saturation of these works, and especially of the solo instrument's line in relation to the surrounding ensembles, with a semblance of subjectivity and, indeed, personification. The Mozartean solo instrument is heard to think and say "I." The fully developed Mozartean operatic character functions in the same way.

When Mozart matches dramatic characters to his music, he is building people, not, as in opera seria, for example, reproducing types. The music says "I," operates in the first person. At stake is not the musicalization of a person, as theatrical convention might suggest, but rather the personification of a musical language. For this reason, we are talking about Mozart's music when we talk about an operatic character. Figaro, as a character, stands also for the life and fate of an operatic genre—namely, opera buffa and its capacity, exceeding that of its sibling opera seria, to adapt to bourgeois modernity.

Just as the purely musical realizations of Mozart's clarinet and piano lines do not claim personification, neither are they encumbered with the other burden of theatrical representation, namely that of dissimulation and make-believe. If Mozart's opera theater produces subjectivity through the musical definition and portrayal of persons, then it carries the ironic and possibly self-contradictory burden of, precisely, the staging of subjectivity: the theater of authenticity. This problem introduces the last degree of distinction between these works and the other Mozart operas. The three Da Ponte operas embrace the irony of the theater of authenticity by a consistent awareness of the problem. They offer a critique of theatricality from the stage. They do so by working with and through the knowledge that the conundrums of theatricality and authenticity are cultural, ideological, and highly charged in the Europe of the late 1780s. At stake are of course old and new political regimes and agendas, but these are in turn hostage to cultural, ideological, and religious cultural systems. The Habsburg perspective that binds Vienna to Venice and Mozart to Da Ponte also binds Italy to Spain as the sites of baroque power and energy. In these operas' referential world, old-regime Europe is a function of the Catholic baroque. Consequently, modernist antagonists of the baroque regime often invoke the gestures and categories of Protestantism, even when an explicit avowal of a new religion is completely irrelevant. Protestantism provides a rhetoric of antibaroque resistance, even when its own structure of belief is not avowed or relevant. As Catholicism figures as the language of old regimes, Protestantizing gestures become markers of modernity in its cultural and rhetorical multiplicity.

Don Giovanni *and the Scene of Patricide*

Don Giovanni's stage action opens with a scene of patricide and ends (excluding, for the moment, the epilogue or so-called *lieto fine*) with the revenge of the father's ghost, in the form of a statue. A tangling with patriarchal order is at the center of the opera's confrontation with history. An initial question for the interpreter is at what level to understand this historical allegory. Mozart's personal biography provides more than one cognate to the case of the Commendatore, the murdered patriarch. The best known is his father, Leopold Mozart, who died in May 1787, five months before the Prague premiere of *Don Giovanni*. Father and son had been estranged since early 1781, when Mozart left Salzburg for Vienna against his father's wishes. He staged this move directly following the successful Munich premiere of *Idomeneo*, his first operatic success on a major scale and the work that catapulted him to independence. The move to Vienna meant autonomy both from his father and from the princely archbishop of Salzburg. "Mozart's task," Maynard Solomon suggests in this context, "was harder than Hamlet's, who at least had his father's spectral authorization, whereas Mozart had to defy both his father and the head of state."[7]

It cannot have escaped the attention of insiders to the Mozarts' domestic drama of 1781 that the plot of *Idomeneo* echoes that drama in concerning a father and king who has agreed to the terms of a curse requiring him to execute his own son. At this opera's happy end, a magical voice releases the king from the curse against his agreement to abdicate in favor of the previously doomed son. King Idomeneo happily agrees to these terms. It does not seem irresponsible to assume that this father's choice of abdication and filial succession over the infanticidal alternative must at least have resided in Wolfgang Mozart's fantasmatic projection for the resolution of the conflict with his father.

The Leopold/Wolfgang relationship is the central story of many Mozart biographies, most recently that of Solomon.[8] Solomon passionately reverses the long-lived nineteenth-century paradigm of the father devoting himself to the prodigious career of his genius son.[9] He begins with a profile of the young

---

[7] Maynard Solomon, *Mozart: A Life* (New York: Harper Collins, 1995), p. 246.

[8] Ibid.

[9] This argument was made in Otto Jahn's "definitive" (Solomon's words) biography (Leipzig, 1856) and was heightened by Hermann Abert in his amended fifth edition of Jahn (Leipzig,

Leopold that draws him as an opportunist and schemer—a humorless and more anxious version of Lorenzo Da Ponte. Born in Augsburg in 1719 and tracked for the priesthood by his family, he "hoodwinked the clerics about becoming a priest," according to the reminiscences of a schoolmate. In 1737 he matriculated at the Benedictine University in Salzburg, from which he was expelled for poor attendance. He became a musician in Salzburg, to the fury of his Augsburg family, in the wake of his own father's death. In 1747 he petitioned the town council of Augsburg to marry and to establish residence in Salzburg but maintain citizenship in Augsburg; in doing so he mendaciously and mysteriously asserted that his father was alive.[10] The subsequent forty years of Leopold's life in Salzburg involved the drive for professional and cultural legitimacy. For Solomon, that dual end motivated the nurturing, international exportation, and general commodification of his son.

Leopold Mozart's negotiation of the religious culture of Augsburg and Salzburg prove both fascinating and incoherent. Clearly, religious affiliation amounted to an exchange value for him, a terrain of opportunism. But whether it amounted only to that is a judgment call to be avoided. He arrived in Salzburg a few years after the expulsion of the city's Protestant population. He did not hesitate to pursue his alliances with the princely archbishops by regularly attending mass and confession. At the same time, Solomon speculates whether Leopold might not have undergone a sincere "crisis of faith, or even contemplated conversion."[11] The speculation, however, seems not to jibe with the picture of religious and moral incoherence. In 1763 Leopold took his seven-year-old son to perform in Augsburg; his estranged family did not attend the concerts. The audiences were composed, Leopold noted, of "almost all Lutherans."[12] Did he mean "only outsiders," or did the Lutheran label connote some kind of positive attraction? A month after the Augsburg concerts, Leopold visited shrines of Luther's life in Worms and Cologne. Augsburg itself holds a unique place in the history of German principalities as an explicitly and contractually biconfessional city. This plurality seems to have given Leopold Mozart a rhetoric with which to stage the resentment against the family he abandoned and whom he now accused of abandoning him. It may have given him the grounds for a fluidity or at least a flirtatiousness of faith and practice. The adoption of a Protestant position, strategic as it may have been, requires interpretation beyond the insufficient binary opposition of opportunism and faith. This consideration, important to the strategies of Leopold Mo-

---

1919–21). Solomon describes the long-lived Jahn/Abert paradigm as an "evolutionist Victorian perspective, which viewed Mozart as embodying the classical ideal of a gifted and harmonious being organically fulfilling his creative potential" (Solomon, *Mozart*, p. 598).

[10] Ibid., pp. 22–25.
[11] Ibid., p. 29.
[12] Ibid., p. 27.

zart, will prove all the more crucial to the musical-dramatic rhetoric deployed by his son.

Solomon's emplotment of generational warfare in the Mozart family is largely a personal story, but it does not ignore political and structural levels. Leopold's personal patriarchal politics involved an alliance with Salzburg's Prince Archbishop Colloredo, who employed Wolfgang Mozart. Wolfgang's protracted, five-month process of separation from the archbishop's service in 1781 was also a separation from his father, a process completed at the end of the year with his marriage to Constanze Weber without his father's consent. Now Mozart added the erotic to the professional and political fields of filial transgression.[13]

The musical and dramatic passage from *Idomeneo* to *Don Giovanni* is that from renounced infanticide and filial forgiveness to enacted patricide and patriarchal revenge. The character Don Giovanni is not literally the son of the father he murders, and that displacement allows the historical and allegorical foci of his energy and motivation to shift. These remain focused, I would argue, on the revolt against baroque patriarchy. But the opera forms a new vocabulary of modernist resistance, self-assertion, and guilt. The fact that *Don Giovanni*'s energy is focused on the erotic, whose energies are presumably not historically specific, need not diminish the historical and allegorical specificity of the opera's critique of power.

Don Giovanni was written for Prague and was a hit there in a way that it was not, a season later, in Vienna. The reasons for this discrepancy are intricate, and have a great deal to do with Viennese political circumstance in the aftermath of the Turkish war, and the ensuing illness and unpopularity of Emperor Joseph II, Mozart's patron. But there is also the question of what might be called macrocircumstantial evidence, having to do with long-term Bohemian-Austrian tension and the consequential differentials in ideology and cultural taste between Prague and Vienna. Prague, the Bohemian capital, had been the seat of the Holy Roman Empire until 1612. Its religious and linguistic duality had done much to launch the conflict, in 1618, that became the Thirty Years' War. In defeat, Bohemia was systematically reduced to the status of a marginal Habsburg province, controlled by imperial power, German language, and Jesuit educational policy. This situation still held in the late eighteenth century. The Josephinian reforms were considered foreign impositions by many Bohemians—as Napoleonic reform would be several decades later by many Germans. When the Prague musical public praised Mozart as a "German Apollo," they clearly had in mind an energy outside the Habsburg orbit, a combination of Germany and Italy, of cultural richness and political

---

[13] Robert Gutman cites evidence for the robust sexuality of the relationship between Wolfgang and Constanze Mozart. See Robert W. Gutman, *Mozart: A Cultural Biography* (New York: Harcourt, 1999).

marginality, that might inspire German culture in Prague in a non-Viennese manner—perhaps in an anti-Viennese manner.[14] The most interesting mystery—and it remains, I think, a mystery—is the extent to which Mozart and Da Ponte complied with the complicated and contestatory spirit of Prague. That Mozart had suffered, in Andrew Steptoe's words, "a catastrophic decline in popularity" among the Viennese in 1786 is relevant, but not sufficient as an explanation.[15]

The result is the principle of "*Don Giovanni* against the baroque," the result of which is the opera's punishment not of its protagonist ("il dissoluto punito") but of the dominant culture it portrays.[16] Mozart's journey to Prague was a journey to a theater not under imperial control, to a place where he could look back on Habsburg culture and, with the opening chords of *Don Giovanni*, hurl modernist thunder at Habsburg society. In *Figaro* he teased ("If you want to dance . . ."); in *Don Giovanni* he accused, claiming for himself the last laugh, even if the last laugh were to come from hell.

Contrary to the morality play that Mozart and Da Ponte inherited from their sources, and into which latter day Austrian audiences have at times tried to redefine the opera *Don Giovanni*, the hero of Mozart and Da Ponte's work is not so much the punished as he is the punisher. His powers, sensuous energy and affective manipulations, are musical powers as well. The often-repeated comment that Don Giovanni scores no sexual victories during the course of the opera is accurate with regard to the plot and characters. It also opens the possibility of an element of his own dysfunction in the aftermath of the killing of the Commendatore. In this respect, the opera is the story of his demise. At the same time, he exerts power from beginning to end over the world around him through an erotic power musically defined. Although he is not identical to musical energy in the opera's cosmos—Joseph Kerman and others have argued convincingly that his own music is the opera's least innovative—he is at least *simultaneous* to the opera's musical and emotional energy. After his demise, the surviving characters sag and droop—like Wagner's gods in the absence of Holda's apples. They regain life only in their memory of Don Giovanni, even if they censor their own memories into a collective, moralizing posture.

Don Giovanni's challengers and victims are the representations of cultural authority. First, the representation of patriarchy: the Commendatore. His sec-

---

[14] See the discussion in Volkmar Braunbehrens, *Mozart in Vienna, 1781–1791*, trans. T. Bell (New York: Harper Collins, 1991), pp. 293–316.

[15] Andrew Steptoe, *The Mozart–Da Ponte Operas* (Oxford: Clarendon Press, 1988), p. 59. In his discussion of "Opera in Context: Vienna, Prague, and *Don Giovanni*" (pp. 115–20), Steptoe suggests (but in my opinion does not support the view) that the success of *Don Giovanni* in Prague but not in Vienna resulted from the relative unsophistication of the "backwater" audiences in Prague, who could still be entertained by the prerationalist hocus-pocus of the plot.

[16] The following discussion of *Don Giovanni* draws and expands on a previous essay, "*Don Giovanni* Against the Baroque, or, the Culture Punished," in *On Mozart*, ed. James M. Morris (Cambridge: Cambridge University Press, 1994).

ond series of challengers, the three women under his spell, embody in different ways the collaboration, or compromise formation, of sexual desire with social, cultural, and religious order. Because of their own desire and their resulting inner conflict, at least two of the three women—Anna and Elvira—become intricate characterizations and figures of considerable dramatic power and agency. In their public personae, nevertheless, they represent the culture of the baroque, which in its Habsburg articulation is the culture of Catholic power, both sacred and secular, of cosmic control through the authority of its static and totalizing representation. Don Giovanni confronts this authority with the energies of dissolution and movement, with those qualities of transience, flux, and contingency (le transitoire, le fugitif, et le contingent) that for Baudelaire formed the defining principles of modernity.[17]

In Don Giovanni, Mozart moved his cultural critique of baroque patriarchy and ideology into the music, and made music into a critique of the ideology of representation. The music of Don Giovanni foregrounds a voice of negation, with Habsburg culture as its specific referent and target. The character of the Don cannot of course be said to possess the critical and cultural self-awareness that inhabits his music and the voice of the orchestra. The music seems to me to carry a mind of its own. Don Giovanni carries a negativity of his own, but it is not a highly self-conscious one; it resembles the diabolical spirit that Goethe invested in the figure of Mephistopheles, who describes himself as "the spirit that always desires evil and always creates goodness [der Geist, der stets das Böse will, und stets das Gute schafft]."[18]

How do these opposing energies play themselves out through the course of the drama? The overture, where the interpretation of drama and the aesthetic of absolute music converge, has been the predictable locus of philosophically oriented interpretation of the work, with Kierkegaard and Wagner providing early and powerful readings. Wagner wrote on the Don Giovanni overture briefly in 1841; Kierkegaard's Either/Or, published in 1843, treats the overture and the work itself at length.

For the young and angry Wagner, writing in Paris, the allegro of the overture represented "the struggle between inexorably opposing forces."[19] But what about the overall duality between the overture's opening andante and the allegro section? As post-Wagnerian listeners, we have grown accustomed to hearing the opening of the overture according to a Wagnerian musical aesthetic, which I would argue is both anachronistic and wrong. We assume that

---

[17] "Modernity [Baudelaire coined the term] is the transient, the fleeting, the contingent; it is one half of art, the other being the eternal and the immovable," from "The Painter of Modern Life" (1859) in Baudelaire, Selected Writings on Art and Literature, trans. P. Charvet (London: Penguin Books, 1992), p. 403.

[18] Goethe, Faust I, lines 1339–40.

[19] The phrase is from Daniel Heartz's summary, in Mozart's Operas, p. 176. The original essay is "De l'ouverture" (1841).

the opening chords represent the Commendatore, the statue, and the punishment he metes out on Don Giovanni. After all, the entrance of the statue into the Don's dining room recapitulates these opening chords. But in this way we give these chords the status of a leitmotiv. I would argue for a much more primitive, musical definition of these chords and the sequences of ascending and descending chromatic runs that follow them. They establish the opera's principal musical language as one of austerity, fury, negation and extrahuman power. In the description of Géza Fodor, "This wholly musically conceived beginning is at the same time one of the most fantastic visions of musical literature: a true apparition. The mass of dominant chords, developed with inherent asymmetry, voiced in the tonality of D minor by the entire orchestra, evoke inarticulate monumentality, a sort of massiveness. The intonation is chilling: it is not without justification that Abert likens it to the concept of Medusa's head."[20] The avenging statue is allowed, in his second appearance, to inhabit this external fury, but he is not identical to it.

Like a true apparition, the meaning of the overture's opening two chords can never fully be known. But I am going to make a more dire assertion: their power lies in the fact that they can never truly be *heard*. These sounds are shocks. They are acoustic impositions, originating and remaining outside the symbolic order that the opera will soon define through music, words, and action. Structurally and retroactively they can be incorporated into a surrounding harmonic logic, but that incorporation functions itself as an ideological absorption of their externality and violence. They assert themselves first as a foreign force, in the way that divine law is inscribed as both absolute and absolutely foreign. What we have here is an instantiation of a Reformation and Old Testament idea of divine authority, musically prefiguring and opposing a Catholic representational world. The chords have the status of divine force, which is foreign and inappropriable, as opposed to mythic force, which is, dangerously, appropriable by human agency. (This distinction between the divine and the mythical is Walter Benjamin's, from the 1921 essay "Toward a Critique of Violence.") Now, when, at the opera's end, these chords return to greet the return of the Commendatore, this force is personified—and at the same time depersonified—in the figure of the avenging statue. The overture's opening chord structure returns now precisely as the voice of the symbolic order—the voice and transformed body of the dead father (as in the case of Hamlet's ghost). Retroactively, we can say, lamely, that the music represents the statue. But we are not so informed at the first hearing of the overture, and that is the significant experience of its dramatic force. In this sense of the listener's time-bound consciousness, there is no such thing as repetition in music.

---

[20] Géza Fodor, "Don Giovanni," in *Reconstructing Aesthetics*, ed. Agnes Heller and Ferenz Feher (Oxford: Blackwell, 1986), pp. 150–51.

The second section of the overture, in contrast, embodies worldly energies, with suggestions of pomp and ceremony provided by its instrumentation. These are the energies of everyday social life, compatible with the empire's official representational content and style, from the Catholic aristocracy (Anna and Ottavio) to the productive, and reproductive, peasantry (Zerlina and Masetto). In Fodor's words again, "As the apparition disappears, the world-stage is occupied by the realm of sensuality, in complete ignorance of the forewarning." The two parts of the overture thus inscribe, for Fodor, Kierkegaard's opposition between the spiritual and the sensual—the sensual defined as a realm "created by Christianity through its exclusion by the spirit."

Compatible with Fodor's and Kierkegaard's descriptions of spirit versus sensuality is the more conventional program given to the two sections of the overture, positing the contrast between death and life, the Commendatore's claim and Don Giovanni's prior exploits. But I would place the Commendatore and Don Giovanni together in the overture's opening D minor andante, and the social world in the D major allegro that abruptly follows. I see, therefore, a dramatic and musical alliance between the Commendatore and Don Giovanni as negative forces. Joseph Losey, in his 1979 film of the opera, displays the same alliance, as manifest in the dire disposition of Ruggero Raimondi's Don. Don Giovanni is possessed of an essential negativity—some might call it a death wish: a force that is not seen again on the operatic stage until Carmen. Don Giovanni and Carmen alike are possessed of a sexuality that is extrasocial and antisocial, and only generations of sedate opera audiences have been able to redefine their sexual danger as lyrical charm. (The prelude to *Carmen* is sequentially different from the *Don Giovanni* overture—the worldly allegro comes first, the ominous adagio second—but it juxtaposes similarly opposing representations of negativity and the social world.) Losey and Raimondi got it right: the opposition that inhabits the drama from the opening bars of the overture is not so much that between spirit and sensuality as that between otherworldly negativity and worldly affirmation.

If Don Giovanni and the Commendatore are immediately allied in the opening energy of the overture, a third musical spirit must be added to them, and that is the voice of the composer. Once again, we must reject the received clichés. If the andante embodies austerity and negation and the allegro embodies worldliness and sensuality, then two centuries of popular Mozart reception will place the Mozartean spirit comfortably in the second mold. But this is the result of inattentive listening. Mozart is able to compose, as in the allegro, within the paradigm of worldly entertainment, but his truest voice stands in critical austerity and remove of the opening andante. How can we be sure of this? Perhaps in the fact that the andante is built on a generative exploration of a single D minor tonality. What unfolds is the birth of consciousness through the spirit of music, in a Kantian dynamic where the critical subject stands apart from and prior to the experience of the world. Wagner will begin *Das Rheingold* with a similarly fundamental elaboration of a tonality—E flat major—but his universe is a Hegelian one, in which consciousness and world germinate simultaneously.

What I want to insist on at this point is the specific historical, cultural definition given by Mozart to the worldly, sensual realm inhabited by the overture's second half and the entire stage action up to the statue's arrival at dinner. It is clear that the historical Austrian association with Spain gives an internal, Habsburg, and even Austrian guise to the literal Spanish locale of the drama. Although the action is entirely secular, the secular culture is deeply inhabited by Catholic ritual practice and behavioral stricture. Religious example is set by the aristocracy, and Donna Anna is the prime carrier of the Catholic aura, its power as well as its fissures.

On the social scale, Anna and Ottavio stand opposite Zerlina and Masetto. As the opera's two ongoing, intact couples, they exhibit opposite patterns of erotic investment in their partnerships. Zerlina and Masetto may reflect a conventional bourgeois cliché about the "natural" sexuality of the peasantry, but their sexuality is evident nonetheless (Zerlina's possible willing infidelity notwithstanding). Zerlina's two arias of consolation amount to scenes of seduction. Anna and Ottavio, on the other hand, obey the various ideological prohibitions on sexual pleasure associated with the religious and class structures from which they seek recognition. The first prohibition is premarital sex; the second is marriage itself during a period of mourning. Donna Anna's Electra complex extends the patriarchal pull on the opera's characters and plot. Significantly, her second aria, "Non mi dir," in which she asks Ottavio to forgive her continuing abstinence, immediately precedes the banquet scene and the return of the statue of her father. Equally significant is that the aria's cabaletta section exhibits the very *jouissance* that the initial exposition disavows, but textually and musically. (The transition is so abrupt that Peter Sellars thought to rationalize it by having his Donna Anna, a heroin addict, shoot up just before the cabaletta, so as to motivate its sudden burst of energy.)

On the issue of class as well as on issues of emotional, erotic, and musical focus, the most difficult and persistent question about the characters seems to remain "Who is Elvira?"—the character invented by Molière. She is the energy of ambivalence, the messenger between the worlds polarized in the opera. She admits to her own internal conflict between religiosity and sensuality with more honesty than Anna will ever have. Her musical style is the most wide-ranging in the opera. When, in her warning to Zerlina ("Ah! fuggi il traditor!"), she defends the strictures of the spirit against the temptations of the flesh, she sings an accomplished baroque opera seria aria, a parody of Handel.[21] The rhetorical move seems to be hers even more than Mozart's; she

---

[21] This last point is an issue of considerable debate, as recounted by Heartz, *Mozart's Operas*, pp. 208–9. Heartz supports Georges de Saint-Foix's defense of the aria "Ah! fuggi il traditor"

seems to understand the expressive as well as the cultural style she is quoting. Elvira and Mozart are here neither parodying nor plagiarizing Handel; they are quoting him. The gesture of quotation implies both alliance and distance in relation to the quoted source.[22] The emotional, indeed repressive distance that Elvira performs in "Ah! fuggi il traditor!" in relation to Don Giovanni is reversed in the second-act aria in which she surrenders to her desire, "Mi tradì quell'alma ingrata" (added for the Vienna premiere). The wish to preserve the Handelian posture might provide one argument for the integrity of the Prague version of the opera, without "Mi tradì." On the other hand, if the Handelian quotation is understood as a repressive gesture, it is so on Elvira's part, not Mozart's. In this case, the counterpart to repressed desire, namely its overabundance, is signaled by the quotation itself, and exhibited finally in "Mi tradì."

As for Elvira's social position, I would argue that her independence speaks to a protobourgeois identity, even if she is formally identified as a noble woman. Her autonomy, mobility, and stylistic eclecticism make her the protobourgeois foil to the patriarchally dominated Anna. In Elvira, we have the makings of Fiordiligi and Dorabella.

It is Elvira's temporary alliance with Anna and Ottavio that gives the forces of the baroque world their strongest moment in the reaction against Don Giovanni's negativity. Again, Losey's instincts are to be given credit. In his film, the three masked figures arriving by gondola from a dock on the Brenta and approaching Don Giovanni's villa provide the true mystery and terror that their collective apparition demands. (Palladians will know, furthermore, that the Villa Rotunda is in fact not on the Brenta at all and that Losey's moment has therefore an aura of surreality about it.) Don Giovanni must be understood to be genuinely afraid of this avenging trinity, as this first act finale prefigures the second act finale, and as this trinity prefigures the avenging statue. The musical moment that embodies the trinity's collective identity is the trio, marked adagio, in which they call on the heavens to protect them in their mission. Musically, we have the return here of the realm of the spirit, a music purged of all sensuality. But this is the spirit of the baroque in its fullest union of sacredness and political power; it is not the critical spirit of the Mozartean voice.

There is another element at work here. Purged along with the sensual are the attending formal qualities of temporality and movement. The senses, time,

---

against "the frequently heard charges that is sounds archaic and somehow like a parody of Handel." The problem in Heartz's summary is the conflation of archaism and parody. A parody would imply distance from the source and thereby an antiarchaic posture.

[22] Mieke Bal has mapped the various meanings and functions of quotation in this regard. Conventional quotation "is a form that reinforces mimesis" (as in my quotation of Bal right here). In a second form, however, and one relevant to the quotation of opera seria in play above, quotations as "fragments of reality . . . function as shifters, allowing the presence of multiple realities within a single image." Bal, *Quoting Caravaggio* (Chicago: University of Chicago Press, 1999), p. 10.

and motion are all arrested in this prayerlike utterance. The sudden suspension of action is all the more striking in its separation from the movemented party music that surrounds it. The musical and dramatic effect of the interrupting trio corresponds to what Joseph Frank called "spatial form in modern literature."[23] The modernist writers whom Frank examined in his essay of that name "ideally intend the reader to apprehend their work spatially, in a moment of time, rather than as a sequence."[24] But where Frank's concern was to identify spatial form as a modernist technique, my purpose is to identify it here, precisely because of its limited and strictly demarcated appearance, as the injection into the music and drama of austere, conservative ideological power— specifically, the ideology of the baroque, the energy of the Counter-Reformation, as rationalized in Habsburg imperial politics, which wants to hold still the world against the modernizing and dissipating momentum of the Reformation.[25]

Under the white masks and black robes of Venetian commedia dell'arte figures, the grim trio of Ottavio, Anna, and Elvira lead Losey's camera into the foyer of the Villa Rotunda. The camera then appears to be inspired by their physical and musical presence to track the structure of the rotunda itself, following the cupola from heaven down to earth. Architecture and musical architecture converge as the trio of voices unfolds.

Don Ottavio does not seem to be interesting to Mozart at this point; if we remember that the aria "Dalla sua pace" was added for the Vienna premiere, we realize that (as the part was first written) he has not yet had an aria, has been given no individual attention. In the trio, his voice serves as an obbligato, a grounding principle.[26] Baroque politics and baroque musical aesthetics converge in the shape and function of Ottavio's musical line. The character Ottavio is thoroughly repressive—successfully, in his effect on Donna Anna.

---

[23] Joseph Frank, "Spatial Form in Modern Literature," *Sewanee Review* (1945); reprinted most recently in Frank, *The Idea of Spatial Form* (New Brunswick: Rutgers University Press, 1991), pp. 5–66.

[24] Ibid., 10.

[25] Ivan Nagel thus summarizes "the dilemma of *Don Giovanni*: to spatialize time or to temporalize space—to side with fate or with emancipation." *Autonomy and Mercy: Reflections on Mozart's Operas*, trans. M. Faber and I. Nagel (Cambridge: Harvard University Press, 1991), p. 42. "Mercy" is a less felicitous translation of Nagel's "*Gnade*" than "grace," which implies the aesthetic and indeed the sensual aspect of the gesture along with the judicial and the forgiving. The binary is a very fruitful one for the tracing of political tensions in Mozart's operas. Nagel ends up with a substantial degree of nostalgia for the word of grace and its aura, all the more so as he repeatedly equates autonomy with bourgeois modernity and the preponderance of instrumental reason associated with the "businessman" (pp. 33, 43).

[26] The *obbligato* (obligatory) refers to a written part, distinct from its close antecedent the thoroughbass or figured bass, an independent bass line that continues throughout a piece in a set pattern. The "baroque era" in musical-historical periodization is often referred to as the thoroughbass period (*Generalbass-Zeitalter*), a term coined by Hugo Riemann.

Figure 1   Andrea Palladio's Villa Rotunda (Vicenza).

His musical line grounds the women's voices, reminding them of their musical, social, and indeed behavioral grounding.

Ottavio's obbligato supports the two women's bid to weave together their melodic lines in a competitive determination to express and suppress their own desire. An ascending, chromatic run is answered, perhaps annulled, by a corresponding descent. The cumulative effect is the construction of musical arches that accumulate structurally to form a perfect, enclosed musical space: to form—stretching my image a bit, but not irresponsibly—a baroque cupola created out of music. For an instant, pious terror displaces sensuality, and a cathedral seems to displace both Don Giovanni's palace, his party, and the opera house itself.

The baroque architecture of domed interiors, especially in cupolas over altars, integrates sensuality and its possibilities of excess into the shape and ideology of its overall scheme of divine totality and power. This baroque—perhaps Mozart and Da Ponte's idea of the Spanish baroque—is unable to do so. The sensuality of Don Giovanni is too blunt for social integration. Elvira's voice is here entirely absorbed into the baroque totality shaped by Donna Anna. Her Handelian moment, with its surfeit of repression suggesting a surplus and indeed a release of desire, is absent.[27]

Don Giovanni was originally conceived in four acts, and the ending of the third act was to come with the sextet following the unmasking of Leporello, who has wooed Donna Elivra while disguised as his master. Daniel Heartz describes the music of the sextet and its effect on contemporary audiences as follows:

> It relies for its music on several characteristic turns of phrase or rhythms that Mozart has used earlier in connection with the same personalities. Moreover, it relies heavily on the recurrent use of a single motif, the descending chromatic fourth.
>
> To Mozart's audience, the motif meant pain, suffering, and death—it could not be otherwise, since they and their forebears had for several generations heard similar chromatic descents in mass settings to convey the words "Crucifixus, passus et sepultus est," corroborating their experience in the opera house on the demise of heroes and heroines (e.g., Dido).[28]

---

[27] In the Franco Zeffirelli staging of *Don Giovanni* produced by the Metropolitan Opera in 1990, the opera's entire action proceeds under the protective form of baroque arches, which define the proscenium space. Zeffirelli, who includes in his curriculum vitae the choreography of large-scale Vatican ceremonies, understands well the theatrical power of Catholic baroque spectacle. In its relation to the opera as a whole, this particular representation is a serious mistake, as it claims, through baroque gesture, to impose form and impose theatrical coherence on a music drama that shreds and negates all such ideological pretenses. The previous Metropolitan production, set within Eugene Berman's constantly moving and changing drops, showed a far superior understanding of the drama's character. But the moment of the Anna–Elvira–Ottavio trio is the one moment where the baroque enclosure fits. The moment provides, to use Géza Fodor's term, an apparition, and thus the enemy of the senses, of time, and of movement.

[28] Heartz, *Mozart's Operas*, p. 210.

Elvira begins the sextet in flirtatious conversation with the man she thinks is Don Giovanni. Heartz ferrets out of Mozart's chromaticisms the double nature of Elvira's passion: the sensual censored by the sacred. When she talks of the terror that makes her feel like dying ("un tal spavento, che mi sembra di morire"), an ascending chromatic run in the violins suggests the sexual subtext of the verb "to die." "The perceptive listeners among Mozart's audience," adds Heartz with high expectations of the late-eighteenth-century ear, "must have relished this point."[29]

Elvira's passion shifts from desire to suffering with an attendant refocusing of the dynamics of theatricality. At first she and Leporello are pursued by Anna and Ottavio, and by Zerlina and Masetto, but as Leporello reveals his identity, she is of course driven away from him to join the other four in a new condemnation, first of Leporello but then again of the now absent Don Giovanni. In other words, the five become an audience, watching in horror and anger as Leporello plays out his—and Don Giovanni's—little costume play. In becoming an audience, the five characters are as manipulated by the drama as the actual opera audience, watching from the other side of the footlights.

At this moment, Losey again chooses to interrogate the opera's critique of baroque ideology. He sets the scene not in a Vicenza street, in a villa, nor on the Brenta, but on the stage of the Teatro Olympico, Palladio's last structure and the architectural apotheosis of the baroque theater. The stage is actually inhabited by a permanent set, duplicating in fact the streets of Vicenza that lie outside it, using carefully angled ramps and trompe l'oeil murals to create an illusion of size and depth—and in effect to parody Renaissance perspective. At the sextet's opening, Losey uses the space as if it were the real space of the city streets, having the three pairs converge from the side ramps. But as the unmasking of Leporello proceeds at the footlights, the characters are represented as if *performing* the work for an invited, aristocratic, possibly even clerical, audience. As the five victims of Don Giovanni condemn him, first believing him to be at their mercy and then knowing him once again to have escaped, the rage of the baroque is thus revealed not only to be theatrical, inhabiting the world-stage, but self-consciously so. The plot moment, like the stage of the Teatro Olympico, comments on the phenomenon of the vanishing point—in this case Don Giovanni himself.

Time, temporality, movement, and sensuality inform the musical side of *Don Giovanni* that carries the Mozartean energy of modernity. It is a dangerous energy that targets baroque authority as its specific, political, and ideological enemy. The modernist spirit moves; the baroque spirit holds still and claims authority over the world theater. Indeed the baroque spirit defines the world as a world theater, as a delimited space, as a way of claiming totality. So it is

[29] Ibid., pp. 212–15.

neither an accident nor a trivial occurrence that the dialectics of modernity and baroque, world and spirit, motion and stillness, and time and space finally converge in a last battle between the two sides, and that the personification of a petrified culture appears onstage as a statue, the stone guest. The grasp of the baroque is the staying hand of death. In a fascinating study, Malcom Baker has suggested that the conceit of the speaking statue spoke itself to the profusion of lifelike imagery on eighteenth-century tomb sculpture. Styles of mediation between life and death reflected the changes in and challenges to Christian belief. An audience to *Don Giovanni* could still be expected to take very seriously an appearance onstage "of tomb sculpture which for so long had been the static intermediary between the earthly and the eternal."[30]

When, clairvoyantly, Don Giovanni agrees to accompany the statue, he does so in formal tones that have recently prompted musicological comment:

> Ho fermo il core in petto.
> Non ho timor. Verro.
>
> Stout-hearted,
> Unafraid: I'll come.

Joseph Kerman, echoing Julian Rushton, comments as follows: "These four bars could never have been predicted. Their unexpected features—stiff, pompous dotted rhythms and baroque-sounding counterpoint, provided by the strings alone—are also features of Donna Elvira's Act I aria 'Ah, *fuggi il traditor.*' "[31] What do we make of the Don's late baroque gesture? Is he assuming the rhetoric of the culture that punishes him for his punishment of it? He says he will never repent: does this baroque gesture belie his claim, or, with final parodic scorn at his worldly surroundings, reinforce it? I would argue for an opposite reading. The baroque rhetoric here is Handelian, but now with the added inflection of Protestantism—the Handel of the oratorios, to which Mozart was devoted.[32] Elvira's first-act aria is rhetorically analogous in its sudden

---

[30] Malcolm Baker, "Odzooks! A Man of Stone!" in *Don Giovanni: Myths of Seduction and Betrayal*, ed. Johnathan Miller (New York: Schocken Books, 1990), p. 68.

[31] Joseph Kerman, "Reading *Don Giovanni*," in *Don Giovanni: Myths of Seduction and Betrayal*, ed. Johnathan Miller, p. 124. The translation of the four lines is uncredited and I therefore assume Kerman's own.

[32] Mozart reorchestrated four of Handel's choral works, including the *Messiah*, for Baron Gottfried van Swieten's *Gesellschaft der Associerten Cavaliere*, a society of aristocratic music patrons, between 1788 and 1790. Van Swieten (1733–1803), born in Leiden, was musical patron and progressive policy maker in the court of Joseph II. A patron also of C.P.E. Bach, he was key to the J. S. Bach revival in Vienna around 1800 and the dedicatee of Forkel's Bach biography of 1802. Ironically, German congregational music and style had also been promoted in Salzburg by Archbishop Colloredo himself who, as Solomon recounts, "in an archepiscopal letter of 19 June 1780 . . . had called for the elimination of complex forms of church music and the substitution of German congregational singing" (p. 271). The new policy "limited duration to forty-five minutes and abolished solo singing and fugues," a direction Mozart explicitly disavowed with his

importation not only of Handelian style but of oratorio. Her drive to unmask Don Giovanni involves a purging of theatricality.

The statue's admonitions can be glossed with the phrase "Recant or burn": the litany of the Inquisition, of Catholic terror. This is a Catholic ghost who knows where to draw his fire. What is the cultural vocabulary from which the doomed Don Giovanni draws his responses, with their mixture of defiance and abjection? "Giovanni does not entreat," Ivan Nagel observes, thereby foreclosing on the baroque alternative to hellfire, namely, *Gnade* (grace, mercy).[33] Does Don Giovanni die a Protestant?

Resistance to baroque patriarchy knew how to draw on the Protestant rhetoric of interiority and autonomy. In describing Mozart's own final days, Solomon—perhaps unwittingly—turns him into quite literally a Protestant: "His faith was so profound that it had no room for pomp, hypocrisy, and especially for the mediation of clerics between individuals and their God."[34] Though there is insufficient evidence that either Mozart or Don Giovanni died as Protestant believers, there is enough to attribute to both of them the Protestantizing stances of antibaroque cultural resistance. Let me shore up this possibility by way of some recent scholarship on a dramatic and biographical precedent.

The dramatic precedent is Shakespeare's ghost of old King Hamlet. The precedent was well known to Mozart and Da Ponte; the ghost of Shakespeare's ghost can be said to haunt the Commendatore's statue. Mozart knew Shakespeare through Wieland's prose translations of 1763–66. He saw *Hamlet* performed in German in Salzburg by Emanuel Schikaneder's troupe and the actor / translator Friedrich Ludwig Schröder. As early as 1789, a Frankfurt critic suggested that the scene of Don Giovanni's removal by the statue had been "learned from Shakespeare."[35] At the same time, Mozart expressed a conventional classicist's impatience with Shakespearean proportion. Most interestingly, he complained: "Were the ghost's speech in *Hamlet* not so long, it would have better effect."[36] Is this judgment the result of literary measure or anxiety?

King Hamlet's ghost has long been analyzed for its rhetorical position on political-religious conflict in late Elizabethan England.[37] The traditional question is whether the ghost "is" Catholic or Protestant. In a recent study called *Hamlet in Purgatory*, Stephen Greenblatt refocuses the question away from the theological pigeonholing of a fictitious character and toward the interrogation

---

mass in C minor. In this switch of positions worthy of *Così fan tutte*, Mozart took the Catholicizing path in opposition to Colloredo's Protestantizing move! Van Swieten had more of an effect.

[33] Nagel, *Autonomy and Mercy*, p. 46.

[34] Solomon, *Mozart*, p. 497.

[35] See Gutman, *Mozart: A Cultural Biography*, p. 685.

[36] See ibid., pp. 320n, 591.

[37] For a selected bibliography of this scholarship see Stephen Greenblatt, *Hamlet in Purgatory* (Princeton: Princeton University Press, 2001), p. 308 n. 46.

of the ambiguities of early-seventeenth-century religious belief. The first question involves King Hamlet, the ghost, in Purgatory. He is condemned to languish in Purgatory, he tells his son, until his murder is avenged. To Elizabethan audiences, the doctrine of Purgatory was a Catholic holdout, associated with the buying of indulgences. The redemption of his father's soul through the purchase of an indulgence does not occur to Prince Hamlet (there would be little room for the play if it did), who may thus show his own Protestantism. (He is a student at Wittenberg, the city of Luther's Ninety-five Theses.) More centrally, young Hamlet suspends his own confidence in the veracity of the ghost's account, moving him to test not only his father's account and authority but the legitimacy of patriarchy in general. The point here is that Hamlet's aggravated interrogation of patriarchy is, in Greenblatt's formulation, connected to his "distinctly Protestant temperament." One might add that this temperament stands in opposition to the at once Catholic and paternally enslaved temperament of his antagonist Laertes, who studies not in Wittenberg but in France. If Greenblatt is right, then the Purgatory occupied by the ghost of King Hamlet is newly inflected, not as a Catholic residue but as a cultural and historical middle ground between Catholic and Protestant cosmologies.

The contours of Hamlet's possible Protestant temperament inform not only his theology but also his take on theatricality. He is consistently and repeatedly obsessed by the problem of the authenticity of action. His ensnarement on the boundary between the authentic and the theatrical, between acting and "acting," doubles the ideological boundary between Catholic authority as the authority of representation and Protestant authority as a referential invocation of an unknowable absolute. Baroque legitimacy requires theatricality. Protestant legitimacy requires authenticity and thereby the disavowal of the theatrical, even if through the performative contradiction of a theater of antitheatricality. If Hamlet honors his father's ghost, he must believe that the latter is consigned to Purgatory: a Catholic plot. The court of King Claudius's brother is Catholic as well. When Hamlet declines to murder Claudius at prayer, he obeys a Catholic tenet that a victim slain while in the performance of good works will be saved. At the same moment, Hamlet obeys his own drive to theatricality, waiting to fulfill the murderous act until, in the following scene, he performs in front of his most desired audience, his mother. Hamlet cannot reconcile theatricality and authenticity, and he cannot therefore reconcile obedience to his (Catholic) father's demand for revenge and his own requirement that the avenging act be authentic and autonomous as criteria of truthfulness. The problem writ large, writ historically, addresses the Elizabethan problem of a Protestant present with regard to a Catholic past.[38]

---

[38] As mentioned earlier, Hamlet's melancholy is at the core of Walter Benjamin's 1924 analysis *Usprung deutscher Trauerspiel*, translated as *The Origins of German Tragic Drama*. Benjamin's readers have paid insufficient attention to the fact that the repertory of baroque drama he engages

An additional dimension of the problem concerns Shakespeare himself. In 1757, Greenblatt recounts, a document found in the ceiling rafters of Shakespeare's birthplace in Stratford was identified as a "spiritual testament" of his father, John Shakespeare, "conspicuously Catholic in content; written by the celebrated Italian priest Carlo Borromeo." Greenbatt concludes: "There is a clear implication to be drawn from this document: the playwright was probably brought up in a Roman Catholic household in a time of official suspicion and persecution of recusancy. And there is, for our purposes, a further implication, particularly if we take seriously the evidence that Shakespeare conformed to the Church of England: in 1601 [the year *Hamlet* was written] the Protestant playwright was haunted by the spirit of his Catholic father pleading for suffrages to relieve his soul from the pains of Purgatory."[39]

The biographical detective work adds a decisive supplement to the religious conflicts raging under *Hamlet*'s surface. I would suggest, however, that those conflicts as constitutive to the plot and meanings of *Hamlet* were more obvious to audiences for whom the politics of confessional difference and rhetoric was itself closer to the surface. I would certainly include Mozart and Da Ponte in this category. At the moment of his demise, Don Giovanni is too busy to consider theological debate or cultural resistance. His character's subjectivity remains here, as earlier, a function of eros and anger. But the cultural work the opera *Don Giovanni* advances engages an intricate referential world that may exceed the intentions of its two authors.

Le nozze di Figaro *and the Scene of Emancipation*

The eros and anger that dominate *Don Giovanni* foreclose on any chance of social integration, and no social integration of any kind is posited. Don Giovanni dies, and the surrounding characters droop in their acceptance of the political, emotional, and, in the case of Leporello, professional status quo. The nineteenth-century performance convention that omitted the *lieto fine* may have been onto something: notably, the possibility of the work's mendacity along with that of its characters, its indulgence of the survivors' advocacy of an exhausted social ideology. At the same time, libertinism is not identical to liberty. The work of *Le nozze di Figaro* is to tie together liberty and marriage. At what price desire?

Leporello's professional analogue in the Mozartean dramatis personae is Figaro, manservant and intriguer in the house of Count Almaviva. This is an opera about a household that, in its elaborate infrastructure of class, gender,

---

here is Protestant, and that the theatricality / authenticity question is constantly at stake. Hence the centrality of the figure of Hamlet to his largely German frame of reference.

[39] Greenblatt, *Hamlet*, pp. 248, 249.

and professional difference, serves as a social microcosm. In the conventional terms of its comedic form, the work's telos is, first of all, marriage, but more importantly marriage as a synecdoche of harmonious social integration. But the opera raises the stakes on marriage, asserting its normative status as a union not only of emotional and political equals, but as the institution where subjectivity and society—desire and stability—converge. Thus, the stakes of social integration are also raised. These high demands on both marriage and society produce a very uncertain finale. Unlike the finale of *The Magic Flute*, in which the declared resolution of both marriage and social order has a prison house aura, the finale of *Le nozze di Figaro* is utterly fragile in its implied foundationalism.

For Mozart and Da Ponte, the time of *Le nozze di Figaro* is now. As a historical piece, *Don Giovanni* focuses on the burdens of history: the memory of fathers and the return of patriarchal power. In *Figaro*, the political and emotional regimes of patriarchal domination have been displaced by a structure of difference within the same generation. Patriarchy persists in the political and indeed sexual authority of Count Almaviva. The central plot stages the marriage of Figaro and Susanna without submitting to the Count's sexual desire and sexual authority. These together threaten the reinstatement of the feudal *droit du seigneur*, which the Count had himself renounced, as the last available means of gaining Susanna's sexual favor. Alain Boureau has recently argued that the *droit du seigneur* (*droit de cuissage/ius primae noctis*) is hard to find in historical fact, and exists rather as an eighteenth- and nineteenth-century projection on the feudal past. Beaumarchais, Da Ponte's source, turns out to be a principal promulgator of the myth. If Boureau is right, then the discourse of political and sexual freedom at the end of the old regime projected a retroactive historical foil of patriarchal sexual crime.[40] According to this projection, unjust patriarchs were also to be understood as sexual predators.

The plot of the bad patriarch has a comic counterplot: namely, that of the restored father. We have seen the plot of the restoration of the *good* father in the finale of *Idomeneo*, where it jibes with a likely fantasy of Mozart's. Here, at the opera's most comic turn, Figaro's absent parents, mother and father, are restored *tout court*. This most humorous plot twist turns out to be not only the structural foil of the plot of the *droit du seigneur*, but also the most historically rich and symptomatic plot line as well. In the replacement of the bad patriarch with the good father we have a slightly disguised but entirely fungible performance of the basic bourgeois myth known as the family romance.

The trope of the family romance was developed by Sigmund Freud. Its basic articulation, as Freud explains it in his short paper "Family Romances" ["Der Familienroman der Neurotiker"] (1909), involves the fantasmatic ennobling

---

[40] See Alain Boureau, *The Lord's First Night: The Myth of the Droit de Cuissage*, trans. L. Cochrane (Chicago: University of Chicago Press, 1998).

of one's father, resulting as it does from the pressures of the Oedipus complex.[41] Thus, an adolescent or young adult who has failed to achieve freedom from parental authority fantasmatically replaces his father with another, more noble one. These imaginary replacements occupy "as a rule, a higher social station" than the subject's true parents. Yet the ennoblement also stands for an idealization of the true parent, "so that in fact the child is not getting rid of his father but exalting him. Indeed the whole effort at replacing the real father by a superior one is only an expression of the child's longing for the happy, vanished days when his father seemed to him the noblest and strongest of men and his mother the dearest and loveliest of women."[42] On the one hand, the family romance liberates its holder from origins by asserting that he or she comes from a different and more attractive source; on the other hand, by idealizing origins, it reaffirms not only actual origins but the idea and validity of origins themselves.

Two family romances explode in quick succession in the third act of *Le nozze di Figaro*. First, Figaro fabricates one as a ploy to release him from the obligation (against a bad debt) to marry Don Bartolo's housekeeper Marcellina. Following Freud's formula, he claims to be the abandoned child of noble parents, without whose consent he cannot marry. A real family romance is then delivered to him with the revelation that Bartolo and Marcellina are his natural father and mother. The revelation solves four problems. It gives him parents, it gives him legitimate parents (as Bartolo and Marcellina avow their alliance and agree to marry), it motivates them to switch allegiance from the Count to Figaro, and it provides Figaro with parents who will bless his union with Susanna, thereby releasing him from the trap he had unwittingly stepped into by insisting that his marriage (never mind to whom) requires parental consent. Figaro's magical entry into the bourgeoisie coincides with his adoption of the family romance—the need for origins, noble ones if possible—as the bourgeois cultural neurosis, the foil to emancipation.[43]

On one level, Figaro's activation of the family romance is entirely cynical, the instrument of a desperate maneuver. But its unintended and magical result has a profound dramatic, indeed musical-dramatic, result. Figaro's instant nu-

[41] This short paper was first published as a note to Otto Rank's book *Der Mythus von der Geburt des Helden* (1909). The English version was translated as "Family Romances," in Freud, *Collected Papers*, ed. J. Strachey (London: Hogarth Press, 1950), V:74–78.

[42] Freud, "Family Romances," pp. 74–78; esp. p. 78.

[43] For an emplotment of the French Revolution in relation to this trope, see Lynn Hunt, *The Family Romance of the French Revolution* (Berkeley and Los Angeles: University of California Press, 1992). Hunt inflects the category of the family romance with a looser and more positive connotation than Freud's, using it to refer to "the collective, unconscious images of the familial order that underlie revolutionary politics" (p. xiii). Her story involves the fall of the good father and mother, namely the branding of Louis XVI and Marie Antoinette as sexual criminals, a sexual and political delegitimation that enables regicide, which is in turn followed by social reconstitution in the form of a band of brothers.

clear family places his domestic and political plot on new structural ground, as he now campaigns with three allies: his betrothed and his "parents." But just as the goal of marriage functions dually as a marker of political autonomy and personal fulfillment, the instant family also gives Figaro emotional as well as political ballast. In other words, the family romance really works here, as Figaro is accorded the security to develop his own emotional investment. The opera itself legitimizes the family romance by grounding a deeper emotionality in and from the moment of its resolution in the middle of the third act. This new emotional dimensionality is a musical turn, and thus the work of Mozart.

The emotional vocabulary of Figaro in the first two acts is consistent between music and text, and thus consistent with the texts of both Da Ponte and Beaumarchais. As is well known, Beaumarchais was a watchmaker as well as a playwright. The Figaro that emerges from his pen, from Da Ponte's, and from Mozart's in the initial acts, is a counter and quantifier. In the opera's opening moments, we see and hear Figaro counting and measuring: "Cinque ... dieci ... venti ... trenta ... trentasei ... quarantatrè." Unlike Beaumarchais's Figaro, who has finished measuring, Mozart and Da Ponte's Figaro, as a musical personality, measures, sings, and beats time. He is measuring the room for the marriage bed he will share with Susanna. This is, as opera dictates, done to music. And music has the same potential as Figaro for counting and measuring. The music that Mozart supplies for this scene, like Figaro, is functional, rational, and instrumental (in the sense of instrumental reason). At the same time, Mozart has Figaro make subtle and telling errors in his counting and in his music. He starts in increments of five, then jumps to thirty-six (a possible final measurement?) and then to forty-three (which makes no sense). This diagnosis is David Lewin's, who has called these errors "Freudian errors," suggesting that Figaro's numerical slippage reveals that the referent of his increment of increase is something more phallic than the bed. Lewin also shows Mozart's musical absorption of (presumably) Da Ponte's joke: Figaro begins his singing and measuring with an interval of a major fifth on the word "cinque." The interval then stretches and breaks down as the counting proceeds and goes awry. Susanna's response, Lewin argues, "directs his therapy in a manner both manipulative and helpful. The brief scene," Lewin concludes, "is paradigmatic for the opera as a whole."[44]

The "Freudian" gloss supports the two characters' unawareness of these psychic disturbances and corrections. At this point in Figaro's life, the symbolic sphere of the marriage bed is one of counting and measuring, scheming and planning. Figaro and his music go through motions, not emotions. Susanna responds in kind: while he measures the bed, she tries on a bonnet and asks Figaro how she looks. But she is not really interested in his opinion, and he

---

[44] David Lewin, "Figaro's Mistakes," in *Current Musicology* (New York: Columbia University Press, 1995), pp. 45–60; here at pp. 47–49 and 60.

is not really paying attention. One might therefore question Lewin's understanding of her initial corrections as therapy; might they just as well be censorious? In that case, we might have here a pessimistic formula for bourgeois marriage based on instrumental reason and mutual commodification. Figaro's first aria, "Se vuol ballare, signor Contino," instantiates musically the political and emotional bind into which Figaro is currently locked. The words declare "I'll call your tune" to the machinations of the Count, but the music suggests otherwise. The three-beat, mock minuet shows that Figaro is not only using the Count's tune but depending on it. He hasn't found a musical idiom of his own; his political and emotional vocabulary suggests a similarly unfortunate mimetic duplication of the Count's. This mimetic dynamic is repeated at the end of the first act, when Figaro mockingly ratifies the Count's punishment of the errant page Cherubino. Here, in the aria "Non più andrai," Figaro again sings in the Count's voice, miming the authority with which the latter has just dispatched Cherubino to serve in one of his regiments, forming his phrases from the relevant military march.

As Figaro's character deepens, his music modulates from one of measurement to one of emotional depth and authenticity. Susanna's character and music follow a similar path. The question of authenticity has been raised throughout the opera, through the theatrical conventions of stealth, disguise, and discovery. Who is hiding in and behind the armchair or in the closet? Who wrote a letter, who forgot to provide the seal, who dropped the letter? Who jumped out the window? Who is Figaro's father? Who is Figaro's mother? Who is wearing the Countess's dress? The trope of marriage comes to stand for a level of emotional authenticity, a bond sealed by a combination of intimacy and autonomy. Marriage, as the institutional ratifier of subjectivity, must also serve as the paradigmatic social bond. In this ambitious frame, the socially progressive, proto-bourgeois marriage of Figaro and Susanna surpasses the conventional and tired marriage of the Almavivas.

Emotional authenticity is obviously much harder to define, all the more difficult to portray onstage, through simulation. The opera confronts this problem by highlighting the dimension of simulation practiced on the stage. Figaro and Susanna are asked by the opera to hone the emotional authenticity that will bring them into a successful marriage by withstanding tests of simulation. If the motivation of the couple's sentimental education resides, as I have suggested, in the magical denouement of the family romance, then that education has only the final act in which to unfold. Both plots—the political and the sentimental—culminate in the various revelations of the final act, where the literal darkness of the Almavivas' garden creates first confusion and then understanding. In this scene of darkness and shadows, emergent clarity is not coupled with metaphors of light or enlightenment.

The Enlightenment is flagged here as a twin of Figaro: a discourse of measurement and transparence that must be redirected as a discourse of subjectivity. The performative desire of the opera *Le nozze di Figaro* is the union of musicalization and subjectivization. Darkness, or, rather, invisibility works as a corrective to the Enlightenment conceit of transparence. The alternative is a clarity that is neither visual nor transparent: the clarity of the ear.

Mozart seems here to refine through instinct what, seventy years later, Wagner worked into a highly theorized practice of music drama: namely, the designation of music as the carrier of emotional truth, the solvent of masquerade. Music thus dissolves the emotional masquerade in which Figaro and Susanna find themselves entrapped. Their plot depends on Susanna's pretended seduction of the Count through a serenade. Hiding, Figaro listens, as the audience does, to Susanna's unquestionably erotic and tender invitation to a lover. As a result of excess confusion and underconfidence, Figaro becomes convinced that Susanna's serenade to the Count is sincere. Indeed, in the aria "Aprite un po' quegl'occhi [Open your eyes for a moment]," the panicked Figaro shows as a symptom the ocularcentric Enlightenment's abiding contradiction: clairvoyance as the claim of the blind. At this late point in the opera, Figaro's music and character remain exhilarating but obtuse. He then listens to Susanna along with the audience:

> Deh vieni, non tardar, o gioia bella.
> Vieni ove amore per goder t'appella,
> Finchè non splende in ciel notturna face,
> Finchè l'aria è ancor bruna e il mondo tace. . . .
> Vieni, ben mio, tra queste piante ascose,
> Ti vo' la fronte incoronar di rose.

> Oh come, do not delay, beautiful joy,
> Come to where love calls you to bliss,
> Before night's torch illumines the sky,
> While the air is dim and the world is silent. . . .
> Come, my love, amidst these sheltering greens,
> I will crown your brow with roses.

The operatic audience is intended to remain a step ahead of both protagonists here, hearing the underlying sincerity in Susanna's masquerade as she may not hear it herself, and knowing, as Figaro does not yet know, that her sincerity and erotic attachment, and indeed the erotic animus of the serenade itself, are addressed to him and not to their putative recipient, the Count.

In the line of musical aesthetics that prizes melody more than harmony, music comes from song.[45] Here, at the fusion of musicality and subjectivity,

---

[45] Rousseau is this argument's best known proponent, especially in his polemics against Rameau and in his preference for Italian music over French. The argument has been revived recently

subjectivity comes from song. Susanna's serenade is thus a performative utterance, providing the musical/subjective vocabulary and maturity that she comes to inhabit while singing. The song sings Susanna, one might propose, rather than the other way around. Compositional clues indicate the aria's steady deconstructive momentum, as a rhetoric of coy simplicity reverses into one of self-critical earnestness and as seduction becomes desire. The first of the two six-line stanzas proceeds as a relatively conventional serenade, except for a surprising vocal dip to a low A-natural on the words "notturna face." The signal here is opaque, but it is clearly a signal of something, perhaps of its own opacity. A "descent" into interiority is a possible reading. The second stanza addresses the lover directly, and thus carries a higher dramatic and emotional stake. As the address to the lover takes on a double identity—a simulated address of seduction to the Count, and a sincere address of desire to Figaro—the musical line expands and hesitates. The final, long syllable on "coronar" twice generates a delaying vocal ornamentation—the first time a broken F-major (tonic) chord, the second time a sustained F-major note. The third utterance of the word is followed by an eighth-note rest (a full beat, since we are in 6/8 time) marked with a fermata, or long pause. This signal appears clear: Susanna pauses to reflect and take stock of the itinerary from simulation to sincerity that she has just traveled. I will risk an overwhelming generalization here: from Mozart to Mahler, the rest, the musical pause, the moment of silence is the indicator of a first-person musical voice taking stock of itself. Music stops to think.

A parallel performative event grips Figaro moments later. Still ostensibly obsessed by catching Susanna and the Count in illicit embrace, Figaro resorts to words that are themselves costumed in Greek mythological reference, a level of masquerade then trumped incommensurably by the music, which resonates from a new source of emotional depth and authenticity.

> Tutto è tranquillo e placido
> Entrò la bella Venere
> Col vago Marte prendere
> Nuovo Vulcan del secolo
> In rete la potrò
>
> All is tranquil and peaceful
> Beautiful Venus has entered
> To take Mars upon a wave
> Like the Vulcan of a new century
> I'll catch her in my net

---

with a pro-song polemic. See Gary Tomlinson, "Vico's Songs: Detours at the Origins of (Ethno) Musicology," *Musical Quarterly* 84:2 (Fall 1999): 344–77.

Figaro's erudition is notable here, as he refers to the myth of Aphrodite (Venus), Ares (Mars) and Hephaestus (Vulcan), as told in the *Odyssey*.[46] Hephaestus violently traps both lovers in a net; Figaro speaks of catching only Venus (that is, Susanna), and the net may be a snare of love rather than force. He has just heard Susanna's anticipation of being in her lover's arms. Figaro perhaps confuses himself with his lofty reference. His words accomplish the same shift of address that Susanna's did minutes before. A musical intensification underlies the shift. The utterance follows immediately on a vocal ensemble (Figaro, the Count, Susanna, the Countess, and Cherubino) in which disguises and unreadable erotic motives confuse everyone. Figaro's words greet a sudden harmonic shift from G-major (of which the rhetoric is clarity, contradicting the action of the ensemble) to E-flat minor, connoting darkness, mystery, and/or interiority. The music modulates with these lines from an indication of the agitation that offsets the peaceful garden into a lush and exquisite musical phrase that seems to signal his emotional fulfillment and confidence. The music seems to anticipate the reconciliation with Susanna that comes seconds later, as they unite to generate not further embarrassment for the Count, but his own reconciliation with the Countess. The music performs and produces the convergence of desire and tranquility with which the opera attempts to frame the good marriage.[47] At the same time, Figaro's music here resembles Don Giovanni's (allegedly disingenuous) entreaty to Elvira ("Discendi, o gioia bella"!) the guileless and erotically ardent prefiguration of the more disciplined, formal serenade (to Elvira's maid) that is to follow.

In his emotional maturity, Figaro is awarded by Mozart with a musical sensuality that departs from his earlier, metronomic ditties. I suggested earlier that the metronomic pacing of Figaro's two first-act arias are also socioeconomic signals in their miming of and dependence on the metric and social "voice" of the Count. At this fourth-act moment Susanna recognizes Figaro by his voice ("È Figaro"), the analog to his desire. Vocality is thus matched with authenticity, and authenticity with object-desire, that is, non-narcissistic desire. Recall that Figaro's first act "farewell" to Cherubino, which involved the miming of the Count's posture and tone, labeled the young page "Narcisetto, Adoncino d'amor [little Narcissus, little Adonis of love]." The narcissistic here unites the amorous with the political; Cherubino is indeed a young Count in his self-centered pursuits. The alliance of subjectivity and hearing, rather than seeing, as a way into object-relations and out of narcissism follows closely the myth of Narcissus, whose self-love was generated by a visual error. (Cara-

---

[46] See *The Odyssey of Homer*, trans. Richmond Lattimore (New York: Harper and Row, 1965), bk. 8, lines 266–366; p. 128.

[47] For a critique of the opera's heterosexual normativity with regard to this same point, see David J. Levin, "Gender, Translation, and the Dramaturgy of Excess: Peter Sellars Stages Mozart's *Marriage of Figaro*," forthcoming in *Unsettling Opera: Staging Mozart, Verdi, and Wagner*.

Figure 2   Caravaggio, *Narcissus*.

vaggio's painted *Narcissus* of 1598 makes an uncannily similar point, its own visual medium notwithstanding. Narcissus gazes at his own reflection, but the one body part apparently unreproduced in the reflection below him is his abundant, fleshy ear. Narcissus's unreflected ear appears to signal the vanishing point of visuality—the passage to the interior where narcissistic as well as mimetic desire are rechanneled, and where subjectivity resides.)

Since the Countess and Susanna are still in each other's clothes, the Count flirts with his own wife while thinking he is seducing Susanna. Figaro and Susanna watch the spectacle separately, but their musical ensemble tells us that they are reacting with shared pleasure, and Figaro's suspicion seems to evaporate. Nevertheless, a final prank is not beyond him, as he can tease Susanna by making a pass at her, and having her think that he thinks he is making a pass at the Countess. Susanna has a moment's rage, but Figaro reassures her by telling her he knew it was she all along, because he recognized her voice. The depth and conviction of harmony and reconciliation in the finale of *Le nozze di Figaro* reside in the insistence that harmony and reconciliation with another—erotic, political—presuppose the emergence of an articulated, artful self.

Subjectivity has now been staged, in the sense that performance has modulated into the performative, dissimulation into action. What is still at stake is the fragility of the subjectivity that has been achieved by Figaro and Susanna. Daniel Herwitz has in fact observed that *Le nozze di Figaro* is about the possibility of the continuation of desire after marriage.[48] This psychic question is immediately contingent on politics, specifically on the question of the Count's authority. That authority survives as an ominous signal, like the survival of Alberich at the end of the *Ring*.

Of the three Mozart/Da Ponte operas, *Le nozze di Figaro* alone points to a new order of modern subjects. But that formation remains contingent on the position of persistent traditional authority. If marriage and bourgeois autonomy converge in the Figaro/Susanna coupling, what is the prognosis for the marital and social legitimacy of the Count/Countess pair? Is the Count sincere in his apology to the Countess? Does his gesture promise a new beginning in fidelity and social justice? Will the *droit du seigneur* (still real in the opera's imaginary) remain abjured? Will marriage and social justice unite the Almavivas and the Figaros as spouses, citizens, and equals? Is he acting or "acting"? How to read the moment's ambiguity?

The musical-dramatic intensity of his moment of repentance is built on its isolation from what comes before and after it and from what surrounds it. The moment is exceptional. Whether it is "historical," in the sense of marking change, is unclear. Mozart inflates a standard question into a moment of great poignancy. As a musical phrase, the Count's line "Contessa perdono" is answered appropriately by the Countess—in music as well as in words. But the audience possesses evidence of the Count's serial repentance; it has been witnessed in act 2. So at the very least there is something new and something old in the Count's plea: something performed, repeated, as well as something performative and original.

The Count's record of sincerity is not good, and his rhetorical means are limited. To what extent do his musical line and rhetoric convince his audience and the opera's of his sincerity and thus of the transformative power of the moment? The musical line leaves behind the gestures of authority with which

---

[48] See Daniel A. Herwitz, "The Cook, His Wife, The Philosopher, and the Librettist," *Musical Quarterly* 78:1 (Spring 1994): 64.

the Count has consistently asserted his power and at the same time undermined his credibility.

The musical language for the Count's authority has been (in musical terms) baroque—Mozart's consistent stylistic choice for the rhetoric of traditional power and for his mockery of it. The Count's third-act aria ("Vedrò mentr'io sospiro felice un servo mio [Must I see a servant of mine made happy while I am left to sigh]"), blurted on his discovery of Figaro and Susanna's plot against him, spoofs the vengeance aria. It contains an overabundance of baroque ornament for the baritone voice; cruelly, in a way, its vocal undoing of the singer duplicates the psychic pressures on the character. The character, however, succeeds in disavowing the logic of vocal pressure and proceeding as if he were driving an opera seria aria in which da capo repetition (even the musical term resonates politically!) signifies the reinforcement of authority.[49] The Count possesses the authority to drive away the modern anxiety that dismantles his baroque politics and baroque style. (His vengeance aria has a descendent in Ford's soliloquoy "È sogno? O realtà?" in act 2, scene 1 of Verdi and Boito's *Falstaff* [1893]. Here, a bourgeois husband duped by his Elizabethan costume into thinking he can access baroque rhetoric is also undone by his own music. Verdi's orchestra seems first to allow him his declamations, supporting the central phrase "E poi diranno che un marito geloso è un insensato [And then they'll say that a jealous husband is crazy]." But when at the end of the soliloquy the orchestra repeats this phrase, pretending to support its earnest emotion, it mocks it, as the fanfare of ascending trumpets is countered by a staccato trombone on the phrase's descent, as if a bloated orchestral inhalation were being released by farts.)

Count Almaviva, in the finale of *Le nozze di Figaro*, abandons baroque postures and politics, including sexual politics. In his final solo utterance, to which Mozart gives the opera's final musical idea for solo voice, he seems to generate an authentic voice for the first time. Mozart gives his sincerity the benefit of the doubt, rewarding him with fermatas and with the invitation to linger on the half-step, chromatic passage from A sharp to B natural between the second and third syllables of "perdono." The arduous half-step passage combines a certain pained eroticism with a purposive political ardor. The moment expresses at least a flash of hope that the Count and the social system he exemplifies have made a similar "small step for man" onto new emotional and political ground. The Count's tone supplies the Countess with the unimpeachable sincerity of her forgiving response, "Più docile sono e dico di sì," as well as the vocal ensemble's brief development of her remark. Alternatively, ardent sincerity can amount to a deceptive artifice.

[49] See Ellen Rosand, "It Bears Repeating, or Desiring the *Da capo*," *Opera News* (July 1996), pp. 18–20.

In any case, the Count's repentant moment duplicates Figaro's rhetorically complicated passage, "Tutto è tranquillo e placido," discussed above. At these junctures both men introduce into their own discursive repertories as well as into that of the opera itself a differentiating tone that *Don Giovanni* can be said to possess all along. That tone might be described as a "differential heaviness," with which these characters, making subjectivity, confront their surrounding political and discursive ideologies.[50] Beyond the reliability of the Count's sincerity, the opera itself ratifies, through his voice, an erotic investment in sincerity and intimacy.

Mozart wrote *Le nozze di Figaro* in 1786 in response to a much-needed commission following the decline of his five-year popularity as a composer and performer of piano concertos for the Viennese public. The dialectic of solo voice and ensemble that becomes the dramatic principle of this opera is the same formal principle that generates the piano concerti of 1781–86 and hence Mozart's transformation of the genre itself.

The dialogue between piano and orchestra in the piano concerti of the 1780s has been interpreted as a metaphor for that between Mozart and his audience, and by extension that between self and society.[51] In an article called "Mozart's Piano Concertos and Their Audience," Joseph Kerman argues that these works form collectively a musical and biographical arc representing the formation and defeat of dialogical subjectivity.

Kerman describes the pre-Mozartean concerto according to the relationship between discourse (the role of the ensemble) and display (the role of the solo instrument).

> But Mozart added another element to the concerto that is of major aesthetic importance. The two concerto actors, so dissimilar in some respects, nonetheless enter into dialogue. The relationship established between them is not adversarial but something much richer and more interesting, and the art of the concerto now devolves upon that relationship.

Kerman associates this sequence with

> the underlying theme of comedy, the "myth of spring," as Northrop Frye expounded it many years ago. In this myth, the individual is incorporated into society and

---

[50] I borrow the phrase "differential heaviness" from Joseph Litvak's analysis of Jane Austen's *Pride and Prejudice* in *Strange Gourmets: Sophistication, Theory, and the Novel* (Durham: Duke University Press, 1997), pp. 21 and 24. Litvak cites Austen's recorded "disgust" with her own novel for its failure to activate such a differential heaviness against its own ideological matching of a lightness of tone with the bourgeois respectability encased in the teleology of the good marriage. Litvak uses the phrase "Mozartean perfection" (his quotation marks) to mark the tone that combines a "distinctive lightness" with "a symbolic economy of *privation*."

[51] See Susan McClary, "A Musical Dialogue from the Enlightenment: Mozart's Piano Concerto in G Major, K. 453, Movement 2," *Cultural Critique* 4 (1986): 129–68, and Joseph Kerman, "Mozart's Piano Concertos and Their Audience," in *On Mozart*, ed. James M. Morris pp. 151–68.

society is transformed. In one Mozartean comedic fiction, Tamino sues and wins entrance to the social order by playing on a magic flute. In seventeen others, Amadeus plays the fortepiano.

But this formation of dialogical subjectivity on the levels of the compositional and the personal is short-lived. With the C minor concerto, K. 491, Mozart "put his tacit contract with [the Viennese] at risk," Kerman asserts. He describes the work as disturbed and disturbing, monumental, austere and abstracted, not really much fun, strangely cold, deeply subversive, and forbiddingly magnificent. It has thus been perennially unpopular, and yet a favorite of musicians.

> As I imagine it, the whole communal exercise had begun to strike Mozart as hollow, irrelevant to his developing needs as man and artist. It was first Mozart, not his audience, who had begun to experience alienation.[52]

Fair enough, but I would amend Kerman's final insight with the alternative that the work of dialogical subjectivity was not so much abandoned as it was displaced, around 1786, to the more intricate genre of opera. Specifically, the solo voice, with its capacity for dialogue but also for alienation, becomes personified. There is no better example of this situation than the personality and formal placement of the Countess in *Le nozze di Figaro*. Her initial statement at the opening of the second act, the cavatina "Porgi amor," is analogous to the entrance of a solo instrument in a concerto form following an opening ensemble, here corresponding to the first act. (Subjectivity, the placement of the Countess would seem subversively to suggest, is an attribute of the idle rich, which needs to trickle down to the working classes.) If the Countess is the one character who seems not to go anywhere psychologically, this may be because the Mozartean imagination in 1786 cannot transcend this melancholic stance; it can only surround it.

Così fan tutte *and the Scene of Instruction*

The political reality that clings to and outlives the domestic plot of *Le nozze di Figaro* is the persistence of class difference as the displacement of patriarchal hierarchy. Patriarchy and class are both suspended in *Così fan tutte*. The suspension of patriarchy is played out domestically by the conspicuous absence of parents. In a simultaneous enactment and spoof of an Enlightenment trope, patriarchal transmission is replaced by the scene of instruction. Don Alfonso is a Voltairean cynic and pessimist, but the drama that he unleashes is Rousseauian. Mozart's music might be understood to transform Da Ponte's Voltairean treatment into a Rousseauian one. The result is a prismatic investigation

---

[52] Kerman, "Mozart's Piano Concertos," pp. 154, 162, 167, 166–67, 168.

of the authenticity of desire and desire's incommensurability with social order. The postpatriarchal world comes to be defined as undisciplinable. There are two kinds of reason—*ragione*, a word Da Ponte highlights—in *Così*. There is the Voltairean, d'Alembertian reason of the formulaic Enlightenment, and there is the Rousseauian reason of the post-Enlightenment, which is erotic, musical, and socially inchoate.

Rousseau's presence is empirical. Lorenzo Da Ponte had begun his peripatetic career as a professor of Italian and Latin literature at Treviso. He was fired in the summer of 1776 for a transgression that he recounts as follows in his *Memoirs*:

> It was incumbent upon me . . . to have the pupils under my instruction recite on the last day of the scholastic year, compositions written by me on some scientific theme. The one I chose that year was, to my misfortune, the following: whether mankind had attained happiness by uniting in a social system, or could be considered happier in a simple state of nature.[53]

Brazenly, Da Ponte represents as his own one of the most celebrated points of debate of the time, namely the very question Jean-Jacques Rousseau proposed in his so-called Second Discourse, *On the Origins of Inequality Among Men*, of 1754. In a Rousseauian manner, Alfonso undertakes the education of desire. He endeavors to instruct two young men in the laws of nature, the laws of desire. The cosmos he releases is one of unleashed desire. The formula is socially dangerous, as desire cannot be integrated into moral or behavioral institutions. Thus, the dramatic as well as political plot of *Così* involves the staging of subjectivity as constituted by desire. The Rousseauian incommensurability between the state of nature and the social contract is activated. The social order is no longer limited to the old regime.

For Rousseau, the authenticity of the state of nature is irretrievable, but it provides an essential heuristic for the potential corrections of the crimes of culture. Authenticity becomes therefore the legitimizing principle of a society at least minimally aware of the grace of nature.

The grace of nature is only a reference; it must be constructed through thought. The cultural tools required, and employed by Rousseau, are eclectic and potentially contradictory in their dependence on incompatible rhetorics from Catholic and Protestant contexts. Grace and sensuality as bearers of the state of nature are attuned to a Catholic aesthetic. Authenticity and the disavowal of artifice carry Protestant critical investment. The polarities remain as unresolved in Rousseau's thinking as they do in his life. Born into a Calvinist milieu in Geneva, he converted to Catholicism as a nomadic sixteen-year-old in Turin in 1728; he converted back to Protestantism in 1754. His account of a peripatetic adolescence reels between the pulls of (Protestant) law and (Catholic) eros. The two salient facts of his recollected child-

---

[53] Lorenzo Da Ponte, *Memoirs*, trans. E. Abbott (New York, NYRB Books, 2000), p. 52.

hood are the sensual deprivations associated with motherlessness and the bonds to "the religion of my fathers," which left him with an early "aversion to Catholicism." Conversion to Catholicism comes with sensual education, in the company of Madame de Warens.[54]

Rousseau's return to Calvinism is theorized in 1758 in his *Letter to d'Alembert*, whose gist is the rejection of the Encyclopedist's call for the foundation of a theater in Geneva. Playing the Calvinist card of the native Genevan, Rousseau argues that the new moral city conceived, in the mode of Plato's Republic, by the Enlightenment (in whatever legitimacy it retained) should not have a theater, as the theater is a mirror, a representation of reality rather than an aspect of reality. In producing illusion, it confounds education. Appearance, in a formula that runs through Rousseau's work, is fundamentally at odds with reality, all the more so when it celebrates itself. Though aware, he writes on the opening page, of the good things d'Alembert has said of "my country," Rousseau suggests that his readers will share his astonishment at d'Alembert's zeal in focusing on the one institution that Geneva lacks, namely, the theater. Adding a theater to Geneva, d'Alembert had written, would help in forming taste, tact, and delicacy of sentiment in the citizenry. Rousseau calls this advice seductive and dangerous. He can dismiss these virtues as performance arts. The delightful surface of theatrical performance flatters manners and cannot reach morals. Here Rousseau's argument suffers from a fascinating, endemic lexical self-contradiction, as his word *moeurs* can mean both "morals" and "manners," thereby signifying each end of a binary opposition he struggles to maintain.

Rousseau's Genevism marks his discourse as Calvinist as well. Disagreement on the specific nature and social desirability of the theater is one of the most abiding issues in the post-Reformation divide between Catholic and Protestant culture. For the Catholic world, the theater represents the world, but more than that it reflects the authority to represent and thus to order the world. Mimetic authority is not only shared by politics and theater but constitutive of both of them as well as of their interpenetration. In Protestant culture, it is that second claim that is to be rejected, since only God can be understood to possess the ability to represent the world.

Contrapuntal to Rousseau's attack on the theater is his ongoing validation of music as an art of authenticity, indeed, as the art of authenticity. Musicality, for Rousseau, is a double principle, signifying an explicit musical aesthetic that valorizes melody over harmony, Italian practice over French, music as affect rather than music as science, and focuses on the foundation of music in the singing voice.[55] The focus on voice links musicality to its second valence, and that is as a metaphor of an authentic subjectivity that remains opaque to

---

[54] Rousseau's autobiography is of course entitled *Confessions*: an ironic reference to Augustine.

[55] Such are the concerns of the early writings on music, written between 1749 and 1753 and including some 400 articles for Diderot and d'Alembert's *Encyclopédie*.

itself. Musicality as a principle of subjectivity involves clarity without the claim of transparence. Indeed, in valorizing the musical Rousseau devalues the visual world, arguing that the ear and music reproduce the animate quality of nature, whereas the reproductions of vision remain inanimate.

Music, for Rousseau, defines the affective dimension of subjectivity as authentic; the art of desire. Can subjectivity and the art of desire survive and serve the social world in the form of social institutions and stability?[56] Against the cautious affirmative answer offered in *Le nozze di Figaro*, *Così fan tutte* offers a more careful investigation.

Desire itself consititutes the subject and agent of *Così fan tutte*. Desire, in turn, is musically constituted and articulated. Subjectivities constituted by desire destabilize conventional subjects defined by social position, honor, and respectability. The opera's danger resides in its failure—or indeed refusal—to reconstitute a new regime of stability, order, and respectability. In the course of the opera, eros disciplines itself but produces no viable social contract.

The setting is the bourgeois household of two Neapolitan sisters, Fiordiligi and Dorabella, betrothed to Guglielmo and Ferrando. These characters live in a no-man's-land between old and new regimes, social and personal. They are bourgeois figures invested in pseudoaristocratic gestures of honor: military glory for the men, and aristocratic pretension, including feigned madness, for the women. They seem also to be floating between adolescence and adulthood. Half the opera takes place in the Naples home of the sisters, populated by a maid but without sign of or reference to parents.[57]

The two pairs of lovers begin with self-involved posturing: the men bragging about their female possessions, the women looking at locket-portraits of their love objects as if they were looking at themselves in mirrors. Throughout the opera, the women and men search for the gestures and rhetoric appropriate to their positions and situations. In the beginning they pose, unable to find an expressive language. The men claim heroism and honor, the women claim beauty and virtue. Musically, they are stuck in the formulas of baroque opera, or opera seria, the seventeenth- and eighteenth-century style or aristocratic,

---

[56] In his recent study called *Jean-Jacques Rousseau: Music, Illusion, Desire* (New York: St. Martin's Press, 1995), Michael O'Dea comments on the divergence between social order and affect in Rousseau as follows: "The socio-political ideal reestablishes a lost cohesion and secures human freedom, but threatens to push intimacy and the emotions to the margins of life. The affective ideal guarantees intimacy but carries with it the threat of alienation and loss of identity in the surrender to the passionate accents of another person's voice. Is there for Rousseau some larger ideal in which all three can be subsumed? I do not believe so, and instead would argue that much of the energy of his work comes from the tensions inherent in each of these ideals and in the movement between them" (p. 6). Rousseau is at his politically most aggressive and portentous in his retention of a category of desire as formative to the social contract, that is, in the notion of the general will (in *On the Social Contract*).

[57] Their predicament recalls a standard commentary on Charles Schulz's comic strip *Peanuts*: that it portrays a world caught between childhood and adulthood.

court opera that Mozart broke away from and always loved to mock. Unlike the Count in *Le nozze di Figaro*, they have no baroque authority to vaunt or maintain. In this respect they resemble Donna Elvira. The gestures and rhetoric of opera seria, like late baroque painting, are mannered and exaggerated to the retrospective eyes of later observers. Fiordiligi and Dorabella are bourgeois women in a period when the bourgeoisie has not formed a cultural language of identity, gesture, or rhetoric. This adds to their burden. Their dramatic task is not only to find selfhood, but to find a historically and socially valid form of selfhood and expression, and to match this with the satisfaction of desire.

When the women return home after their lovers' feigned departure, Dorabella demands solitude and declares, in an aria that parodies not only opera seria but opera seria arias that Mozart himself has written, that she will go mad. She speaks of her "smanie implacabili": implacable mania. What is really at work is not madness but the release of desire.

That desire had already been mentioned, in a veiled way, in the trio in which the women and Don Alfonso say farewell to Ferrando and Guglielmo. At the same moment, Alfonso speaks of his intrigue in terms of the snaring of Venus and Mars—clearly a trope of which Da Ponte was fond. And just as in *Figaro*, the ensnarement of Venus and Mars carries erotic desire within its net of intrigue. The obbligato sustaining the vocal trio that follows is a tremolo that undermines the very ground it provides through the quivering erotic energy.

> Soave sia il vento,
> Tranquilla sia l'onda
> Ed ogni elemento
> Benigno risponda
> Ai vostri desir.

> May the wind be gentle,
> The waves calm;
> And may every element
> Respond kindly
> To your desire.

The manifest and socially proper meaning of this entreaty is the benign "may your desires, that is, wishes, be granted." But the subtext of the fulfillment of desire is evident enough. Whose desire is in question? Ostensibly, the desire of all four lovers for the safety of the men; just as clearly, however, the sexual desire of all four now liberated from the presence of the betrothed. The logic of Alfonso's ruse is the unfettering of the id in the suspension of the superego. What may be less obvious but equally important is the equation of sexual desire with subjectivity. This moment's musical rhetoric reveals it as a moment of unmasking and sincerity in the course of the opera. Various levels of masking and artifice are seemingly stripped—the costumes of the men (military, so far) and the manners and mannerisms of both the men and the women. The journey in question at the manifest level of the words is the journey (fraudulent, as only the men now know) of the men to war. The latent journey in question, engaged perhaps only by the unconscious voices, is the journey to realization of desire.

The dramatic formula for what follows is a known trope: dissimulation as a means of (censorable) sincerity. The men's reappearance as "Albanians" suffuses the scene with Orientalist sensuality, a signal to stage players and audience alike that the sexual economy has suddenly swollen. When the "Albanians" mention the word "love"—*amor*—the music swells and shivers with erotic tension. After the initial encounter of the foursome, Ferrando sings of the amorous aura ("Un aura amoroso") by which he allegedly refers to his sustaining love for Dorabella, but without ever referring to her. This perfect vagueness was undoubtedly in Da Ponte's plans. What we have is a web of desire without the establishment of the object of desire.

The chiasmus—or switching of the partners—is accomplished steadily. It is also musically programmed. The new combinations of the (Albanian) Ferrando with Fiordiligi and the (Albanian) Guglielmo with Dorabella are more harmonious to the ear, as they match a tenor with a soprano and a baritone with a mezzo-soprano. The long duet that attracts and combines Ferrando and Fiordiligi unites two compatible voices, who are speaking with each other (I will push the pun here) on the same level. Their exchange proceeds from innuendo and sexual tension to confession and union. Fiordiligi says she awaits the arms of her returning lover. She mentions no name. Ferrando answers: "Ed intanto di dolore, Meschinello, io mi morrò [And meanwhile of sorrow, wretched, I shall die]." The word order is important, paving the way for the unmistakable sexual pun on "I shall die," just as we heard it from Donna Elvira in *Don Giovanni*. The same holds for the phallic swordplay between and for Fiordiligi's self-contradictory order to Ferrando to "rise" ("Sorgi, sorgi"), effectively, and possibly consciously, asking him both to desist and to perform sexually. Finally, in a phrase as ardent and sincere as anything uttered in *Figaro*, Ferrando wins Fiordiligi by offering to be both her husband and her lover: "Sposo, amante, e più se vuoi." Now the combination of spouse and lover speaks to the harmony of marriage and desire to which the psychological and musical energies of *Figaro* are addressed. *Così*, one can argue, introduces the "e più" to this economy, a degree of supplementarity. It is precisely the opposite supplement to the one Ottavio offers to Anna, namely the presence of the dead father in the husband ("Hai sposo e padre in me.") This idiotic offer raises the specter of incest; of course Anna will now reject him. In *Così*, supplementarity is pure desire; it therefore destabilizes the opera.

Così ends with a double promise, of which half is realized.[58] Realized is happy mise en jeu of a self-regulating economy of desire. Unrealized is the reattachment of this economy of desire to subjects—that is, to the four characters. Subjectivities, in other words, are not reattached to subjects. The happy end resides in the music, the music drama, and its claim to have reconciled reason and desire. The operatic text (music and words) gives no clue about the reconfiguration of persons that is necessary if the plot is to resolve itself with two marriages. The opera's closing ensemble depicts the four lovers to be sincere and satisfied in their integration into the musical texture of self-regulating desire. But these characters are allowed to suspend the decision necessary for a reincorporation of subjectivity into subjecthood: Whom do I marry? How do I reenter the social order? The structural potential for marriage—a union of legal autonomous subjects as well as a bond of desire, so immanent in *Le nozze di Figaro*, is nil at the end of *Così*.

The musical-visual dialectic overlays that of subjectivities (psychic conditions) and subjects (bodies). The dramaturgy of bodies is a problem. Singing bodies must be physically placed somewhere on a stage, and that decision will communicate the chosen resolution. We can see bodies and their alignments; we cannot see psychic states. An important exception to this assumption arises from the context of mesmerism and animal magentism, sciences—not pseudo-sciences in the later eighteenth-century context—invoked by Despina's antics at the end of act 1 and probably familiar to initial audiences. According to these discourses, attractions are physical and involve material energies and fluids that are potentially visual.[59]

Until a staging of *Così* elects to render visible mesmeric fluid or the visual traces of desire and subjectivity, we can only hear the energies of the continuing work of desire, the continuing work of aesthetic self-formation, and the formations of erotic attachment. According to this musical idea, the work of desire for another person does not result in the positing or the possession of that person as the object of desire.

[58] What "happens" in the end? How are the final couples configured? Music and text remain opaque on the issue. Stage directors have tended to assume that a final decision rests with them. The result is a directorial repertoire of three choices: return to the *status quo ante*, avowal of the new combinations, or general disintegration. But what fourth and largely ignored alternative might result from a serious reading of the stunning dramatic vagueness? Edward Dent argues that the libretto renders the final matching undecipherable. Kerman argues that the return to the *status quo ante* is implied. Solomon asserts that Kerman "is surely right" but adds, "it may not make much difference how the couples are matched. The worm is deep within the apple: after the intervening betrayal and recognition scenes, none of the pairings can be satisfactory" (Solomon, *Mozart*, p. 509).

[59] See Alison Winter, *Mesmerized: Powers of Mind in Victorian Britain* (Chicago: University of Chicago Press, 1998). On the connection between Franz Anton Mesmer and Leopold Mozart, see Gutman, *Mozart*, pp. 241–46.

But is the economy of desire stabilized at the opera's end? The music and text argue yes: "da ragion guidar si fa." At this level, mutuality of desire, mutuality of voice, like two musical lines, combine in harmony and autonomy as a partnership of subjects. What we have in the end of *Così* is what Ferrando promises and what Figaro and Susanna achieve: the synchrony of stability and desire. Desire is primary in the construction of subjectivity but it is not necessarily undisciplined. It is sexuality's discipline—rather than the discipline imposed on sexuality by authority—that this opera defines as enlightenment reason. The sisters have learned that love is not an object—a locket, a portrait. It is no longer a question of the object of desire being locked into a portrait. There is indeed a promiscuous traffic of images in *Così*, from Fiordiligi's opening "Ah, guarda sorella" to the transferred locket that signals Dorabella's betrayal of Ferrando. The concluding maxim of the importance of reason is a post-Rousseauian position that presumes the reason of eros: musical reason. The logic of *Così*'s ending involves the constitution of musical and erotic reason. I would argue that the invocation of reason—"da ragion guidar si fa"—is sincere and unironic, just as the tone of the first-act trio "Soave sia il vento" was unironic.

Musical subjectivity resists incorporation into (human) subjects. The four lovers are allowed, so to speak, by the opera to remain subjects *of* desire in the sense of being subject *to* desire. But that desire is self-regulating as late-eighteenth-century ideas of a naturally ordered economy are self-regulating—as if, in Adam Smith's notion, governed by the just and benevolent authority of an invisible hand. The ending of *Così* thus suspends the return of a political and social reality principle—namely, the question of how such a natural economy will be administered. In the political, social, and indeed patriarchal no-man's-land of this opera, no structure is available on which a social order of responsible subjects can be founded.

Chapter Two

BEETHOVEN: HEROISM AND ABSTRACTION

Heroism and Abstraction

In the preface to his 1987 study *Ludwig van Beethoven: Approaches to His Music*, Carl Dahlhaus made an empirically sound and nonetheless arresting observation. There has never been a "'great' biography of Beethoven," he wrote, "fit to stand beside Philipp Spitta's *Bach* and Hermann Abert's *Mozart*." Moreover, he asserted, there is likely never to be one. These biographies combine "life and work" into a total and coherent whole, and into a cultural monument. The biography and history of the cultural icon itself—"Beethoven"—is perhaps the third element in the equation of life and work. Beethoven is a key figure in this configuration. In the nineteenth century, the "life and work" formula was supplanted by the "myth": "Beethoven hero," in Scott Burnham's formulation.[1] If anything, then, the Beethoven myth may have proven too big for the discursive contours of even the most monumental biography.

The age of monumental biography, Dahlhaus observed, "came to an end with the First World War."[2] The age of the cultural icon, however, did not. In the archive of Western music, Beethoven has remained an icon more so than any other composer. As Burnham suggests, Beethoven is the hero of Western music. His predominant style is dubbed "heroic"; that style's representative work is the Heroic (*Eroica*) symphony. In Beethoven scholarship, the "heroic style" is an increasingly controversial category, now used more as a periodizing epithet than as a general sobriquet. It is used to describe the so-called middle period, with the *Eroica* and the Fifth Symphony the major mile-

[1] Scott Burnham, *Beethoven Hero* (Princeton: Princeton University Press, 1995).

[2] Carl Dahlhaus, *Ludwig van Beethoven: Approaches to His Music*, trans. M. Whittall (1987; Oxford, 1991), p. v. (The original German title, *Beethoven und seine Zeit*, was dictated by the series into which the study fit, and stands in possible contradiction to the principles of the study, as the translator points out. The English language title fits the study better.) Inside German literary circles, the debate over the validity of monumental biography raged into the Nazi period, at which point the genre may be said to have been finally discredited. The cult of genius, the genre's motivating principle and value, was deliberately nurtured by such groups as the Stefan George circle. Some of the most trenchant critiques of the ideology of genius and the resulting genre of heroic biography were leveled against the George Circle by critics such as Walter Benjamin. Thus Benjamin's essay on Goethe's *Elective Affinities* challenged the "biography of the genius" as the basis of literary analysis. Benjamin's bête noire was Friedrich Gundolf's Goethe biography.

stones.[3] Burnham's analysis begins with a chapter on Beethoven's hero, in other words, with an analysis of the hero as a topic or depiction of Beethoven's symphonic writing. In the case of the *Eroica*, the "default" inhabitor of the position of the hero in this work is Napoleon. (Arnold Schering heard the story of Achilles in the musical narrative; more recently, Peter Schleuning proposed hearing it as the story of Prometheus.)[4] The famous vignette of Beethoven crossing out his dedication to Napoleon on receiving the news that he had crowned himself emperor survives as an irresolvable overlay of biography and apocrypha. I will return to the story and its interpretive challenges later in this chapter.

Burnham concludes with a consideration of his titular trope, "Beethoven hero," in which he analyzes Beethoven's heroic status in the history of music, as accumulated by nineteenth-century critics. As his chapter titles indicate, Burnham's study follows the nineteenth-century progression from music's alleged depiction of the hero to the idea of music-as-hero to the ideology of the composer-as-hero. Another and more cynical option in the sociology of reception is the possibility that the heroic style allows its nonheroic listeners to identify with a heroic musical rhetoric, which in turn comes to resemble a deluded sense of the listener's own heroic self. As Burnham speculates: "we will find that we ourselves appear to become mythologized in the process of identifying with this music."[5]

If Beethoven himself became the hero of Western music, the question remains whether that distinction flags the man or the music. For Dahlhaus, Beethoven the republican, Beethoven the revolutionary, and Beethoven the apostle of human freedom are dubious attributions. But these historical and biographical untruths are belied by the attributions' presence as an "aesthetic truth" of the music.[6] The trajectory of "the heroic" in Burnham's analysis, from Napoleonic default to music itself, doubles another historical trajectory, analyzed by Dahlhaus as *The Idea of Absolute Music*.[7] The story of absolute music is the story of how musical form became itself a cultural hero. The story has several key shifts and ambiguities. Beethoven—or perhaps more accurately "Beethoven"—is consistently invoked through these shifts and ambiguities, with a high degree of interpretive uncertainty the result.

The aesthetic valorization of music alone dates from around 1800. As Dahlhaus points out, it emerges less from musical compositions than from aesthetic writings about music by figures such as E.T.A. Hoffmann, Ludwig Tieck, and

---

[3] On the heroic style as a principle of periodization, see James Webster, "The Form of the Finale of Beethoven's Ninth Symphony," *Beethoven Forum* 1 (1992): 25–62.

[4] See Burnham, *Beethoven Hero*, pp. 9, 10.

[5] Ibid., p. 24.

[6] Dahlhaus, *Beethoven: Approaches to His Music*, p. 1.

[7] Carl Dahlhaus, *The Idea of Absolute Music*, trans. R. Lustig (1978; Chicago: University of Chicago Press, 1989).

Wilhelm Wackenroder. Their writings focus on the symphony as the mark of musical integrity, with the Beethovenian symphony as the paradigm.[8] In 1859, the critic A. B. Marx added a Hegelian, teleological gloss to the judgment when he asserted that Beethoven's *Eroica* symphony marked the consummation of music history.

Crucially, the actual term "absolute music" was coined by Richard Wagner in an 1846 description of the fourth movement of Beethoven's Ninth Symphony, in which the bounds of instrumental music are allegedly broken. Wagner's language is infused with a paradigmatic contradiction, as he refers at once to the limitations of instrumental music and to its capacity, now dubbed "absolute," to reach the infinite. This contradiction became the cornerstone of Wagner's aesthetic of music drama. Wagner was not the first to employ that fundament of Romantic metaphysics whereby aesthetic value is measured according to its grasp of the infinite. Indeed, Hoffmann used the same word in his 1813 article "Beethoven's Instrumental Music."[9] But Wagner did shift the ground under the concept "absolute music" at the same time as he coined the phrase that would continue to mark the (changing) concept. Wagner effected the shift from a concept of autonomy and independence in general— music as autonomous from language (the language of words) and representation (the mimetic reproduction of stories and images)—to a concept of authority. To Wagner's as to our ears, the "absolute" still carries a gloss of political authority. Thus, for Wagner, and for the aesthetic of music drama, music that is absolute is also absolutist.

In this regard, Dahlhaus may have done better to call his study "*Ideas of Absolute Music*," even if its generations of theorists cannot be completely separated. The first generation, according to this argument, produced a theory of abstract music. The second generation produced a theory of absolute music indeed, in which authority had supplanted autonomy. After Wagner—until 1945—musical authority often became synonymous with national authority, absolute music, paradoxically, with German music. The realization of absolute German music was narrativized according to various tripartite schemata: Bach–Beethoven–Brahms for Hans von Bülow, Bach–Beethoven–Wagner for Nietzsche, and Bach–Beethoven–Bruckner for August Halm.[10]

In this chapter, I stake out the terms of analysis of Beethoven's musical aesthetic as an aesthetic of abstraction. Abstraction, I will argue, is the key element of his heroic style. Moreover, Beethovenian abstraction must be understood as compatible with the first-generation argument about autonomous

---

[8] See ibid., p. 10. Representative works include Wackenroder's *Psychology of Modern Instrumental Music*, Tieck's essay "Symphonies," and Hoffmann's 1810 review of Beethoven's Fifth Symphony in the *Allgemeine Musikalische Zeitung*.

[9] See J. Hermand and M. Gilbert, eds., *German Essays on Music* (New York: Continuum, 1994), pp. 59–64.

[10] Dahlhaus, *The Idea of Absolute Music*, p. 119.

music, and thus as different and distinct from the idea and ideology of absolute
music as codified by Wagner. What this means is that Beethovenian autonomous music refuses and resists absolutist postures. It does so formally through
a critique of representation in music. In this way, a musical aesthetic becomes
a form of political engagement and political critique, and as such overrides
the incompatibilities in the politics of Beethoven the man. Heroism and abstraction thus form together as a rhetoric of refusal. Similarly, Beethoven's
heroism is itself abstract. If it feeds no political ideology, it likewise provides
no concrete charter of political emancipation. Reducing the claims of musical
heroism may thus buoy its integrity; this is indeed a political integrity but one
that remains a politics of form.

If Beethoven's music is heard to argue or assert a position, it does so autono-
mously from nonmusical utterances. Here, another distinction of Dahlhaus's
is key: that between the aesthetic subject and the biographical subject.

> A proper definition of the relationship between the "aesthetic" subject and the
> "biographical" subject—between the hypothetical first person discovered in the
> scores and the no less hypothetical human being discovered in the documentary
> evidence—is essential, for without such a definition it is frankly impossible to arrive
> at a valid interpretation of works.[11]

Dahlhaus equates the first-person, aesthetic subject with subjectivity. Though
subjectivity, he continues, "is not always or necessarily implied by musical
expressivity, it is all the more marked as a characteristic of the music of Beethoven." Nineteenth-century Beethoven reception, he reminds us, equated
the aesthetic subject with the biographical subject. Thus August Wilhelm
Ambros wrote in 1865 that "[t]he picture of the mighty inner life of a Titanic
soul is unrolled before us—we are no longer interested in the tone poem
alone—we are also interested in the tone poet. We already stand . . . with
Beethoven as we do with Goethe: we survey his works as the commentary on
his life."[12]

If Dahlhaus corrects the chronic fusion of aesthetic and biographical subjects, he does not address the fusion of subjectivity with heroic subjectivity,
or with the Titanic soul of Ambros's not atypical rhetoric. Thus the abiding
centrality of "Beethoven hero" has perpetuated the identification of musical
subjectivity with Beethovenian heroic subjectivity. I hope that the preceding
chapter on Mozart's critical yet nonheroic musical subjectivity has shown the
inaccuracy of this assumption. That inaccuracy may also shed light on the
ideological investments that led nineteenth-century criticism to trivialize Mozart in comparison with Beethoven.

[11] Dahlhaus, *Beethoven: Approaches to His Music*, p. 31.
[12] Ibid., p. 30.

If Beethovenian heroic subjectivity, as a characteristic of the musical subjectivity in his works, is abstract, then by definition it cannot tell a concrete story, cannot represent a concrete self. Beethoven's music does not have the Mozartean capacity for personification. I see no reason not to perceive this noncapacity as a principle of style and aesthetic choice, rather than as a detriment. The issue becomes central to any discussion of his opera *Fidelio*. Sharply distinct from its Mozartean models, *Fidelio*'s music does not itself personify to build musical correlatives of psychologically nuanced characters. In the language of my discussion of the opera below, the music does not seek or find "voice." This tendency needs to be understood as an aesthetic principle rather than a flaw, unique and odd as the resulting opera may be in relation to others. Moreover, just as Beethoven's music refuses to personify a psyche, it also refuses to claim the status of a collective voice. In nineteenth-century terms, and in opposition to the stakes of Beethoven reception, the music does not and will not fuse with or infuse a national music. Against Wagner's view of Beethoven, it must be asserted that Beethoven's works neither achieve nor portend the making of a national music.

At the same time, abstraction as a category only makes sense as a negation of the concrete, and therefore with reference to the concrete, if only as a system of perception and representation that it chooses to disavow. Thus, as a rhetoric of refusal—the refusal of representation—abstraction emerges as a deliberate counterpode to the representational world that surrounds it. Abstraction is culturally informed. Abstraction does therefore refer to, and perhaps oppose, the representational world that it will not engage through mimetic representation.

In a 1985 article called "Beethoven's 'Orpheus in Hades': The *Andante con moto* of the Fourth Piano Concerto," Owen Jander advanced a controversial thesis about this movement's status not only (as Liszt and Marx suggested) as "Beethoven's most elaborate venture into the realm of program music" but (in Jander's judgment) as "the most totally programmatic piece of music—great art music—ever composed."[13] The music thus tells "the story of Orpheus taming the wild beasts with the music of his lyre." Beethoven sketched the concerto soon after he had begun using the new Viennese six-octave fortepiano, which enabled him to evoke the sound of the harp—in other words, Orpheus's lyre. Moreover, the Orpheus story had returned to Vienna in multiple genres in the preceding decade. Ovid's *Metamorphoses* was printed there for the first time in 1791 as a result of Josephinian reform and the lifting of censorship. Gluck's Viennese opera *Orfeo ed Euridice* was staged in 1774, followed by operas on the Orpheus theme by Johann Gottlieb Naumann in 1786 and Friedrich August Kanne in 1807. The fourth piano concerto was first performed in 1807 in the palace of Franz Joseph von Lobkowitz, who had been

---

[13] *Nineteenth-Century Music* 8:3 (Spring 1985): 195–212; here pp. 195 and 197.

involved in the publication of the *Metamorphoses* along with Josef Son-
nleithner, the librettist of *Fidelio*.

Jander's dramatic claim, regarding one of the most loved and most played
works in the repertory, was made at a time when the musicological establishment, the guardians of interpretation, remained defensive about the distinctions between so-called absolute and so-called program music. The music criticism and especially the philosophical music criticism of Beethoven's time,
which focused on Beethoven's music, had split into two directions: the advocacy of abstraction, soon called "absolute music," and the advocacy of a music
of ideas. The abstract faction, led by Hoffmann and his milestone essay on
the fifth symphony, won out over the "music of ideas" paradigm of A. B. Marx.
Marx's principles are analogous to the critical tropes of his contemporary
Robert Schumann, who attached emotional correlatives to musical utterances
according to the vocabulary of *Seelenzustände* (conditions of the soul) or *Stim-
mungen* (moods). The "absolute" faction inspired the conservative, anti-
Wagnerian faction in mid-nineteenth-century musical scholarship, as led by
Eduard Hanslick and later by Heinrich Schenker in Vienna. In the aftermath
of the Second World War, the Holocaust, and the migration to England and
America of large numbers of distinguished music scholars, this paradigm again
asserted itself as formalism, directed once again against program music and
Wagnerism, both of which had become toxically associated with the ideologies of fascism and the Third Reich. Formalism and positivism, and their
underarticulated historical contingencies, set the stage for the current patriarchs of music scholarship reared after 1945. "When I was young," writes
Joseph Kerman, more symptomatically than analytically, "analogical or metaphorical efforts of this kind were taboo in academic music studies. The manda-
rin, Miltonian position was to dismiss such discourse as 'incorrigible' and 'literally meaningless.' In today's musicology, though, meanings are discovered
everyway." For Marx, musical forms and structures are often inspired by or
associated with an extramusical idea, such as the life of Napoleon that guides
and finally names the Heroic symphony. But the music of ideas functions as
a commentary, not as a narrative, as in the case of program music. Jander's
position is thus more radical than Marx's.

The musicological establishment has reacted to Jander's claim with skepti-
cism but perhaps without the resolve required to work through its challenge.
Two examples have been Kerman and Leon Plantinga, who both spent much
of the last decade completing major studies of the concerto form.

Kerman's book, *Concerto Conversations*, offers a survey of the concerto as a
principal genre of the music of dialogue.[14] For Kerman, concerto conversations

---

[14] The praise of music as conversation comes from Goethe, who suggested in a letter to Zelter
that the string quartet recounted a conversation among four rational voices. *Briefwechsel Goethe
Zelter*, ed. W. Pfister (Zurich and Munich: Athenien, 1987) p. 304; cited in Joseph Kerman,
Concerto Conversations (Cambridge: Harvard University Press, 1999) pp. 38, 132 n 1.

offer three modes of duality: polarity, reciprocity, and reconciliation.[15] Kerman cites Jander's claims without taking a clear position, but in the following passage he seems to settle into a Marxian understanding of a music of ideas:

> listen to Beethoven's Piano Concerto No. 4 in G major, the Andante con moto movement, a work which has so often been held up as a paradigm of concerto aesthetics. All the way through this much-discussed piece, until just before the end, piano and orchestra have completely different music. Yet generations of listeners have heard these different musics not as independent, but as a precisely modulated series of responses—piano to orchestra, and orchestra to piano. From early times this musical conversation has been read, with a unanimity very rare in Beethoven reception, as a specific narrative: a narrative of harshness and appeal, acquiescence and release, crisis and reconciliation. A narrative of Orpheus, of course, and the Furies.[16]

In 1999, Plantinga published a thorough and systematic study called *Beethoven's Concertos*.[17] The full chapter devoted to the fourth piano concerto carries the decidedly programmatic title "To Sing of Arms and Men." It begins by asserting this work to be "Beethoven's most captivating work in the genre" and by claiming that its most arresting attribute is the brevity of the middle movement, the andante con moto.[18]

Plantinga's account of its dialogical mood is more austere than Kerman's: the movement "offer[s] us a vividly sketched dialogue between piano and strings, one that seems to begin in dead earnest discord and distance but in the end achieves at least an uneasy resolution." The movement, Plantinga continues, "joins many other among Beethoven's instrumental works that conjure up *the idea* of voices and song and dramatic situation. . . . The sort of musical rhetoric Beethoven gives us seems intimately bound up with situation, character, speech. . . . And there can be no doubt about elements of implied human drama here: a protagonist and antagonist, a relationship between the two that changes over time from implacable opposition—even their very worlds of discourse seem at first opposed—to some agreement, reconciliation, maybe sympathy."[19]

In an essay of 1859 cited by both Jander and Plantinga, Marx had suggested that the andante con moto movement is analogous to the episode of Orpheus and the Furies, as mediated by Gluck's operatic setting. Jander, however (in Plantinga's summary), "proposes that what Marx made was not an analogy but a discovery: he discovered the 'truth' that Beethoven, in composing this

---

[15] Ibid., p. 21.

[16] Ibid., p. 42.

[17] Leon Plantinga, *Beethoven's Concertos: History, Style, Performance* (Cambridge: Harvard University Press, 1999).

[18] Ibid., p. 185.

[19] Ibid., pp. 186, 189; emphasis added.

movement, consciously set about to create a detailed and specific musical counterpart to the story of Orpheus and the Furies."[20] And, for Plantinga, this claim lacks evidence. Neither Beethoven nor his contemporaries said anything about such a program. For Plantinga, Jander goes too far, and should have limited his reading to the appreciation of a Marxian idea or analogy.

In my reading, Jander's argument fails because it doesn't go far enough. Amply supported in its circumstantial and formal thesis that this movement tells the story of Orpheus in Hades, it strays, I would argue, in calling the result program music. This argument is a one-way street. It doesn't return to the music. What Beethoven does is flag and absorb the Orphic program, and return it to the discourse of music alone. He does so—or, rather, the movement does so—by flagging and absorbing not the Orpheus story alone but the story as a vessel for the tropes of music and modernity that date back to Monteverdi's adoption of Orpheus as the mascot and allegory of the musically new.

The movement is not *telling* Orpheus but *being* Orpheus. In addition to Marxian analogy, we have here an allegory. Indeed, it is a double allegory. The music offers an allegory that allows it to return to a discussion, in music, of itself. The music is talking about itself as music; it is speaking in the first person. In doing so, finally, it is foregrounding representation in order to offer a critique of representation. It is, one might say, setting precisely the trap into which Jander's explication will fall.

This claim—that the music *is*, that it embodies, Orpheus and that this turns it into first-person music—is key to an assessment of Jander's analysis. To my ear, Jander shares one error with his critics, and that is the habit of hearing the narrative of this movement as a third-person narrative: the music is *telling* the Orpheus story (Jander), *referring* to it (Marx, Kerman), or not (Plantinga). In contrast, I would propose that the drama of this movement resides in the piano's stealthlike and subversive appropriation of the work's narrative voice as a first-person voice. This can be understood as a form of quotation, specifically that form, in Mieke Bal's explanation, that functions as a "shifter" of the original meaning, thus "allowing the presence of multiple realities within a single image."[21]

The concerto is quoting the Orpheus story in order to set up a music of subjectivity, a music that engages the world in a first-person voice. Why is this important? Because the first-personhood of the music transforms its historical position, and in its wake, that of the other music of the long nineteenth century. For such a first-person voice accrues as a kind of awakening critique of (baroque) power—again, Orpheus and the Furies, not represented or repeated

[20] Ibid., p. 192.

[21] See Mieke Bal, *Quoting Caravaggio* (Chicago: University of Chicago Press, 1999), p. 10. See also above, chapter 1, footnote 22.

by or in the music, but quoted, as a correlative to the music's production of subjectivity. The baroque and the modern, intertwined, in polemical dialogue.

If we hear and understand this movement to be quoting the Orpheus story, we also hear it to be positing a distance between itself and that story. Its narrative of the Orpheus story becomes a citation of the story, a marking of its own distance from the original account. Distance, in the sense of the distinction and perspective required for the dialogue between two subjects, is a hallmark of modern subjectivity. In recognition of these qualities of quotation and distance, I should immediately correct the formulation I have just made and argue that the first-person voice of this movement involves not "being Orpheus" but rather "being *like* Orpheus" or "being Orphic," citing the Orphic trope in its cultural-historical availability. Nineteenth-century audiences heard a music talking about itself in a critical and generous spirit, engaged with its world and with its listeners.

Heroism and Anxiety

Beethoven's rhetoric of abstraction, synonymous with the heroic subjectivity in the music, opposes a culture of representation that repeats and reasserts the baroque Imperium. His rhetoric of abstraction thus bespeaks a Protestant aesthetic, often in contradiction to his own professed personal actions, tastes, desires, and claims.

Beethoven the man, as Solomon's work has incisively exposed, was fraught with anxieties and pretenses about his social origins and status. Beethoven the man surfaces as a massive symptom of the European generation of 1789, for whom the historical transition from feudal to bourgeois society opened substantial psychological chasms and anxieties. Just fourteen years younger than Mozart, Beethoven belonged to a European cohort that could not avoid facing and judging the events of the French Revolution and their European aftermath, including the Napoleonic sweep eastward. With every milestone and radicalization of the Revolution—most intensely with the proclamation of the Republic, the regicide, the war with the European monarchies, and finally Napoleon's claim to be conquering Europe in the name of liberty, fraternity, and equality—those very principles appeared more bound up with violence and mass politics. The Mozartean panorama of personal freedom had quickly become obsolete. Historians need to value the extent of political and personal confusion that ensued.

The German world added its own complexities to its hypersensitive reception of the transformations effected in and from France.[22] Liberals who sup-

---

[22] See R. R. Palmer, *The World of the French Revolution* (New York: Harper Torchbooks, 1972).

ported the revolution of the rights of man, the Revolution of 1789–91, tended to balk at the violence of the Terror in 1793–74. For the philosopher G.W.F. Hegel, born the same year as Beethoven, the disintentegration of the Revolution into terror disqualified it as a general turning point in world history.[23] For Beethoven, the crucial event appears to have been Napoleon's auto-coronation as emperor of France in May 1804, in which he symbolically redirected his power and legitimacy away from the principles of 1789 toward a reinvestiture of the old regime.

Bonn, the city of Beethoven's birth and youth, was at that time a court city, housing the Elector of Cologne. From 1784, the elector was Maximilian Franz, a Habsburg, brother to Joseph II of Austria and Marie Antoinette of France. More like his brother than like his sister, Max Franz believed in both enlightened despotism and enlightened religion. The question of the logical and indeed the political validity of such compromise formations is a bane of European historiography. The Beethoven family was a family of court musicians. Beethoven's revered grandfather Ludwig had been *Kappellmeister* to the court; his father was a court tenor, whose career foundered as a result of his alcoholism.[24]

Solomon's psychoanalytically informed biography of Beethoven has little to say on the question of religion. His wise essay of a decade later called "The Quest for Faith" makes up for that gap.[25] It begins: "Little is known about the nature or extent of Beethoven's religious beliefs during his Bonn years. He was born and baptized into a Catholic family, but apart from neighbors' conventional references to his mother's piety there are no reports that his parents were practicing Catholics, let alone that they instilled any of their sons with religious feeling."

It is very difficult to have a sense of the nature of belief in late-eighteenth-century Europe in general. The compromises between religion and secularization and between Catholicism and Protestantism are intricate. Religious difference is no longer organized according to doctrinal difference but according to social, political, cultural, and stylistic difference. Beethoven's adolescence is perfectly dated for maximum ambiguity: during the so-called Josephinian decade (1780–90) of toleration and rational religion. This decade is followed by a quarter-century of revolution and Napoleonic sweep. Paradoxically, the restoration of Catholic regimes after 1815 reestablished the cultural symbolism

[23] See G.W.F. Hegel, *Philosophy of Right*, trans. T. M. Knox (Oxford: Oxford University Press, 1967), and Joachim Ritter, *Hegel and the French Revolution*, trans. R. Winfield (Cambridge: MIT Press, 1982).

[24] In her sociological study *Beethoven and the Construction of Genius: Musical Politics in Vienna, 1792–1803* (Berkeley and Los Angeles: University of California Press, 1995), Tia DeNora argues that, in keeping with his paternal legacy, Beethoven's first decade in Vienna was professionally dependent on court culture and the contexts of private patronage and performance.

[25] Maynard Solomon, "The Quest for Faith," in *Beethoven Essays* (Cambridge: Harvard University Press, 1988), pp. 216–29.

of the Catholic baroque and gave renewed clarity to the Catholic-Protestant divide. Catholic and Protestant cultures are to be understood as cultural, symbolic systems more than as doctrines of belief.

Beethoven's most influential—musical and intellectual—mentor during his Bonn years was Christian Gottlob Neefe, a Protestant with "Masonic and Illuminist propensities."[26] Through Neefe, Beethoven found a work that remained important throughout his life: Christian Sturm's *Reflections on the Works of God in Nature* (Beethoven's most heavily annotated copy is the edition of 1811). Sturm speaks from that underremembered voice of the eighteenth century that reconciled a pantheistic world with the postscientific world. God and science shared the tendency to the well-ordered world. Organized religion has little place in this compact. Such a position on religion has its own politics, which is much more compatible with the internalized world of Protestantism than with the external, representational world of the Catholic baroque.

For the quarter-century following his 1792 arrival in Vienna, Beethoven perpetuated the illusion that he held a patent of nobility: that his bourgeois Dutch "van" signaled an aristocratic German "von." Indeed, he insinuated himself at all points into the aristocratic circles of his patrons, and was on excellent terms with members of the Habsburg imperial family, most notably Archduke Rudolf, brother to Emperor Franz. (The piano sonata op. 81a, titled *Les adieux*, is dedicated to Rudolf on the occasion of his departure from Vienna during the French occupation in 1809.)[27] It is a reality of Beethoven's personality and career that he never bit the hand that fed him. Ironically, as Solomon points out, the nobility pretense secured Beethoven's bourgeois status, as it foreclosed on the possibility of a conferral of a patent of nobility by one of his Habsburg patrons.[28]

This aristocratic insinuation combined with consistent delusional behavior about his birth year and family origins. The result is an intricate set of variations on Freud and Rank's myth of the family romance, in which Oepidal desire for the love of one's true parents is distorted into (and hence allowed by) the fantasy that one is really the child of other parents. The fantasy parents are in turn nobler than one's own; classically, they are royalty. Beethoven's family romance has indeed "nuclear" Oedipal components, but it transcends his private sphere to become exemplary of the cultural, historical myth of the family romance that prevailed across Europe in the wake of the end of the Old Regime in the French Revolution. Especially in France, where in 1792

---

[26] Ibid., p. 217. See also Neefe's memoir: *Christian Gottlob Neefens Lebenslauf, von ihm selbst beschrieben Nebst beigefügtem Karackter 1789*, ed. Walther Engelhardt, (Cologne: Im Arno Volk, 1957).

[27] See Dahlhaus's analysis of this biographical fact in relation to the aesthetic subject, or "lyrical first person" of the sonata, in *Beethoven*, pp. 31, 34–35.

[28] See Solomon, "The Nobility Pretense," in *Beethoven Essays*, p. 47.

and 1793 the monarchy was overthrown and the king beheaded, the postrevolutionary literate bourgeoisie wrestled with its self-conception as an orphaned
class by reading endless novels about orphans.[29] Beethoven was thus a member
of that generation of 1789 whose bourgeois status—in its political and fantasmatic auras—meant both freedom and abandonment.

Beethoven consistently disavowed the year of his birth, a delusion that
Solomon has convincingly interpreted as motivated in the desire to merge his
identity with that of a brother, named Ludwig Maria, who died before the
composer Ludwig's birth.[30] Most notably, late in his life for a period of over
fifteen years, Beethoven did nothing to suppress the rumor that he was the
natural son of King Frederick William III of Prussia. The rumor surfaced in
1810; after repeated queries, Beethoven admitted its falseness in a letter of
December 1826, and then failed to post the letter.[31] Significant in this delusional filiation is not only the formulaic family romance about royalty, but
more specifically the projection of north German, Protestant filiation. The
figure of the Prussian king may be displacing several fathers, from Johann
van Beethoven to Ludwig's Habsburg patrons, but the projected musical (and
thereby also cultural) paternity of another Johann—J. S. Bach—must be suspected to contribute to the compromise formation. The Ninth Symphony, it
will be important to remember, carries a dedication to Frederick William III.

Beethoven's contempt for the baroque Imperium found the perfect displaced target in "Emperor" Napoleon in 1804. As Dahlhaus and others have
cautioned, myth and history are difficult to separate when addressing the leg-
endary revocation of the dedication of the *Eroica* symphony to Bonaparte.
The source is Beethoven's pupil and assistant Ferdinand Ries, who wrote in
his memoir that "I was the first to bring him the news that Buonaparte had
proclaimed himself emperor, whereat he fell into a rage and exclaimed: 'Is he
too no different from an ordinary man! Now he too will trample all the rights
of man beneath his feet, indulge only his own ambition; he will set himself
higher than all other men now, and become a tyrant!' "[32] Neither Ries nor
Dahlhaus appears to have remarked on the contradiction lodging within Beethoven's comment itself: his defense of ordinary men is offended by the realization that Bonaparte has proven himself ordinary. Dahlhaus does not question
the credibility of Ries's account, but points out that Ries did not know when
he wrote his memoir that Beethoven's spontaneous reaction "was not his last
word." Beethoven later reinstated the phrase "Intitulata Bonaparte" in pencil,

---

[29] Lynn Hunt has developed this argument in *The Family Romance of the French Revolution*
(Berkeley and Los Angeles: University of California Press, 1992), as discussed in the previous
chapter.

[30] See Solomon, "The Posthumous Life of Ludwig Maria van Beethoven," in *Beethoven Essays*,
p. 83.

[31] Maynard Solomon, *Beethoven* (New York: Schirmer Books, 1977), p. 5.

[32] Dahlhaus, *Beethoven: Approaches to His Music*, p. 23.

and on 26 August 1804 he wrote to his publishers Breitkopf and Härtel that "the symphony is actually [*eigentlich*] entitled Bonaparte." The eventual published first edition carried the title "Sinfonia Eroica . . . composta per festeggiare il sovvenire di un gran Uomo [Heroic symphony . . . composed to celebrate the memory of a great man]." With this account, Dahlhaus appears almost to retract his own statement that the account of Beethoven's initial gesture was a "myth"; it appears to be a fact, its survival however contingent on an incomplete account of a complicated gestural event. Dahlhaus's conclusion appears sound: "it is as the 'preservation' of 'the spirit of the hero' . . . that 'memory' is to be understood in the 1806 title of Beethoven's symphony. What the *Eroica* realizes aesthetically is not the image but the myth of Napoleon, which was associated with the myth of Prometheus."

Solomon has pointed out that the withdrawal of the dedication had earlier harbingers. It was Napoleon's Concordat with the Vatican of July 1801 that first raised Beethoven's anger, causing him to comment that "everything is trying to slip back into the old rut, now that Buonaparte has concluded his Concordat with the Pope."[33] For Beethoven then, Napoleon abjured his heroic status when he made peace with the Catholic Imperium. If Beethoven's anger in May 1804 showed support for his threatened Austrian inhabitants, there too the cake is sliced in intricate ways. Beethoven was conceivably expressing solidarity with the fellow inhabitants of Vienna in the moment of their siege under an imperial aggressor; that solidarity does not amount to an endorsement of the Austrian Empire against the winds of 1789! Thus the *Eroica* stands both for the identification with Napoleon and the rage against him. This contradiction must be understood to inhabit future traces of the so-called heroic style.

Heroism is assertive. The heroic style is a style of assertion. With the heroic assertion of the two opening blasts of the *Eroica*, Beethoven becomes, as Scott Burnham recounts, "the hero of Western music, 'The Man Who Freed Music.' "[34] According to this trope, music is freed from the eighteenth century, which means from the Old Regimes and from classicism. The "heroic decade" signifies as well Beethoven's transcendence of the classical and its form. The style and structure of the music of the so-called classical period (Haydn, Mozart, Beethoven) have been described as dialogical.[35] A dialogical pattern develops from sequences of musically articulated propositions and responses. An initial phrase is amplified, altered, or contradicted by a responding idea.

With Beethoven, the problem is that the culmination of the heroic style—the *Eroica*—is also its undermining, meaning the withdrawal of the Napoleonic dedication in its rhetorical and cultural context. Moreover, the very

---

[33] Solomon, *Beethoven*, p. 135.
[34] Burnham, *Beethoven Hero*, pp. xv–xvi.
[35] See Charles Rosen, *The Classical Style* (New York: Norton, 1977).

opening bars of the *Eroica* combine heroic assertion with a signal of its own apparent deconstruction. As Burnham writes: "No one denies the overtly heroic effect of the two opening blasts, and it is almost comic to see how programmatic interpreters inevitably rush off with the impetus of these two chords only to stumble a few bars later when they realize that something distressingly less than expeditious heroism is implied by the much-discussed C# in bar 7. The tendency for critical discourse to slow down when passing this spot mirrors the inability of the piece itself to get started in a convincing fashion. What kind of a hero would pause so portentously at the very outset of his heroic exploits?"[36] But is it inability, I would ask Burnham, or is it refusal? Burnham may in fact anticipate this question when he observes that in the movement's ambiguities "we start to understand the power of Beethoven's heroic style as an expression of the conditions of selfhood."[37] This notion of selfhood includes self-awareness and self-doubt. It thus implies a first-person voice, in the guise of a *presentation de soi* that unfolds through time. Simultaneously, the hero who is thinking and speaking in this movement is thinking about its own heroic status, and the music that is thinking and speaking is thinking about its own heroic style.

In this way, the very opening of the *Eroica* can be heard to contain the proposition of its deconstruction, of the deconstruction of the heroic style and its rhetoric of subjective assertion.[38] The later Beethoven, the postheroic, if that term is meaningful, involves the reinscription of the dialogical and critical rhetorics of classicism into a music of profound self-consciousness—and that in the dual meanings of self-awareness (Hegel's *Selbstbewusstsein*) and self-critique. Through the formal inscription of this interiority, Beethoven reinvents classical rhetorical, as well as North German and Protestant cultural style.

The *Eroica*'s rhetorical agenda abides. A first-person narrative unfolding of heroic subjectivity forms the agenda of the Beethovenian symphony as a series of works and as an accumulating aesthetic. If we shift categories from "style" to "voice," then we can assert that Beethoven's symphonic voice, the companion to heroic style, is a heroic, first-person narrative voice. In the history of reception, the content of the heroic narrative has changed, with particular emphasis on the first movement of the *Eroica*, from the hero himself (vague as that category may be) to the self-aware hero, as Burnham emphasizes. From this stance, Beethoven's music is able to work through cultural contradictions to extents unavailable to Beethoven the man.

After the rejection of Napoleon, what is heroic for Beethoven beyond the abstract idea of heroism? My hypothesis: Leonore. Empowered by the operatic

[36] Burnham, *Beethoven Hero*, pp. 4–5.
[37] Ibid., p. 24.
[38] I understand the term "deconstruction" to refer to an ongoing examination of a work or work-like phenomenon for its multiplicity of meaning, which will still prove to be context-spe-

capacity, since Mozart, of personified music, Leonore becomes the most articu-lated, most personified bearer of Beethovenian heroic subjectivity, which now seems capable of negotiating every obstacle except the politics of gender. For that reason, the figure of Leonore will paradoxically raise rather than reduce the stakes of abstraction.

Fidelio

In 1804–5 Beethoven was occupied with the composition of his opera *Leonore*, the first version of *Fidelio*. The first performance took place in November 1805, soon after the French occupation of Vienna. It was revised in May 1806 with a new overture: the heroic orchestral narrative known to posterity as *Leonore* no. 3. The final revision of the work—the name changed by the theater man-agement to *Fidelio*—was revealed in 1814, with a new overture that does not attempt to summarize the narrative content of the opera. These revisions are significant for the understanding of Beethoven's postheroic, or at least post-*Eroica*, voice. They accrue indeed into an ongoing experiment in which pre-cisely the creation of the postheroic heroic voice is at stake. This voice is the protagonist Leonore's voice. The logic that the revisions follow is the difficult rearticulation of the Beethovenian heroic voice as the voice of Leonore. At their prompting we ask what if Beethoven isn't—and has no interest in being—Prometheus? What if Beethoven wants to be—and wants always to remake himself as—Leonore? The final imprimatur on the opera, replete with the later opus number, accompanies the doubling of the plot's gender disguise: Leonore is disguised as Fidelio, *Leonore* as *Fidelio*, a symphony as an opera, and an opera as a symphony.

Fidelio is a moral and political opera about heroic love, marriage, and the integration of private and public life. The generic vocal quartet (such as the one Beethoven will employ in the radical "choral" movement of the ninth symphony) is here personified in the characters of Marzelline, Leonore, Jac-quino, and Rocco. This is the roster of the characters who in fact do sing the quartet that announces the heroic stakes of the opera in the first act's second scene. In the quartet that closes the opera (joining, as in the ninth symphony, the full chorus), the light tenor Jacquino is replaced by the heroic tenor, Flo-restan, whose rescue forms the opera's main plot. *Fidelio* demands that the postrevolutionary, indeed post-Napoleonic bourgeoisie pursue an integrated path of private love and public virtue. It asks Biedermeier audiences not to withdraw into privacy but to bring domestic virtue into political service. To be tendentious, one can say that it asks the question: What happens to Figaro

---

cific and coherent. I do not mean a kind of hostile "dismantling" or assertion of meaninglessness, as is often implied by popular adoptions of the term.

and Susanna between 1789 and 1815? *Fidelio* is about two couples who answer this question in two radically different ways. Conventional—and condescending—opinion holds that the dramatic weakness of *Fidelio* results from its incoherent juxtaposition of the petit bourgeois (Marzelline, Jacquino, Rocco) and the heroic (Leonore, Florestan). But these extremes enclose the cultural space in which the new bourgeoisie is to reside.

Fidelio is, paradoxically, a lone survivor of the French genre of the rescue opera, most current in the revolutionary period. It is based on J. N. Bouilly's *Léonore, ou l'amour conjugal* of 1798, which was in turn drawn from an actual episode from the period of the Terror. So this tale of emancipation is in fact grounded in counterrevolutionary zeal, or at least in the desire to stem French revolutionary excess. This political and nationalistic resonance became much more explicit in the revised version of 1814 and has a great deal to do with the work's success. As Solomon has observed, "if in 1805–06 *Fidelio* could be understood as a rescue opera expressive of Enlightened belief in the triumph of nobility over evil, in 1814 the work unfolded fresh meanings which accelerated its popular acceptance. The new version could readily be perceived as a celebration of victory over the Napoleonic forces by the Allies, and as an allegory of the liberation of Europe from the aggressions of the tyrant/usurper."[39]

The overture to *Fidelio* is the fourth work written for the purpose, this one for the revised version of 1814. Like its predecessors, this overture is an allegory of heroism and liberation. Unlike them, however, it does not build an allegorical narrative of Leonore's heroism and emancipation of her husband. (The narrative drama of *Leonore* no. 3 is so convincing that, in encapsulating the plot of the opera itself, it has been said to upstage the drama itself. Donald Francis Tovey held that it "annihilates the first act."[40] Current performance convention offers it to the audience in between the second act's two scenes—with the function of recapitulating allegorically for the audience the heroic scene that has already transpired onstage.) The *Fidelio* overture of 1814, rather than build an allegorical narrative, offers an allegorical statement. It begins with a proposition (musically unrelated to the music of the opera itself) and continues with its elaboration, much in the mode of the Fifth Symphony. The initial development of this first thematic statement builds in a long crescendo with regular support from the tympani. This crescendo, involving a repetition of a basic theme with its regular beat reinforced by the percussion, forms a

---

[39] Solomon, *Beethoven*, pp. 223–24. The ambiguity between universal and national liberation in *Fidelio* has continued to serve the allegorical investment of German audiences. The most renowned post–World War II performance of the work remains the one that reopened the Vienna State Opera House in 1955, the year of the founding of the Second Republic and the departure of the Red Army from Vienna. The performance was broadcast to the public in the streets around the opera house. What was being celebrated: republicanism or nationalism?

[40] See ibid., p. 200.

rhetoric of interiority and insistence—the inner resolve that Leonore will invoke in her first-act soliloquoy. This crescendo charts the formation of an ethical conviction—indeed of an ethics of conviction. A crucial trope in nineteenth-century German music, it will be revisited notably in the opening measures of the first movement of Brahms's First Symphony. Solomon calls the *Fidelio* overture a "festive curtain raiser."[41] I would disagree, over a fundamental point: Beethoven's intransigent resistance to rhetorics of theatricality. The overture is not, then, an allegory of dramatic action but of the ethical determination that will be at the core of this drama.

The action of *Fidelio* takes place in an ahistorical Seville—in other words it is just far enough removed in place and time not to raise censorial brows. Beethoven's symbolic investment in Seville may involve some distorted engagement with his own encodings of two Catholic cities: his birth city, Bonn, and his adopted city, Vienna. Florestan's Seville and Beethoven's Bonn/Vienna both involve liberation from old Catholic regimes hovering between authoritarianism and enlightenment. (The adolescent Sigmund Freud invested precisely in this displacement of the Austrian Imperium. With his friend Eduard Silberstein he developed a shadow universe, speaking in Spanish and encoding Spanish cities to stand for German capitals. Thus Madrid stood for Berlin, and Seville for Vienna.)[42]

The scene of *Fidelio* is a prison, in which the evil warden Don Pizarro unjustly interns political prisoners. A freethinker named Florestan has been Pizarro's secret prisoner for two years, and his wife Leonore, determined to find out whether he is alive and if so to rescue him, has been hired as a jailor's helper, in the male disguise of Fidelio. The jailor, Rocco, has a daughter named Marzelline, who is betrothed to his other assistant Jacquino, but who has now fallen in love with Fidelio.

The first of the opera's two acts begins at the level of the petit bourgeois and the banal. Marzelline is ironing, and Jacquino is pestering her. He leaves the stage several times to attend to the front gate. His exits and returns make the scene an allegory of the banality of marriage: she does chores, while he leaves in the morning and returns in the evening, always frustrated. Is *this* the result of the domestication and embourgeoisement of Figaro and Susanna between 1789 and 1815? The knocking on the gate, though never concretized by a corresponding stage action, indicates some kind of important intrusion into these small lives. It is signaled by the orchestra—abstract, portentous, and overdetermined. Musically, these blasts recall the stone guest knocking on Don Giovanni's door. In their abstraction and nonpersonification, they

---

[41] Ibid.

[42] For a more thorough account of Freud's friendship with Silberstein and their Spain fantasy, see Phyllis Grosskurth, *The Secret Ring* (Reading, Ma.: Addison-Wesley Publishing Company, 1991), pp. 26–27.

resemble the gesture in the final movement of Schubert's Symphony no. 9, which some interpreters have hastened to allegorize as "death knocking on the door," with a reference to *Don Giovanni*. Like Schubert's noises, Beethoven's are not concretized, despite their operatic context. They allegorize intrusion, but the intrusion remains abstract.

Rocco and Fidelio enter. Rocco tells both Fidelio and Marzelline that he knows what is in their hearts, and that he will ask Pizarro for permission to announce their engagement. In the ensuing vocal quartet, each character ponders his or her domestic fate, from frustration (Jacquino) to bewildered hope (Fidelio) to—for the moment—satisfaction (Rocco and Marzelline). Cleverly, Fidelio presses Rocco to prove his confidence by allowing him access to all the prisoners. Rocco agrees.

In scene 2, Don Pizarro receives a warning of the impending, unannounced visit by an emissary of the king; he resolves to have Florestan murdered. Leonore overhears him, but doesn't know whether he is referring to Florestan. With added urgency, Fidelio persuades Rocco to let the prisoners into the fresh air for a moment, her ulterior motive being her desire to scan the prisoners for her husband. The prisoners emerge and with great dignity sing a melancholy but increasingly resounding hymn to the sun and to freedom. A solo tenor voice elaborates on this paean, and a bass voice cautions the others to keep their voices down, as they are being "watched with ear and eye [Wir sind belauscht mit Ohr und Blick]." The surveillance of prisoners operates with eye and ear, but especially through the ear, as the prisoner's concern is that the chorus is too loud. The sonic arch of the prisoners' hymn, having stretched from melancholy to joy and from piano to forte, now returns again to the dissipating piano of resignation, as Leonore is forced to help herd them back into their cells.

The emergence and reincarceration of the prisoners is musically and symbolically potent. These are, of course, literal prisoners. But they carry in their voices multiple cultural and symbolic associations. The group of harmonized male voices refers, in both musical and extramusical contexts, to the army and the church—to a solidarity of power and a solidarity of faith. Beethoven consistently mixes his references to faith and power, to peace and to militancy. (A clear example is the "alla Marcia" section with tenor solo of the Ninth Symphony's choral movement.) These prisoners represent the subjection and suppression of male harmony. They are—as Leonore understands—Florestan multiplied by a hundred, and thus harbingers of his own decomposition.

The prisoners' recognition of their position as objects of surveillance fits into a well-known trope of the equation of modern society with the destabilization of the ego. An illustration of Bentham's panopticon and Foucault's resulting general metaphor of surveillance, this scene combines the surveillance of the eye with the surveillance of the ear. The prisoners' recognition that surveillance operates "with the eye and the ear" signals the overdetermined cultural authority in which they are caught. They are caught in an ideological apparatus that is premodern and modern, Catholic and Protestant, baroque and administrative, spectacular and surveillant.

Foucault's parable of modernity as a system of surveillance argues that surveillance has replaced spectacle by internalizing it. Foucault's model of internalization is Catholic: baroque spectacle is internalized as amour propre. In the reliteralization of modes of modern surveillance—as in the prison—Foucault, following Bentham, identifies control with a regime of the eye.[43] Also following Bentham, John Stuart Mill in *On Liberty* (1859) defines the modern loss of individuality as the condition whereby "everyone lives as under the eye of a hostile and dreaded censorship."[44] From Mill to Foucault, the terror of modernity lies in the availability to hegemony of both literal and projected surveillance.

Freud uses similar terms to address the psychic dynamics of the internalization of authority. In his 1914 essay "On Narcissism" he writes that "a power of this kind, watching, discovering and criticizing all our intentions, does really exist; indeed, it exists with every one of us in normal life. The delusion of being watched presents it in a regressive form, thereby revealing the genesis of this function and the reason why the patient is in revolt against it."[45] But Freud makes a significant move here, in combining, like the prisoner in *Fidelio*, the internalization of authority in both visual and auditory metaphors. And whereas the internalization of visual authority produces the anxiety of being watched, the internalization of auditory authority produces the sensation of hearing inner voices. Thus, conscience is the internalization of surveillance, just as in the broader cultural and historical context Protestant interiority is the internalization of baroque spectacle and visual control. The inner voice may remain the voice of external authority. The task of emancipation is to free subjectivity, to free the voice from the bonds of those forms of external authority that are politically and psychologically harmful.

The surveillance of the ear is especially horrifying here, as it a fortiori subsumes music. The freedom of these prisoners from their surveillance becomes essential as it becomes equated with the freedom of subjectivity and the freedom of music. The overcoming of a surveillance of the ear is achieved through the regaining of voice: the ability and the courage to sing loud. This restoration is the task—Leonore's task—in the second act.

Act 2 begins in Florestan's dungeon cell. The starving, isolated prisoner consoles himself with the knowledge that he has done his duty to speak out

[43] See Michel Foucault, *Discipline and Punish: the Birth of the Prison*, trans. A. Sheridan (New York: Pantheon Books, 1997) [translation of *Surveiller et punir: naissance de la prison*] (Paris: Gallimard, 1975).

[44] John Stuart Mill, *On Liberty* (1859; Harmondsworth: Penquin Books, 1982), p. 125.

[45] Sigmund Freud, "On Narcissism: An Introduction," in *General Psychological Theory*, ed. Philip Rieff (New York: Macmillan, 1963), p. 76.

against Pizarro. Florestan's recitative ("O Gott! Welch' Dunkel hier! [Oh God! What darkness here!]") defines a foundational moment not only for the opera itself but for the genealogy of political rhetoric in German Romantic opera in general. It takes a tripartite structure similar to Leonore's first-act aria. Both begin with denunciation of the current injustice, continue in a mood of consolation and dignity in the memory of past justice and public and private happiness, and conclude in a mood of hope. Leonore's hope is resolute and practical: conjugal love will inspire heroic rescue. Florestan's hope has given up the possibility of action. His aria concludes with a hallucinatory conjuring of "the angel Leonore," accompanied by a rhapsodic oboe obbligato. The oboe is an odd sound in Beethoven's orchestra. Its oddness is acute in this scene as it generates a kind of psychotic music, hovering between inner experience and external phenomenon, in the ambiguity that produces hallucinations. This obbligato marks the broken boundaries between sanity and delirium, mind and word, and imprisonment and emancipation. (Wagner will develop a similar effect with the English horn in the third act of *Tristan und Isolde*.)

Beethoven creates an uncanny effect here, as the passage is both exquisite and in an important way unlistenable. Florestan and his oboe—the voice of his desire and his delirium—are in sonic texture and harmonic line both compatible and contradictory. The listener must in some way choose which voice to follow. The listener is strained by the interpretive decision as to whether Florestan himself hears the oboe or not, in other words, as to whether the oboe signifies an experienced auditory delusion, or whether it in fact signifies the opposite—namely, Florestan's inability to grasp the (auditory) world around him. The mad scene in Donizetti's *Lucia di Lammermoor*, with its solo flute accompanying Lucia's coloratura, is in some way a bizarre younger sibling to Florestan's music here, but a vastly less interesting one. Lucia's flute is a voice of external, penetrating madness, taunting and torturing like a Hitchcockian bird; Florestan's oboe is an internal voice of both madness and ecstasy. Lucia's voice and her flute alternate, enabling the listener to give the combination coherence, to tame it. The counterpoint of Florestan and his oboe allows the listener no such smug superiority.

Significantly, this passage was added for the first time in the revised version of 1814. William Kinderman comments that "[t]he final section of this aria is one of Beethoven's most significant monuments to the Romantic tenet that the current of subjectivity, of spiritual activity, of the individual's apprehension of *value*, is more real than external reality."[46] I would interpret the moment's importance to Romantic rhetoric differently and more negatively. This moment enacts and thereby warns of a simultaneous breakdown of psychological and political integrity. Florestan's psychotic separation from his own voice,

---

[46] William Kinderman, *Beethoven* (Berkeley and Los Angeles: University of California Press, 1995), p. 106.

his acoustic as well as visual hallucination, will be relieved twice: for the first time through his hallucinatory *jouissance* and delirium, and for the second through Leonore's actual intervention and rescue.

The politics of hallucinatory satisfaction are interesting, especially in relation to Romantic aesthetics. In 1808, Friedrich Schlegel converted to Catholicism along with his wife Dorothea, the daughter of Moses Mendelssohn. The aesthetic motivation of religious converson carried political ramifications, as the Romantic generation shifted from a discourse of liberation to one of guardianship and conservatism. Between 1831 and 1833, the poet and critic Heinrich Heine (born in Düsseldorf, exiled in Paris; born Jewish, converted to Protestantism) wrote a savage essay called "The Romantic School." Written over the cusp of the deaths of Goethe and Hegel, the essay faced the predicament of the future of German intellectual life. In it, Heine took to task both the Romantics themselves and their European popularity on the grounds of the reactionary slippage mentioned above. The French in particular, Heine wrote, had been hoodwinked into philo-Germanicism by Mme de Staël's book *De L'Allemagne*, and Mme de Staël had herself been hoodwinked by her association with August Wilhelm Schlegel, whom she had engaged as tutor to her son. Heine's contempt for the Schlegel brothers and for the Romantic School in general focused on their peculiar German brand of medieval and Roman Catholic revivalism, which the French, he argued, had no way of understanding.

Heine defines the Romantic School as "a passion flower rising from the blood of Christ . . . a strange flower of unpleasing color, in whose chalice can be seen depicted the instruments of torture used at the Crucifixion of Christ, namely, hammer, tongs, nails, etc., a flower that is by no means ugly, only eery, indeed, the sight of which even arouses in us an uncanny pleasure like the convulsively sweet sensations which result even from suffering itself. In this respect the flower would be the most fitting symbol of Christianity, whose most gruesome attraction consists in this very ecstasy of suffering."[47] Heine thus sees the ecstasy and mortification of the flesh as a peculiarly German Catholic mode of aestheticization. The sublime is thus revealed in its two opposing yet complementary guises: the ecstatic, and the melancholy and/or uncanny.

Florestan's initial, hallucinatory satisfaction is thus symptomatic of the transposition of Romantic political rhetoric from a rhetoric of emancipation to one of redemption, a transition that *Fidelio* does not advocate. In the deliberations of the self-proclaimed Romantics, the desire for reenchantment was answered by the allure of conversion to Catholicism. (Hence the conversion of the Schlegel circle, and Heine's vilification.) After the restorations of 1815,

---

[47] Heinrich Heine, "The Romantic School," trans. Helen Mustard, in *The Romantic School and Other Essays*, ed. Jost Hermand and Robert C. Holub (New York: Continuum, 1985), p. 3.

Catholicism remained the most tempting option until it was surpassed, after the failures of 1848, by the next form of opera: Wagner's music drama and the new totalizing genre of the *Gesamtkunstwerk*.

Fidelio is a political opera; it is about the demand for justice in the public world. Justice must be obtained—demanded—through the ethical action of ordinary people. Such action must reach heroic proportions when necessary. The shrinking of the political world after 1815 displaces the efficacy of political action in the public world to a subinstrumental hopefulness. In this way, emancipation is displaced to a rhetoric of redemption. To an extent this change involves the nostalgia for magical, divine intervention. The historical passage from emancipation to redemption is marked by the transition from *Fidelio* to Carl Maria von Weber's *Der Freischütz* of 1822. Here, a woman must be prepared to sacrifice herself to tame demonic forces (magic bullets) uncontrollable by men. The final step in the replacement of political emancipation by magical redemption is taken by the women who traverse Wagner's music dramas, in which the active, heroic, rescuing woman (Leonore) is replaced by the passive, neurotic, redemptive woman (Senta, Elisabeth, Elsa, Kundry). Even the truly heroic Brünnhilde is tripped up by the plot around her, and can regain a heroic posture only in suicidal ecstasy. It is indeed therefore significant—as Kinderman notes, but for this more complicated, contextual reason—that "Florestan's aria is among those parts of the opera that most deeply impressed Wagner; and traces of its influence are felt in Tristan's 'delirium' scene in the last act of *Tristan und Isolde*."[48]

Florestan's hallucination is followed by the appearance of the real Leonore. We might pause here for a moment to analyze how this passage from illusion to reality is informed by Beethoven's hierarchy of the senses—precisely, by his valorization of hearing over seeing. Florestan, as he presents himself to us, lives in a visual universe defined by two kinds of privation: darkness and hallucination. He laments the darkness and says that nothing around him lives or moves. He lives also in complete silence but says nothing about that. His own reliance on visuality becomes truly psychotic as he sees, or at least claims to see, an angelic Leonore. To return to the question of the oboe obbligato, it might then be the case that Beethoven wrote this voice precisely not as an inner voice of Florestan's but as the opposite, as an external voice that he does not hear. Florestan's imprisonment is about deafness and voicelessness. The dark dungeon of Florestan/Beethoven's being involves the inability to hear. (The composition of *Fidelio*, between 1804 and 1814, coincides with the finality of Beethoven's deafness.) Metaphor meets physiological literality as Florestan's real freedom—Beethoven's most ardent desire—becomes the restoration of hearing. There is coincidence here, deserving of respect, between

---

[48] Kinderman, *Beethoven*, p. 106.

Beethoven's existential silence and his allegorical emplotment of silence as a political metaphor.

Rocco and Fidelio enter with the task of digging Florestan's grave. Leonore leads with a lamp; she sees, but in the darkness she is more attuned to what she hears. She is descending into psychically as well as politically defined depths. The dungeon is also the depth of the psyche, where id, ego, and super-ego compete for control and where internalized authority competes with voices and images. Leonore recognizes Florestan first by his voice. Florestan, however, does not recognize his wife's voice, but sees something uncanny in her face. (His reduced state apparently compromises his deployment of the operatic rule of sound's superior reliability to sight. Leonore, on the other hand, deploys the operatic hierarchy of the senses correctly.) Rocco hurries Leonore in the digging of the grave, and accuses her of lagging in her work. She protests that she is not lagging, but seems immediately to realize that what she is insisting on is her participation in the digging of a prisoner's—perhaps her husband's—grave. Motivated perhaps by this thought, and per-haps also by the memory of her complicity in herding the other prisoners back to their cells, she now turns to the still unrecognized crouching prisoner and declares in the name of God that she will free him whoever he may be:

Wer du auch seist, ich will dich retten!
Bei Gott! Bei Gott! Du sollst kein Opfer sein!

Whoever you may be, I will free you!
By God! By God! You shall not be sacrificed!

Universal emancipation means redemption from sacrifice. Florestan stirs, speaks, and is recognized by Leonore with ear and eye—"mit Ohr und Blick." Rescue is, after all, a fantasy of benevolent surveillance: someone to watch over me, as the song says. Continuing to traffic in emblems of sacredness, Fidelio persuades Rocco to give the prisoner water and bread. Through the course of these exchanges, in other words, at the foundation (in the depths) of material and spiritual life and ritual, she already—and prematurely—acts within the material and sacred symbolic structure of the domestic, conjugal scene her rescue seeks to restore.

Pizarro enters with a dagger, and shouts that his moment of triumph has come. As he raises his arm, Fidelio intercepts him. Pizarro shouts at Fidelio to get out the way, upon which Fidelio cries "First kill his wife!" Leonore does not sentimentalize her own position, and expects Pizarro to try to kill her along with Florestan. As he moves to stab them both, Leonore pulls a pistol from her vest. A trumpet sounds, announcing the arrival of the king's minister. Numerous critics have commented on this deus ex machina moment, either with disapproval (Bertolt Brecht) or with approval, the latter exemplified perhaps most famously by Ernst Bloch's designation of the trumpet call as "the aesthetic anticipation of social hope."[49]

At this point I must say something about the music, or, more precisely, about a moment to which Beethoven gave no music. The rescue scene has been carried out to excited and exultant orchestral and vocal sound. Left alone in the cell, Florestan turns to his wife and, in a spoken and unaccompanied voice, asks rhetorically "Treues Weib! Frau ohne Gleichen! Was hast du meinetwegen erduldet? [Faithful wife! Woman without equal! What have you endured for my sake?]" Leonore replies, also with unaccompanied speech: "Nichts, mein Florestan [Nothing, my Florestan]."[50] Now, here is what Beethoven *wants* to become of Figaro and Susanna, of bourgeois marriage, after 1815. What he portrays here is the union of conjugal love and moral heroism in a self-understood, a priori manner that defies articulation. Beethoven the artist withholds his art to literalize Leonore's statement of "That goes without saying." Beethoven's practical translation of this notion is "That goes without music." Leonore's sublime (in the Kantian sense) word "Nothing" is said against the aura of silence, and not against music, which would in an important way be self-contradictory. The move is especially radical in the context of audience expectation; according to the aesthetic of the Singspiel, which would inform the mixing of speech and song, the higher the moment's dramatic stakes, the more intense the music. Here Beethoven does indeed represent nonrepresentation.

This moment of musical silence is followed by an exultant duet: "O namenlose Freude! [Oh indescribable (nameless) joy!]" With a clear gesture in the words to indescribability, namelessness, and unrepresentability, Beethoven restores to Leonore and Florestan the powers of music, voice, and listening:

Nach unnennbarem Leide
So übergrosse Lust!

After unnamable suffering
Such infinite joy!

Leonore sings these phrases first and Florestan repeats them. First his wife and his liberator, Leonore is now also his music teacher. That lesson taught, she leads him out of the darkness of hallucination and into the light.

There are further resonances to this sequence of musical silence and the restoration of voice and hearing. They involve the different ways—musical,

---

[49] Ernst Bloch, *Das Prinzip Hoffnung* (Frankfurt, 1959). See the discussion in Dahlhaus, *Beethoven*, p. 182.

[50] These cumbersome words have many performing variants and are usually updated somehow; often this spoken exchange is (unfortunately) omitted altogether, in breathless anticipation of the sung duet that follows.

symbolic, and political—in which Leonore's heroism restores voice both to herself and to Florestan. In *Fidelio*'s final scene, Leonore's vocal writing is resplendent and utterly singable (as opposed to the vocal line in her first-act "Abscheulicher!" ["Villain!"] aria); and it is, the dense ensemble writing notwithstanding, audible (as opposed, for example, to the buried alto voice in the final movement of the Ninth Symphony). The triumph of Leonore—more vis-à-vis Beethoven than vis-à-vis Pizarro—is her voice: vocal, musical, and political. Her singing instantiates Kant's use of the German language's equation of maturity and the right to speak: *Mündigkeit*.[51] By not allowing her to sing in her most sublime conjugal moment—"Nichts, nichts, mein Florestan"—Beethoven subjectivizes her own recognition of the transendence of art by ethics. The ethical voice can then, with new glory, incorporate—that is, literally, embody—the aesthetic, *sung*, voice.

The privileged voice and the privileged subjectivity in *Fidelio* is Leonore's. Hers is the opera's guiding voice. For Beethoven, the voicing of Leonore becomes an act of radical otherness. That otherness is first instantiated in the trope of the heroic-as-woman. The heroic woman relegitimates the postheroic, post-Napoleonic, post-1815 man's world. Having thrown off her Fidelio disguise, Leonore remains a hero; she is never a "heroine." She is a manly woman, inappropriate to male fantasies of and desires for grace, for mothering, or for seduction. She does not save the world for men; perhaps she saves men for the world, which is unquestionably the ethically and politically superior action. In the multiply displaced pantheon of modernity, Leonore is the most austere of bourgeois, Protestant goddesses. She is Athena.

Where is Athena's place in the City of Man? The emancipation of the other prisoners, along with Florestan, is brought about through the beneficence of an unnamed king, via his representative Don Fernando. Shocked to find that Florestan is alive, Fernando greets him as "the giant who strove for truth." Made aware by Rocco of Leonore's deeds, Fernando asks her to remove her husband's shackles. Beethoven confirms the sacredness of the moment with a general hymn to God's judgment (*Gericht*)—not mercy. Florestan, his voice having been restored in the "Namenlose Freude" duet but only in imitation of Leonore's, is now unchained, literally, as a musical and political agent. He initiates a round of praise for Leonore that the chorus repeats, ending the opera. At this moment, audiences might legitimately be moved to understand and indeed honor the deaf Beethoven's titanic investment in restoring to Florestan in a single stroke his political voice and his ability to hear. At the same time, we might be sensitive to Leonore's silence in the restored City of Man.

[51] The reference here is to the first line of Kant's 1784 essay "What Is Enlightenment?" ["Was Ist Aufklärung?"] in which enlightenment is defined as the emergence from self-imposed immaturity (*Unmündigkeit*).

Fidelio's difficult combination of the abstract and the concrete poses a dramaturgical challenge, and the decisions and values of a production that manifestly takes on the issue may prove instructive. I would therefore add a postscript to my treatment of *Fidelio* in response to Jürgen Flimm's highly interesting production for the Metropolitan Opera, which premiered in October 2000. Flimm's direction, together with Robert Israel's set design, places the action in a mythical present-day landscape. Seville, as a default operatic place symbol, is replaced by a visual world rendered familiar by recent cinematic style. The prison is a contemporary one, a Benthamite panopticon, where isolation and dungeons have been replaced by systems of surveillance. The guards' weapons are contemporary; the domestic scene is slightly antiquated, reminiscent of postmodern revisitations of film noir, or indeed of early television's domestic comedies.[52] The fact that this visual world is familiar but not real adds up to an alienation effect, in which scenic abstraction returns the action to the level of the music. The spectator is recast as a listener. Unexpectedly, this aesthetic of visual abstraction is abandoned in act 2, scene 2, with a turn to concrete historical allegory. The liberation of the prisoners is cast as a multireferential gloss on the fall of communism in 1989, with Don Pizarro suddenly transformed from film noir warden to the generic communist potentate, from Lenin to Ceausescu. Here, an insistence of visual specificity intrudes on the general aesthetic of abstraction through which the visual world of act 1 had grasped the work's musical-dramatic principle of abstraction.

The Symphony No. 9

The locus classicus for the confrontation of "absolute" and representational music is the fourth movement of Beethoven's Symphony no. 9. In adding a chorus, four vocal soloists, and hence words to a symphonic work, Beethoven appeared to his nineteenth-century music scholars to undermine the aesthetic of abstraction in whose name he himself had developed the symphony. Heinrich Schenker's 1912 monograph *Beethoven's Ninth Symphony* is particularly interesting on this point. As a successor to Eduard Hanslick in the valorization of the musical absolute, Schenker is caught between his absolute reverence for Beethoven and for this symphony on the one hand and his contempt for program music on the other. His strategy is therefore to consider the "nonmu-

---

[52] I have in mind David Lynch's *Blue Velvet* (1986) and Curtis Hanson's *L.A. Confidential* (1997), as well as *The Honeymooners*, for example. If these associations are apposite to Flimm and Israel's conception for this production, then their sensitivity to predictable visual associations of an American audience in the year 2000 is on the mark. The fact that Israel teaches scenic design at UCLA is relevant here.

Figure 3   *Fidelio*, act 1, Metropolitan Opera, 2000.

Figure 4   *Fidelio*, act 2, scene 2, Metropolitan Opera, 2000.

sical" elements of the symphony's fourth movement as a brute fact of history, as if Beethoven simply had no choice but to assimilate it. "To be sure," Schenker writes, "Beethoven found himself as he began the finale in an extraordinarily difficult situation. To have singing voices enter out of nowhere after three movements filled with the most highly developed instrumental arts ran counter to his natural disposition, just as it also runs counter to the psyche of the listener to accept such an act of force unless the composer's justification for it is provided simultaneously."[53] Beethoven justifies the arrival of this intrusive element (words) by attempting to declare its necessity in musical terms alone. Schenker ultimately throws up his hands at this impossibility of justifying words from within music, as "[t]he persuasive power of music has force only in its own realm."[54]

In arguing at once for the rhetorical force and futility of Beethoven's announcement of the arrival of an external element, Schenker invokes and then rejects a parallel from drama. The example is illuminating.

> Shakespeare . . . often enough confronted assumptions that were, to be sure, intrinsically impossible and unbelievable, but which, since they formed the point of departure of the drama or appeared somehow necessary on other grounds, he wanted nevertheless to have accepted by the viewer as possible and probable. He made it his business in such cases to validate the dubious assumptions for the viewer in some way, and to make them digestible.
>
> Thus he lends credibility to the "ghost" in *Hamlet*, for example, simply by establishing at the very outset, even before we ourselves and Hamlet have seen it, that the ghost has already been seen by Horatio, Marcellus, and Bernardo, and thus certified as real precisely by this fact![55]

Thus, in the world of absolute music, programmatic content is an intruder, the ghost of an antiquated authority, the ghost of a king, and King Hamlet at that! An aesthetic old regime of representation is equated with a political one. Beethoven the modernist can by sheer force declare the old regime to be present, but even he cannot provide a reasoned argument for its legitimacy or indeed for its integration. Beethoven emerges as the victim (rather than the agent) of the material presence of words, with no choice but to deal with them. His compromise, in Schenker's unwitting political allegory, is the Biedermeier compromise whereby the aesthetic modernist accommodates the persistence of the old regime and its ciphers.

Schenker's own analysis of the fourth movement proceeds in functional disavowal of the intrusive presence of words. Taking another approach, we

---

[53] Heinrich Schenker, *Beethoven's Ninth Symphony*, trans. J. Rothgeb (New Haven: Yale University Press, 1992), pp. 231–32.

[54] Ibid., p. 234.

[55] Ibid., p. 234.

might ask how Beethoven's musically constituted announcement of an aesthetic change of course actually functions. What is being rejected? What is being promoted? Beethoven's choice of Friedrich Schiller, author of *An die Freude*, signifies.

Beethoven had been exposed to Schiller early. His early plays were staged in Bonn in 1782–83, in the theater where Beethoven's teacher, Christian Gottlob Neefe, served as music director. Following his early death in 1804, Schiller's aura survived as that form of radical early Romanticism that withstood the pressures and indeed the seductions of conservatism. Schiller, from whom Beethoven borrowed the text for the Ninth Symphony's finale, was a vehement opponent of the Catholic Imperium and its potential returns in European politics. Two of his most popular dramas, *William Tell* and *Don Carlos*, continued to figure as political allegories against the old regimes and returns of the Catholic Imperium. *Don Carlos*, finished in 1786, the same year as the publication of *An die Freude*, was a favorite text of many of its generation, including Beethoven. When Beethoven left for Vienna in 1792, as Solomon observes, three friends "chose passages from *Don Carlos* for their entries in his farewell book (*Stammbuch*)."[56]

Don Carlos is the errant son of King Philip II of Spain, and the grandson of the Holy Roman Emperor Charles V, who ruled over Austria, Spain, and their imperial possessions. In portraying personal and political corruption in Philip's court—of which Carlos is the victim—Schiller levels a blow at Habsburg authority and its trappings. Carlos's alienation from his father is assured by his closest emotional alliances. He has long been in love with Elisabeth de Valois, whom his father has forced into marriage with himself as a means to peace with France. His closest friend is the Marquis of Posa, who is agitating for the liberation of Flanders from Spanish rule. King Philip is beholden to the spiritual and political power of the Church, as personified by the Grand Inquisitor. When Carlos joins Posa, the Inquisitor demands that both Posa (whom the King admires) and Carlos himself be executed for treason. Philip accedes to the clandestine murder of Posa and, in the drama's final lines, hands over his son to the Grand Inquisitor with the chilling line "I have done my duty; now you must do yours [Kardinal! Ich habe das Meinige getan. Tun Sie das Ihre]."

Schillerian anti-Catholicism is a critique of the cultural system of the baroque, of the Imperium. Schiller wants a sublime that is not Catholic—that does not claim divine authority in the exertion of questionable earthly power. But can he have it? Is it a possibility in historical and in formal terms? The unfolding personal and intellectual biographies of Schiller's closest colleagues and collaborators would suggest that it is not. In their search for the sublime, a significant number of the so-called Romantic generation chose to convert

---

[56] See Solomon, "Beethoven and Schiller," in *Beethoven Essays*, pp. 205–15; 206.

to Catholicism. We can thus ask whether the enormous attraction of the Romantic generation to Catholicism resulted from the historically Catholic aura of the category of the sublime.

The "Romantic generation" refers specifically to a group of literary friends in the town of Jena, at whose distinguished university Schiller occupied a professorship of history in 1793. (The institution of the university was central to Romantic ideals, its implicit goal being the universal representation of the world and knowledge of it: a "systematic totalization of the multiple," in Luc Ferry's phrase. The idealist philosopher Schelling formulated a program of the university as a unified totality. The idea of the university as a totality is a component of Catholic totalizing aestheticism, as Heine implied venomously in his repeated invectives against Schelling as the "professor in Munich," "headquarters" of German Catholicism.)[57]

In Jena, Schiller held the center of two groups that formed, successively, two journals. The group around the journal *The Graces* included Goethe, Herder, Kant, Fichte, Klopstock, Jacobi, the two Humboldt brothers (Wilhelm and Alexander), and the two Schlegel brothers (Friedrich and August Wilhelm). The second group and its journal, the *Athenäum* (intact from 1798 till 1800), was led by Schiller and the two Schlegels. Schiller died in May 1804 at the age of forty-four.

The violent fanfare (the *Schreckensfanfare*, as Wagner called it) that opens the final movement of Beethoven's Symphony no. 9 asserts itself as a kind of acoustical shock; a gesture of disorientation rather than orientation. It thus differs from the heroic blast in the mode of the opening phrase of the *Eroica* and resembles more, as a kind of foreign interruption, the opening chords of the *Don Giovanni* overture, later to be associated with the figure of the Commendatore. Schenker compared it indirectly to the appearance of King Hamlet's ghost, as we have seen. To have made the comparison more direct would have undermined his nonrecognition of the programmatic element in the movement. The initial fanfare is followed by quotations of the principal themes of the preceding three movements. Each quotation is negated by the repetition of a fragment of the fanfare. When this process is complete, the fanfare is repeated, followed by a recitative statement by the solo bass, with the words: "O Freunde, nicht diese Töne! [Oh friends, not these tones!]"

There is a certain incommensurability here as the words address and admonish the music. But, in fact, the words are redundant, because in the move-

---

[57] For a discussion of the role of the university in German idealism, see Luc Ferry, *Philosophie politique* (Paris: Presses Universitaires de France, 1984), 1:98ff. The Catholic ideology of the university remained a topic of considerable debate in Germany. See, for example, Max Weber's 1917 polemic "A Catholic University in Salzburg," in which the equation of Protestantism and rational modernity, a staple theme in Weber's work, is revived with topic and political relevance. See Weber, "A Catholic University in Salzburg," in Edward Shils, ed., *Max Weber on Universities: The*

ment's orchestral opening Beethoven has already claimed, *through music alone*, to negate the validity of the previous three movements. He does this by working into the opening exposition clear quotations of their principal themes, and then cutting them off with combinations of silence and interruption. The musical phrase that does the interrupting returns as the musical line undergirding the words "Not these tones." The movement adds a chorus and a quartet of vocal soloists to the musical language of the work as heard so far. From their mouths comes not only music, but words. This of course throws the symphony's rhetorical system entirely off balance, as a discourse of absolute music and implied referentiality is upstaged by words.

The *desired* tones that the symphony's now dominant voice (in the sense of subjectivity and actual sung voice) asserts resound in Schiller's words:

> Freude, schöner Götterfunken,
> Tochter aus Elysium:
> Wir betreten feuertrunken
> Himmlische, dein Heiligtum!
> Deine Zauber binden wieder
> Was die Mode streng geteilt;
> Alle Menschen werden Brüder
> Wo dein sanfter Flügel weilt.

> Joy, beautiful spark of the gods,
> Daughter of Elysium:
> Drunk with fire
> We enter your holy realm!
> Your magic reunites
> What was torn apart by custom;
> All men become brothers
> Under the sway of your gentle wings.

The tone and the human emotion that the symphony advocates, now in music and words, is joy. But what kind of joy, and whose? Intimate or publicly exultant? The joy of love, say, or military victory? The continuing verses—not Schiller's finest—persist on a level of abstraction that leaves such questions unanswered. For the grandeur of its scale, and its combination of literality (the presence of words) and abstraction (their message), the movement threatens to undermine the reconciliation of truth and grace that the preceding one has achieved. The words continue with a call to exultation set for tenor solo to the accompaniment of an aggressive beat in the winds, brass, percussion, and male chorus that is not distant from the style of military fan-

Power of the State and the Dignity of the Academic Calling in Germany (Chicago: University of Chicago Press, 1976).

fare. This passage compares the reign of joy to the conquest of a hero. The words' final message is one of universal brotherhood:

Seid umschlungen, Millionen,
Diesen Kuss der ganzen Welt . . .

Be embraced, millions
By this kiss to the whole world . . .

Again, the level of abstraction disturbs. The total effect of the work is overwhelming, and one feels the need to wonder whether the enraptured state of its listeners accompanies a level of seduction that is politically dangerous. Is the listener being asked to submit to an aggressive collectivity that operates in the name of universal brotherhood and joy?

The celebration of mass exultation carries danger. But the exultant and even militant tone and scale of the movement is countered, perhaps even transcended, by a corresponding emphasis on expressive intimacy. Toward this end the individual voices of the four soloists offset the power of the collectivity. Beethoven seems to be concluding the movement with a forceful recapitulation of the first verse, cited above. But then he deliberately reopens and reexplores individual phrases in the orchestra and chorus, recombining them into a momentum whose resolution is not given to the chorus or to the orchestra but, rather, to the four soloists. This unexpected and dramatic highlighting of the four interwoven voices restores a dimension of individuality and intimacy. The work is thus halted from "straying into the gigantic," as Hermann Broch commented about Wagnerian music drama. It is also halted from straying into the oceanic—the term Freud used to describe dangerous religious or political rapture—into the ideological, and indeed into the violent. The work's final impression is thus a calibration of intimacy and solidarity. I am tempted to say that intimacy and solidarity are reconciled, but I am not as convinced of the success of the integration as I am in the case of the third movement's reconciliation of truth and grace. Here, the stakes are higher.

Insofar as such integration is signaled, however, the weaving of solo quartet and chorus points to a symbolic integration of an aesthetic of community and solidarity and the real thing. Only on this symbolic plane of projection and desire was nineteenth-century Europe, and Germany in particular, able to expand the bourgeois sphere of family and community into the collectivity and totality of the nation without violence. Only symbolically can the nation be coherent without violence—in a symbolic formulation that internally and formally shows itself to be self-conscious of its restriction to the symbolic realm, and carries no desire to be applied to the dimension of the real that is social and political.

The Ninth Symphony points to a realm of transcendence and resolution that it cannot represent. Again we have an ethic of reference as opposed to an aesthetic of representation. Beethoven points to an extrahuman plane of representation and allows his material to spin out of its own orbit. Ultimately, in line and scale, the movement spins out of control and, rather than ending, bursts. (I believe this hearing can be sustained despite, indeed even because of, the musicological assertion associated with Schenker and, more recently, James Webster of a "super-closure" in the movement's final cadences. Perhaps the movement's apparent structural insistence on closure spirals rhetorically into its own opposite—a musical example of a double positive making a negative.)[58] On the question of representation and its legitimacy, this work is as self-conscious as it is jubilant. What Solomon says about the *Hammerklavier* sonata (op. 106) is true also for this work, however more accessible it may be: "Never before had Beethoven attempted so difficult an affirmation."[59]

Moreover, the abstraction of the affirmation is matched by the uncertainty as to what is being negated to make way for it. To what does the plea "Nicht diese Töne!" refer? Does the phrase repeat the message and function of the *Schreckensfanfare* and the latter's successive interruptions of the quotations of earlier movements, so that the disavowed tones are those of the preceding three movements and hence the formal vocabulary of the symphony? Or, rather, is it the negation itself, the terror in the *Schreckensfanfare*, that is being negated: not *those* tones? I don't see that the work supplies the answer. This resistance to reconciliation should give pause to the understandable temptation to follow the ecstatic zeal of the movements and its Schillerian text to a claim of reconciliation and totality, that is, to Elysium.

The contemporaneity of the Ninth Symphony and the *Missa Solemnis* tempts the listener further to hear the union of secular and sacred, Utopia and Elysium. Thus Solomon concludes "The Quest for Faith" by reminding us of the interpenetration of the sacred and secular in Beethoven. Together, he suggests, the Ninth Symphony and the *Missa Solemnis* "exemplify Beethoven's desire to hold both religious and secular-humanist ideas in one hand, so it is not surprising that the anachronistic Enlightenment model of 'An die Freude' is penetrated by religious motifs, and the archaic liturgical model of the mass by secular elements. . . . In the end Beethoven drew no distinction between the city of man and the City of God."[60] But there may be a surfeit of reconciliation in this reading.

Theodor Adorno's understanding of the *Missa Solemnis* as an "alienated masterpiece" resists this notion of reconciliation. Indeed, Beethoven's alien-

---

[58] See Heinrich Schenker, *Beethoven's Ninth Symphony*, pp. 223–326; Webster, "The Form of the Finale." I am grateful to Scott Burnham for pointing this issue out to me.

[59] Solomon, *Beethoven*, p. 300.

[60] Solomon, "The Quest for Faith," in *Beethoven Essays*, p. 228.

ation as the mark, for Adorno, of Beethoven's "late style" resists specifically the binding of subject and object with which idealist philosophy claimed to offer a philosophical argument for reconciliation. Adorno writes:

> The musical experience of the late Beethoven must have become mistrustful of the unity of subjectivity and objectivity, the roundness of symphonic success, the totality emerging from the movement of all the parts; in short, of everything that gave authenticity up to now to the works of the middle period. He exposed the classical as classicizing.[61]

Beethoven's late style is thus alienated as well from the work of his own so-called middle period and its "classical" aesthetic of equilibration. The *Missa Solemnis* thus holds onto a message and an aesthetic of negation—"nicht diese Töne!"—that the Ninth Symphony merely flags. This refusal is achieved, for Adorno, through its "archaic methodology":

> The internal construction of this music, its fever, is radically different from everything which distinguishes Beethoven's style. It is itself archaic. The form is not achieved through developing variations from basic motifs, but arises largely from sections imitative in themselves, similar to the method of the Dutch composers around the middle of the fifteenth century, and it is uncertain how well Beethoven knew their work. The formal organization of the whole work is not that of a process developing through its own impetus—it is not dialectical—but seeks accomplishment by a balance of the individual sections, of the movements, ultimately through contrapuntal enclosure.[62]

The resulting esotericism rendered the *Missa Solemnis* unpopular until the 1860s, the same decade that saw the revival of the late string quartets, fellow bearers of "late style." Around 1870, Carl Dahlhaus observes, Beethoven's quartets displaced the symphonies as bearers of the idea of absolute music that had been developed around 1800 with reference to the symphony. The distinction of the quartets lodged in their alleged autonomy from the sensual and from the affective sphere.[63] One might suggest here that the valorization of the late quartets around 1870 corresponded to a deliberate invocation of both an aesthetic and a politics of 1800, that is, a removal from the dominant affective and subject-object reconciliation of 1870, namely, nationalism. Like

---

[61] Theodor Adorno, "Alienated Masterpiece: The *Missa Solemnis*" (1959), trans. D. Smith, *Telos* 28 (1976): 113–24; 122.

[62] Ibid., p. 117. For a discussion of Adorno's "Alienated Masterpiece" in the context of Adorno's music criticism and its reception, see my essay "The Musical Absolute," *New German Critique* 56 (Summer 1992): 17–42. Dahlhaus offers a tacit commentary on this assertion of Adorno's in the section "What Is a Late Work?" of his *Beethoven* (pp. 219–21). He suggests that the past is not so much "summoned up" by an archaizing style as it is shown to have remained present.

[63] Dahlhaus, *The Idea of Absolute Music*, p. 17.

the short passage for solo vocal quartet in the final moments of the Ninth Symphony, the quartet sui generis offered the contemporaries of Wagner and Bismarck a respite from the prevalence of large forces and totalizing identities: aesthetic, personal, and national. In this return the promise of subjectivity remains viable. Its itinerary between Beethoven and Wagner is the topic of the next chapter.

Chapter Three

CANNY AND UNCANNY HISTORIES
IN BIEDERMEIER MUSIC

Biedermeier Music

Early in 1839, Ferdinand Schubert consigned the unknown manuscript of his deceased brother's C major symphony (currently known as no. 9 or "the Great") to three musical authorities: Robert Schumann, Felix Mendelssohn, and the publishing house of Breitkopf and Härtel. Schumann was traveling in Vienna at the time. Mendelssohn was in Leipzig, where he would conduct the premiere of the work in March. Mendelssohn dubbed the work "the Great" ("die Grosse") on the occasion of its second Leipzig performance on 22 March.[1]

This triple transmission of the text of Franz Schubert's C major symphony strikes me as an anchoring moment in German music and musical culture between Beethoven and Wagner and between 1815 and 1848, the period often referred to with the sobriquet "Biedermeier." In history and in music history, the Biedermeier category and period conventionally imply the need for an apology. So, it often seems, does Biedermeier music itself. Both period and music conventionally seem caught in a no-man's-land between the age of revolution and heroism on one side and the age of national self-fulfillment on the other. Yet it is precisely the narrative and teleology of national fulfillment, dominant in the years after 1848, that puts into place the persistent judgment of the inconsequentiality of Biedermeier period and style. Indeed the fictional schoolmaster Gottlob Biedermeier, who traversed the pages of the satirical Munich rag *Die Fliegenden Blätter* between 1855 and 1857, and who gave his name to an era, reveals more about the melancholy condescension of his post-1848 inventors than he does about the period to which he gives his name.

The dual teleology of German music and the German nation is contingent on Wagner's self-placement as the voice of music and empire across the threshold of 1870. Indeed, Beethoven's power and Wagner's claim as its absolute inheritor leave little apparent room for greatness between them. Wagner's proposed history of music as a Mount Rushmore-like trio of Bach, Beethoven, and himself remained fundamental to succeeding modernists' understanding of their own inheritance. (Schoenberg may have replaced

[1] See Marie Luise Maintz, *Franz Schubert in der Rezeption Robert Schumanns* (Kassel: Bärenreiter Verlag, 1995), p. 66.

Wagner with Brahms in his own Wagnerian gesture, by which he also completed the course of German music with himself; but in his model as in
Wagner's the passage from Beethoven to the next holder of the mantle, be
that Wagner or Brahms, is direct.) This procession of giants of German music
duplicates a historiographic ideology of the procession of grand German moments—grand moments, that is, in the making of the German nation.
Wagner's famous pamphlet on Beethoven dates from 1870; the year of German unification was not incidental to the new pantheon of German music.
From the vantage point of 1870, German nationalism has two phases: cultural
heroism before the political fact (Beethoven, Goethe, and Hegel) and national self-realization (Wagner—no one else need apply, as Nietzsche
learned). In this sequence, the middle generations are lost. Politically, the
liberalism of 1848 is lost. Musically, the generation between Beethoven and
Wagner is disenfranchised.

According to this teleology, born of the hubris of 1870 and long obsolete,
the "greatness" of Schubert's C major symphony would lodge in its successful
assumption of Beethovenian heroism. I do not believe that Mendelssohn had
such an evaluation in mind. I believe he heard something quite different, and
more closely associated to his own aesthetic as well as historical sensibilities.
Bach holds a more important place than Beethoven in Mendelssohn's musical
pantheon, but the argument for Mendelssohn's autonomy lies deeper than
that. It is Mendelssohn's multiple sense of history that produces this autonomy, his sense of the autonomy of a present moment that at the same time
communicates profoundly with the past. Schumann's equally strong attachment to Schubert's C major symphony is more vexed, as Schumann's relation
to Beethoven and to history in general reveals a persistent nostalgia, a desire
for a return. Mendelssohn made peace with history; his reputation has suffered
from that biographical achievement. Conceivably, his music did as well. As I
will suggest, Mendelssohn may have worked through too many issues outside
the boundaries of music, causing, from within, his compositional posterity to
suffer. The superiority, in Schumann's case, of music to extramusical thinking
may have sealed his musical greatness as it compromised his intellectual—
and indeed his mental—sagacity. Harbingers, one is tempted to observe, of
the Wagnerian behemoth to come.

Biedermeier music sounds an awareness of its past; its interpretation involves qualifying the terms of the relation to the past. "For Beethoven," Walter Frisch wrote recently, "there is no question of pausing to recollect."[2] "In
Schubert, unlike in Beethoven," wrote Carl Dahlhaus, "the most lasting impression is made by remembrance, which turns from later events back to earlier

[2] Walter Frisch, " 'You Must Remember This': Memory and Structure in Schubert's G-Major
String Quartet (D. 887)," *Musical Quarterly* 84:4 (Winter 2000): 582–603.

ones, and not by goal consciousness, which presses on from earlier to later."[3]
"From Robert Schumann on," Frisch writes, "commentators have resorted to
metaphors of memory to capture in prose the special qualities of Schubert's
mature instrumental works. Recollection, retrospection, association, nostalgia: these are some of the concepts which float through Schubert criticism."
John Daverio has suggested that Schumann was "acutely aware of what might
be called the temporality of pastness in Schubert's music and its bearing on
the composer's handling of large-scale temporal spans." This view relates to
Schumann's well-known praise for Schubert's C major symphony (now num-
bered no. 9) for its "heavenly lengths." Daverio continues:

> [T]o put it in terms of a comparison: whereas Beethoven, especially in the symphonic
> works of his "heroic" phase, drives headlong from the present into the future, thus
> emulating the teleological thrust of drama, Schubert treats the present as a pretext
> for summoning up or mulling over the past.[4]

An interpretive focus on the presence and predominance of memory articulates a cognitive shift between Beethoven and Schubert. Beethoven is a generation older than Schubert, though their deaths are separated by only twenty
months. Beethoven's maturity begins in the revolutionary age, Schubert's after
the Congress of Vienna. For the Biedermeier generation, musical history and
political history can be understood to pull backwards toward a more heroic
past. Beethoven's rhetoric involves living in the present and asserting a template for the future. The musical arguments of Biedermeier music are not often
understood to do the same. Rather, they have seemed to look back on the
past—whether that past is defined politically (the emancipatory claims of
1789 and the Napoleonic age) or musically (Beethoven).

This chapter interrogates the standard reception of Biedermeier political
and aesthetic culture as melancholic and nostalgic. It does not doubt the Biedermeier focus on the past, on history, and indeed on "pastness" as a cognitive
and emotional category. But it seeks to complicate these categories as categories of cognitive, emotional, and political experience. First, the Biedermeier
period is varied in its political contexts and possibilities. North German cities
differ from Austrian ones, especially from the imperial capital of Vienna under
Metternichian rule. Cities like Leipzig operated at the level of what Hegel
called civil society—*bürgerliche Gesellschaft*. But whereas for Hegel the social
and cultural patterns of civil society would gain maturity under the organiza-
tional and political umbrella of the central state, this teleology can be profit-

---

[3] Carl Dahlhaus, "Sonata Form in Schubert: The First Movement of the G-Major String Quartet, op. 161 (D. 887)," trans. T. Reinhard, in *Schubert: Critical and Analytical Studies*, ed. Walter
Frisch (Lincoln: University of Nebraska Press, 1986), p. 8.

[4] John Daverio, " 'One More Beautiful Memory of Schubert': Schumann's Critique of the Im-
promptus, D. 935," *Musical Quarterly* 84:4 (Winter 2000): 604–18; 605.

ably abandoned by historical work. The civic life of Biedermeier Leipzig stands in productive autonomy from the authority of Vienna, which cast its shadow under Metternich, and from the authority of Berlin, which swelled under the authority of Frederick William IV and later under Bismarck. Second, the proliferation of historical consciousness and scholarship in the Biedermeier period formed ways of linking the past with the present and future that complicated and criticized the mentalities of nostalgia and conservatism. What we may too easily assimilate as a rhetoric of memory, replete with melancholy, nostalgia, and wistfulness, may in fact approximate a rhetoric of history and historical argument: a conscious, processed, considered discourse about the past in its relation to the present and future. The past does not live only in the past or for it.

Mendelssohn's Canny Histories

In the summer of 1829, the twenty-year-old Felix Mendelssohn traveled through Scotland, a trip that provided him not only with the moment of his self-perceived maturity but also with the metaphors with which to engage it musically. The clearest musical transcription of this complicated moment is the so-called *Hebrides* overture, also known as "Fingal's Cave," composed and revised between 1829 and 1835.

On 7 August, Mendelssohn, an accomplished watercolorist, produced a pen-and-ink drawing that he called "Ein Blick auf die Hebriden": a view of the Hebrides. It depicted a tree, Dunillie Castle, and the outlines of Morven and the Isle of Morn. The following day, the composer set out to see Fingal's Cave. But, as his traveling companion Karl Klingemann recounted, he did not see the cave due to an attack of seasickness. Whatever record of the celebrated cave may inhabit the music, it is a record of a thing unseen.

As a musical recollection, the *Hebrides* overture alternates between a recollection of seeing and one of not seeing. Its opening statements seem to set, perhaps to paint, a scene. This is not the case with the work's celebrated second theme, which Donald Tovey described as "quite the greatest melody Mendelssohn ever wrote." This one is stated first in measures 47–56 by the bassoons and cellos, and repeated in measures 57–66 by the violins. It is the subject of a recent essay by Jerrold Levinson called "Hope in the *Hebrides*." Levinson argues in fact against the formalist position associated with Eduard Hanslick and holds first that music can express emotions and, second, that the *Hebrides* overture expresses hope. Though Levinson does not deny the music's programmaticity, he chooses to analyze it as "absolute music." To this end he quotes Hans Keller's observation that "all the sea-gulls and salt-fish in the Hebrides did not prevent Mendelssohn from designing a complex sonata structure such as many a fanatically 'absolute' musician would have been proud of;

if the sea-gulls helped, so much the better."[5] For Levinson, the second theme's alleged expression of hope is carried by its upward and forward movement, as hope accompanies aspiration and "a little touch of faith as well." Finally, Levinson argues that this expression of hope is unique, as other examples of positive motion and emotion in Mendelssohn do not express hope: the first movement of the octet is "too febrile, too controlled, to contextless"; the opening theme of the *Italian* symphony "contains no element of straining," etcetera.[6]

Levinson and Keller's observations are on the right track but both miss, to my ear, the shape of the overture's dramatic unfolding. Combining the tripartite sequence of sonata form (exposition, development, and recapitulation) with the Hegelian dialectic (thesis, antithesis, and synthesis), the work offers an initial tableau of scene painting, then, in the second theme, offers a highly movemented set of phrases that cannot be heard to paint, or to imitate a visual experience. Finally, in the third part, the scenic and antiscenic, visual and antivisual, and mimetic and antimimetic elements are combined into a texture that is formally masterful but dramatically unsatisfying.

If the second theme is the work's and possibly—if Tovey is right—Mendelssohn's greatest melody, then I would suggest that its greatness lies in its original Romantic gesture of the disavowal of vision and thus, in musical terms, in the disavowal of music as a mimetic substitute for vision. It is a Romantic gesture in its engagement of the natural world as a metaphoric landscape of inner life. In the now classic terms of the literary historian M. H. Abrams, Romanticism replaces the mirror of nature with the lamp of existential truth. Even a Romantic landscape painting—Caspar David Friedrich's oeuvre provides the most sustained example—is not merely a landscape. Rather, it engages nature as a way into inner nature, into the making of existential authenticity. In this sense, the *Hebrides* overture is not a mirror (of nature) but a lamp. It engages a scene of nature, a picture, but then, abetted by the circumstantial record of a thing unseen, is born as music and musical drama as it transcends the scaffold of its ostensible representations.[7]

Richard Wagner, Mendelssohn's most abiding detractor, esteemed the *Hebrides* overture, calling it a "masterpiece" of a "landscape painter of the first order." But Wagner was damning with faint praise; the composer as landscape painter was the one restricted to mimetic imitation and hence incapable of authentic invention. Such were the alleged limitations of the Jews, which Wagner spelled out in his 1850 essay "Judaism in Music." Wagner, who remains the greater musical dramatist, failed to hear—or perhaps was threatened

[5] Jerrold Levinson, "Hope in the *Hebrides*," in *Music, Art, and Metaphysics: Essays in Philosophical Aesthetics* (Ithaca: Cornell University Press, 1990), pp. 336–75. See also Hans Keller, *Of German Music*, ed. H. H. Schoenzeler (London: O. Wolff, 1976), p. 207.

[6] Levinson, "Hope in the *Hebrides*," pp. 370, 372.

[7] See M. H. Abrams, *The Mirror and the Lamp: Romantic Theory and the Critical Tradition* (New York: W. W. Norton, 1953).

by the hearing of—the power of the *Hebrides*'s second theme as an articulation of the emancipation from mimesis and the instantiation of musical subjectivity. The theme's dramatic thrust, I would argue, hails from a switching of voice, from the sudden and indeed urgent instantiation of a first-person declarative utterance, distinct from the third-person voice of narrative scene painting already heard.

In Mendelssohn's music, Scottish metaphors remain key to inscriptions of leave-takings of image and mimesis. Generally, early-nineteenth-century evocations of Scotland conjure foggy texts even more than they do foggy pictures. Most notoriously, the German Romantics were enchanted by the figure of Ossian, the alleged third-century Celtic poet and northern partner to Homer. By the beginning of the century, Ossian had been definitively exposed as the fabrication of his ostensible "translator," James Macpherson. One of the best-known "Ossianic" texts was the epic poem "Fingal." The first Leipzig performance of the *Hebrides* overture, on 4 December 1834, carried the title "Ossian in Fingalshöhle": Ossian in Fingal's Cave. The epithet suggests the poetic presence in the image of a cave not only unseen but known not to exist. This cave invokes Plato's from Book 7 of the *Republic*: the cave of mimesis, out of which leads the path to knowledge.

For Mendelssohn, more than signifying rocks and fish, Scotland clearly signified Protestant culture and enlightenment. Thus the meaning of his Scottish journey was informed by the triumphant revival of Bach's *St. Matthew* Passion in Berlin the previous March.[8] Scotland-as-metaphor returns, of course, in the *Scottish* symphony, completed in 1842 and misnumbered as Symphony no. 3. The way the metaphor works is crucial to a perception of this work's coherence. The initial three movements and the opening of the fourth can once again be heard as a form of musical scene painting, as if the Scottish journey of 1829 were once again being invoked and described. The final movement continues in this general descriptive mode in its first half but then gives way to a conclusion, marked allegro maestoso, in which the musical voice and rhetoric clearly change. The change recapitulates, on a larger scale, the move to the second theme in the *Hebrides* overture. The final section resounds like a militant hymn. It has sounded out of place and indeed even embarrassing in its proto-Elgarian pomp to many conductors; in a notorious decision, Otto Klemperer deleted it altogether. The aesthetic debate notwithstanding, the movement and the symphony's coherence are clear. The resolution of the Scottish metaphor lies in the reunion of two Leipzig institutions: the Gewandhaus and Bach's Thomaskirche.

---

[8] This famous performance was thought at the time to mark the centenary of the work's first performance in Leipzig. That event is now generally agreed to have taken place on Good Friday 1727, not 1729. See Christoph Wolff, *Johann Sebastian Bach: The Learned Musician* (New York: W. W. Norton & Sons, 2000), pp. 288, 295.

Mendelssohn's lifelong engagement with the music of J. S. Bach provides the key to his historicism, which was in turn formulated in dialogue with his tutor Johann Gustav Droysen. Through Droysen, Mendelssohn's engagement with Bach modulated from one based on historical legacy to one based on dialectical engagement. The young Mendelssohn wrote home from Paris in April 1825: "You also write me that I should set myself up as an evangelist and instruct Onslow and Reicha . . . how to love Sebastian Bach. I'm already doing that, as far as it goes. But just think, dear child, that the people here take Sebastian Bach to be a powdered wig properly stuffed with learning."[9] As so often with Mendelssohn, a seemingly precious gesture carries analytical riches. The comment reveals at least three things: that the young composer had long integrated an important and unusual esteem for Bach; that he learned this taste from within his family; and, most significantly, that Bach was, for him, not a relic or an ancestor, but a modern composer.

The corrective work that Arnold Schoenberg did for Brahms in his essay "Brahms the Progressive" still needs doing for Mendelssohn, and it can be begun with the recognition of what Mendelssohn did for Bach. In other words, each generation has recognized an element of hidden modernism in a preceeding master whom contemporary taste wrongly considers old-fashioned. To put the issue another way, did Mendelssohn prefigure the view of Bach that Theodor Adorno would elaborate, a century later, in the celebrated essay "Bach Defended Against His Devotees"? In this well-known essay of 1956, Adorno addresses a polemic against two ideologies of authenticity: musical antiquarianism, which he calls historicism, and existentialism, by which he means the ideology of cultural authenticity he later attacked in his book on Heidegger. Musicology, he argues, has transformed Bach from a dynamic explorer of musical modernity to a neutralized cultural monument, a final survivor of the static and secure middle ages. What is neutralized in the process is Bach's own subjectivity, and this is the principle that connects musical antiquarianism with existential ideology. The dismissal of subjectivity transforms life into Being. In Adorno's formulation: "To sacrifice the subject in such works, to hear in them nothing but the Order of Being and not the nostalgic echo that the decline of such an order finds in the mind, is to grasp only the *caput mortuum*. The phantasma of Bach's ontology arises through an act of force mechanically performed by the Philistines, whose sole desire is to neutralize art since they lack the capacity to comprehend it."[10] Bach's modernity, for Adorno, is found in the fugue, in counterpoint and polyphony, and

---

[9] Letter of Felix Mendelssohn, New York Public Library, quoted by R. Larry Todd, "Me voilà perruqué: Mendelssohn's Six Preludes and Fugues, op. 35 Reconsidered," in *Mendelssohn Studies*, ed. R. Larry Todd (Cambridge: Cambridge University Press, 1992), p. 162.

[10] Theodor Adorno, "Bach Defended Against His Devotees," in *Prisms*, trans. S. Weber (Cambridge: MIT Press, 1981), p. 137.

in the "duality of mind" revealed by basso-continuo harmony. The art of the fugue is an "art of dissection; one could almost say, of dissolving Being, posited as the theme, and hence incompatible with the common belief that this Being maintains itself static and unchanged throughout the fugue."[11] But he goes further, to an interpretation of the cultural meaning of Bach's modernity, and that is to the interpretation of Bach's musical voice as that of the emancipated subject, "for only it can conceive music as the emphatic promise of objective salvation."[12]

The musical ego as the emancipated subject is a trope fundamental to nineteenth-century German musical aesthetics. It is the tradition that Dahlhaus, to a great extent in the shadow of Adorno, analyzed in his book *The Idea of Absolute Music*. But Adorno parts from tradition in his use of the trope. Dahlhaus shows how the idea of absolute music became, in fact, an ideology of absolute music where the autonomous musical ego in fact came to signify the German national spirit. For Adorno, the trope of the emancipated subject, musical or otherwise, emerges from and strives to recuperate the subjectivity of the Jewish *Bildungsbürgertum*. "Bach defended against his devotees" means music and spirit defended from German nationalism. Adorno's valuation of Arnold Schoenberg carries the same task.

When we look at Mendelssohn's sensibility, we must alter significantly our own sense of historical context to a prenationalist period in which the Jewish *Bildungsbürgertum* was in its cultural prime. For Mendelssohn, subjective autonomy and an ideal of community were fully compatible in a way that became impossible after the mid-nineteenth century. Mendelssohn heard in Bach the same spirit of subjective modernity that German musical aesthetics from Wagner through Pfitzner would fail to recognize and that Adorno recovered. At the same time, he combined that principle of subjective modernity with an ideal of community that would in turn connect the private and female family tradition that had nurtured his love and knowledge of Bach with an overall cultural ideal. Thus, in hearing in Bach a straightforward rhetoric of individual emancipation, Adorno overmodernizes Bach's music and intentions.

Mendelssohn's youthful musical aesthetic grew from a dual context of family life and community. His early initiation into the north German Bach tradition, as the historian John Toews has recently written, "was nurtured almost in cult-like fashion" at home and within the *Singakademie* led by his composition teacher, Carl Friedrich Zelter.[13] As a Christmas present in 1823 he received a score of the *St. Matthew* Passion—a rare collector's item at the time, as Toews

---

[11] Ibid., p. 139.

[12] Ibid., p. 138.

[13] John Toews, "Memory and Gender in the Remaking of Fanny Mendelssohn's Musical Identity," *Musical Quarterly* 77:4 (Winter 1993): 727–48. In this issue of the *Musical Quarterly*, see in general the special section called "Culture, Gender, and Music: A Forum on the Mendelssohn Family," pp. 648–748.

points out—from his maternal grandmother, Babette Salomon, née Itzig. Babette and even more so her sister Sara Levy, a patron of Bach's son Wilhelm Friedrich, were responsible for the transmission of the Bach tradition in the Mendelssohn family. (Through her collection of scores and her patronage of composers, Sara Levy was instrumental in the creation of musical taste in late-eighteenth-century Berlin, and her library formed the initial archive of the *Singakademie*.)[14] Outside the home, Zelter's *Singakademie* provided not only a model for music-making but a model for community building through the collective pursuit of music, specifically of choral singing. The chorale was the musical form that both symbolized and actually enacted the creation of a community through music.

But how was this community defined: as one of art, faith, or politics? Toews has argued for the slow accumulation of all three characteristics in Felix's generation. The Mendelssohn circle included at its core Felix and his sister Fanny, the singer and actor Eduard Devrient, the family classical language tutor, Droysen, and the music critic Adolph Bernhard Marx. For them, J. S. Bach provided a model not of musical and formal complexity but rather a font of spirituality and emotional expression. When, in 1827, in this company, Mendelssohn began to rehearse portions of the *St. Matthew* Passion, he did so against the will of his teacher Zelter, who had doubts about the music's performability. The Mendelssohn circle strove to unite the aesthetic and confessional legacies of Bach into a newly formed and newly potent ethical community. Formally, the chorale was the vehicle of this community making. As Toews writes:

> Bach's arrangements of the chorales were imagined as an emancipation of the salvational process from the specific confines of traditional confessional liturgies. The art work universalized the particular confessional form, transforming the church congregation into a more inclusive cultural community. Although the *St. Matthew* Passion was performed in a neo-classical temple of art by lay musicians at a benefit concert for a ticket-holding, paying audience, both Fanny and Felix thought that the music had transformed the attenders of a secular concert into participants in a sacred service.[15]

In a letter to Franz Hauser in 1830, Mendelssohn wrote of the 1829 *St. Matthew* Passion: "Sie sangen mit einer Andacht, als ob sie in der Kirche waren [They sang with a devotion, as if they were in church]." The community of north German music and its pious context clearly posited a countermodel

---

[14] See Peter Wollny, "Sara Levy and the Making of Musical Taste in Berlin," *Musical Quarterly* 77:4 (Winter 1993): 651–88.

[15] Toews, "Memory and Gender," p. 736.

to the French-Italian tradition represented in the 1820s by Rossini, and by another German Jew: Giacomo Meyerbeer, born Jacob Beer.[16]

The sacred musical community, secularized in its indication of a cultural rather than a religious identity, is represented musically by the chorale. Certainly, the chorale is a form that Mendelssohn borrowed from Bach with deep recognition of its historical and communitarian symbolism. But where, then, is Adorno's Bach, the Bach of musical modernism? Or, to put the question differently: alongside the chorale, what are we to make of the fugue, as well as other musical indications of movement and counterpoint? Is the fugue a musical metaphor for modernism, movement, and the recognition of temporality? In a more general sense, my question can be posed as follows. If we agree that Mendelssohn absorbed the German Bach tradition not so much as a way of returning to past traditions but as a way of defining a new cultural identity in music, then to what extent can we argue that this birth of cultural identity through the spirit of music was in fact a modern discourse: an inscription of a modern subjectivity that exists in movement and constant self-reformation?

For clues to this side of Mendelssohn and his Bach reception, we can turn to Michael Marissen's work on the 1829 performance of the *St. Matthew* Passion. Marissen has reconstructed and interpreted Mendelssohn's performance version of the *St. Matthew* Passion, speculating on the meaning both of Mendelssohn's choice of this work and on the reasoning behind the substantial excisions he made in its performance. We might recall that the year 1829 was held to be the centennial of the work's premiere, but it was also the centennial of the birth of Moses Mendelssohn.

Marissen begins his inquiry with an obvious but neglected question, and that is, "Why the *St. Matthew* Passion?" He suggests that no aesthetic criterion presents itself that would clearly distinguish this work from other great Bach choral works, but that religious and cultural criteria do become evident. The *St. Matthew* Passion tells a story of a universal community and religion. Rather than focus on the culpability of the Jews in the trial and crucifixion of Christ, it focuses, in Marissen's words, "much more on Christ as 'suffering servant,' one who is guiltless and whose death is brought on by the guilt of *all*."[17] The tone is set in the opening chorus, the E-minor lament and procession toward death, which Marissen describes splendidly as a "musical equivalent of a *Trauerspiel*." The inscription of a universal community is achieved through reference to Zion, understood both as the Christian Church and the people of Israel.

---

[16] See Arno Forchert, "Von Bach zu Mendelssohn," in *Bachtage Berlin*, ed. Günther Wagner (Neuhauser: Hänssler, 1985), pp. 211–33.

[17] Michael Marissen, "Religious Aims in Mendelssohn's 1829 Berlin Singakademie Performances of Bach's St. Matthew Passion," *Musical Quarterly* 77:4 (Winter 1993): 720.

Marissen also investigates Mendelssohn's performance version of the *St. Matthew*. Why did he cut all the arias, except "Erbarme dich," as well as six chorales and some recitatives (in the arrest and trial scene)? There is some evidence from Eduard Devrient, who reports that the work had to be shortened, and moreoever that it was unthinkable to perform the entire work, not only because of its length but more so because it "showed so many signs of the tastes of its times." Marissen argues that Mendelssohn's reading of Schleiermacher is evident in the reshaping of the work, with its stress on the congregation rather than on the religious experience of the individual. Through a thorough analysis of the cuts, which I will not rehearse here, Marissen arrives at a view of Mendelssohn's *St. Matthew* Passion as an aesthetic expression of open community. We can speculate further that the excision of arias favors the presentation of a collectivity, and thus an implicit rejection of the theatricality of the so-called French and Italian tradition.

By 1829 and the revival of the *St. Matthew* Passion, the Bach-Mendelssohn dialogue had produced an ongoing dialectic of community and modern temporality in the young composer's music. A third element is added to this constellation, and that is the mature Mendelssohn's sense of musical allegory. When Mendelssohn leaves choral music and its communitarian symbolism, he turns to the orchestra with a nonrepresentational musical discourse, yet an allegorical one all the same, in its inscription of an open, time-bound subjectivity.

The nineteenth-century antipathy to Mendelssohn was set by Wagner, but it was initiated by Marx, the theorist from whom Mendelssohn developed early ideas of programmatic music. Mendelssohn's friend turned foe, Marx finally described Mendelssohn as a talent, but no genius.[18] In a friendlier time, Marx shared in the paternity of the music to *A Midsummer Night's Dream*, composed in 1826, during the peak years of their friendship, which lasted until 1830. Why did Marx turn against Mendelssohn? Or, rather, why did Mendelssohn turn away from Marx and his aesthetic of musical allegory?

The *Reformation* symphony is the watershed work for this problem. It presents a programmatic allegory of Reformation—that is clear, but its paradoxical quality lies in its reminiscence, in Judith Ballan's analysis, "of the so-called 'Palestrina school,' that musicians of Mendelssohn's time commonly associated with Catholicism."[19] For example, A.F.J. Thibaut, in his widely read treatise *Über Reinheit der Tonkunst* [*On Purity in Musical Art*](1824), urged Protestant composers to adopt the Catholic aesthetic of Palestrina and Lotti.[20] In

---

[18] See Judith Silber Ballan, "Marxian Programmatic Music: A Stage in Mendelssohn's Musical Development," in Todd, *Mendelssohn Studies*, p. 149.

[19] Ibid., p. 154. See also Judith Silber Ballan, "Mendelssohn and the Reformation Symphony: A Critical and Historical Study" (diss., Yale University, 1987).

[20] See Ballan, "Marxian Programmatic Music," 154n. Anton Friedrich Justus Thibaut, *Über Reinheit der Tonkunst* (Darmstadt: Wissenschaftliche Buchgesellschaft, 1967); idem, *On Purity in Musical Art*, trans. W. H. Gladstone (London: John Murray, 1877). It is worth noting here that J. S.

following Marx's charge, Mendelssohn gives us a Catholic-style musical allegory of a Protestant event.

Thibaut was a professor of jurisprudence—Schumann's law professor, in fact—in Heidelberg. Purity in music, as his translator suggests, meant for Thibaut not technical but moral purity, with church music the moral model for musical expression.[21] A Lutheran himself, Thibaut mourned the loss of musical inspiration that the Lutheran church allowed, despite the fabled devotion to chorale singing of Martin Luther himself. Sectarianism, he argued, had caused the dissipation of Catholic musical integrity, and as Luther had himself argued for the retention of Catholic music, that music should now be recovered for the Lutheran church.[22] Thibaut's agenda was to rescue the oratorio style from the clutches of the operatic and to return it to the church style: It was this authentic church music, he argued, that Mozart went to the Sistine Chapel during Holy Week "for the purpose of purloining." Music, he concluded, is a gift from God, and "the divinity of music is only revealed when it transports us into an ideal state of being."[23]

Thibaut deified Handel, but for his parity with Palestrina and hence with an appreciation of his music for its devotional rigidity. Such an aesthetic did not long please or serve Mendelssohn. In this context we can invoke another milestone of 1842. This is the initiation of Mendelssohn's association with the *Berliner Domchor* within the responsibility of his position as *Generalmusikdirektor* to the court of Frederick William IV. The association proved unhappy, largely because of a controversy between Mendelssohn and the clergy over the difference between *geistliche Musik* and *kirchliche Musik*.[24] This distinction and the resulting conflict duplicates that between Mendelssohnian musical allegory and the Catholicizing allegory of Marx, and the line from Palestrina to Pfitzner.

In 1835, Mendelssohn moved to Leipzig as the director of the concerts of the Gewandhaus orchestra. As a musical and civic institution, the Gewandhaus instantiates the triangle of music, commerce, and religious and civic devotion. When the new textile guild hall (*Gewandhaus*) was inaugurated in 1781, a wing was dedicated to a concert hall and to the continuing patronage of the orchestra that had been founded in 1743 with the backing of eight merchants and eight noblemen. (Each had subsidized one musician to make an ensemble of sixteen.) The spatial organization of the hall's interior reveals

---

Bach himself had turned to figures such as Palestrina and Lotti in the last two decades of his life, as well as to the (Catholic) genre of the mass itself. See Christoph Wolff, *Der Stile antico in der Musik Johann Sebastian Bachs* (Wiesbaden: Steiner, 1968).

[21] See W. H. Gladstone, Preface to Thibaut, *On Purity in Musical Art*, p. xiii.

[22] Thibaut, *On Purity in Musical Art*, pp. 23–25.

[23] Ibid., pp. 55, 102, 194, 85.

[24] See David Brodbeck, "Mendelssohn and the *Berliner Domchor*," in Todd, *Mendelssohn Studies*, p. 23.

the visual and cultural symbolism of north German musical experience. The cultural prototype for the concert hall of the first Gewandhaus is not a theater but rather a church: specifically, a choir. The listeners sit facing each other exactly as in the choir of the Thomaskirche. While listening to music, their visual referent is the community, not the music or its performance aspect. Above the musicians, the Gewandhaus motto is carved into the balustrade: RES SEVERA VERUM GAUDIUM: True joy is a serious matter. Seneca's phrase appears on the frontispiece of a locally published hymnal in 1783, and it has served as the Gewandhaus motto ever since. Aesthetic pleasure, it holds, is legitimized through internalization, meditation, and hence compatibility with devotion. Art does not supplant religion; art follows religion's rules. Music's mediation between subjectivity and community was a paradigm central to the Mendelssohn household and to Felix's upbringing. From 1835 until his death in 1847, he felt at home in Leipzig, as he did not in Berlin.

A period watercolor of the concert hall in the first Gewandhaus supplies an iconography of the social relations it stood for (fig. 5). In anticipation of a concert, listeners enter and take their seats in the organization described above. Some linger and speak with each other in groups of two and three. One man reads. With the exception of the two women on the image's left side and the figures on the balcony, there are no signs of spectatorship or a stress on the visual at all. Visuality exists in the decoration of the room, and of course in the presence of the stoic motto.

(Compare this image with a more famous analogue: Gustav Klimt's 1888 painting of the Old Burgtheater [fig. 6]. The preperformance situation is the same. But here, everything is spectacle. Everyone is watching and desirous of being watched. The artist's vantage point is the stage, rendering the painting itself into a kind of performance.)

Mendelssohn's attachment to the musical and civic culture of Leipzig did not prevent him from accepting the position of court composer to King Frederick William IV, who ascended the Prussian throne in June 1840. On 28 October 1841 a performance of Sophocles' *Antigone* took place in the palace of Sans-Souci, with incidental music by Mendelssohn. The enterprise originated in the taste and wishes of the King. Mendelssohn's music is not among his most memorable. As an event, however, *Antigone* provides a *mise-en-jeu* of Mendelssohn's deepest convictions and conflicts. In Sophoclean terms, these can be categorized as kinship, civic life, and the state.[25]

The Prussian sovereign's taste in drama was shared by the thinkers of Romantic Germany. Hegel's claim is perhaps the best known: "Of all the masterpieces of the classical and the modern world—and I know nearly all of them and you should and can—the *Antigone* seems to me to be the most magnificent

---

[25] The juxtaposition of kinship and the state generates Judith Butler's recent analysis of the *Antigone* problem. See Butler, *Antigone's Claim* (New York: Columbia University Press, 2000).

Figure 5   Concert hall in the first Gewandhaus (1781–1884).

Figure 6   Gustav Klimt, *Interior of the Old Burgtheater.*

and satisfying work of art of this kind."[26] Hegel's judgment remained uncontested for a century. With reference to it, George Steiner began his 1984 book *Antigones* with the suggestion that from about 1790 (the year of Friedrich Schlegel's *History of Attic Tragedy*) to the turn of the twentieth century (when the Freudian referent of Oedipus claimed the spotlight), "it was widely held by European poets, philosophers, scholars that Sophocles' *Antigone* was not only the finest of Greek tragedies, but a work of art nearer to perfection than any other produced by the human spirit."[27] The generation of the German idealists and Romantics were perhaps the most ardent *Antigone* fans. Kant, Schelling, and the Schlegel brothers, as well as Hegel, all revered the play. In 1787 the seventeen-year-old Hegel translated a portion of the play while a student at Tübingen; he returned to it in the *Phenomenology of Mind* of 1807,

[26] See *Hegel's Aesthetics: Lectures on Fine Art*, 2 vols. (given between 1823 and 1829, published posthumously in 1835), trans. T. M. Knox (Oxford: Oxford University Press, 1975), p. 1218.

[27] George Steiner, *Antigones* (Oxford: Oxford University Press, 1984), p. 2.

in the *Philosophy of Right* of 1821, and in the *Lectures on Aesthetics* of the 1820s. Friedrich Hölderlin, Hegel's intimate friend during their student days in Tübingen, ended his career in 1804 with a "translation" that has redefined the poetics of translation for modern criticism. August Boeckh and his pupil Droysen—contributing founders not only of modern classical scholarship but of modern historiographical practice—came back to Sophocles' drama time and again throughout their long careers. The 1841 *Antigone* was a group effort involving the patronage of the king, general mediation and staging by his court "reader" (*Vorleser*) Ludwig Tieck, J. J. Donner's translation, and the music of Mendelssohn. As a collective project, this *Antigone* addresses questions fundamental to German Romantic and liberal culture, such as the cultural and political place of classicial tradition, humanism, and scholarship, and—for Mendelssohn and Droysen—the cultural place of the Jews in both the classical and contemporary worlds, as well as in scholarly and cultural discourse about those worlds.

The 1841 *Antigone* instantiates the conjunction in German history that Thomas Nipperdey has called "Bürgerwelt und starker Staat."[28] Significant in this dialectic of "bürgerlich" society—the adjective connotes bourgeois society but also the civil society which for Hegel mediates between the family and the state—and the state itself is the place of the assimilating, post-Enlightnment German Jewry. Its most renowned representative had been Moses Mendelssohn, the composer's grandfather. The father, Abraham, had chosen the path of full Protestant assimilation, including conversion and the change of the family name to Bartholdy. Felix's relation to the predicament of German Jewry coincides with the increasing complications of the issue in his generation. He kept the name Mendelssohn against his father's explicit and stern wishes. The maturity that generated this decision is simultaneous with his devotion to Lutheran music. His relation—aesthetic, cultural, and religious—to Protestant music foreshadows Mahler's relation to Catholic culture and music two generations later. Subtlety can generate silence, and Felix Mendelssohn's relation to Judaism operated at a level of sensitivity approaching taboo.

In Sophocles' play, the modern state opposes the intransigence of traditional morality—and hence the definitions of legitimacy and authenticity—in the persons of Creon and Antigone. Creon is the restoring king who brings Thebes out of a threatened revolution led by Polynices, brother of Antigone. To show that legitimacy rests with the state, Creon has forbidden burial ritual for the slain Polynices. Antigone resists and attempts to bury the corpse, in an insistence that legitimacy rests in a morality that is prior to and more

---

[28] Thomas Nipperdey, *Deutsche Geschichte 1800–1866: Bürgerwelt und starker Staat* (Munich: C. H. Beck, 1984). The terminology and tone of the phrase translate only with great difficulty. "Bürgerwelt" means "the world of the middle class," or the bourgeoisie, but with the positive connotation of citizenship and solidity. "Starker Staat" means, literally, "strong state."

constant than the life and the rights of the state. Creon remains confident in his attitude until the moment of the death of his son Haemon (a suicide for love of Antigone—pace Hegel, who said that the Greeks did not know of love in the Romantic sense and that the suicide is not owing to love).[29] The filial connection, and its loss, are ultimately more primal than the logic of the state. But Creon's grief does not solve the dramatic and political problem of the play. His grief may not necessarily prove the falseness of his prior position; it may indeed only call into question its intransigence and thus his ultimate incapacity to rule. In this way, the moral choice between Creon and Antigone occupied nineteenth-century readings of the tragedy.

For Hegel, the tragedy shows the way to synthesis and resolution of value conflicts (family versus city, and moral law and tradition versus political necessity) beyond the abilities of the characters, and hence of the possibilities of the drama.[30] For both Friedrich and August Wilhelm Schlegel, Antigone is the hero and Creon the villain; for Hegel the opposition is morally symmetrical and for that precise reason tragic. The harmonization of the ethical life of individual persons, families, and religions with the life and exigencies of the state is the process of history worked out throughout Hegel's work, with the references to *Antigone* a recurring presence. Hegel's reading cannot itself be read simply as an endorsement of Creon's position, just as his emerging philosophy of the state cannot be read simply as an endorsement of state (that is, Prussian) power. But such a simplified reading was prevalent in the 1830s and 1840s, as it is still today. Steiner therefore talks about the conservative, pro-Creon Hegel paradigm; such a paradigm belongs more accurately to the reception of Hegel than to his own position. This pro-Creon paradigm remained dominant, Steiner argues, until O. Ribbeck's *Sophokles und seine Tragödien* (1869) and Wilamowitz-Moellendorf's late nineteenth-century designation of Antigone as a religious martyr.[31]

The classicist August Boeckh (1785–1867), Hegel's colleague and personal rival at the University of Berlin, worked as well within a state-oriented reading of *Antigone*. Boeckh's essay "On the *Antigone* of Sophocles" dates from 1824 and was presented again in a Berlin seminar in 1828—a span simultaneous with Hegel's Berlin *Lectures on Aesthetics*.[32] The crucial point Boeckh makes in this essay is that Creon's position is morally complicated and cannot be dismissed as that of the tyrant. Opposing the position of Schönborn, for whom Antigone was the clear heroine in a stand against tyranny, Boeckh argues that

---

[29] See Hegel, *Aesthetics*, p. 564.

[30] See the discussion in Martha C. Nussbaum, *The Fragility of Goodness: Luck and Ethics in Greek Tragedy and Philosophy* (Cambridge: Cambridge University Press, 1986), p. 52.

[31] Steiner, *Antigones*, p. 41.

[32] August Boeckh, *Über die Antigone des Sophokles* (1824); 2d ed.: *Abhandlungen der historisch-philologischen Klasse der königlichen Akademie der Wissenschaften zu Berlin aus dem Jahre 1828* (Berlin: Akademie der Wissenschaften, 1831), pp. 49–112.

the line between legitimate state power and illegitimate tyranny is not clear. Antigone is not simply an innocent battling tyranny; she also undermines the state: "the action of this tragedy shatters the royal house and the state."[33] Boeckh continues: "I do not have to restate that I have not ignored the tyrannical aspect of Creon; but who can ignore the fact that Sophocles represented him as a noble, solitary ruler in search of law and order?"[34]

The relative conservatism of Hegel and Boeckh's "Creonism" certainly inhabits the production of 1841, at least as far as Ludwig Tieck's participation is concerned. Steiner, for example, states that "There is, unquestionably, a Creon after Hegel. Already the celebrated Tieck-Mendelssohn staging of *Antigone* presents Creon as a noble, tragically constrained, defender of the law."[35] But the scenario is complicated by the plurality of participants; not only Mendelssohn, but also Frederick William IV may be responsible for a larger degree of political ambiguity in the 1841 production than Steiner allows. There is a strong and a weak interpretation of this ambiguity. The strong interpretation insists on an element of liberalism on the part of either Mendelssohn or the king, or both, which militates in favor of Antigone. The weak interpretation suggests that by 1840 the Hegelian promise of synthesis—the promise that the *Antigone* at least points the way to the resolution of morality and state power—has faded, and that the indecision, and hence the tragedy, of Sophocles's cosmos must control the principles of its representation.

To pursue the question of the identity of "Mendelssohn's *Antigone*," we can, first, follow two chronologies—those of Mendelssohn and those of Droysen, his friend and teacher. As to the question of the work's political valences, the reception of the work in the line of Hegel and Boeckh shows profound political ambivalence, and we are in a position to see how Mendelssohn adds to such ambivalence new refractions.

Felix's cultural and religious sensibilities can be understood according to (at least) three issues: his relationship to Judaism and to Jewish assimilation, his growing devotion to Protestant music, and the social taboo of the discussion of Jewish matters among the assimilated, largely converted Berlin intelligentsia. Abraham Mendelssohn's famous letter to his son of 8 July 1829 amounts to a stern charge that his son adopt the name Bartholdy and drop the name Mendelssohn. Only thus could Felix reap the benefits of the Lutheran identity to which the family conversion entitled him. The letter bears quoting:

[M]y father felt that the name Moses ben Mendel Dessau would handicap him in gaining the needed access to those who had the better education at their disposal.

---

[33] Ibid., p. 77: "die Handlung dieser Tragödie erschüttert Königshaus und Staat."

[34] Ibid., p. 87: "Dass ich nun das Tyrannische in Kreon nicht verkannt habe, brauche ich nicht zu beweisen; aber dass ihn Sophokles als einen edlen, Recht und Ordnung suchenden Alleinherrscher darstellte, wer kann das verkennen?"

[35] Steiner, *Antigones*, p. 182.

Without any fear that his own father would take offense, my father assumed the name Mendelssohn. The change, though a small one, was decisive. As Mendelssohn, he became irrevocably detached from an entire class, the best of whom he raised to his own level. By that name he identified himself with a different group. Through the influence which, ever growing, persists to this day, that name Mendelssohn acquired a great import [*ein grosses Gewicht*] and a significance which defies extinction. This, considering that you were reared a Christian, you can hardly understand. A Christian Mendelssohn is an impossibility. A Christian Mendelssohn the world would never recognize. Nor should there be a Christian Mendelssohn; for my father himself did not want to be a Christian. "Mendelssohn" does and always will stand for a Judaism in transition, when Judaism, just because it is seeking to transmute itself spiritually, clings to its ancient form all the more stubbornly and tenaciously, by way of protest against the novel form that so arrogantly and tyrannically declared itself to be the one and only path to the good.[36]

This passage is a profound reflection of and on Jewish assimilation in Prussia in the first half of the nineteenth century. The historical logic is Hegelian: assimilation represents historical development and the maturation of spiritual life. Abraham did not see his conversion and name change as a rejection of his father's path, but precisely as a continuation of it. Moses had changed his name in accordance with the social changes of German Jewry; Abraham took the process one significant step further and expected his own son to respect this historical trajectory. Felix's rebellion must therefore be seen in terms of his general rejection of a Hegelian historical linearity. Felix thus recomplicated the cultural identity in relation to which his father and grandfather had sought harmony and resolution.

With regard to this spirit of complication, Felix's determination to remain Mendelssohn must be understood in conjunction with the growing devotion to Protestant music—as a mark of his increasing insistence on a critical and self-forming cultural identity. The 1829 revival of the *St. Matthew* Passion is the strongest example. One might argue that Mendelssohn's relation to Protestantism and the integrity of its aesthetic representations foreshadows

---

[36] Eric Werner, *Mendelssohn: A New Image of the Composer and His Age* (Glencoe: Free Press, 1963), p. 37. The phrase "a great import" carries an alteration of Werner's translation in order to parallel more closely the German original, which appears in brackets. Werner's translation—"a Messianic import"—is overinterpretive, in the words of Peter Ward Jones, librarian of the Music Section, Bodleian Library, Oxford University (personal correspondence, 16 December 1998). In 1998 and 1999, a relevant debate on the merits of Eric Werner's scholarship unfolded in the *Musical Quarterly*. See Jeffrey S. Sposato, "Creative Writing: The [Self-]Identification of Mendelssohn as Jew," and Leon Botstein, "Mendelssohn and the Jews," *Musical Quarterly*, 82:1 (Spring 1998): 190–219; Peter Ward Jones, letter to the editor concerning Michael P. Steinberg, "Mendelssohn's Music and German-Jewish Culture: An Intervention," and Leon Botstein, "Mendelssohn, Werner, and the Jews: A Final Word," *Musical Quarterly*, 83:1 (Spring 1999): 27–50.

Mahler's attachment, two generations later (however more conflicted the latter's may be), to Catholicism and Catholic theatricality. Mahler roamed the contours of the German world, holding positions in Prague, Budapest, and Hamburg, and craved the return to the center, which meant the cultural, musical, and symbolic world of Vienna. His own conversion to Catholicism must therefore be understood as a dimension of a desire to participate in the majority culture of the Austrian Catholic baroque.[37] Similarly, Mendelssohn's itinerary had taken him from Hamburg, Düsseldorf, and Leipzig to the new cultural center of Berlin, and his Protestant devotion represented also a devotion to cultural traditions of northern Germany, with Bach as the main cultural as well as musical hero.

Nevertheless, the confidence and mastery Mendelssohn showed in 1829 were not free of Jewish self-consciousness, as noted in the memoirs of Eduard Devrient. Devrient, an actor (Haemon in the 1841 *Antigone*) and close friend of Mendelssohn's, recalled Mendelssohn's remarks on the success of the *St. Matthew* Passion: "To think that a comedian and a Jew must revive the greatest Christian music for the world."[38] The fact that the performances took place in the *Singakademie* generated the recurring disapproval, in the nineteenth-century literature, of the alleged secularization of Bach.[39] Such uncertainties persisted. The *Singakademie*'s rejection of Mendelssohn's candidacy for the directorship in January 1833 clearly had something to do with his Jewish origins.[40]

By 1833, one can suggest, the Jewish-Protestant symbiosis that Mendelssohn had internalized was in jeopardy on the outside as well. Another example of the inner symbiosis of Jewish memory and Protestant culture that became increasingly embattled from without appears in Eric Werner's perceptive reading of the Jewish subtext in a January 1831 letter disparaging the frivolity of New Year's celebrations. The days around the turning of the year, wrote Mendelssohn, are *"real days* of atonement." Werner attributes these thoughts to "his parental home, where the very serious attitude towards the New Year had simply been transposed from Jewish to Christian practice."[41] The same sensibility is revealed in the words to the concluding hymn of Goethe's "Erste Walpurgisnacht" (1831):

---

[37] See my discussion of this issue in its relation to Mahler and other thinkers in the chapter "The Catholic Culture of the Austrian Jews" in Steinberg, *Austria as Theater and Ideology: The Meaning of the Salzburg Festival, 1890–1938* (1990; Ithaca: Cornell University Press, 2000), pp. 164–95.

[38] Eduard Devrient, *Meine Erinnerungen an Felix Mendelssohn* (Leipzig: J. J. Weber, 1869), p. 56.

[39] See Werner, *Mendelssohn*, p. 100.

[40] Ibid., pp. 230–31. On the issue of the *Singakademie* election and Werner's account of it, see William A. Little's essay "Mendelssohn and the Berlin *Singakademie*: The Composer at the Crossroads" in *Mendelssohn and His World*, ed. R. Larry Todd (Princeton: Princeton University Press, 1991), pp. 65–85.

[41] Werner, *Mendelssohn*, p. 171.

Und raubt man uns den alten Brauch,
Dein Licht, wer kann es rauben?

And if we are robbed of our old customs,
Who can rob us of thy light?[42]

The Sophoclean theme of the robbing of custom must have been evident, perhaps even disturbing, to Mendelssohn. We can recall that for Hegel, the family as carrier of moral and religious values is illustrated in two relationships: brother and sister (Polynices and Antigone), and also father and son (Creon and Haemon). The latter relationship cannot survive the destruction of Antigone's family values. Where are we, then, on Hegel's historical path: at a point where the family and its values are at odds with the state, or integrated within it? I would suggest that Abraham Mendelssohn was in this sense the perfect Hegelian, and that he read the resolution of the Hegelian-Sophoclean dialectic of family and state in terms of the succesful assimilation of the Berlin Jewish intelligentsia. By the time of Felix's maturity in the 1830s and 1840s, the synthesis had begun to show cracks. (It is worth remembering that Mendelssohn heard at least some of Hegel's lectures on aesthetics at the University of Berlin. According to a letter that Mendelssohn's teacher C. F. Zelter wrote to Goethe, Mendelssohn offered an accomplished imitation of Hegel's lecturing style.)[43]

Who is Mendelssohn's Creon: Moses Mendelssohn or Frederick William IV? What is the nature of "law" in his symbolic discourse: universal principle, custom, or bondage? And whose laws are in question: those of ancient religion or those of the modern state?

Felix Mendelssohn had, apparently, little sympathy for his patron Frederick William IV.[44] The king's political and cultural tastes remain underresearched and hard to fathom. The historian Heinrich von Treitschke called his entire reign, from 1840 to 1861, a "long chain of misunderstandings."[45] The association with Mendelssohn occurred during the early years of the reign. These early years were popularly successful, as the king's determination to be well liked led him to take the posture of the reformer. He thus reversed many of the repressive policies of 1819 and after. Censorship was "at least somewhat mitigated," three of the liberal "Göttingen Seven" professors were called to Berlin, etcetera. At bottom, however, Frederick William IV was a Romantic conservative who believed in the divine right of kings and whose model of

[42] Ibid., p. 203.

[43] Ibid., p. 79. Werner's summary of Hegel's ideas on the aesthetics of music and their possible influence on Mendelssohn's developing aesthetic is not convincing. Romantic platitudes about the emotionality of music form the principle of connection.

[44] Werner cites an unpublished letter of 27 Oct 1840 (held, according to Werner, by the Library of Congress) in which Mendelssohn derides the king. Ibid., pp. 82, 85.

[45] Nipperdey, *Deutsche Geschichte*, p. 397.

the Prussian state was grounded in an idea of a "Christian-German" moral community.[46] To that end he relied, in the 1840s, on the advice of Friedrich Julius Stahl, a converted Jew who worked out the model of the "evangelical state."[47] When, for example, David Friedrich Strauss wrote an essay called "Ein Romantiker auf dem Throne der Caesaren," the ostensible subject of Julian the Apostate was easily recognized as Frederick William IV. Nevertheless, the first years of his reign provided a certain honeymoon period for reinstated liberal intellectuals. The constitutional and parliamentary challenges culminating in the events of 1848 and after undid the king's liberalizing pretentions and persona.

How the king's taste brought him to Antigone is a difficult question but an interesting one. Apparently he found Donner's translation of *Antigone* himself and gave it to Tieck.[48] This was the king's first exposure to Greek tragedy, and the Berlin Orientalist Christian Josias Freiherr von Bunsen reported him to be "delighted as with a new and brilliant discovery."[49] Tieck had argued to the king for a reading of *Antigone* as a work presaging Christianity, an approach that irritated the historicist Boeckh. The spatial symbolism of Tieck's staging emphasized the orchestra while at the same time reflecting his view of the tragedy as pre-Christian. From the proscenium he built a double set of stairs leading down to the orchestra, which held the instrumentalists as well as the chorus and an altar.[50] Thus, the stage action deferred to the levels of commentary emanating from the music and musical chorus; Greek drama deferred to the aesthetic forms of Lutheran church music. Tieck, who found "already the later Haydn too noisy, and Beethoven beyond the pale," did not like Mendelssohn's music.[51] Boeckh, on the other hand, defended the music as a legitimate evocation of the Attic poetic—metric—and cultural origins.[52]

One can reasonably assume that the king's personal wish to have *Antigone* staged in Sans-Souci presupposed a given sympathy for the plight of Creon. How sensitive the king was to the text and what kind of political message he may have hoped it would give to the court audience are difficult questions to answer. The Mendelssohn-Tieck *Antigone* did originate with the king's own attraction to Sophocles' tragedy. What is the place of the person and moral intransigence of Antigone within the tastes and forms of a royal entertainment? Is the royal intention the tragedy of Creon, as Steiner suggests? Is it

---

[46] Ibid., pp. 396, 397.

[47] See Walter Bussmann, *Zwischen Preussen und Deutschland: Friedrich Wilhelm IV, Eine Biographie* (Berlin: Siedler Verlag, 1990), pp. 159–90.

[48] Roger Paulin, *Ludwig Tieck: A Literary Biography* (Oxford: Clarendon Press, 1985), p. 336.

[49] Werner, *Mendelssohn*, p. 374.

[50] Paulin, *Ludwig Tieck*, p. 336.

[51] Ibid., p. 337.

[52] Wulf Konold, *Felix Mendelssohn-Bartholdy und seine Zeit* (Regensburg: Laaber Verlag, 1984), p. 215.

the Hegelian Antigone-Creon synthesis realized, a fitting aesthetic representation of a new liberal beginning? And how did Mendelssohn negotiate this hazy but high-staked symbolic context?

Where Mendelssohn's relationship with the classical world is at issue, his friendship with Johann Gustav Droysen is relevant, not only for his knowledge of classical literature but also for his sense of the contemporary political ramifications of classical allusion. The friendship dates from 1827, when Droysen, one year Mendelssohn's senior, replaced Karl Wilhelm Ludwig Heyse as the tutor for both Felix and Fanny Mendelssohn. They remained in regular contact until 1840, when Droysen was called from Berlin to a professorship in Kiel. Their closeness is revealed in their published correspondence, with the first extant letter from Mendelssohn to Droysen written in November 1829: a tourist report from London, with first names and the familiar address used throughout.[53]

Like Mendelssohn, Droysen had heard some of Hegel's Berlin lectures of the 1820s, in his case the lectures on world history. These lectures contributed to the formation of Droysen's early conception of the history of fifth-century Athens as having "attained and set in motion a consciousness of freedom." "The conception of Athenian history as the manifestation of the idea of liberty," James McGlew has written, "is the basis of Droysen's interpretation of Athenian tragedy."[54] In 1832 Droysen published his two-volume study of Aeschylus (*Des Aischylos Werke*), and, in 1833, his life of Alexander the Great (*Geschichte Alexanders des Grossen*). The latter work displayed the first use of the term Hellenism in its now standard usage to mean the general culture of the period between Alexander and the rise of Christianity. The prior, traditional usage of the term had denoted the Greek dialect spoken by Jews in Egypt.[55] The work initiated a life-long interest in Hellenism, which yielded paradoxical results. On the one hand the idea of Macedonia as an ancient model for modern Prussia remained constant. On the other hand, the study of the Hellenistic period was never finished. Arnaldo Momigliano has suggested that this noncompletion had to to with Droysen's difficulty in engaging the question of the role of the Jews in the Hellenistic period. To be sure, the category of the Jews and its modern resonances complicate the linear sense of history grounded in liberal Hegelianism. But in the case of Droysen, as with Mendelssohn, there are personal and social criteria at work as well.

The first volume of the history of Hellenism (*Geschichte des Hellenismus*) appeared in 1836, the second in 1843. In the second volume's last chapter,

[53] Rudolf Hübner, ed., *Johann Gustav Droysen, Briefwechsel*, 2 vols. (1929); Osnabrück: Biblio-Verlag, 1967.

[54] Droysen, *Des Aischylos Werke*, I:163–64; James F. McGlew, "J. G. Droysen and the Aeschylean Hero," *Classical Philology* 79:1 (January 1984): 4.

[55] Arnaldo Momigliano, "J. G. Droysen Between Greeks and Jews," in *Essays in Ancient and Modern Historiography* (Middletown: Wesleyan University Press, 1977), p. 310.

Momigliano points out, "Judaism is mentioned for the first time as an important factor in the origins of Christianity. . . . [A]t least from 1838 onward Droysen became more interested in Judaism. He included books in the popular literature of which he intended to make a special study. He was not indifferent to the mounting research on Alexandrian Judaism, on the Essenes and on Paulism. He seemed to be preparing himself for the next volume of the *History of Hellenism*. Yet nothing happened. . . . Once again we are faced with the question: why did he not pursue this obviously fruitful line?"[56] Momigliano's answer has to do with the "taboo . . . deeply ingrained" within the converted German-Jewish community of Berlin and their discussion of—and their silences about—Judaism.[57] Droysen's personal circle included many Jews and Jewish converts to Christianity. His first wife was Marie Mendheim, daughter of a bookseller, né Mendel. Other friends and associates, in addition to Mendelssohn, included E. Bendemann, Heine, Eduard Gans, and the classicists G. Bernhardy and August Neander (né David Mendel).[58] Momigliano comments: "Droysen did some work on Jewish texts, but he never brought himself to face the whole problem of the relation between Judaism and Christianity. It was the problem which at a personal level had deeply concerned his best friends, his wife and his relatives—and it was going to affect his own children. He must have known that his friends were thinking about it in their silences. He remained silent, too. The *History of Hellenism* was never finished."[59] In March 1842, Droysen wrote to Mendelssohn of the success his oratorio *Paulus* was enjoying in Kiel. (The audience was particularly enthusiastic, Droysen wrote, about the rendition of "Jerusalem" by Amalie Niebuhr, "the daughter of the old Niebuhr.") Droysen heralded the return of "Protestant music" for the first time since Bach and Handel.[60] In view of Droysen's research on Paulism as an element of the Hellenistic transition from Judaism to Christianity, the silence on the work's Jewish references is significant.

On the occasion of Droysen's 1834 engagement to Mendheim, Mendelssohn wrote a letter of congratulation that expresses nonetheless a sense of loss: "if we can no longer live in each other's company, let us not grow distant from one another."[61] Their next recorded correpondence occurs after a gap of almost three years. In December 1837 the two men correspondended about a possible Mendelssohn opera on the *Odyssey*. Droysen was interested in supplying the libretto, and entreated Mendelssohn not to plan an English opera:

[56] Ibid., p. 316.

[57] Ibid., p. 318.

[58] Ibid., p. 317.

[59] Ibid., p. 318.

[60] Hübner, *Johann Gustav Droysen*, 1:211.

[61] Ibid., 1:71: "wenn wir auch wohl nicht wieder miteinander leben werden, so lass uns darum doch nicht voneinander entfernen."

"Was haben wir schon alles in der Musik an das Ausland verloren! [Haven't we already lost enough music to foreigners?]"[62]

Droysen first heard of the 1841 *Antigone* after the Potsdam premiere. In a letter to Mendelssohn of 1 November, he expressed astonishment that Mendelssohn had set the choruses to music, and great interest in hearing them. "You must have truly penetrated to the innermost core of this ancient splendor to be able to say just how they are musical. I cannot yet grasp it. . . . I have absolutely no idea how the ancient forms can adapt themselves to your sounds, something no musician has yet accomplished." The letter ends with the entreaty not to follow the inclinations of the Tieck circle and produce Euripides for the stage. It would be better, Droysen advises, "to bring to the boards the full preserved trilogy of Aeschylus; I think that this would provide the most powerful theatrical effect, and a great opportunity for music." A Wagnerian prophecy![63]

Mendelssohn answered (on 2 December) as follows:

> Should I tell you about the *Antigone*? Yes. If only you had been there! The thing was in fact a private amusement which I undertook, and which came out so well, that I have no desire to repeat it (you know my *esprit de contradiction* in such matters). There's no question of Euripides. . . . Deep in his soul even Tieck had no real interest in the thing [*Antigone*], and then it was a question only of Count Redern and the actors! They all talk about it, because the King "wished" it, and for their part they wished only that I declare the music for such a thing an impossibility, as you do. But then one fine morning I read the wonderful three plays and thought the devil on all this dumb talk and was beside myself with the desire to see it before my eyes (for better or worse) and I was most of all enchanted with the life that inhabits them still today, and that the choruses are still today what we call musical . . . and here the wonderful, natural, aboriginal verse made a more overwhelming impression than I had ever dreamed possible. It gave me a boundless joy which I will never forget. The more or less jolting words do not inspire concern; but the mood and the verse rhythms are everywhere so truly musical, that one need not think about the individual words but rather compose only for those moods and rhythms—and the chorus is finished. Even today one could hope for no richer a task than these multifaceted choral moods: victory and daybreak [Mendelssohn's chorus no. 1], peaceful reflection [no. 2], melancholia [no. 3], love [no. 4, first part], mourning [no. 4, second part], Bacchus's song [no. 6], and the earnest warning at the end [no. 7]—what more could one want?[64]

A public forum for Droysen's reception of *Antigone* came in a newspaper essay following the public premiere of the work in the Berlin Schauspielhaus

---

[62] Ibid., 1:130.
[63] Ibid., 1:200.
[64] Ibid., 1:203.

on 13 April 1842.[65] The essay is a charged and multifaceted polemic about the necessity of public culture and public memory. Mendelssohn is embraced to those ends, but his name is never mentioned.

Droysen's opening sentence exemplifies the cushioned political barb, in this case directed against the king and court: "The *Antigone* must not be a mere masterly and brilliant court festival, an artistic pleasure for the small, select circle of the highly cultured. The work is intended for the public theater, for the whole public." Attic tragedy was a dimension of public culture, and its contemporary nineteenth-century reprise is to serve the same ends. In this first of several instances in this piece, Droysen's argument anticipates Nietzsche's. Cleverly, Droysen flatters the members of Frederick William's circle by referring to them not as the powerful or the privileged but as the "Hochgebildeten"—the highly educated/cultured. There may of course be an element of personal resentment at work here—with regard to Mendelssohn as well as the court—as Droysen only heard of the *Antigone* project after the Sans-souci premiere. The Berlin performances, Droysen continues, became an event of great public interest: "the city is full of talk about the piece." "The city" refers to Berlin, but the category recalls Athens (or Thebes).

Antigone, Droysen continues, explodes "the renowned trivialities of the artistic taste [die bekannten Trivialitäten der Kunstkennerei]" of the Berlin public. He credits royal taste with the revival: "It was a royal idea to revive for our time the most splendid creation of Greek poetry." Here, Droysen makes an impassioned argument for the place of interpretation as opposed to the illusory insistence on the literal representability of ancient forms. This argument for the place of interpretation is highly interesting as an early document in Droysen's developing ideas of historical methodology—the aspect of his work, culminating in the *Historik*, for which he is most remembered:

> Nicht die abgestorbenen Vergangenheiten sollen uns wiederkehren; aber was in ihnen Grosses und Unvergängliches, das soll mit dem frischesten und lebendigsten Geist der Gegenwart erfasst, von ihm durchdrungen zu neuer, unberechenbarer Wirkung in die Wirklichkeit geführt werden; kein Babel toter Trümmerstücke, sondern ein Pantheon der Vergangenheit sei unsere Gegenwart.

> It is not the extinct ages of the past which are to be brought back to us; rather, it is for the freshest and liveliest minds of the present to grasp what is great and enduring of those ages and to bring this to incalculable present-day effect. Our own time should not be a Babel of dead lamentation plays, but a pantheon of the past.

Mendelssohn was pleased with his *Antigone* music and remained closely identified with it during the final years of his life. An excerpt was played at

[65] The review is in the *Spenersche[n] Zeitung* of 25 April, reprinted as "Die Aufführung der Antigone des Sophokles in Berlin," in *Kleinere Schriften zur alten Geschichte* 2 (Leipzig: Veit, 1893–94), pp. 146–52.

his funeral in Leipzig's Paulinerkirche in 1847. What the piece—his music, its relation to the drama, and the drama itself—actually meant to him cannot be clearly understood. I would insist, however, that the resonances of this work are broad, even if they cannot be precisely determined. They start, but do not end, with the political ambivalences of Sophocles' text, its tradition of reception in Romantic Germany, and its relationship to the court of Frederick William IV in the early years of his reign. The theme of eternal, religious law and custom versus the vagaries of the political and of the state recalls the Mendelssohn family saga of Jewish enlightenment (Moses), Protestant assimilation (Abraham), and subtly distributed loyalty (Felix). We surely have the right to ask whether Felix's view of the character Antigone might have resonated with his own discomfort with the previous generation's modernizing, secularizing, state-oriented practice. This deep personal involvement with the Antigone problematic informs the sensitivity of the musical settings, and it also sheds light on the clear difference in compositional style between this work and the *Lobgesang* (Symphony no. 2) of the previous year.

John Toews has interpreted the *Lobgesang* in a convincing argument that places Mendelssohn in a position entirely different from the one I am ascribing to him in the context of his *Antigone*. For Toews, the *Lobgesang*, like the oratorio *Paulus* (also known as *St. Paul*) (1836), reveals the public ethic of Christian reform, community, and adherence to the state. Mendelssohn's public musical ethic, which led Alexander von Humboldt and Christian Bunsen to recommend to Frederick William IV that he be brought to Berlin, corresponded to Bunsen's view of music as, in Toews's formulation, "a significant component of religious reform by [its] recreating and revitalizing for public consumption the emotive core of traditional religious forms, both specifically liturgical and more broadly 'national' or communal."[66] This musical and moral-political ethic intensified, as Toews points out, after the sudden death of Abraham Mendelssohn in 1835. In a letter of December 1835 to Karl Klingemann, Mendelssohn wrote of the wish to "become like his father."[67] His determination to marry and to build a family thus spoke to his father's "longstanding wish"—again in Toews's formulation—"that he might emancipate himself from the subjective world of romantic fantasy and attain the solid ground of ethical responsibility." For his father, romantic, subjective solipsism was the partner of the cultural isolation of the Jew, as he had made clear in the famous letter of 1829.

Written just after Abraham Mendelssohn's death, *Paulus* stands as a tribute to his memory. It transmits Abraham's conviction of a linear realization of

[66] John E. Toews, "Musical Historicism and the Transcendental Foundations of Community: Mendelssohn's *Lobgesang* and the 'Christian-German' Cultural Politics of Frederick William IV," in *Rediscovering History: Culture, Politics, and the Psyche*, ed. Michael Roth (Stanford: Stanford University Press, 1994), pp. 183–201.

[67] *Felix Mendelssohn Bartholdys Briefwechsel mit Legionsrat Karl Klingemann in London* (Essen, 1909), p. 195; quoted by Toews, p. 187.

history through synthesis, and, a fortiori, conversion. The work's narrative of the conversion of Paul tells this story in a transparent way. But it does not do so without representing as well the inner conflict required—and required of Felix—in telling and advocating his father's story. The father/son inscriptions are multiple, as the Abraham/Felix axis is doubled by the Bach/Mendelssohn one and the division of male voices into bass (Paul) and tenor.

In the second part of *Paulus*, the tenor and bass soloists have two duets. The first is a duet for Paul and Barnabas to the words (Cor. 5:20): "So sind wir nun Botschafter an Christi Statt [Now we are ambassadors of Christ]." The second duet carries a similar statement. Finally, the tenor has a last cavatina, with cello obbligato, to the words "Sei getreu bis an den Tod, so will ich dir die Krone des Lebens geben! Fürchte dich nicht, ich bin bei dir! [Be faithful unto death, and I will give you the crown of life. Do not fear, I am with you.]" Dramatically, it is unclear who is speaking here, and to whom. But the tenor voice and rhetoric resonate with the consolation offered by a son to a father—a situation awkward and indeed atypical in the relationship of a father and son but possibly invoked with commemorative affection by a son for a dead father. If the bass-tenor duets in the second half of *Paulus* can be understood as projections of harmony between father and son, then they perform, in musical terms, the alliance between Abraham and Felix that the composition of the oratorio explicitly expressed. The oratorio, named for the father, is concluded musically and dramatically by the son. In a way, Felix anoints himself the successor in Christian music that his father had wished him to be. But the duet form that is so prominent within the work speaks to a different result. The duet form speaks to a synchrony of generations and cultures rather than to the linear sequence that Abraham advocated. But this act of memory, inscribed as harmony, gives up the other projection of the grateful son: namely, the recognition of the generous father who encourages individuation in his talented son.[68]

The enormous public success of *Paulus* and the successful relationship with the Leipzig Gewandhaus orchestra generated the aesthetic of the *Lobgesang*, which combines the Protestant ethic and the spirit of music with, in Toews's words, "a self-conscious attempt to remake or revise Beethoven's choral symphony in a manner which resolved its problematic relations between vocal and instrumental forms, and between immanent structures and transcendent yearnings."[69] There is certainly a convergence, in the years between 1836 and 1840, of a psychological internalization of Abraham's Protestant ethic and Felix's own aesthetic maturation as an independent musical presence, the lat-

---

[68] The tangestial issue here is the way in which Abraham most explicitly discouraged autonomy in his talented daughter, Fanny Mendelssohn, and the way his prohibition on her public display of talent was seconded by Felix.

[69] Toews, "Musical Historicism," p. 191.

ter bolstered by his success in Leipzig. One is led, therefore, to speculate whether the call to Berlin and to the court of the new king might have reactivated the rebellious individualism of the young Felix, and caused him to view the fatherly, Christian-German state of Frederick William IV with all the political, ethical, and psychological ambivalence evident in the *Antigone*—that of Sophocles and that of Mendelssohn.

Schumann's Uncanny Histories

Mendelssohn's music may lack intensity because he often worked through so many issues outside music, rather than in or through music. To emulate a Nietzschean cadence with respect to Wagner ("as a musician he was an actor"): as a musician Mendelssohn may have been a historian. As the student and friend of Droysen, and as the contemporary of Ranke and the young Burckhardt, the grandson of Moses Mendelssohn may have brought to his music his own resolution of past and present. Like them, he understood history as a dimension of living consciousness that can be ordered.

This early- and mid-nineteenth-century paradigm of the meaning of history produced two results. The ordering of history produced the modern historical profession, in which the name of Leopold von Ranke (1791–1886) remained dominant first in Germany and then in the United States well into the twentieth century. Ranke championed a doctrine of historical accuracy and specificity, which evolved into the principle of objectivity in its American reception. At the same time, he championed national teleology as the grand narrative of German history.[70] The second tendency, the service of history to the formation and legitimation of centralized power structures such as capitalism and nationalism, provoked a reaction against the authority and teleological drive of history itself. Thus, Karl Marx, in the opening pages of *The Eighteenth Brumaire of Louis Bonaparte* (1852), berated the authority of historical precedent as the weight of the dead that incapacitates the living. In the wake of 1870, Friedrich Nietzsche warned of the "disadvantages of history for life," arguing that historical antiquarianism and monumentality alike both generate and legitimate creative impotence. For Nietzsche, "history" as both the record of events and a mode of knowledge was exhausted. The variant of this position (which is one that may get this chapter's discussion a bit ahead of itself, but not by much) is the psychoanalytic argument founded by Sigmund Freud in

---

[70] For an analysis of Ranke's career and importance according to these two divergent principles, see Leonard Krieger, *Ranke, or, The Meaning of History* (Chicago: University of Chicago Press, 1977). Ranke was the first honorary president of the American Historical Association, founded in 1884. For the role of Ranke and Rankeanism in the American historical profession, see Peter Novick, *That Noble Dream: The "Objectivity Question" and the American Historical Profession* (Cambridge: Cambridge University Press, 1986).

The Interpretation of Dreams (1900). Freud's developing model of the mind portrays consciousness as a historical and historicizing structure in which the historical record of experience, where culture and subjectivity are intertwined, *cannot be ordered.* Quantitatively, the past contains too much; qualitatively, it contains too much conflict. The past surfaces in waves of overabundance, overstimulation, and overdetermination. This last concept, one of Freud's key terms, denotes the surfeit of meaning in surface signs and symptoms, whereby what lies beneath the surface of, for example, consciousness and art is larger and more multiple than is made manifest by the order of the surface.

Freud offered psychology a Napoleonic civil code of the mind, codifying its operations according to a record accumulated throughout history but peaking in the nineteenth century. Freud's examples highlight classical literature and Shakespeare (Oedipus and Hamlet) but are most saturated by instances from Romantic literature (which include citations of the ancients and Shakespeare). Here he shares a circumstantial trait with Robert Schumann, who is often described as the most literary-minded of composers. But the tie is deeper than that. Schumann, unlike Mendelssohn, produces in music a sense of the past more redolent of surfeit than order. Where Mendelssohn's histories are canny, reflecting the ordering and solution of the subtle legacies of the past, Schumann's histories seem organized around one of Romantic literature's most fruitful categories, on which Freud built a key component of his interpretive and scientific edifice: the idea of the uncanny.

Schumann first chose law, not music, for a profession. He was a law student in Leipzig in 1828–29 and in Heidelberg in 1829–30. At Heidelberg he was taught by Thibaut, professor of law and the author, as we have seen, of *Über Reinheit der Tonkunst* (1825). In October 1830 Schumann gave himself up to music and returned to Leipzig to study and live with Friedrich Wieck, piano pedagogue and father of piano prodigy Clara Wieck, who after much domestic tumult became Clara Schumann.

On his 1829 arrival in Heidelberg, Schumann recorded a humorous remark that carries resonance for ongoing questions of music and cultural ideology: "My lodgings face the asylum on the right and the Catholic church on the left, so that I'm really in doubt whether one is supposed to go crazy or become Catholic."[71] Whether Thibaut and his views played an important role in this configuration is unclear, but Schumann reveals here an unmistakable sensitivity to the cultural ramifications of the Protestant-Catholic, north-south distinction that continued to inform nineteenth-century musical aesthetics and taste. The issue of Catholicism remains a consistent, overdetermined cultural category for its association with theatricality against the Protestant inclination to inwardness. This distinction later pitted Schumann as guardian of the north

[71] See Peter Ostwald, *Schumann: Music and Madness* (London: V. Gollancz, 1985), p. 51.

German Bach-Mendelssohn tradition against Liszt and Wagner and their theatrical styles.

Schumann's cultural adherence is revealed in a programmatic article "Frag-
mente aus Leipzig," published in 1837 in his *Neue Zeitschrift für Musik*. Here
he opposed Meyerbeer's *Les Huguenots*, which made him "weary and faint with
anger," to Mendelssohn's oratorio *St. Paul*.[72] This identification with the Leip-
zig-Mendelssohnian aesthetic intensified, especially after Mendelssohn's death
in November 1847. At the end of his active career, his installation in Düsseldorf in 1850 left him highly conscious of his Protestant status in the Catholic
Rhineland; in this context Schumann planned a gigantic oratorio on the life
of Martin Luther, a project he mused over for two years without result.

Loyalty to Mendelssohn's legacy provoked a skirmish with Liszt and an
awkwardness, at least, with Wagner. Liszt was the guest of honor at the Schumann home in Dresden in 1848. Wagner was among the guests. On hearing
Schumann's piano quintet, Liszt irritated his host by calling it too "Leipzig-
like," a veiled slur against Mendelssohn that also activated the cultural divide
between the Catholic-theatrical and the north German introverted aesthetics.
Later in the evening Liszt spoke highly of Meyerbeer at Mendelssohn's expense, upon which Schumann told him to shut up and then stormed out of
the room.[73] (On such occasions, we might speculate, the young Wagner may
have learned how and why to straddle the two aesthetics.)

Musical inwardness travels with the sonic language of the piano. The piano
moves on ambiguous terrain between privacy, domesticity, and performance.
On one extreme is Liszt. In the middle is the discourse of the piano concerto
as honed by Mozart. Here, a solo voice converses with a more public collectivity in an elaborate metaphor of passage between the private and the public.
At its most socially withdrawn is the style of "esoteric" music, the term aptly
used by Gerhard Dietel to describe Schumann's music for solo piano.[74] Schumann's pianistic voice not only releases an esoteric language but invokes that
realm of secrecy, security, and terror that is contained in the protopsychoana-
lytic word *heimlich*, or "homely." Schumann's piano is the site of the private,
the secret, the *heimlich*, and thereby also of the *unheimlich*: the uncanny, the
unhomely, the radical defamiliarization of the most familiar.

Schumann's separation from Clara in 1836 inspired the composition between 1836 and 1838 of the ambitious and psychologically complicated fantasy in C major, op. 17. The second context for the fantasy is the project for
a Beethoven monument in Bonn, inaugurated on what would have been his

[72] See Leon Plantinga, "Schumann's Critical Reaction to Mendelssohn," in *Mendelssohn and
Schumann: Essays on Their Music and Its Context*, ed. Jon W. Finson and R. Larry Todd (Durham:
Duke University Press, 1984), p. 15.

[73] See Ostwald, *Schumann: Music and Madness*, pp. 221–22.

[74] Gerhard Dietel, *"Eine neue poetische Zeit": Musikanschauung und stilistische Tendenzen im Kla-
vierwerk Robert Schumanns* (Kassel: Bärenreiter, 1989), pp. 296–390.

sixty-fifth birthday in December 1835. In April 1835 Schumann dedicated the front page of his *Neue Zeitschrift* to the public fundraising appeal of the *Bonner Verein für Beethovens Monument*. Is the fantasy's passion directed at Beethoven or at Clara, at public or at private monuments? The answer, of course, is both.[75]

The work's epigraph cites Friedrich Schlegel's poem "Die Gebüsche" ("The Bushes"):

> Durch alle Töne tönet
> Im bunten Erdentraum
> Ein leiser Ton gezogen
> Für den der heimlich lauschet.

> Through all sounds resounds
> In earth's many-colored dream
> A soft sound drawn out
> For the secret listener.

Schumann, lover of puzzles, invested Schlegel's stanza with his own secret. The Schumann interpretive canon, beginning with the work of his first biographer, Wilhelm Joseph Wasielewski, has placed Schumann's secret reference in the words *ein leiser Ton*, "a soft sound," which they assume must refer to Clara. But I would suggest that Schumann was both cleverer and less in control with regard to his own secrets and that the secret of the motto lodges in the word "secret," *heimlich*. Its interpretation requires reference to the literary tradition extending from Schlegel and E.T.A. Hoffmann to Freud.[76]

First, the final line's extra syllable sets it apart metrically from the preceding three and gives it a hushed, private quality, separating it from the declamatory, public tone of the first three lines. That is the onomatopoetic work of the word *lauschet*. More important for the epigraph as a whole and for this internalizing effect in particular, we must parse the word *heimlich*—with its marking of an emotional space that is secret, intimate, homely—in the way readers since Freud have analyzed its partner and antagonist, *unheimlich*.

In his essay "The Uncanny" ("Das Unheimliche") of 1919, Freud defines the uncanny as the lexical opposite of the *heimlich* (the homely; now, after Freud, also the canny). But the lexical opposites converge in the psychological definition of the uncanny as "that class of the terrifying which leads back to something long known to us, once very familiar."[77] And: "What is *heimlich*

---

[75] See the discussion of this and other interpretive issues in Nicholas Marston, *Schumann: "Fantasie," Op. 17* (Cambridge: Cambridge University Press, 1992), pp. 2–3.

[76] For a historical survey of the category of the uncanny, see Anthony Vidler, *The Architectural Uncanny: Essays in the Modern Unhomely* (Cambridge: MIT Press, 1992), pp. 1–66.

[77] Sigmund Freud, "The Uncanny," in *Collected Papers*, vol. 4 (London: Hogarth Press, 1925), pp. 369–70.

thus comes to be *unheimlich*. . . . *Unheimlich* is in some way or other a sub-species of *heimlich*. . . . [S]omething familiar and old-established in the mind that has been estranged only by the process of repression."[78] The homely is the site also of the unhomely, the uncanny: *heimlich* and *unheimlich* coincide, and that is the root of terror, especially in childhood. Freud locates the modern archetype for the uncanny in the literary corpus of Hoffmann, a figure of great importance to Schumann as well, and for similar reasons.

An entry in Schumann's diary from 1831 reads, "One can barely breathe when reading Hoffmann. . . . Reading Hoffmann uninterruptedly. New worlds."[79] In 1838 he wrote the *Kreisleriana*, eight piano fantasies inspired by Hoffmann, which portray a combination of Hoffmann's mad musician Kapell-meister Johannes Kreisler along with strong doses of Liszt, Paganini, and Rob-ert and Clara themselves.

For Freud, the locus classicus for the categories of *heimlich* and *unheimlich* is Hoffmann's story "The Sandman," written in 1815, which contains the por-traits of Nathaniel, Professor Spalanzani, and his "daughter," the doll Olympia. Peering through the professor's window, Nathaniel falls in love with the doll, which disintegrates into its component parts, including bleeding eyes that have been procured by Dr. Coppelius. The same Coppelius had been present at the death of Nathaniel's father in an explosion, during a period of his childhood when Nathaniel was especially vulnerable to the Sandman, the figure of German legend who steals the eyes of children who refuse to go to sleep at night. In Nathaniel's adult psychosis, Coppelius is the Sandman, who has provided Olympia with eyes stolen from children.

In the context of Schumann's reading of Hoffmann, the opening of "The Sandman" is truly uncanny, *unheimlich*. It takes the form of a letter from Na-thaniel to his best friend, Lothario:

> You must all be very worried that I have not written for such a long time. I expect mother is angry, and Clara may think I am living here in a state of debauchery and altogether forgetting the dear angel whose image is imprinted so deeply into my heart and mind. . . . But, ah, how could I have written to you in the utter melancholy which has been disrupting all my mind?[80]

Nathaniel's engagement to Clara is undermined by his obsession with Olympia and the Sandman. Waking from delirium, he pushes the horrified Clara away, calling her "you lifeless accursed automaton."[81] Finally, in a har-binger of Hitchcock's *Vertigo*, he nearly throws her to her death from a tower.

---

[78] Ibid., pp. 375, 377, 394.

[79] See Ostwald, *Schumann: Music and Madness*, p. 77.

[80] e.T.A. Hoffmann, "The Sandman," trans. R. J. Hollingdale, in *Tales of Hoffmann* (Harmonds-worth: Penguin Books, 1982), p. 85.

[81] Ibid., p. 106.

Now, for Nathaniel, Spalanzani, and Olympia we might be prepared to read: Schumann, Wieck, and Clara. In "The Sandman," Nathaniel's horror peaks when he learns that Olympia's eyes are in fact his own, previously stolen by the Sandman. If Schumann was anxious about Clara as a puppet of her father, can we also extend this speculation of "puppet anxiety" to the most familiar, or *heimlich*, sphere—himself? Did he worry about himself as a puppet of Wieck's, and might this be a context in which to understand the well-known and disastrous fourth-finger contraption with which he attached his finger to a string suspended from the ceiling, allegedly intending to strengthen it but instead causing permanent muscle damage that ended his performing viability? If, finally, we take the aspect of sexual anxiety from Freud's analysis, we can extend Freud's equation of eye anxiety with castration complex to the pianistically appropriate fear for the fingers.

In March 1838 Schumann wrote to Clara, "I have completed a fantasy in three movements which I had sketched down to the last detail in June 1836. The first movement is probably the most passionate thing I have ever written—deep lament for you—the others are weaker, but need not exactly feel ashamed of themselves." Passion may be proud so long as it is strong; the association of weakness and shame is notable. In January 1839, however, Schumann described the work to Clara as "excessively melancholy" (*übermelancholisch*).[82]

If we can assert that the fantasy builds an elaborate musical discourse of desire, then we can suggest that it does so in all three of its expansive movements through a complex incorporation of Beethovenian tropes. For Schumann, Beethoven's voice suggests, first of all, masculinity, perhaps masculinization. The first movement—marked *leidenschaftlich vorzutragen*—has a heroic energy, the heroism for which the dominant contemporary aesthetic lionized Beethoven. (For this reason the implied "program" allegedly inherent in symphonic form was held to be the heroic journey, a model that listeners would attach to Schumann's own C major symphony, as we shall see.) This heroic voice is a first-person voice. The second movement offers an internal dialectic that comments on the initial first-person heroic voice from, as it were, two opposing perspectives. The first is external: the movement begins in an unmistakably third-person narrative posture, with the telling of the story of the hero. It is formal and declamatory without assuming the emotional stance of the first-person voice. But this narrative is quickly and repeatedly infiltrated by a second voice that evokes the "jazz" variation from the second movement of Beethoven's last piano sonata, op. 111; the suggestion is of an inner, psychological destabilization of the conventional narrative. The final movement reins in these distinct voices and, perhaps with echoes of the triplet motion in the first movement of Beethoven's *Moonlight* sonata (albeit now in the

[82] See Marston, *Schumann: "Fantasie," Op. 17*, pp. 6 and 98.

major mode), transforms desire into a projected state of shared intimacy while retaining the imprimatur of masculinity.

In March 1839 Schumann abandoned his intention to move to Vienna, where Clara was to join him, when the Bureau of Censors refused to grant him permission to publish his journal there. In *Faschingsschwank aus Wien*, he teased Metternich's censors by mixing a quotation from the *Marseillaise* into the opening allegro. This gesture also served as a greeting to Clara, who was in Paris at the time. Thus Metternich and Wieck converged as Schumann's impediments. Wieck explicitly engaged politics to insult Schumann; early in 1841 he called the first symphony, still in progress, an "opposition symphony." In response, Schumann dedicated the work to King Friedrich August II of Saxony.[83]

This gesture is at least as interesting psychoanalytically as it is politically. When Schumann returned to Leipzig in 1830 to study with Wieck, he clearly looked to his teacher for the union of fatherhood and music that he had lacked. The souring of the relationship with Wieck, complicated by the presence of Clara and the hints of incestuousness in her attachment to Wieck as well as to Schumann (who had first filled the place in the household of an older brother) represents the betrayal of a substitute father. The king of Saxony would seem to be a ceremonially appropriate, emotionally uninvested, and rhetorically powerful figure to mark the usurpation of Wieck's paternal position. But no one could absorb the paternal authority of Beethoven, Schumann's Commendatore.

In early 1839 Schumann, we can recall, remitted from Vienna the manuscript of Franz Schubert's C major symphony, D. 944. The following year, he wrote a celebrated essay extolling the work but also investing it with the fear that evolved from his association of Schubert with the feminine, and thus the counterpart to Beethoven. Susan McClary has cited Schumann's essay with comments that bear quoting:

> The essay carefully establishes a dichotomy between the masculine example of Beethoven and the more sensitive, romantic Schubert, and throughout the essay, Schumann shields himself from Schubert's influence by calling upon Beethoven's 'virile power' at moments when he is about to be overwhelmed by Schubert's charm. At the end, after he has succumbed to a rhapsodic account of what it is like to listen to the Schubert symphony, he seeks to recover his masculine authority by abruptly informing the reader: "I once found on Beethoven's grave a steel pen, which ever since I have reverently preserved. I never use it save on festive occasions like this one; may inspiration have flowed from it."[84]

[83] See ibid., pp. 147, 169–70.

[84] Susan McClary, *Feminine Endings* (Minneapolis: University of Minnesota Press, 1991), p. 18. The Schumann article appeared in the *Neue Zeitschrift für Musik* on 10 March 1840. It is

Beethoven thus provided Schumann with a personal "tonic." I apologize for the musical pun, but it seems apt. Beethoven's masculine voice was therapeutic, and it represented the desired home position for Schumann's own musical and emotional voice. Schumann's ego ideology can be described according to the notion of "masculinity as home."

Schumann relied heavily on this posture as he endeavored to become a public figure in Leipzig, Dresden, and Düsseldorf between 1840 and 1852. Here again the closest model was Mendelssohn, whose public and performing gifts Schumann could not match. "The year of the song," 1840, commenced with the lawsuit against Friedrich Wieck, for the right to marry Clara, still pending. The song literature offers a discourse of focused desire, for Clara and also for subjective autonomy. Thereafter, the genres of choice are large-scaled and public: the symphony first, the hybrid oratorio (such as *Das Paradies und die Peri*) in second place.

Clara's favorite of the symphonies was the C major Symphony, no. 2. It has not been a favorite of twentieth-century audiences and critics. The twentieth century's leading Schumann commentators, including W. H. Hadow, August Halm, Gerald Abraham, and Mosco Carner, have found the piece seriously flawed and in many instances, including Abraham's 1980 article in the *New Grove Dictionary*, not worth discussing.[85] In an important article, Anthony Newcomb has argued for the distinction of the work and for its recanonization, proposing that a nineteenth-century reception aesthetic is necessary for its appreciation. This aesthetic proposed that symphonies be listened to for their musical embodiments of what Schumann and others called *Seelenzustände*, or psychological states. The leading models are the Beethoven symphonies. Comparisons to literary forms, especially to the novel, were common. Wilhelm Fink, as Newcomb recounts, "compared the *grosse Symphonie* to the 'dramatically constructed *Gefühlsnovelle*,' " and A. B. Marx called the symphony "a living image [*Lebensbild*] unfolding in a series of psychologically natural steps."[86] For Newcomb, the musical portrayal of a psychological state involves a journey in time and can therefore be understood in terms of a narrative. The narrative of the C major Symphony is that of the journey from despair to healing and redemption. For the work's form and inferred story, it was compared by mid-nineteenth-century interpreters to Beethoven's Fifth and Ninth Symphonies.

The problem with a general narrative model is the implication of a consistent narrating voice. The problem with this specific model of a narrative of

---

perhaps only pointing out the obvious to say that Schumann rediscovered the phallus in Beethoven's steel pen, but then Schumann's own sexual and gender position is again rendered unclear.

[85] See Anthony Newcomb, "Once More 'Between Absolute and Program Music': Schumann's Second Symphony," *Nineteenth-Century Music* 7 (1984): 239.

[86] Ibid., p. 234. I have adjusted the translation of *Lebensbild*.

redemption is its teleology. When the story is one of redemption, everything points to the end. With such a telos in mind, and at the same time with perhaps too much faith in its legitimacy, Newcomb directs his own analysis to the final movement.

Although many twentieth-century critics of this symphony have found particular fault with the disjointed final movement, this is not the only place in the work where Schumann's form seems stretched, out of order, or possibly incoherent. One such problem is the unconventional placement of the scherzo as the second movement, followed by the slow movement marked adagio espressivo. Presumably, the redemption narrative would not itself determine the placement of the two inner movements, so long as the narrative were able to transcend the melancholy of the adagio. Aside from the opening, transitional phrase (which Brahms may have been invoking in the opening of the final movement of his Fourth Symphony), the final movement, beginning as it does with, in Newcomb's phrase, "a rough shout of affirmation," is completely unconnected in rhetoric and mood to the adagio. But the adagio is voiced in direct relation and response to the preceding scherzo. I would suggest an allegorical reading of the adagio in relation to the scherzo and argue accordingly that the middle movements of the work enable a reading in terms of allegory that is more helpful than one conceived in terms of narrative.

The scherzo is clearly and brilliantly a Mendelssohnian movement, and no less so for the layer of melancholy that underlies its jocularity. Newcomb speaks of the "inactive, somewhat melancholy character and crawling chromaticism [that] lie behind the vigorous athleticism of the scherzo theme, and help to give it the unstable, contradictory character remarked in many early reviews." He suggests that the "antic scherzo is in fact not quite what it pretends to be."[87]

The exquisite adagio espressivo unfolds in a confessional, first-person mode. The music says "I"; the investment in the musical first person of Robert Schumann is certain but not readily decipherable. The overall posture of the movement seems to impart the thought—part confession, part defense, part self-assertion—"I am not Mendelssohn." In a way the movement turns away from—unwrites—the work of the scherzo. This internal unwriting of previous movements may be figured in the work's tendency to quote Beethoven, central as this rhetorical property is to the Ninth Symphony. The adagio's first-person utterance offers a consistent melancholic mood but does not progress in a unified voice; multivocality is made clear by varied orchestration and the use of solo instruments, especially the oboe and bassoon, in sequences of short figures and phrases that appear and withdraw. Schumann himself wrote in a letter of his affection for "my melancholy bassoon."[88] The main theme reorga-

---

[87] Ibid., p. 242.
[88] See Ostwald, *Schumann: Music and Madness*, p. 205.

nizes material from the two principal thematic groups of the preceding two movements.[89] It adds to these materials the central gesture of the falling diminished fourth, which Newcomb identifies in a fascinating way as "a figure from the *Figurenlehre* of the Baroque music in which Schumann had immersed himself for months before writing the C major symphony"—another connection, perhaps, to Mendelssohn.[90] If we hear this movement's rhetoric in a larger frame of reference, we might suggest that its inscription of melancholy works as well through invocations of Mozartean as well as Schubertian gestures, especially in solo wind lines, in the fragmentary quality of phrases passed from one wind instrument to another, supported by syncopations. (I am thinking, for example, of the larghetto of the clarinet quintet, K. 581.) The movement ends—again, in Newcomb's felicitous description—"not in an atmosphere of triumph; rather, in an atmosphere of resignation and near stasis." Nothing is worked through.

The finale reclaims an extroverted, public voice, yet it does so not by transcending the private, interior, unresolved melancholy of the adagio but rather by momentarily suppressing it. For this reason the reading of the symphony as a salvation narrative is unconvincing. If the final movement is itself structurally and emotionally unconvincing, this may have to do with the authenticity of the melancholic state it has somewhat glibly left behind.

Back to Schubert

The C-major key signature of Schumann's Second Symphony may imply a reference to Schubert's "Great" symphony, which Schumann had transmitted from Vienna in 1839; but the tone does not. For Schumann, melancholia and the burdens of history predominate as they do not in the larger Schubert work. The comparison gives Schubert's work a more Mendelssohnian subject position. Thus, the circumstantial contingency of Schubert's C major symphony on its reception, valorization, publication, and performance by Schumann and Mendelssohn may hold a key to its interpretation as well. In other words, the life of the Schubert Ninth unfolds in the context of the north German symphonic tradition: that of Leipzig, not Vienna. This tradition is also a historicizing tradition, but not necessarily one of memory or nostalgia.

Heard in this context, the Schubert Ninth, distinct from Schubert's other symphonies, works intensely to find its place in a historical continuum. In his famous review of the work in the *Neue Zeitschrift für Musik*, Schumann described it as "a thick novel in four volumes as if by Jean Paul."[91] As many

---

[89] See Newcomb, "Once More 'Between Absolute and Program Music,' " p. 243.

[90] Ibid., p. 243.

[91] Schumann, *Neue Zeitschrift fuer Musik* (1840), pp. 81–83; cited in Maintz, *Franz Schubert, in der Rezeption Robert Schumanns*, pp. 250–51.

scholars have remarked, the abiding importance of Jean Paul in Schumann's aesthetic stems from the former's insistence on originality and individuality as principles of aesthetic expression. For Jean Paul, suggests Leon Botstein, "the act of reading inspired, as it did in Schumann, the individual's own novel of self-creation."[92] The psychological depth that Schumann heralded in Schubert's music—with the Ninth Symphony as the ultimate case—formed, in Marie Luise Maintz's felicitous phrase, through the "resumption of the principle of individuation."[93]

Schumann's hearing of Schubert's Ninth Symphony as an argument of individuation, an experience that would in turn be shared, as Botstein suggests, by the listener, coincides with the antimimetic subjectivity constructed—as discussed above—in Mendelssohn's musical arguments. At the same time, Schubert's texture is thicker, his sense of dramatic unfolding more portentous. Finally, the last movement would seem to ask, with the listener as witness, whether a canny narrative is overtaken by an uncanny presence and therefore whether the capacity of historical analysis is bound to be overwhelmed by the momentum of unresolved history. Thus, the listener is left with the question of whether history has caught up with and overwhelmed this music and its argument for its own subjective integrity, or whether the work and its implied subjectivity has succeeded in integrating history in its overabundance.

The structure of the allegro vivace finale is founded on a phrase constructed of four repeated half notes (each taking a full measure in 2/4 time), usually sounded by the winds, with a string accompaniment of triple eighth-note figures. As the four-note figure repeats and returns, it gains in intensity. Its final hearing—marked "*fff*"—is intoned by the full orchestra without the triplet accompaniment, as if the latter had been scared away. Many hearers have given a programmatic content to this insistent phrase. The most basic is "death knocking at the door." Related and more interesting is the possibility that the phrase quotes the Commendatore's quadruple knock on Don Giovanni's front door. The effect of the movement's unfolding is one of a reversal of control between the movement, its narrative voice, and the four-note figure in its increasingly aggressive insistence. If at the beginning the movement's pulse and narration use and include the figure, by the end the figure takes over to intimidate and control the overall process: the return of the repressed. Although the balance between the figure and its context, between interruption and continuity, remains to a great extent the conductor's call, the repetition, orchestration, and dynamic markings controlling this phrase suggest that the narrative order of the symphony is being unhinged. The canny is dislodged by the uncanny; individuation is overcome by history.

[92] Leon Bostein, "History, Rhetoric, and the Self: Robert Schumann and Music Making in German-Speaking Europe, 1800–1860," in *Schumann and His World*, ed. R. Larry Todd (Princeton: Princeton University Press, 1994), p. 16.

[93] Maintz, *Franz Schubert*, p. 84: "die Fortsetzung des Prinzips der Individuation."

Chapter Four

THE FAMILY ROMANCES OF MUSIC DRAMA

Ob euch gelang
ein rechtes Paar zu finden,
Das zeigt sich an den Kindern.
Den Stollen ähnlich, doch nicht gleich,
An eig'nen Reim und Tönen reich;
Dass man's recht schlank und selbstig find',
Das freut die Eltern an dem Kind:

Und Euren Stollen gibt's den Schluss,
Dass nichts davon abfallen muss.

If you've succeeded
In finding a true pair,
It will show in the children.
Similar to the stanzas, but not exactly
    the same,
Rich in its own rhyme and tones;
So that one will find it slender and
    self-sufficient—

Thus are parents proud of the child:
Your stanzas will have their conclusion,
With nothing falling off the mark.
    —Wagner, *Die Meistersinger von Nürnberg,*
    act 3.

The Family Romances of Music Drama

Wagner's *Ring of the Nibelung* tells the stories of two families, or rather two kinds of families. The first story follows the extended family of the god Wotan, including those who share in his accession to power and pomp (his wife's family and his illegitimate daughters) and those who are fundamentally excluded (his twin children and, eventually, their son) or at one time banished from its aura (his favorite daughter). Wotan's nemesis, the dwarf Alberich, the Nibelung who gives the whole enterprise its name, generates a family tree of his own, a more economical one that highlights the resentful bond with his son Hagen. Alberich's family is not structured fundamentally so differently from Wotan's; it is, rather, only less lucky and less tragic. The second family saga I have in mind is, then, not inhabited by dramatic characters but rather by musical and dramatic forms. This is the family history of music drama, in which the *Ring* itself figures as the most prominent progeny. The first story unfolds in a manifest way and, at least to a degree, intentionally; the second, latent story emerges symptomatically.

In the first story, the *Ring* follows the decline of a powerful family dynasty: a *Buddenbrooks* avant la lettre. (Of course, as Thomas Mann would have been the first to confess, the historical fact is inconveniently the reverse: his own novel of 1901, *Buddenbrooks: The Decline of a Family,* is a *Ring* après la musique.) Like Mann's novel, moreover, Wagner's *Ring* can be understood as a historical epic specific to the life of the *Grossbürgertum* in nineteenth-century Germany, a period in which the family occupies a crucial position in the unfolding of modernity as the mediating entity between traditional and rationalized social structures and relations.

The debate over the *Ring*'s historicity has taken place on altered ground since 1976, when Patrice Chéreau staged it for the centennial of the Bayreuth Festival. In Chéreau's understanding, which he later recorded in a memoir of the origins and life of his production, the *Ring* is constructed allegorically and not symbolically.[1] In other words, any claim to universal signification is produced through a referential world that is culturally and historically specific. Chéreau's *Ring* is conceived as a historical epic about three generations of a family and three paradigmatic generations in the rise, crisis, and fall of a society and a nation. Calling characters "gods" serves to identify the extent and style of their conceits and rhetorics of prominence. Chéreau thus literalized for the stage an idea as old at least as George Bernard Shaw's *The Perfect Wagnerite* (1901), which opened with the assertion of the *Ring*'s contemporaneity. The *Ring*, Shaw wrote, "is a drama of today . . . and could not have been written before the second half of the nineteenth century, because it deals with events which were only then consummating themselves."[2]

In his production, Chéreau placed the young Wotan and the building of Valhalla in the context of German industrialization and nation- and empire-building—in other words, in the *Gründerzeit* of the 1870s. The building of Valhalla became synchronous with the building of Bayreuth as well as with the building of Bismarckian and Wilhelmine Germany. Wotan's self-institutionalization came to parallel Wagner's, as the wandering god with an uncertain and transgressive past resolved to install himself as a monument to himself. In this historicized reading, if the founding generation is that of the *Gründerzeit*, the generation of crisis thus becomes the generation of the 1890s, a periodization that allows for the conjunction of incest (Siegmund and Sieglinde) and the decade of decadence and preoccupation with degeneration. Finally, the age of the twilight of the gods fits into a Weimar context, with its straddling of the two German debacles of 1918 and 1933–45.

Scenically, the *Ring* of Chéreau and his designer Richard Peduzzi combined the romantic visual allegories of loneliness of a Caspar David Friedrich with the industrial, urban bleakness of film noir and the visual universe of Fritz Lang's *Metropolis*. If Alberich's theft of the Rhinegold is conventionally understood as the rape of an innocent and ahistorical nature, in the Chéreau/Peduzzi opening tableau, the Rhinescape has already been absorbed by modern history.

---

[1] Patrice Chéreau, *Lorsque cinq ans seront passés* (Toulouse: Editions Ombres, 1994).

[2] George Bernard Shaw, *The Perfect Wagnerite: A Commentary on the Niblung's Ring* (London: Constable and Co., 1901), p. 1.

It has been industrialized. If the Rhineland is an industrial landscape, as it was swiftly becoming during the decade of the *Ring*'s premiere, then there is no unspoiled state of nature to be represented at the opening of *Das Rheingold* but, rather, only the desire for a return to such a state. Brünnhilde's rock, from *Die Walküre* to *Götterdämmerung*, another of the production's more renowned tableaux, allegorizes the desire to return to nature with an alternative visual vocabulary. This set is punctuated by a scenic quotation not of a natural setting but of a prominent romantic trope of the desire for the return to nature, namely the visual tropology of Friedrich. Peduzzi's set evokes several important Friedrich canvases, including *Abbey in an Oak Forest* (1809–10), *Monastery in a Graveyard* (1817–19, destroyed in World War 2), and the *Ruin at Eldena* (1825).

Chéreau's combined historicization and allegorization of the *Ring* marks the most recent watershed in the history of Wagner staging. Since its introduction in 1976, its allegorical argument and visual iconography have edged out the reigning postwar Bayreuth antihistoricist style (associated mostly with Wieland Wagner) as the zero degree of the Wagnerian visual universe. (After 1945 and the prominent position of both Wagner and Bayreuth in Nazi cultural mythology, the relegitimation of Wagner depended on radical dehistoricization. Wieland Wagner's style and statement were consistent across the Wagnerian canon. Perhaps the most aggressive intervention was his *Meistersinger* of 1956, popularly dubbed "the mastersingers without Nuremberg" for its dehistoricization of Wagner's only explicitly historicizing opera.)

In my own discussion, I will adopt Chéreau's historicizing logic but at the same time advance and expand his historical template. The span of Chéreau's generational narrative, stretching from 1870 to 1920, may not have been big enough for the family history recounted in the *Ring*. The *Ring*, I will argue, covers a larger trajectory of nineteenth-century German history and crisis. The *Ring*, as Wagner's life work, covers the period of his own lifetime (1813–83) from the liberation of Germany from Napoleonic rule to the Wilhelmine period.

With this revised trajectory, a second question presents itself. If the nineteenth century marks the rise of Germany, how can the *Ring* follow the historical model and at the same time, like *Buddenbrooks*, trace a story of decline? The *Ring*, and the phenomena of Richard Wagner and music drama, must be understood as gigantic symptoms of a crisis and at the same time as bearers of critical analysis of that very crisis. The *Ring* confronts that trajectory of modernity that builds institutions and places human subjectivity in what Max Weber called the iron cage. Simultaneously, the *Ring*—like music drama as ideology, like Valhalla and Bayreuth—strives to redeem a certain heroic subjectivity against the alleged restricting agencies of modernity (material power, wealth, and corruption) and strives itself to become the kind of institution (music

Figure 7 Das Rheingold, act 1, Bayreuth Festival, 1976.

Figure 8 Die Walküre, act 3, Bayreuth Festival, 1976.

Figure 9   Caspar David Friedrich, *Ruin at Eldena* (1825).

drama, Bayreuth, etcetera)—that is the structural and ideological product of precisely this desubjectivizing regime of modernity. The *Ring* at once narrates and symptomatizes the rise and decline of subjectivity, both as a historical phenomenon and as a principal aspect of musical form and musical culture.

The *Ring* as symptom: this allegation invokes the second family history and family crisis at play. This is the story of music drama itself. This story produces the work's unconscious narrative. At this level, the *Ring* drives the culmination and crisis of music drama. The music itself, closely related to the genre (in principles and practice) of music drama, contains a family saga of its own. This is also a historical issue, specific to the period of the work's composition through the third quarter of the nineteenth century.

Music drama is conceived by Wagner, both theoretically and practically—in other words, both in his prose writings and in his music dramas—as a music-driven system. I take this to be a relatively straightforward yet often misunderstood principle. Consistently, for Wagner, music must generate drama. Music's telos is drama, but drama's principal source is music. This issue has claimed significant attention in recent Wagner scholarship. Two concerns, related but distinct, have been highlighted. The first concerns the privileging of music in an aesthetic that also involves text and stage. The issue here is the extent to which the drama is contained and privileged within the musical writing for orchestra and voices. The second issue involves Wagner's relationship to the ideology of "absolute music," a term he coined in 1846.[3] This is by far the more vexed of the two issues for at least two reasons. First, Wagner is understood to comment on a tradition he himself names, and thus to shift the ground under the historical formation he engages. Second, this shifting of ground (which I addressed in chapter 2 as the shift from the abstract to the absolute) constitutes a political act. The absolute nationalizes the abstract. It makes the abstract signify, and signify absolutely, as the voice of the nation. Thus, the musical values of the aesthetic of music drama must be understood, in my view, to be a priori political in their definition. The nationalization of music engages only German music, and it makes Germanness into an internally coherent and therefore into an essentially exclusionary category. Moreover, it does so (or claims to do so) retroactively, investing Beethoven as the father of the national tradition.

At the level of the music, we have the desire to reconcile precisely music and drama: the absolute and the signifying/representational. Wagner, Carolyn Abbate has written, "saw himself as Beethoven's only legitimate son, the symphonic opera composer born of the last great symphonist."[4] For Abbate, Wagner's self-investiture as Beethoven's son parallels his investiture of music drama as symphonic opera. For Wagner, "*symphonic* referred to . . . a continuous network of interrelated thematic ideas, which he regarded as characteristic both of Beethoven's symphonies and of his own operas."[5] As Abbate notes, the analyst to run furthest with this idea was Alfred Lorenz, who argued that Wagnerian operas and their individual acts could and should be analyzed as literal symphonic structures, replete with sonata form, adagios, rondos, and so forth. Abbate argues for a loose application of the symphonic metaphor, "in which a discursive music that takes its shape and voice from words becomes a symphonic music that pursues its own sonorous logic." Does she give the words too much credit?

Wagner's 1851 manifesto *Oper und Drama* argued for a dramatic aesthetic of music as the superior heir to a music of mere notes. Ten years later, in the essay "Zukunftsmusik," Wagner "rejected" (Robert Bailey), unconsciously revised (Carl Dahlhaus), or reexamined (Abbate) *Oper und Drama*. He thus reinvigorated the category of the symphonic, arming it, suggests Abbate, with a Schopenhauerian conceit—gleaned in the mid-1850s—that pure music con-

---

[3] See Thomas S. Grey, *Wagner's Musical Prose: Texts and Contexts* (Cambridge: Cambridge University Press, 1995), pp. 1–6 and passim. Wagner used the phrase in a program note to his performances of Beethoven's Ninth Symphony for the Dresden Palm Sunday concerts. This work would remain the lodestar for Wagner's repetitions and mutations of the term.

[4] Carolyn Abbate, "Opera as Symphony: A Wagnerian Myth," in *Analyzing Opera: Verdi and Wagner*, ed. Abbate and Roger Parker (Berkeley and Los Angeles: University of California Press, 1989), pp. 92–124; quotation from p. 92.

[5] Ibid., p. 93.

stitutes a representation of the Will.[6] In this later essay, as Klaus Kropfinger has suggested, the symphonic in the sense of "mere notes" and the dramatic in the sense of music drama are mediated by the thematic, the weaving of "musical motives." For Wagner, "theme" and "motive" are synonyms.[7]

Wagner's equation of theme and motive can be understood either to resolve or to gloss the difference between music and music drama. This poses an interpretive problem for the basic Wagnerian tool of the leitmotiv, which is both musically and textually generated and contingent, and which does not function consistently across the Wagnerian canon. In the *Ring*, due certainly in part to its enormous scale, leitmotivs perform a large amount of narrative and dramatic work. Their function and importance do not disavow the myth of symphonic opera; at the same time, however, they create a mnemonic language of musical pictures through which the listener can reduce musical structure and temporality to repetitions of static figures. Indeed, Theodor Adorno accused Wagner of intentionally building the listener's acoustic experience in this way.

Through the course of the *Ring*, leitmotivs are introduced and combined in groups, and these groups are often referred to as families. Thus, the tetralogy's prelude, *Das Rheingold*, as is well known, begins with a slowly-forming chord, generating a system of musically related phrases that signify nature in their upward-moving formations and human downfall in downward moving analogues. The leitmotivs that give dramatic meaning to musical phrases, as many Wagner scholars have argued, form an elaborate system of signification and intersignification. When a lone leitmotiv "speaks," it—to bracket the issue of the gendering of the leitmotivs for the moment—speaks as a member of a family. The "educated" Wagner listener is likely to be competent in the identification of leitmotivs in two ways. First, he or she will identify individual motives: nature, Rhine, gold, sword, etcetera. Second, and in a more sophisticated manner, the listener will understand the family structures and interdependencies of the motives. Thus, the sword is a close derivative of nature, differing only in its distribution of the broken major triad and octave. As these musical

[6] Robert Bailey, "The Genesis of *Tristan und Isolde*" (diss. Princeton University, 1969); Carl Dahlhaus, *Wagners Konzeption des musikalischen Dramas*, cited in Abbate, "Opera as Symphony," p. 97. Schopenhauer's assertion of music as representation of the Will (from *Die Welt als Wille und Vorstellung* [*The World as Will and Representation*] of 1819) codified for the nineteenth century a misreading of Kant, whereby the Kantian noumenal and phenomenal were remapped as the will and its representation. Schopenhauer misunderstood the central Kantian principle of the unrepresentability of the noumenal. Martin Heidegger and Hermann Broch both accused Nietzsche of repeating Schopenhauer's error. See my introduction to Hermann Broch, *Hugo von Hofmannsthal and His Time: The European Imagination, 1860–1920* (Chicago: University of Chicago Press, 1984), p. 186 n. 25.

[7] Klaus Kropfinger, *Wagner and Beethoven: Richard Wagner's Reception of Beethoven*, trans. P. Palmer (1974; Cambridge: Cambridge University Press, 1991), p. 160 and passim.

families become musical-dramatic associations, they tell the true, ratified story that is being experienced epiphenomenally by the characters onstage.

It seems to me that musicological scholarship has tended to make a choice in its treatment of Wagner's musical idiom, specifically the systems of leitmotivs. Thus, scholars as different as Lorenz in the 1920s and Abbate in the 1980s have argued for the minimization of signification/representation in the leitmotivic systems, in favor of a more "absolute" musical texture and sequence.[8] For Lorenz, that absolute narrative signified nationally; for Abbate it did not. Conversely, scholars as different as Adorno and Robert Donington (both writing in the 1960s) emphasized the importance of the leitmotivs as signifying principles. For Adorno, the signifying leitmotivs formed the key to Wagner as a composer for regressive listeners whose memories could rely on musical pictures. For Donington, they built a sublime symbolic universe, delivering what Carl Jung had only dreamt of. Divergent scholarly musicological arguments, one might argue, relate to the reception of Wagner's music as diverging staging practices relate to the reception of the drama.

Thus, the *Ring*'s two family stories have, then, two family romances. At the level of the plot, we have the romance of the gods—or rather the "gods," to cite the Chéreauvian return to history. The desire that motivates the romance—as all family romances are structured by desire—is the wish for the patriarch to reconcile history and individuality. The character who stands as both the object and subject of this desire is Siegmund, the free agent who is also an ethical agent. In plot terms, Siegmund's death can be understood as the death of subjectivity. The generational passage from Siegmund to Siegfried accompanies the passage from subjectivity to identity. Finally, this double passage constitutes the devolution of music drama into a system, where fissures begin to open. In what follows, I will analyze several moments in musical and dramatic unfolding of the *Ring* that emphasize the conjunction of its two family romances.

---

[8] Alfred Lorenz, *Das Geheimnis der Form bei Richard Wagner*, 4 vols. (Berlin: M. Hesse, 1924–33). A concise summary of some of the legacies of Wagner scholarship appears in Grey, *Wagner's Musical Prose*, p. xii. Lorenz's scheme was unraveled by Rudolf Stephan and then, more famously, by Carl Dahlhaus. Abbate begins her argument in "Opera as Symphony," cited above, by rejecting a simple model of "symphonic opera" that would ignore the ways the music symbolizes text, poetry, and story. Her detailed reading of the conspiracy scene from act 2 of *Götterdämmerung* reinstates the notion of "symphony's triumph over poetry" in its argument, based on sketches and other evidence from the compositional process, that ostensibly text-driven interruptions of musical sequence turn out, on close analysis, to be musically driven. The implied "story" that Abbate tells about the conspiracy scene could be emplotted as the revenge of music drama, Son of Symphony. Abbate engages this scene as an autonomous example and does not address the dramatic context of the scene at the end of the extraordinary act 2, extraordinary for precisely the concerns under examination, namely the shape and limits of music drama. This issue will be addressed later in this chapter. What is virtually ignored by all the scholars mentioned in this footnote is the political dimension of the debate about Wagner and absolute music.

Siegmund's Death

For the nineteenth century, the multigenerational family emerges at once as the compromise formation and the breaking point between the traditional world of community, honor, and affect and the contemporary world of society, exchange, and commodification. When the family turns inward, it experiences and represents itself according to bonds of affect—perhaps love. When it turns outward to the world, or indeed when it conducts its own internal relations according to its internalization of external worldly rules, it becomes an organ of power. According to this economy, love and interiority are feminized, while power and self-assertion are masculinized. Generational continuity is defined patriarchally: a continuation of name, capital, property, and power. The continuity of love is much more difficult to trace rationally, as love depends on the subjective energy created by specific personal relations.

In the nineteenth-century bourgeois family, bonds of love appear in configurations and tropes that go against the grain of the generational transmission of power and capital. A principal site of this kind of relationship is that between brother and sister. In nineteenth-century literature, the brother-sister relation is indeed a classic site of the countermodernizing affective bond. Sibling relations don't fit into the rationalization of the family as a post–Adam Smithian political economy of productivity—of dynasty- and capital-creation. The affective bonds of the relations between brothers usually collapse into violence as one brother claims the mantle of capital formation: Fafner against Fasolt, Alberich against Mime, even Siegfried against his phony brother Gunther. The relationship between brother and sister comes to be understood as a place of true impasse between affective and rationalized relations.

The intensity of the brother-sister relationship in this period and its erotic charge often leads to the classification of incest. David Warren Sabean has suggested the following, in an article called "Fanny and Felix Mendelssohn-Bartholdy and the Question of Incest":

> The relationship between brothers and sisters was an absolutely central theme for the post-Napoleonic German family. Heinz Reif in his study of the Paderborn nobility demonstrates that the new bourgeois family ideals during this period became characteristic even of the provincial nobility: Domesticity (*Innerlichkeit*), friendship, marriage and courtship based on emotion and individualization and sentimental cohesiveness were valued. Familial relations came to be marked by intense inner experience and the construction of personal connections based on feeling, with a tendency to develop individualized ways of expression. In this period appears among families from the nobility to the *Bildungsbürgertum* a new emphasis on dyadic relationships, which partly at least excluded others in the family. There was a great interest in letter writing to address individuals in the family and to construct special

relations among those of the same age. Above all, this was a time for brothers and sisters to construct individual emotional relationships.[9]

In 1800, Sabean writes, the Wittenberg theologian Carl Nitzsch contrasted the purity of brother-sister love with the impurity and selfishness of marital love, in which lust is associated with egotism. Paradoxically, the designation of brother-sister love as the purest love functions as an eroticizing agent. German literature between 1770 and 1830 was saturated with stories of conscious and unconscious incest. The actual relationship between Goethe and his sister Cornelia has been dubbed incestuous by psychoanalytic observers, and has been called the "very nerve center of Goethe's creativity" by one of them: Kurt Eissler. Only slightly less renowned—and no less significant—are the cases of Felix and Fanny Mendelssohn-Bartholdy and Heinrich and Ulrike von Kleist. In all cases, sympathy and attraction were nurtured by a sense of equality in education and temperament in childhood. And in both cases, as Sabean points out, the male sibling reserved the mantle of public life for himself.

Erotic affectivity between brother and sister is further coded as a specifically early nineteenth-century phenomenon in its incorporation of the romantic notion of androgyny. In the musings of the Schlegels' Athenäum circle, androgyny was prized as the harmonization of male and female personae that is the richest fount of creativity. For bourgeois brothers and sisters slotted into a socially and patriarchically sanctioned protocol of aesthetic education, the recognition of a counter-gendered version of the self in the sibling provided a flirtation with androgyny. The twin becomes the literary ideal type for this potential: the face that is the cross-gendered replication of the self. In Wagner's Siegmund and Sieglinde, as we shall see, we have thus a late—and not a first—instance of this ideal type. For the male sibling (for Goethe and Mendelssohn, for example), the culturally sanctioned course of this aesthetic education and its flirtation with androgyny was the final resumption of a secure masculinity—a separation from the sister that involved precisely the insistence that she restrict her talents to the home, while he takes his out into the world.

The incestuous union of Siegmund and Sieglinde that lies at the plot center of the *Ring* thus also places the *Ring* at the center of nineteenth-century familial and social discursive and material networks. In this historical network, Siegmund in his unique psychological delicacy and complexity embodies precisely the complexity and vulnerability of the middle transitional generation—what I am tempted to call the Mendelssohnian generation. His life traces the cultural and political transition in mid-century Germany from liberal hope to violent betrayal. His personality marks the hope and defeat of subjectivity. So does his music. That subjectivity lodges musically and dramatically in the sym-

[9] David Warren Sabean, "Fanny and Felix Mendelssohn-Bartholdy and the Question of Incest," *Musical Quarterly* 77:4 (Winter 1993): 712.

bol of "Nothung": the name of Siegmund's sword, a word that is a slight sonic variant of "Not" (need, despair) and the marker of a subjectivity that is distinctly phallic but with an extraordinary degree of complication. Indeed, Siegmund's intricate subjectivity complicates his phallic determinism in the same way that an allegorical, historical reading of the *Ring* complicates references to symbolic orders on which transhistorical authority is often conferred.

The character Siegmund appears at the opening of *Die Walküre*. (He appears as a wholly musically conceived premonition in the final scene of *Das Rheingold*, as will be discussed below.) I would suggest here only half-seriously a hyperformalizing template that would embarrass Alfred Lorenz: if we imagine the shape of the *Ring* as a concerto (we lose Lorenz here, who looked for symphonies), then Siegmund enters in the position of the solo instrument. Here he resembles the Countess in *Le nozze di Figaro*. But whereas Siegmund's entrance, like the Countess's, comes at the opening of the second opera qua second part of a four-part structure, it carries additional privilege as the opening gesture in the first of three music dramas, as preceded by a prologue—the status Wagner accords explicitly to *Das Rheingold*.

In this first act of *Die Walküre*, Siegmund is granted exceptional privilege in the tuning of his first-person voice. He is given permission, one might say, by music drama to construct carefully his own musical and psychological subjectivity. This "permission" can be understood as a gesture of temporary hospitality on the part of music drama, a parallel to the momentary hospitality granted by his hostile host, Hunding. Siegmund is both at the center of music drama and its guest. He finds his voice, through the course of the first act, through two sudden and conflicting engagements: with an erotic counterpart and with his paternal inheritance.

In his narrative to Sieglinde and Hunding, Siegmund recalls his wandering childhood with his father, whom he refers to as Wälse. His youth seems a classical example of filiation as apprenticeship: training in the art of masculinity. Moreover, Wälse and Son are pariahs to the social world they border. They intervene to impose justice. They have different values. They are, as Hunding states in growing agitation, "a wild breed [ein wildes Geschlecht]," hated by all.

Siegmund's nobility, to Wagner's eye and ear, seems clear enough. What is less clear is the content of Wagner's identification with Siegmund. An initial element is a projection of the thwarted revolutionary: Siegmund and Richard as impeded heroes of the 1848 revolts and their agendas. More mysteriously, Wagner's identification with Siegmund conjures the trope of the social pariah as wandering Jew. Wälse the Flying Dutchman (alias Ahasuerus, the Wandering Jew) has a son, whom he loves, trains, abandons, and finally kills. The structure of Wagner's own fantasmatic relation of issues of paternity and filiation with regard to this cluster is rich. Wagner's own biography involves anxiety about the biological paternity and abandonment, through death, by his father Karl Friedrich Wagner. It involves his anxiety about possible paternity of his mother's second husband, the actor Ludwig Geyer. Geyer was, technically, a mime. From mime to Mime—to the allegory of the false, Jewish father—the distance is small. Wagner suspected that Geyer was his father and that Geyer was Jewish, which he was not. Resonating here as well is the vexed musical filiation of two prominent composers of Wagner's youth, Meyerbeer and Mendelssohn, whom Wagner disowned in the wake of his sense of having been abandoned by them. Finally, there is Wagner the megalomaniac, identifying with Christ himself, the original and absolute Son abandoned by his Jewish father: the old God, to use Nietzsche's label for Wotan. Wagner–Siegmund–Christ: the son trained, loved, and killed by the Jewish father in the name of justice. (Not coincidentally, during the years of the initial sketches for the *Ring*, Wagner worked as well on a spoken drama called *Jesus of Nazareth*.)

This Jewish component of Wagner's symbolic investment in Siegmund brings up an important issue, an important reversal, in the history of nineteenth-century German Jewish relations and symbolic constructions of Selves and Others. The loading of Siegmund with a Jewish fantasy brings out not the phantasmagorical construction of the Jew as Other, but the obverse: the fantasy construction of the Jew as innermost, and most dangerous, Self. As we know, the fantasmatic "Other" becomes most threatening when it seems to embody the innermost and most repressed aspects of the Self.

Siegmund is thus the embodiment of a complicated and ambivalent Jewish fantasy. This fantasy is both philo-Semitic and anti-Semitic—two postures that also turn out to be more alike than different. Siegmund is a noble outsider and also, if we believe Fricka, a defiler of community and a seducer. He is a complicated character, and taking his name in vain can be treacherous.

The young Thomas Mann—aesthetically precocious and ideologically confused—fell head-first into the maelstrom of fin de siècle fantasy of the Jewish Siegmund. In his 1905 story "The Blood of the Walsungs," a more neurotic variant of "The Philadelphia Story," Mann portrayed a hard-working Teuton named Beckerath, a cultural philistine engaged to the highly refined Sieglinde Aarenhold, whose primary loyalty is to her twin brother named—Siegmund. Beckerath is Hunding and Mann himself, and Sieglinde holds inevitably the position of Katia Pringsheim, twin sister of Klaus and Mann's wife that same year, whose family was not pleased by this story. We should not be pleased with it either, because its equation of Jewishness with racial separateness and incest is so clear that it has no need to be explicit.

The story opens at an afternoon dinner chez Aarenhold, as Siegmund and Sieglinde ask Beckerath if he will permit brother and sister to attend a performance of *Die Walküre* that evening, as a last act of sibling intimacy before Sieglinde's wedding. The two hear the performance alone in the family's box. Mann then narrates the plot of *Die Walküre*, as witnessed by the twins.

Siegmund gave a moving account of the hatred and envy which had been the bane of his life and his strange father's life, how their hall had been burnt, his sister carried off, how they had led in the forest a harried, persecuted, outlawed life; and how finally he had mysteriously lost his father as well. And then Siegmund sang the most painful thing of all: he told of his yearning for human beings, his longing and ceaseless loneliness. He sang of men and women, of friendship and love he had sometimes won, only to be thrust back again into the dark. A curse had lain upon him forever, he was marked by the brand of his strange origins.[10]

The erotic charge between Siegmund and Sieglinde Aarenhold increases through the evening's performance, and when they return home they not only consummate their love just like their Wagnerian models, but they do it on a bearskin. Mann closes the story with the observation that, in Siegmund's postcoital agitation, "for a second the marks of his race stood out strong upon his face." Racial Jewishness can no longer be concealed, Mann tells us, in the natural, bearskin state of incestuous sex. Narratorial legitimacy seems suspended in the story's shocking closing gesture.

The anti-Semitism in Mann's portrayal should not obscure the equally strong proclivity of German Jewish audiences to identify with Siegmund. Fin de siècle Jewish audiences certainly caught the sting of the stereotyping in Alberich, Mime, and, more subtly, in Loge. But just as certainly they did not identify with these characters. If they accepted the anti-Semitic stereotype, they are more likely to have identified with the producer of the stereotype, and to connect these characters with their idea of culturally inferior Eastern European Jewry. They identified with Siegmund, and named their sons after him.[11] Like Lohengrin's origins, Siegmund's origins were noble, but irrelevant to his position in the outside world; his heroism was self-produced, as was his personality in general.

Indeed, that inner identification continued past 1933. Ernst Bloch wrote that Siegmund and Sieglinde must be understood as refugees, as the love-motive expresses a profound solitude. Siegmund, Bloch says, comports himself as the most lucid, the most free, and the least conformist of all the heroes of the *Ring*, completely different from the "free" Siegfried, who remains content to follow ingenuously his own nature. These observations are found in Bloch's *Philosophy of Music*; just as interesting is the fact that they are cited by Chéreau in his memoir of his Bayreuth production of the *Ring*.[12]

---

[10] Thomas Mann, "The Blood of the Walsungs," in *Death in Venice and Seven Other Stories*, trans. H. T. Lowe-Porter (New York: Vintage Books, 1954), p. 309.

[11] And their daughters. The poet Richard Beer-Hofmann remarked that a friend had stopped him on Vienna's Ringstrasse to offer congratulations on the birth of his daughter, whom he had named Miriam. The friend inquired why Beer-Hofmann had not chosen a more explicitly Jewish name, such as Elsa.

[12] Chéreau, *Lorsque cinq ans seront passés*, p. 17.

Die Walküre's act 1 prelude had scene-painted a storm through which Siegmund ran en route to Sieglinde and Hunding's hearth. The prelude to act 2 is more abstract in its imposition of violence; even so, variations of the sword motive persist through both preludes and make close siblings out of them. When the curtain is raised on act 2, however, we realize that the musical differences announce a different set of characters—namely, Wotan and Brünnhilde. Brünnhilde, the Valkyrie, is a horsewoman, and the final cadenzas of the prelude include a heavy equestrian program. But even this music becomes metaphorical, suggesting the overtaking of the transgressive son Siegmund by the punishing father Wotan, that is, the traumatic reversal of generational inheritance.

Siegmund's iteration of "I" is overtaken as Siegmund himself is killed. The *Ring* thus symptomatizes at the same time as it performs the death of subjectivity in the post-1848 generation. Siegmund is the beloved subject not only of the story but of music drama as a form. Musical subjectivity does not recover from this emplotted death. Siegmund's offspring, namely Siegfried, stands for an entirely new musical as well as political aesthetic, namely, the passage from subjectivity to identity.

Siegmund is a '48er; Siegfried is a son of the Wilhelmine epoch, of the *Gründerzeit*, of empire. Siegfried achieves both maturity and vocality—the two attributes that jointly make up Kant's *Mündigkeit*—in the summer of 1876.[13] The sequence of the *Ring* requires us to do a kind of historian's new math: if Siegfried first sings in 1876, we must infer that his father Siegmund met his death at the complicitous hand of his own father Wotan twenty years before. In truth, Siegmund first sang in Munich in the summer of 1870—a not insignificant date for the symbolic death of the generation of 1848. Whether early audiences of *Die Walküre* felt the resonance of such symbolism remains our guess.

Siegfried, we can recall, is the pure instrumental object of Wotan's scheme to regain the Ring and its power. Forced through contract and law to relinquish Alberich's Ring to the giant Fafner, Wotan must create a "free agent" who will repossess the fetish object with no knowledge that he is working for his own family business. In Wotan's imagination, Siegfried is a thing, not a person. It is Siegmund whom Wotan loves—and kills, Siegmund who is the mid-century bourgeois son in this fundamentally bourgeois epic of a social, industrial, and politically climbing family.

---

[13] Lutz Koepnick has tied the *Ring* to 1848 with the felicitous phrase and chapter title "Der *Ring* als emanzipatorische Wunschbiographie, oder der Geburt der Wälsungen aus dem Geiste des Barrikadenkampfes" [The *Ring* as emancipatory biographal wish-fulfillment, or the birth of the Volsungs from the spirit of the barricades], chapter 2 of *Nothungs Modernität* (Munich: Wilhelm Fink Verlag, 1994), pp. 43–89. Koepnick's focus on the sword Nothung as the carrier of the story as political allegory leads him to combine Siegmund and Siegfried as its finder and reforger, and thus apparently to ignore the generational difference that I am stressing here.

In the generational passage from Siegmund to Siegfried, from 1848 to 1870, from liberal hope to nationalist power, the nineteenth century is lost. The death of Siegmund at the hand of his self-entrapped father Wotan is a horrendous allegory for the destruction of subjectivity at the hand of a self-entrapped modernity, where rationality has produced not freedom but Weber's iron cage. The pathos of Wotan's Farewell at the conclusion of *Die Walküre* resides in its overdetermination: it is Wotan's farewell to the promise of a subjectivity that he has never understood and that he has failed through arrogance. It is at some level Wagner's farewell to a world that he has similarly failed, and thus at some level a farewell to music. As Brünnhilde tells Wotan, he has become his own enemy, a predicament that is also Wagner's. Brünnhilde is herself not exempt from Valhallic hegemony, that is, she is not yet a woman and thus not even she understands at this point that, even more obviously, Wotan's farewell involves the subjection of Woman. Siegmund, finally, is the only man in the *Ring* who knows how to treat a woman.

Why, then, in his phallic exhuberance, does Siegmund extract the sword Nothung from the ash tree to the orchestral motif of the renunciation of love, first heard in Alberich's curse? Daniel Foster has made the following observation, in defense of Alberich: "What exactly is noble in Alberich's sacrifice of love? One answer to this question can be found in the specific moment of his sacrifice. Insofar as Alberich, at the moment of his declaration, is specifically renouncing the 'escapist fantasies' which the love of these three mermaids seductively offer, he is thereby renouncing the infantile longing for an earthly paradise which all immature men, in their unconcsious mother-longings, still pursue in one woman after another. In other words, he is nobly rejecting the path of a Don Giovanni who would undoubtedly have kept flitting from one mermaid to the other for the rest of the opera—until he got caught off course."[14]

For Alberich, love is no different from lust. In his economy, therefore, the renunciation of love is the renunciation of desire. It is traded for power. Power, then, exists as a precise parallel to the work of culture as sublimation.

A social and ethical evolution resides in the generational passage from Alberich and Wotan to Siegmund; from the renunciation of love to the renunciation of a certain kind of love—that utopian dream of love (Alberich) or power (the young Wotan) that is made of pictures and eludes both subjectivity and accountability. Siegmund's grasp of the sword is, literally, his grasping of Need (*Nothung*).

This process is revealed by the gradual matching of Siegmund with the sword Nothung through the work of the leitmotiv associated with the sword— the clarion broken major chord that appears in a sudden and uncontextualized

---

[14] Daniel Foster, "The Sacrifice of Love for Power in the *Parados* of the *Agamemnon* and *Das Rheingold*" (unpublished essay, 1995).

manner at the end of *Das Rheingold*. It appears—according to Wagner's own declared aesthetic of the leitmotiv—as a premonition. But we must ask, as a premonition of what? Of Nothung? Of Siegmund? Of Wotan's scheme to engender Siegmund? All of these answers seem to me like rationalizations of the uncannily external quality of this intrusive phrase. It seems rather that the externality of this first hearing of the sword motive is precisely about its own externality. It signals something that does not exist. As a musical gesture, the appearance of the unidentified sword motive resembles the unprocessed, presymbolic opening chords of the *Don Giovanni* overture, discussed in chapter 1. Just as the force of those chords will later be associated with the Commendatore, the "sword motive" will later be understood as such, when in Siegmund's musings it combines with explicit references to it. On first hearing, it is a wholly musical construction. At the same time, by this late point in *Das Rheingold*, the listener has learned how to listen, knows to press for the identification and interrelation of leitmotivs. The listener wants this phrase to signify, if only to ratify his or her own understanding of the musical *parole* within the musical *langue* that is underway. Wotan's desire (for the return of the Ring) together with the listener's desire (for musical signification) can be argued to confer a desiring subjectivity on the musical phrase itself. This music strives for something, and does so, I would argue, in a first-person voice.

That something might be articulated as subjectivity itself. In Wotan's structure of desire, subjectivity corresponds to a free agency that exercises autonomy and achieves social order. That social order is reactionary, however, with respect to the division of labor and economic welfare, as Loge recognizes and bemoans to the violated Rhinemaidens at the end of *Das Rheingold*. As a son at once loyal, sentimental, and rebellious, Siegmund wants to combine freedom with social justice; hence his narrative—in the first act of *Die Walküre*— of the failed attempt to save a forced bride against Hunding's kinsmen. The new man is to find the newer and gentler phallus in the sword Nothung, left for him (with Arthurian resonances) by his father. Nothung and Siegmund himself embody, ultimately, musical-dramatic allegories of subjectivity. The sword motive first appears as an unprepared premonition of an unformed quality of subjectivity. As a normative characteristic that exudes balance and harmony, subjectivity is musically pictured as a mediation between nature and culture. Thus the broken chord of its leitmotiv is a compromise formation between the ascending broken chord associated with nature and the descending, chromaticized formations associated with counternatural forces: law, decadence, and, ultimately, the twilight of the gods.

When the sword music returns, in the first act of *Die Walküre*, it returns not only as Siegmund's music but produced by Siegmund's own mind. The sword motive thus emerges in a musically woven pattern through Siegmund's monologue of memory: "Ein Schwert verhiess mir der Vater; ich fänd' es in höchster Not." Finding the sword is an operation in the subjunctive: contingent on

subjectivity and situation. In this monologue, the sword motive teases itself
out of the narrative, forming itself as an instrument of subjectivity. The sword
music, the sword itself, is a transitional object, just as Siegmund can be described historically as a transitional subject.

Siegmund is defined by vulnerability and accountability. "Not führt' ihn ins
Haus [need led him to this house]," says Sieglinde to Hunding. He is a pre-
1848er, perhaps a self-portrait of the young Wagner and the young Wotan at
the level of ethical potential neither ever reached. A loner, he acts for social
justice, as his account to his hosts of his day in the forest attests.

In finding Sieglinde and copulating with her, Siegmund fulfills his father's
plan. The desire he brings to this endeavor is, perhaps, excessive and transgressive—not only with relation to Fricka's laws but to his father's Oedipal
competition. We have every right to wonder whether Wotan may not bear
real anger at his phallically gifted son, a self-generated, emotional anger that
is tapped and given social, legal legitimacy by Fricka's intervention. And we
can wonder as well whether Siegmund's belated erotic self-discovery (he has
been with women before, he tells Sieglinde and Hunding, but has not found
joy) constitutes a first and decisive refusal of obedience to his remembered but
perhaps fetishized father-image, Wälse. We can recall here the Rat Man's famous remark to Freud. "Several years after his father's death," Freud writes in
his case history, "the first time he experienced the pleasurable sensations of
copulation, an idea sprang into his mind: 'This is glorious! One might murder
one's father for this!' "[15] Siegmund's union with Sieglinde does compromise
his father's legal-contractual legitimacy, as Fricka makes clear. But it may also
compromise Wotan's psyche, his masculinity, and his monopoly, in the plot
of the *Ring* so far, on male desire.

Siegmund's extraction of the sword from the tree in Hunding's house is
clearly the discovery of the transgressive phallus. But it is at the same time
the discovery of the transitional object representing his own subjectivity. This
ambiguity was visually realized by Chéreau in Bayreuth and subsequently imi-
tated in August Everding's staging in Chicago in 1994 and 1996. Here, Siegmund stood facing the audience, grasping the hilt of the sword just over his
head behind him. Thus the moment of his greatest prowess doubled visually
as that often repeated moment in bourgeois childhood when physical growth
is measured against a mark on the wall. Moreover, Siegmund appeared to be
pulling the sword out of his own head. The pull of subjectivity became defined
visually as the pull of memory: Siegmund's mental, subjective grasp on the
recollected promise of his father.

But, as with other bourgeois sons, Siegmund's internalization of his father's
promise may play itself out as the superego rather than as the materialization
of desire—father's or son's. Wotan's promise becomes identical to his entrap-

<hr />

[15] Sigmund Freud, *Three Case Histories* (New York: Macmillan, 1963), pp. 42–43.

ment of his son. The entrapment of Siegmund as middle generation, caught between Wotan and Siegfried—between founding and decadence—seals his own destruction. Moreover, Siegmund's destruction lies in his refusal to make the choice between obedience and rebellion, in his drive to hold to a middle ground that his culture in turn withholds from him.

Siegmund's love and desire for his twin is, incest paradoxically notwithstanding, the perfect allegory of romantic-bourgeois desire: the finding of the true Self in a real Other. Siegmund alone attains the most elusive goal of romantic-bourgeois sensibility: the combination of autonomy and intimacy. Wagner honors the first hints of this process through a delicate marshalling of solo instruments. Solo strings begin the scene as the markers of intimacy; solo brass answer as the markers of autonomy. The reuniting of Siegmund and Sieglinde introduces the erotic as the power regulating the boundaries of sameness and difference, Self and Other, intimacy and autonomy. Their mutual attraction has to do, in Wagner's text, with each one finding at once Self and Other in the face of the other. They acknowledge their likeness after declaring their love in the following paradoxical exchange:

> SIEGMUND:
> Du bist das Bild, das ich in mir barg.
> [You are the image that I hid in myself.]
>
> SIEGLINDE:
> O still! Lass mich der Stimme lauschen:
> mich dünkt, ihren Klang hört' ich als Kind.
> [Be still! Let me hear the voice:
> it seems to me, I heard its sound as a child.]

Siegmund acknowledges that Sieglinde's face is a mirror of his own, and does so by making his voice into an echo of hers: the line carries the musical phrase of Sieglinde's "Du bist der Lenz [you are the spring]," which we listeners are sure to have retained in our ear. This is the musical picture that Siegmund—like us—has absorbed into his memory. Sieglinde at once tells him to be quiet and then says she wants to hear his voice. How do we explain this contradiction? At one level, she displaces their exchange from one about images to one about sound, from seeing to hearing. They look alike, but the true memory of likeness resides in the memory of voice. (We can be reminded of the fourth-act reconciliation of Susanna and Figaro in *Le nozze di Figaro*, when after succumbing to confusion and distress brought on by too many visual masquerades, Figaro consoles his lover by telling her he had recognized her voice.) Authentic recognition and love are here achieved as sight is transcended to sound, from face to voice.

The fulfillment of the dialectic of intimacy and autonomy is so fragile and so exquisite that Wagner can barely represent it. But he does so, in Siegmund's vocal caress "Schwester! Geliebte!" just before the apparition of Brünnhilde in act 2. Siegmund's gesture embodies a nonmasculine masculinity, a nonphallic eroticism, and thus an instance of the ethical erotic—namely, the supreme moment of romantic-bourgeois hope. It is the instance of hope that Luce Irigaray describes in her essay "The Fecundity of the Caress." The caress is that threshold gesture where subject and object converge but remain autonomous; it is "like an amorous impregnation that seeks out and affirms otherness while protecting it."[16] Brünnhilde confesses to Wotan that she was moved by Siegmund's *Leid* (passion/sorrow) and *Not* (need, despair), and that he "breathed love into my heart"—in other words, that she was also erotically touched by him. Siegmund's seduction of Brünnhilde makes her disobedience even harder for Wotan to bear. He persists in punishing and disgracing her, but allows her the possibility of experiencing desire in her humiliation: the man who awakens her from her forced sleep will be Siegfried. She would have preferred his father.

Siegmund's need, so attractive to Brünnhilde, is his need for Sieglinde. Because of Sieglinde, he will not follow Brünnhilde alone to a hero's welcome in Valhalla. For this position, Siegmund earned a place in a different Valhalla: inclusion in the repertory of examples cited by Max Weber in his historical sociology of religions. Thus, in *The Protestant Ethic and the Spirit of Capitalism*, Weber interprets Siegmund's rejection of Brünnhilde's call to Valhalla as an indication of a lack of selfish interest in his own salvation that distinguishes his worldly behavior from the symptomatic behavior of those Protestants concerned only with their own salvation. Calvinist anxiety, expressed most decisively in Bunyan's *Pilgrim's Progress*, is self-absorbed. "Only when he himself is safe," Weber writes of the pilgrim, "does it occur to him that it would be nice to have his family with him." This tendency, Weber argues, is "worlds removed from that spirit of proud worldliness which Machiavelli expresses in relating the fame of those Florentine citizens who, in their struggle against the Pope and his excommunication, had held 'Love of their native city higher than the fear for the salvation of their souls.' And it is of course even farther from the feelings which Richard Wagner puts into the mouth of Siegmund before his fatal combat, 'Grüsse mir Wotan, grüsse mir Walhall—doch in Walhalls spröden Wonnen sprich du wahrlich mir nicht.' "[17]

Siegmund's refusal to enter Valhalla without Sieglinde involves another complicated transgression. Most immediately, he is willing to kill Sieglinde himself in order to assure her presence in Valhalla—an impossibility according

---

[16] Luce Irigaray, "The Fecundity of the Caress: A Reading of Levinas, *Totality and Infinity*, 'Phenomenology of Eros,' " in *An Ethics of Sexual Difference*, trans. C. Burke and G. C. Gill (Ithaca: Cornell University Press, 1993), pp. 185–217.

[17] Max Weber, *The Protestant Ethic and the Spirit of Capitalism*, trans. T. Parsons (New York: Charles Scribner's Sons, 1958), p. 107.

to Valhalla's noncoeducational policy. But if we go back for a moment to our initial discussion of the male trajectory of *Bildung*, in which the flirtation with androgyny is supposed to result in the mantle of masculinity and the separation from the feminine alter ego, we see that Siegmund's refusal to part with Sieglinde is also a transgressive refusal to shed a feminine alter ego—a refusal to become a conventional hero. It is this gesture that confuses and moves Brünnhilde, and that insures Siegmund's father Wotan's direct participation in his son's murder. To make sure that Brünnhilde's spontaneous interference on behalf of Siegmund is overridden, Wotan must aid in Hunding's killing of Siegmund. Siegmund is thus killed (penetrated) by the force of law (the spear) as agent of both Father (Wotan) and Mother (Fricka—not his natural mother, but the structural representative of Mother as partner of Father rather than as nurturer of the son). Incest and too large a dose of androgyny become the cumulative crime that results in Siegmund's death at the hand of his father.

Subjectivity and Identity

In the general plot of the *Ring* and in the shape of Wotan's schemes, the death of Siegmund is the turning point—the peripeteia in the Aristotelian lexicon of the structure of tragedy (*Poetics* 6). But in the *Ring* as a work of historical allegory it is also the moment of the failure of the joint promise of modernity and subjectivity. Wagner himself, for all his clear sympathy for his character Siegmund, appears not to be concerned about this. Perhaps the young Wagner was, but the Wagner of post-1870 who completes the work in the age of nationalism and postsubjectivity—the age of Siegfried—is no longer. Not even he seems to have understood that the Ride of the Valkyries, which follows the murder of Siegmund, is not an innocent frolic but an eruption of hysteria—a foretaste of the Norns' realization that doom is imminent. And if we the audience are appropriately distrubed by Siegmund's death, how can we retain, or redevelop, the sympathy for Wotan that Wagner clearly wants to have as we experience his conflict and grief in taking leave of Brünnhilde?

Siegfried's lonely youth and life repeats many of the coordinates of his father's life. But his world is entirely different, as is his character. We have in Siegfried's youth not elements of Wagner's fantasmatic childhood but his memory of a real, nightmare childhood. Mime is the quintessential bad parent, a quasi-male version of the witch in the Hansel and Gretel story, whose purpose in nurturing a child is to kill him. In his own way, Mime has indeed coddled Siegfried, and his self-pity at the boy's ingratitude is the self-pity of the bourgeois parent whose flaw is in the fact that his only expectation is gratitude. Siegfried's suffocating childhood found brilliant materialization in John Conklin's stage design of act 1 for Chicago. Everything in Mime's hut is scaled to Mime's size and therefore much too small for Siegfried, including a bunk bed and a rocking horse with a dragon's head.

Mime is also mocked as the quintessential bad teacher. He has taught Siegfreid neither to fear nor to forge. When he and the Wanderer test each other's knowledge, Mime makes the prime pedagogical error of asking only questions to which he already knows the answer. Through the Wanderer's ensuing counterinterrogation, Mime realizes that the ignorant Siegfried, whom he has not taught to forge, may nevertheless be the only one to reforge Nothung. Mime wants Siegfried to reforge his father's sword, but not to reinhabit the sword's symbolic aura—the aura of need, Nothung. There is no danger of that. Siegfried may be the only one able to forge, just as Siegmund was the only one able to extract, but Siegmund's act of extraction was an act of sympathetic union with Nothung as an agent of subjectivity. When Siegfried forges the sword, he finds in it just another toy.

For Siegfried, the sword is an object. For Siegmund, it had been, to invoke D. W. Winnicott's beautiful term, a transitional object. The transitional object, the transitional phenomenon, is that space or symbolic structure in between subjectivity and objectivity through which the boundaries between self and world are discovered and negotiated. The transitional object, in Winnicott's description, "gives room for the process of becoming able to accept difference and similarity." It is "the root of symbolism in time, a term that describes the infant's journey from the purely subjective to objectivity . . . [the] progress towards experiencing."[18] Siegfried's ignorance of fear is the ignorance of how to negotiate with the world. The world remains populated with objects: inanimate, like the sword, and animate, like Fafner and Brünnhilde, but all to be mastered by strength and confidence. Siegfried's sword is therefore not Siegmund's. It is "transforged" rather than reforged, transformed from a transitional object into a purely instrumentalized one. Siegfried's treatment of Brünnhilde (however unwitting) will differ from Siegmund's treatment of Sieglinde according to the same transformation from intersubjectivity to instrumentalization.

Siegfried comes of age in 1876, in a cramped industrial space marked by the two technologies of the take-off period, the *Gründerzeit* of German industrial awakening: steel and chemicals. His guardian, the dwarf Mime, is a smith and a maker of poison. He is the guardian thereby of metals and chemicals, the two industries on Germany's steerage of the so-called second industrial revolution of the late nineteenth century. At the act's end, as Siegfried forges the magic sword and Mime prepares the poison that is to kill him, we have in the scene's furious musical energy the fulminant productive spasms of Krupp and I. G. Farben. Siegfried's forge, one might argue, is industrialized metonymically

---

[18] D. W. Winnicott, *Playing and Reality* (London: Routledge, 1971), p. 6.

through its constitution by the orchestra, which itself breaks out as a full-throttled industrial machine at this moment.

And how unattractive both these characters are! Mime an anti-Semitic Jewish stereotype, and Siegfried a portrait of the hero as a young anti-Semite. In his universal ignorance, Siegfried himself doesn't know he is an anti-Semite, but when he tells Mime he hates him for his nervous ticking and limping and speech, so unlike the graceful movements of the animals in the forest (that is, so contrary to nature), Siegfried displays a masterful passive absorption of anti-Semitic principle and rhetoric.

The stage for Siegfried's coming of age is set (literally) by his return to nature—the escape from Mime's lair, from the scene of a nightmare petit bourgeois childhood, to a site where alleged purity can breed pure ideology: the German forest. As Siegfried relaxes, his ear attunes to the panoramic picture-music of the forest. When he kills the dragon—the monster that pollutes the alleged purity of nature (that is, the monster who is of course the worker-giant Fafner in disguise)—the reflexive tasting of the creature's hot blood enables him to understand the sonic language of the forest-bird, who tells him to scale the rock to find the sleeping Brünnhilde. We have in this episode the symbolic birth of the nation through two interiorities turned into external apparitions: hearing and blood. Not, this time, the Blood of the Walsungs, but the blood of the nation.

Siegfried first tastes Fafner's blood, we can recall, in Bayreuth in 1876. Self-monumentalization is bad for memory; the house of Bayreuth, where the young Siegfried first sang, did not encourage his, or Wagner's, memory of Siegmund. Siegmund is recalled only as a transmitter of the sword, not as a person. And the maturing Siegfried has severe memory problems.

Consider the forgetting potion administered to him in the first act of *Götterdämmerung*. The drink must be chemically related to the potion Brangäne administers in the first act of *Tristan und Isolde*. It has become conventional to understand the *Tristan* love potion as a placebo, a catalyst for the lovers' mutual recognition of their preexisting conditions. A similar reading is possible in the case of Siegfried, with mixed results. Siegfried's personality might be describable from the beginning as one devoid of a sense of the past, of history, of time. No memory; no fear. Thus, the forgetting of Brünnhilde may come naturally, so to speak; he has no sense of why he should remember anything. Without a past there can be no psychologically inhabited present—no mourning, no working through. Without a sense of a past there is no present and no future, no subjectivity, and no ethics. Siegfried's Rhine Journey and arrival at the Hall of the Gibichungs is the journey of unselfconscious national power and capital. As a potential historical allegory, Siegfried's journey might be understood to prefigure the late youth and youthful journey of German imperialism. The Wilhelmine innocent Siegfried now assumes the place of the young imperialist, arriving, let's say, on the coast of German

Southwest Africa with the same ineptitude that dogged German imperialist energies between 1880 and 1914.

The belated nobility of Siegfried's death scene, on the other hand, is its focus on his sudden accrual of a past. Siegfried's narrative to Hagen, Gunther, and the hunters is literally the product of recovered memory. Again following the example of *Tristan*, can this moment be understood as Siegfried's tardy education into subjecthood through the discovery of memory and history?

The part of me that hears suffering and greatness in Wagner's music tells me as well that he must have known all this, must have known that the brat Siegfried is a meager repetition of the hero Siegmund. But Wagner called his own son Siegfried, not Siegmund. The figure of Siegfried is the hero at the ideological origins and core of the *Ring*; hence Wagner's son had to be Sieg-fried. For Wagner, life and theory coexisted on a level of representation and ideology that could be disrupted only by music.

Wagner never allowed himself to have confidence in his son Siegfried, never thought he would be capable of running Bayreuth and Wagner's legacy. A bizarre moment in the father-son relationship, recorded in Cosima Wagner's diaries, brings us back to the cultural conundrum of identifying with Sieg-mund. Wagner apparently thought that his son Siegfried bore a resemblance to Ludwig Geyer. Thus, in some corner of Wagner's imagination, young Siegfried Wagner's face establishes Geyer as the composer's own father. The young Sieg-fried—Siegfried Wagner, that is—causes Richard Wagner to reexperience the abandonment of his desired father (Wagner senior) and the betrayal by his natural father, Geyer, who in Wagner's corresponding fantasy was Jewish. Geyer was in fact a Protestant. But such is the logic of anti-Semitism: fathers do not abandon their children because they are Jewish; rather, they become Jewish because they abandon their children. Wagner, Geyer, Mendelssohn, Meyerbeer—all are fathers, abandoners, and therefore Jews in Richard Wagner's fantasmatic anti-Semitism. In the 1870s, probably leaked through Nietzsche, the rumor circulated among Viennese anti-Semites that Wagner was himself a Jew, and he was given the sobriquet "Geyerbeer."[19] Thus, Wagner remains bound up with the solitary and suffering Siegmund. That identifica-tion, I would suggest, provides a measure of the man's greatness that is always the partner of his monstrousness.

By the summer of 1870 and the vocalization (the German *Mündigkeit* com-bines majority, or coming-of-age, with vocality, or having a mouth) of Sieg-mund, Wagner had made his peace with the new Germany—with the Ger-many, led by Prussian power, that now completed its abandonment of the liberal agenda of 1848. Wagner/Wotan's imperial peace is the uneasy peace

---

[19] The facts referred to in this paragraph are recounted in Jean-Jacques Nattiez, *Wagner Andro-gyne* (Princeton: Princeton University Press, 1993), ch. 8.

of Valhalla, for which the abandonment of Siegmund and his generation of ambivalence and subjectivity is required. The abandonment of ambivalence catapults symptomaticity into ideology—one that is overwhelming in its power if impregnable in its logic.

Siegfried's journey to the Gibichungs, to forgetfulness and betrayal, is also the journey of music drama. Here I recharge the second of the two family romances in play in my discussion: that of music drama itself. I will comment briefly on two successive scenes from act 2 of *Götterdämmerung*: the public reunion and confrontation of Siegfried and Brünnhilde, and the so-called conspiracy scene, which concludes the act with the hatching of the plot by Brünnhilde, Hagen, and Gunther on Siegfried's life.

Siegfried defends himself against Brünnhilde's accusation of betrayal. He attempts inarticulately to assert his innocence, his verbal confusion exacerbated by a crisis of musical incompetence. Still amnesiac, he cannot participate in the ongoing musical vocabulary. He struggles to get on top of the leitmotivs, and he can't. By this point in the action, the listener is likely to be more literate in the recollection of leitmotivs than Siegfried. The listener can thus be expected to hear Siegfried's musical inadequacy, to hold him in some contempt despite his innocence. Indeed, the listener may be counted on to listen to Siegfried's efforts while silently correcting the notes he is singing. This involves a double correction. First, the leitmotivs need to be intoned correctly; second, they and their musical connective tissue need to be rendered with lyrical and harmonic viability. This is precisely what Brünnhilde does in response. Not knowing that Siegfried is ignorant of his own mendacity, Brünnhilde pushes him away from the spear he is swearing with, replaces his oath with her own, and contradicts him. Her music—"Helle Wehr! Heilige Waffe! [Shining weapon! Hallowed blade!]"—instantly claims the level of articulation and lyricism that eluded Siegfried. Brünnhilde easily controls the motivic language and achieves subjectivity and lyricism by liberating herself from the burden of leitmotivic submission; she makes music, yelling herself out of the musical, hegemonic structure of the *Ring* and its musical rhetoric. Paradoxically, Brünnhilde is deluded in words and action but lucid in music.

At this moment, having lost the ring from her hand, Brünnhilde takes control of the *Ring*, qua music drama, plot, and style. Simultaneously, she reinstates music drama (correcting Siegfried) and escapes it. Unlike Siegfried, she gets the musical and dramatic rhetoric right. But at the same moment, she uses that mastery to push aside the strictures of the system. Thus, her position with regard to music drama recalls Walther von Stolzing's to the rules of the *Meisterlied*. In *Die Meistersinger von Nürnberg* (1868), this young singer is educated to respect musical law in order to transcend it. At that opera's end, with an integrative conservatism consistent with its comic form, the young outsider is persuaded to become a complete insider and join the ranks of the mastersingers who once rejected him and whom he continues to disdain.

Brünnhilde, like the tragic epic that surrounds her, never gains reintegration. Related to this eventuality, her externality, at the moment of her rebellion, to the aesthetic system that surrounds her—music drama—is more pronounced.

I would assert that Brünnhilde's rebelliousness gains stature and danger by adopting a style that is literally foreign to the form, namely, the voice of Italian opera. Suddenly, she is Norma. The unlikely parallel has both histrionic and historical validity. Wagner had attended a performance of *Norma* in Riga in 1837. "It is not a crime to believe in this music," he said. "People think that I detest the entire Italian school, in particular Bellini. This is not true—a thousand times no! Bellini is my first preference because there is strength in his vocal writing and his music lends itself so perfectly to the original text."

Brünnhilde performs this heroic masquerade for the first time during the summer of 1876 in Bayreuth. Translating and transforming her music drama into the heroic subjectivity of the Italian opera heroine, Brünnhilde becomes once again the *Ring's* voice of disruption. As the Valkyrie, two operas and twenty years before, she had disrupted Wotan's order by enacting his true will. Now, six years into the German *Gründerzeit* and at the apogee of nationalist swagger, she disrupts again by reinvigorating the beer-hall fraternity that surrounds her with Nietzsche's beloved lifeblood of the south: the transgressive subjectivity of pure voice.

Brünnhilde's life-force of history, her assertion of modernity, of the fleeting, the contingent, and the transitory, is the death-wish of music drama. Brünnhilde's will, like Wotan's, is for the end of the gods whose institutionalization in bourgeois law and society—as Wotan laments—kills the will and kills the voice. Wotan and Wagner think this is the fault of bourgeois society; I think it's the fault of music drama. But Wotan's desire for the bourgeois apocalypse is also the desire for the end of music drama. And Wagner will not allow that.

In act 2 of *Götterdämmerung*, Wagner and the master discourse of music drama cannot control Brünnhilde's escape into voice and Italian opera. She is one of two women in this opera's plot; her foil, Gutrune, proves no challenge either to her or to music drama. Gutrune, as Jean Jacques Nattiez has persuasively argued, is marked as a decadent by a vocal style lifted from French opera. Nattiez identifies Gutrune's melody in her "comic opera exchange" with Siegfried in act 2, scene 2 as a tune lifted directly from Auber's *La Muette de Portici*, which Wagner had heard.[20] The collusion of French opera (Gutrune) and Jewishness (Hagen, son of Alberich) lures music drama (Siegfried) to corruption and doom—a repetition, in Wagner's fantasmatic lineup of cultural criminals, of the alliance of Meyerbeer and Mendelssohn. But in this second act of *Götterdämmerung*, the containment of French opera is outmaneuvered by the temporary resurgence of Italian opera in the voice of Brünnhilde.

---

[20] Ibid., pp. 86–87.

But Wagner, like Wotan, does not cede victory to the transgressive Brünn-hilde. Her Italian moment in act 2 of *Götterdämmerung* also catapults her into the conspiracy on Siegfried's life led by Hagen and (now) Gunther; in ideological terms as well, she joins those marked as foreigners. At the end of the Immolation Scene, Wagner takes back the hegemonic form of music drama by taking away Brünnhilde's voice and, in a well-known change of mind, placing final comment in the narrative voice of orchestral music. Six years later, he fulfills his own reappropriative campaign with *Parsifal*, the final return of music drama through its own sublation into the higher sphere of the festival play for the consecration of the stage [*Bühnenweihfestspiel*], a sacred sonic world where no one can have a voice at all, especially the soprano, who loses hers entirely at the end of act 2.[21] The silencing of the voice, in particular the female voice, signifies the return of the repressor: music drama itself.

Carolyn Abbate has analyzed the final scene of *Götterdämmerung* act 2 for its negotiation with the mantle of symphonic opera that Wagner claimed to inherit from Beethoven. The conspiracy scene, she shows, begins as "a musical argument broken and interrupted by text-incited intrusions of never-changing refrains: an anti-symphonic scene." This situation is illustrated through the repetition of specific words with harsh consonant clusters: *Bruch, Blut, Schmach, Schuld.* "Repetition," Abbate suggests, "has a specific dramatic im-port, as the obsessed, monotonous language of individuals suffering great emo-tional distress." (If Abbate had written a decade later, she may well have used the term "trauma" here, which developed into a prime analytical tool in the 1990s.) Thus, the predicament marking the emotional "break" between lovers (Brünnhilde and Siegfried) and blood-brothers (Siegfried and Hagen) is en-acted from a musical-dramatic style that breaks with the symphonic and the integrity of musical procedure. In play here, Abbate suggests, is "the very an-tithesis of that progressive motivic development and musical interaction Wagner had deemed the essence of Beethoven's symphonic procedure."

But this very scene ends differently, Abbate asserts, as it "veers to the sym-phonic" in the third statement of its two refrains. Here, in an inversion of Wagner's interpretation of the values and sequence in play in the choral movement of Beethoven's Ninth Symphony, the symphonic "overwhelms and defeats the poetic."[22]

What I would add to Abbate's persuasive reading is an argument for the political undergirding of this play of form and value in music drama. The return, indeed the redemption, of the symphonic constitutes a national ges-ture. This gesture coincides with Wagner's 1846 codification of the "absolute"

---

[21] This last point I owe to Suzanne Stewart, "The Theft of the Operatic Voice: Masochistic Seduction in Wagner's *Parsifal*," in *Sublime Surrender: Male Masochism at the Fin-de-siècle* (Ithaca: Cornell University Press, 1998), ch. 3.

[22] Abbate, "Opera as Symphony," pp. 106–18 and passim.

as a national value. Thus the Wagnerian ideology of national identity posits in turn the identity of music drama as a form and as a national identity. The category music drama carries this national, ideological aura. There is no need to place scare quotes around the term in order to flag the aura. When, on the other hand, we refer to the symphonic from the vantage point of music drama and thus from the vantage point of its interpellation, qua absolute music, into the ideological orbit of music drama and national identity, then we might indeed use the scare quotes and refer to the "symphonic."

The redemption of music drama as the return of the repressor—at the end of the *Ring* and in *Parsifal*—relegitimates a national "symphonic" rhetoric at the expense of the human voice: Brünnhilde's and Kundry's. Identity (national and formal) edges out subjectivity and the latter's will toward individuality and indeterminacy.

The comedic happy end of *Die Meistersinger* involves the harmonization between subjectivity and identity, between the human, lyrical voice and its symphonic and choral context. The *Meisterlied* becomes the metonym of music drama, the mastersinger becomes the metonym of the national subject, and the lyrical becomes the partner of the symphonic. Yet the fulfillment of comedic inclusion requires an act of exclusion, a banishment of the threat to unity. In *Die Meistersinger*, that gesture is satisfied by the humiliation of the "marker" and critic Sixtus Beckmesser.[23] The happy end leaves open the possibility that subjectivity and identity will coexist in the future of Walther, Eva, and the people of Nuremberg. At the same time, the new dawn that the chorus intones and that Hans Sachs explicitly outlines in his forcible investiture of Walther as a mastersinger is the dawn of the nation, self-important and xenophobic.[24] Walther has nothing to say at this point; he never voices his agreement. His final absorption into power is at least as silent as Tamino's and Parsifal's; one could even argue that it is as silent as Brünnhilde's or Kundry's.

The enthroning of the *Meisterlied* assures the survival of the lyrical, but only in its absorption into the "symphonic," into music drama as the art of the

---

[23] See Barry Millington, "Nuremberg Trial: Is There Anti-Semitism in *Die Meistersinger?*" *Cambridge Opera Journal* 3:3 (1991): 247–60, for the presentation of Beckmesser as an anti-Semitic stereotype. Millington's persuasive case does not preclude the presence, and indeed the interchangeability, of a larger repertory of "foreign" stereotypes, such as the "Italian" marked by allegedly trivial coloratura ornamentation, which is in turn one aspect of Beckmesser's style. Millington's presentation implies—erroneously, in my view—that Beckmesser's construction out of stereotypes limits him to a stereotype. On this issue see my discussion of Kundry in "Music Drama and the End of History" in *New German Critique* 69 (1996) pp. 163–80. See also Peter Gay, "For Beckmesser," in *Freud, Jews, and Other Germans* (Oxford: Oxford University Press, 1978), pp. 257–77.

[24] See Arthur Groos, "Constructing Nuremberg," *Nineteenth-Century Music* 16:1 (Summer 1992): 18–34, for a discussion of the transformation of the chorus in *Die Meistersinger* from congregation, as they first appear at the opening of act 1, into "Volk," in which guise they conclude the opera.

nation. The banishment of Beckmesser is the banishment of the sublyrical. Sublyricism is the musical crime that excludes him, just as superlyricism is the crime that marks and banishes Brünnhilde. Although both sub- and superlyricism threaten the order of music drama, the former is more present as a Wagnerian type. The recurrent, indeed standard Wagnerian pattern involves the introduction of the sublyrical followed quickly by its correction by the lyrical or superlyrical. Brünnhilde's correction of Siegfried in *Götterdämmerung* act 2 is one such occurrence. Walther's correction of Beckmesser's failed mastersong in *Meistersinger* act 3 is another. The third example I would cite is the English-horn lament in act 3 of *Tristan und Isolde*. This is a shepherd's tune, the correlative to the dying Tristan's melancholy introspection. On his instruction, the lament is to be replaced by a cheerful tune at the moment Isolde's ship is spotted.

The Wagnerian passage across the boundary of 1848, I have argued, is the passage from subjectivity to identity, the reification of music drama as the discourse of the nation. In this way Wagner and music drama both speak to and help constitute a material, historical transformation that is solid and uncontestable. The triumph of music drama—that dimension in which the end of the *Ring* is unambiguously happy—is the absorption of the lyrical into the symphonic. The sublyrical, the truly foreign, is banished. But the sublyrical contains a measure of melancholy and dignity, which may in fact constitute a remnant of the lyrical, once the lyrical has been absorbed into the symphonic. The sublyrical is unabsorbable, both harmonically and rhetorically. Wagner's characters and Wagner's audiences are instructed, trained, to desire its exclusion in the name of harmonization. We want Beckmesser to leave the stage, and we want the English horn to lose the "alte Weise," the old, melancholy tune, and cheerfully announce the arrival of Isolde's ship, an arrival that promises to draw Tristan not only out of misery but out of psychosis as well. At the same time, few would argue that the eventual cheerful tune is musically interesting, while the lament is hauntingly beautiful. Less clear but certainly no less plausible is the argument that Tristan's solitude represents a state of psychic truth for which the English-horn lament is a correlative, whereas the musical triviliality of the corrected tune speaks to the superfluousness of Isolde's arrival.[25] Similarly, in a radical and watershed casting decision, the Bayreuth production of *Die Meistersinger* in 1981 assigned the role of Beckmesser to Hermann Prey, the *nea-plus-ultra* of German lyric baritones. Prey's performance revealed the haunting, melancholic texture of Beckmes-

---

[25] Intensifying this position, Jean Pierre Ponnelle's production for Bayreuth in the 1980s represented Isolde's arrival as a delusion of the dying Tristan, who died in Kurwenal's arms following his fantasy of the two ships' arrival. The fact that Isolde's *Liebestod* became also a fantasy of Tristan's provides a recognition of his imagination's musical sophistication and power, attributes that would have been earned through the course of Tristan's psychic work in act 3.

ser's *music*, a texture not unlike the English-horn lament in the third act of *Tristan*. Moreover, like the *Tristan* lament, Beckmesser's song acquired a psychological and musical edge on the music that allegedly displaces it, Walther's prize song. As the authority of the lyrical becomes complicit in its own absorption into the "symphonic," the sublyrical acquires the dignity of the subject and subjectivity not absorbed into ideology. Nuremberg after *Die Meistersinger* will need its Beckmessers.

Chapter Five

THE VOICE OF THE PEOPLE AT THE
MOMENT OF THE NATION

People and Nations

Between 1868 and 1890 three major composers, emerging from confessionally and geographically diverse areas of Europe and associated with fundamentally diverse compositional practices, departed from their ongoing musical projects and genres and produced large scale works for orchestra, chorus, and vocal soloists in the form of the requiem mass. I refer to Brahms in Germany in 1868, Verdi in Italy in 1874, and Dvořák in Bohemia in 1890.[1] In terms of requisite musical personnel, these are the largest-scale works of their composers' careers. They are also large rhetorically, as massive utterances of collective voices and wills. Emerging from the age, in George Mosse's phrase, of "the nationalization of the masses," these works are commonly associated with national and nationalist consciousness in music. As such, for their sonic power and—at least potentially—political rhetoric, they have all three the makings of sustained ideological embarrassments.[2] Why, then, this chapter asks, do these massive works remain almost uniquely unembarrassing to the late-twentieth-century critical ear, the ear attentive (so at least one would hope) to the respect for subjectivity and suspicious of the absorption into ideology? The answer lies, I will propose, in the ability of these works at once to produce and to restrict a rhetoric of collectivity—a collective voice. I will call this voice the voice of the people, as crucially distinct from the alleged voice of the nation. This is a first-person voice but a first-person plural voice. In all three cases, it is a voice that at once refers to and resists incorporation into the ideological master-category of the period, namely, the nation. The unembarrassing quality of these works has to do with their internal resistance to ideological posturing, and therefore with their politics, a politics of voice.

---

[1] Brahms (born in Hamburg in 1833) composed most of his Requiem in Vienna, where he had mostly lived since 1863; the work was premiered in Bremen and Leipzig. Inversely, Dvořák (born in the Bohemian village of Nelahozeves, near Kralupy, in 1841) was based in Prague when his Requiem was premiered in 1890, but this event took place in Birmingham. Thus, the musical "homes" of works and their composers is a complicated matter, as will be discussed below.

[2] George L. Mosse, *The Nationalization of the Masses: Political Symbolism and Mass Movements in Germany from the Napoleonic Wars through the Third Reich* (Ithaca: Cornell University Press, 1991).

Through the mediation of choral, solo vocal, and orchestral writing, these works produce original rhetorics of collectivity that insist on the survival of authentic forms of subjectivity. All three involve the return of the sacred. The sacred functions not as a herald of institutional, ecclesiastical power, but as a guarantor of subjectivity at the level of intimacy and personal devotion, the cultural complications of modern subject formation. Authenticity relates to what is subjectively lived. In resisting ideological absorption, these works strive aggressively to define structures of personal and collective memory. Memory thus becomes a basis for temporal coherence that can generate the production of a new sense of the future.

The requiem mass is an act of collective rededication and commemoration through the honoring and benediction of the dead. Its performative work involves the fusion of memory (an emotionally, cognitively experienced mental function) and commemoration (a public act involving cultural authority). Since the political power of commemoration involves the didactic control of memory, it is important to distinguish between the two functions. Much of the recent work in the burgeoning "history of memory" fails to make precisely this distinction.

For example, Pierre Nora's four-volume *Realms of Memory* [*Lieux de mémoire*], the locus classicus of the 1980s subgenre of the cultural history of memory, systematically suppresses this distinction. Indeed, that suppression is its purpose, as the places of memory it invokes are mostly national monuments whose intentions are to fuse private memory and subjectivity into national memory and national identity. This collected work of sixty historians was published between 1984 and 1986, motivated, in the words of Nora's introduction, by the "rapid disappearance of our national memory." The work was inspired by the wish to recover the French national memory lost, by implication, to socialist victory in 1981. Moreover, a recovered national patrimony would provide the ballast necessary for the commemorations of the Revolution, which were due in 1989. The organization of the four volumes represented a newly inscribed national teleology from republic to nation. (Part 1 is entitled "The Republic," part 2, in three volumes, "The Nation.") Whose memory is in play? It is the memory of the nation—in other words, a fictional memory that is systematically cultivated by national symbols, monuments, and narratives. National memory is cultivated to meet national ideology: the greatness of France is to be reconstituted through mystification rather than deconstructed through analysis.[3] Memory is fickle; commemoration works to make memory consistent, coherent, and useful.

---

[3] Pierre Nora, ed., *Les lieux de mémoire* (Paris: Gallimard, 1984–86). Nora's introduction is available in article form: "Between Memory and History: *Les lieux de mémoire*," *Representations* 26 (Spring 1989): 7–25. For critiques of the historiographical interest in and valorization of the trope of memory, see Charles Maier, "A Surfeit of Memory?" *History and Memory* 5:2 (1993), and Kerwin Lee Klein, "On the Emergence of *Memory* in Historical Discourse," *Representations* 69 (Winter 2000).

Verdi and Dvořák, both Catholic by confession, used the Latin liturgical text of the requiem mass that had been in place, with deviations, since the fourteenth century, taking the following sequence:

Introit (*Requiem aeternam*)
Kyrie
Gradual and tract (*Absolve, Domine*)
Sequence (*Dies irae, Dies illa*)
Offertory (*Domine Jesu Christe*)
Sanctus
Benedictus
Agnus Dei
Communion (*Lux aeterna*)
[Occasionally] Responsory (*Libera me*)

The liturgical setting had retained its dominance in the late-eighteenth and earlier-nineteenth-century Requiems, including Mozart's (K. 626) of 1791, Cherubini's of 1817, and Berlioz's of 1837. The aura that continues to hover over these works is indicative of the kind of supplementarity that modern reception attaches to this traditional sacred form. In the case of Mozart, that supplementarity takes the form of alleged self-commemoration. Mozart's biographers continue to support the story of the anonymous patron who commissioned the work. That anonymity fueled the suspicion that Mozart had generated the work himself out of a mystical intention to commemorate himself in anticipation of his death. That the work remained unfinished on his death in December 1791 has served to inflate the legend.

In the case of Luigi Cherubini's C-minor Requiem of 1817, commemoration is altogether conventional. Premiered two years into France's Bourbon restoration, the work commemorates the execution of King Louis XVI, older brother of the reigning monarch. Liturgical authority is thus allied to political reaction. Musically, Cherubini's Requiem was esteemed both by Beethoven and by Berlioz, neither of whom commented, to my knowledge, on its political context. The relatively large scale of Cherubini's Requiem anticipates the scale of later nineteenth-century requiems, from Berlioz on. Requiems remain acts of power for their scale alone; Verdi and Dvořák are not exceptions.

Unlike their predecessors, Brahms, Verdi, and Dvořák clearly mark their sacred utterances as distinct from the Church and from ecclesiastic authority. The Requiems of Brahms and Dvořák are sacred, confessionally marked, and nonclerical. Verdi's is anticlerical. None is conceived as a component of a ritual observance and—the location of the premiere of Verdi's notwithstanding—all three are destined for concert halls more than for churches. These works are neither sacred in a conventional sense nor secular in the sense of leaving behind, denying, or displacing sacred claims. Their dignity resides in their internal critical resistance against the standard ideological move of 1870,

which is the displacement of religiously (confessionally) based sacred observance toward the frame of the national. Rather, the works enact—perform—
an original and subtle mediation between the sacred and the secular. Brahms's
Requiem remains Protestant as Verdi's and Dvořák's remain Catholic. In none
of these cases does the religious community become the national one.

In addition to the marked separation from clerical institutions and power,
these Requiems carry an additional burden that Mozart's implied and that
Cherubini's clearly defied. This is the opposition to theatricality, specifically
to theatricality as a bearer of official power and authority. The dominant legend that Mozart wrote his Requiem about himself has tended to diffuse the
question of whether the work was friendly or hostile to the Catholic Church.
(A debate on this issue did erupt with vehemence in Austria in the "Mozart
year" 1991, focusing on the question of whether the bicentennial of Mozart's
death should be commemorated by the Church—in other words, whether
Mozart died in the faith or not. Predictably, the energies of appropriation were
victorious—everyone wants to claim Mozart—and the Requiem was performed and televised from Saint Stephen's Cathedral in Vienna on 5 December 1991.)

If my hearing of *Don Giovanni*, as discussed in chapter 1, is correct, then
Mozart did set himself against the agenda of baroque theatricality and power.
Two thirds of a century later, however, those energies have returned in different guise, through the elevation of theatricality to theatocracy, as Nietzsche
warned in *The Case of Wagner*. The culprits: Bayreuth and *Parsifal*. The power
of the theater involves its ability and authority to perform someone else's
agenda, in the case of *Parsifal* the agenda of German nationalism and racism.
In the age of Bayreuth, the political legitimacy of collective utterances involves the resistance to this kind of performance of exclusionary power. It
was of course not the task of Brahms, and even less so that of Verdi or Dvořák,
to fight the ideology of Bayreuth. The point is that they were not subject to
its claims.

The antitheatricality of the Requiems of Brahms, Verdi, and Dvořák can
be understood according to the distinction between performativity and performance. These works are performative but they are not really performances.
This distinction is crucial to their status as critiques of ideology—nationalist
or clerical—as opposed to their incorporation into ideology. They are performative—in the sense of J. L. Austin's category of performative speech—in that
they produce, enact, the collectivity they refer to, rather than perform it in
the image or name of an external authority. In these works, the principle
of performativity means, moreover, that the collective subjectivity is in fact
produced in the utterances and limited to them. Nothing external to the
works themselves is being represented. There is no representation at work,
only presentation, as it were. The voice of the people is limited to music and

emerges only in music; nothing external to music is represented. This is not the music of the nation.

Let me emphasize the literalness of the assertion I am making. As a modern political "imagined community," "the people" exists categorically as an aesthetic assertion. It exists materially, as an utterance of collective subjectivity by real bodies, only in music. The vocalization of the people, the self-voicing of a collectivity, thus follows the logic of "subjectivity" in the normative usage that governs this book. As identity and national identity become increasingly indistinct, collective subjectivity is attached to a popular voice that insists on an outsider status to the voice of the nation.

Brahms called his Requiem German and Verdi wrote his to commemorate a hero of the Risorgimento. But the nations in question are never named from within the works. Thus Brahms's label "ein deutsches Requiem" is uncorroborated from within the work itself, where the sacred pulls the frame of reference out beyond the nation. Exactly the opposite is the case in another—*the* other—work of 1868, Wagner's *Meistersinger*, where the nation is named and rendered sacred from within the work and as the culmination of the work. As Arthur Groos has shown, the chorus opens the work as the voice of a congregation and concludes it as the voice of a nation.[4] When, in the final scene, the chorus of Nurembergers is bonded in loyalty to what is truly German ("was deutsch, und echt"), performativity is absorbed by performance, of the representation of an external authority. Thus, a nationalism of expressivity and inclusion—honed in language and poetry and welcoming of iconoclasts like Walther von Stolzing and Richard Wagner—is absorbed into a nationalism of oppression and exclusion. When the heretofore conciliatory Hans Sachs agitates the chorus into nationalist militancy, he conjoins the categories of "the people" and "empire" in their redemptive battle against the French.

At the same time, however, the absorption of the congregation into the *Volk* is less perfected, at the end of *Die Meistersinger*, than its culminating nationalist momentum might suggest. There is a remainder, an unabsorbed and unarticulated entity, and that is religion itself. In this opera, the historical moment of 1868 looks to the 1550s for its mirror image. The fit is imperfect. National consolidation in 1868 is reflected by post-Reformation consolidation in 1560. Nuremberg and Hans Sachs are, at this time, solidly Protestant. The finale of *Die Meistersinger* defines the honor of the German nation in terms of what it is protecting itself from. Hans Sachs warns:

Hab' Acht!
Uns dräuen üble Streich!
Zerfällt erst deutsches Volk und Reich

[4] See Arthur Groos, "Constructing Nuremberg: Typological and Proleptic Communities in *Die Meistersinger*," *Nineteenth Century Music* 16:1 (summer 1992).

In falscher, welscher Majestät
Kein Fürst bald mehr sein Volk versteht,
Und welschen Dunst mit welschem Tand
Sie pflanzen uns in deutsches Land!

Beware!
Evil ploys threaten us!
The collapse of the German people and empire
Means false, foreign/French rule
Where no prince understands his people,
And foreign/French deceit with foreign/French sham
Are planted on German soil!

The unambiguous referent of Second Empire France provides the historical heir to the Catholic marked as foreign, whether it lies within or without German boundaries. In the symbolic cultural vocabulary of *Die Meistersinger*, the place of the foreign is filled by Jewish, French, and Catholic placeholders. Thus, in the opera's codification of German virtues and foreign vices, the religious enmities of the sixteenth century are secularized but remain present nonetheless. The parallel between the sixteenth and nineteenth centuries holds, but becomes more complicated as aporias begin to open in this structure of national insiders and outsiders. As a sixteenth-century portrait, *Die Meistersinger* is structured around literal and symbolic absences having to do with the disintegration of the Catholic word and its symbols and practices.

Act 1 opens in the Church of Saint Catherine, whose Gothic architecture lends itself to the surrounding premodern, medieval nostalgia. The *Katharinenkirche* had been recently celebrated as the venue of the mastersingers. In 1839 King Ludwig I of Bavaria wrote an encomium to Nuremberg as the city that offered the true image of the Middle Ages: "des Mittelalters treues Bild." Viollet-le-Duc offered the same opinion on a visit through the city in 1854.[5] In response to Ludwig's text, the city's most prominent planner and architectural restorer, Carl Alexander Heideloff, drew a series of images of the city's most prominent sites, including the Church of Saint Catherine, identified explicitly as the gathering place of the mastersingers.[6] For Ludwig—as indeed for Viollet-le-Duc—medieval unity presupposed the universal, Catholic Church. The Nuremberg personified by Hans Sachs, on the other hand, is decidedly Protestant. The historic Sachs (1494–1576) was one of Nuremberg's most prominent

---

[5] Eugene Emmanuel Viollet-le-Duc (1814–79) was in 1854 at the pinnacle of his career as France's preeminent medieval architectural revivalist and restorer. His aesthetic was mainly Gothic, as exemplified by his placement of the spire atop the Cathedral of Notre Dame in Paris.

[6] Michael Brix, *Nürnberg und Lübeck im 19.Jahrhundert* (Munich: Prestel-Verlag, 1981), pp. 25, 100. Ernest Newman points out that Saint Catherine's hosted meetings of the mastersingers only after 1620. Previously they had met in the smaller church of Saint Martha's. See Ernest Newman, *The Wagner Operas* (New York: Alfred A. Knopf, 1949), p. 304.

early advocates of Martin Luther's reforms, "versifying protestant dogma" in 1523 as "The Wittenberg Nightingale" ["Die wittenbergisch Nachtigall"].[7] The nightingale Luther, in Gerald Strauss's summary of the text, is to awaken believers from the long sleep induced by the moon, an allegory for the cold reason of sophists. Sachs continues with "a long and vituperative diatribe against priests, monks, bishops, and the rest of the clergy" in a tone that prefigures the anti-*welsch* homily of Wagner's Sachs in 1868![8]

The scenic and musical tableau that opens Wagner's opera is explicitly Lutheran, but the rhetoric of this Lutheran scene appropriates the universalizing claim of Catholic medievalism. The orchestral voice of the prelude leads seamlessly into the chorale-singing, united voice of the congregants, a significant passage both musically and ideologically. The four-part Protestant chorale, with organ accompaniment, is in the style of J. S. Bach. Wagner had cited Bach and specifically the chorale form in his early essay "Über deutsches Musikwesen" (1841) as "an exclusively German property," opposing in its solid simplicity the splendor of Catholic ritual as imported from Italy by aristocratic courts.[9] The scene takes place on the eve of the Feast of John the Baptist— *Johannesfest*; the chorale's words cite John's baptism of Christ in terms used previously by both Luther and Bach.[10] As the plot unfolds, Hans Sachs (with Hans a diminutive of Johannes, that is, the name of both John the Baptist and Johann Sebastian Bach) will take up the induction of Walther von Stolzing as a mastersinger and will literally baptize Walther's "child": the latter's mastersong.[11] As a carrier of what Arthur Groos has labeled "cultural unity projected backwards" from the nineteenth to the sixteenth century, Nuremberg's Protestant status is portrayed as absolute and frictionless. The fact that Nuremberg was the site of a divided population and of key conflicts and negotiations of the Reformation is obscured.[12] Wagner's placement of the opera in the

---

[7] Euan Cameron, *The European Reformation* (Oxford: Oxford University Press, 1991), p. 228. Sachs's advocacy preceded the official introduction of the Reformation into Nuremberg by two years. See Steven Ozment, *The Reformation in the Cities* (New Haven: Yale University Press, 1975), p. 11, and Günter Vogler, *Nürnberg 1524/25: Sudien zur Geschichte der reformatorischen und sozialen Bewegung in der Reichsstadt* (Berlin: Deutscher Verlag der Wissenschaften, 1982).

[8] Gerald Strauss, *Nuremberg in the Sixteenth Century* (New York: John Wiley & Sons, 1966), p. 166. Strauss argues that the Nurembergers' wealth precludes an economic argument for the attraction of Protestantism. For Strauss, Sachs and others were motivated by "the quest for certainty and for the removal of doubt" (p. 170), a frame of mind that translated well into the nineteenth century and the motivations for nationalism.

[9] Groos, "Constructing Nuremberg," p. 20.

[10] Ibid., pp. 21, 22.

[11] See Ibid., pp. 23–24.

[12] I will not attempt a summary but will mention, as examples, the Peace of Nuremberg of 1532, which gave Protestant estates the right to combine against their pledge to help the Catholic emperor fight the Turks. For Heiko Oberman the "Nuremberg treaty was in reality little more than an uneasy cease-fire, but it foreshadowed the legal solution of the religious struggle in the empire as it was to be negotiated in Augsburg in 1555 and Osnabrück in 1648." [Heiko A. Ober-

year 1560, five years after the Peace of Augsburg, helped him portray the Reformation as a result rather than as an event.[13]

With the dissolution of the Holy Roman Empire in 1806 (an event referred to—an anachronistic in-joke—in Hans Sachs's closing speech), the free imperial city of Nuremberg was annexed to Bavaria. In July 1866 Wagner wrote of *Die Meistersinger* to his patron, Bavarian King Ludwig II, echoing the words of his character Hans Sachs but with a sharp difference. Sachs praises Nuremberg, in the celebrated *Wahn* monologue, according to the trope of patriotic unity:

> Wie friedsam treuer Sitten
> Getrost in Tat und Werk
> Liegt nicht in Deutschlands Mitten
> Mein liebes Nurenberg!

> How peacefully in its true customs,
> Content in deeds and work,
> Lies in the midst of Germany,
> My beloved Nuremberg!

With similar John-of-Gaunt sentiment, Wagner writes to Ludwig:

> Nuremberg, the old, true seat of German art, German uniqueness and splendor, the powerful old free city, well preserved like a precious jewel, reborn through the labors of its serenely happy, solid, enlightened and liberal populace under the patronage of the Bavarian throne.[14]

As he will do in building Bayreuth, Wagner is serving two masters: the new Germany with its Protestant-based fantasy of unity, and Bavaria with its Catholic history and stylistic propensities. When pushed, *Die Meistersinger* reveals the same cultural dualism. This spells trouble for the proleptic relation of the Protestant community in 1560 to the German nation of 1870.

---

man, *Luther: Man Between God and Devil*, trans. E. Walliser-Schwarzbart (New York: Image Books, 1992), p. 238.] In 1538, however, the Nuremberg League of the Catholic estates was founded against the Protestants. Nuremberg, the alleged site of German unity, is in fact a paradigmatic site of German diversity.

[13] Groos, "Constructing Nuremberg," p. 19. Ernest Newman fixed the date of 1560 from the evidence that Hans Sachs's widowerhood "lasted only about a year from that date" (Newman, *The Wagner Operas*, p. 304). In an article called "Wagner's Nuremberg," *Cambridge Opera Journal* 4:1 (1992), Stewart Spencer surveys the history of Nuremberg as one of increasing prosperity until the Thirty Years' War; he never mentions the Reformation. This account seems unintentionally and indeed symptomatically to duplicate the "backward projection" of the nineteenth-century valorization of Nuremberg as the synecdoche of German unity. That position, as Spencer notes, was expertly seized on by the National Socialist regime after 1933, most prominently by the staging of the party festival in September 1934, filmed by Leni Riefenstahl as *Triumph of the Will*.

[14] *König Ludwig II und Richard Wagner: Briefwechsel*, ed. Otto Strobel (Karlsruhe, 1936–39) 2:78, cited in Spencer, "Wagner's Nuremberg," p. 36.

Before the Church of Saint Catherine was a Protestant venue hosting the meetings of the mastersingers, it was the church of a convent serving wealthy families and young women of Nuremberg. Wagner's setting follows accurately the sixteenth-century documents as revived by Ludwig I and others in the 1830s. At the same time, his deployment of Saint Catherine's participates perforce in a literal manifestation of a widespread symbolic function of the Reformation—namely, the disappearance of women and the repression of the sensual and the erotic. Hans Sachs and Veit Pogner are widowers. Pogner's induction of his daughter Eva into the bridal market sends an erotic frisson into the mastersingers' homosocial world. Sachs's counter-erotic decision not to woo her himself reveals him to be reserving his strength for nation-building—like Parsifal, like the Heldentenor in the famous Tristan joke, as indeed unlike Tristan himself.[15] Beckmesser's drive to woo reveals him to be oversexed, adding another dimension to the anti-Semitic stereotyping in his portrayal. The union of Walther and Eva promises the sexual happiness appropriate to a comic ending but here too a repressive note has already been struck. If we recall the lovely moment (act 3, scene 1) when Sachs tells Eva of his own decision not to court her by quoting the fate (and music) of Wagner's King Marke, we can also infer the accompanying admonition whereby Eva and Walther are instructed not to behave like Isolde and Tristan. "Sublimate!" is the order here, as it continues to be when Sachs drafts Walther into the guild at the end of the opera. The Wilhelmine weight on this couple's shoulders exceeds the Leopoldine burden on those of Tamino and Pamina. It is a late-nineteenth century and a national weight, and also a Protestant one.

Die Meistersinger concludes with a series of perfect equations. German art and German nation are equal to each other and each internally unified. The unity of German art resides in the harmony of tradition and inspiration. The unity of the German nation resides in its love for its own art. Herein lies a tautology. The German nation is in love with itself. Unity is not the harmony of parts but the denial of difference. Anti-Semitism, as exercised against the character Beckmesser, serves to displace and disguise intra-Christian, Protestant-Catholic difference. Thus, the ideological gloss of the *Festwiese* belies and denies a cultural diversity within Germany as great in 1870 as it was in 1550, and which remains so along the same lines. Never was Wagner so humorless, Hermann Broch remarked, as in his only comic opera.[16]

In December 1869, eighteen months after the premiere of *Die Meistersinger*, Modest Musorgsky completed what would come to be known as the first and

[15] The character Tristan, of course, loses himself in eros. In the Tristan joke, a Heldentenor entertaining a woman in a hotel room receives a telephone call, after which he informs his guest, "You have to leave; I've been hired to sing Tristan in six months."

[16] Hermann Broch, *Hugo von Hofmannsthal and His Time: The European Imagination 1860–1920*, trans. M. P. Steinberg (Chicago: University of Chicago Press, 1984), p. 56.

failed version of *Boris Godunov*. The structure of this opera is as vexed and intractable as that of *Die Meistersinger* is clear and perfected. No consensus has emerged as to the optimal performance version of the work, with opera houses tending to prefer a conflation of its two versions, an option decried by scholars. But although this work's cultural and ideological aporias open less readily, they are surprisingly similar to the ones I have tried to bring into relief in *Die Meistersinger*. If the German nation produced in Wagner's work is Protestant with an unabsorbed Catholic remainder, that same Catholic remainder follows the progress and plot of *Boris*. The fact that it opposes an Orthodox norm rather than a Protestant one only reinforces the parallel between the German and Russian predicaments. Catholic style continues to connote sensuality and theatricality; Orthodoxy, like Protestantism, responds with the values of text, reason, and faith.

The 1869 *Boris* evinces two overriding attributes. It is an all-male opera. It is conceived, moreover, according to the deliberately Russianizing and rationalizing aesthetic of the 1860s known as "kuchkism." As Richard Taruskin has shown, the "kuchka" (literally meaning "little heap") understood itself as a "cabal of idealist progressives opposing authority," which translated into the avoidance of academic authority, the praise of formlessness, and the emancipation "from the shackles of the lyric and the beautiful."[17] The aesthetic's antitheatricality emerged in the category of the *opéra dialogué*, one with definite Wagnerian echoes but with a Russian standard-bearer in Alexander Dargomizhky's *The Stone Guest*. The kuchkists' implicit Wagnerism was matched by an explicit anti-Verdianism, expressed most forcefully in their contempt for *La forza del destino* on the occasion of its premiere in Saint Petersburg in 1862.[18]

The rejection of the 1869 *Boris* was sustained in the memoir of Ludmila Shestakova with the question "How can there be an opera without the feminine element?"[19] Musorgsky's substantial pragmatic correction along these lines was the addition of the "Polish act" and the character of Marina Mnichek to the second version of the opera, completed in late 1871 and published in 1874. The Polish act was supported, according to Taruskin, by an entirely new aesthetic, which departed from the principles of the kuchkists in favor of a "rough and gaudy theatricality."[20] The Polish act also introduced the character of the Jesuit conspirator Rangoni, who allowed Musorgsky to indulge, in Taruskin's words, his "xenophobic, rabidly anti-Catholic interpretation of the Time of Troubles."[21]

---

[17] See Richard Taruskin, *Defining Russia Musically* (Princeton: Princeton University Press, 1997), p. xv, and *Musorgsky: Eight Essays and an Epilogue* (Princeton: Princeton University Press, 1993), pp. xxiii–iv, 73, and 280.

[18] See Taruskin, *Musorgsky*, p. 268.

[19] Ibid., p. 251.

[20] Ibid., p. 269.

[21] Ibid., p. 288.

The second, 1871 *Boris* thus offers a fascinating contradiction. It achieved success in the theater through its adoption of (or capitulation to?) grand-operatic style. At the same time, it used that style to present two characters— Marina Mnichek and Rangoni—who embody, in Musorgsky's xenophobic view, precisely the content of the same Catholic world that produces grand opera and theatricality—namely, an allegedly mortal danger to the political and cultural integrity of Russia. If Taruskin is correct in the assertion that the 1871 *Boris* reflects a new grand-operatic aesthetic in toto, rather than deploying it ironically to depict those characters enslaved to Catholic ideology and aggression, then we are faced with the contradiction of an idiom used to portray the attack of the culture embodied by that (false) idiom on a culture (Russia's) that stands for truth and authenticity. In this case, Musorgsky can be understood to escape the contradiction in the new ending, which removes the lament of the Holy Fool from the now excised scene at Saint Basil's to the concluding moments in the Kromy Forest. Can the fool's lament for enslaved Russia, uttered as the Pretender makes his way toward Moscow, be heard to incorporate an ironic lament for the abandoned "Russian" *Boris Godunov* of 1869?

Even more so than *Die Meistersinger*, *Boris Godunov* (in either version) is a choral opera. This attribute, as Taruskin points out, is in fact brought into relief by the symmetrical, palindromic structure of the 1871 version, in which the prologue and four acts deliver nine scenes that alternate in their focus between a principal character and the crowd. Taruskin's skeleton pattern (curiously ignoring Marina, whom I will add in brackets) runs: Crowd, Boris, Pretender, Boris, Pretender, [Marina,] Boris, Crowd.[22] The chorus claims the opening and closing moments as it does in *Die Meistersinger*, but its designation as Crowd rather than as Congregation and *Volk* denotes both its political underarticulation and its lack of progress through the course of the drama. The voice of the chorus remains the voice of the people. It is a beautiful collective voice but an unfulfilled voice, at once coherent and inchoate and consistently opposed to the voices of authority. In the prologue, the chorus (as a synecdoche for the Russian "people") is ordered to implore Boris to accept the crown. This act marks decisively the impossibility of accession of the chorus/"people" to a position of authority, at the same time marking its alleged choral unanimity as the result of coercion. In the final scene in the Kromy Forest, the crowd becomes a mob, following the Pretender to Moscow. But the chorus's place as existential truth-teller is taken by the Holy Fool. In other words, as the chorus/crowd begins to lie, a synecdochal shadow of its

---

[22] Ibid., p. 281. This sequence observes the 1871 excision of the Saint Basil's scene, commonly restored in the "conflated" version preferred by contemporary opera houses. Taruskin decries the "rage to conflate" (p. 290) as a denial of the specific aesthetic idiom and internal coherence of each finished version of the opera.

better self disassociates from the ecstatic collective to tell the truth about the splitting of people and nation. This voice is of course missing from the end of *Die Meistersinger*. Call it the voice of the people at the moment of the nation.

Brahms, 1868

Ein Deutsches Requiem [A German Requiem], opus 45, was composed over an eleven-year period, 1857–68, and premiered incrementally as it took its final form. The first three sections were essayed in Vienna late in 1867, but without success. The first "complete" performance was given in Bremen on Good Friday of 1868, but what has become the fifth section for soprano solo ("Ihr habt nun Traurigkeit") was added subsequently. Thus, the first performance of the final version, in seven parts, took place in Leipzig on 18 February 1869. The work's incremental origins are interesting for various reasons. As the Requiem developed into what would stand as Brahms's largest-scale work, it also developed into his most personal one. It is personal both in its commemorative and confessional aspects.

As a musical act of commemoration, the work's initial motivation, as Brahms's first biographer Max Kalbeck suggested, followed on the death of Robert Schumann in 1856. Brahms had apparently planned a work in a single movement, which he did not complete. The Requiem's commemorative work was overtaken in early 1865 by the death of Brahms's mother, Christiane. Brahms's first musical commemoration of his mother appears in the *adagio mesto* movement of the horn trio, opus 40, with its quotation from the folksong *Dort in der Weiden steht ein Haus*. It is as a further act of musical mourning for his mother that Brahms returned to the Requiem in 1865 and 1866. The addition of the movement for soprano solo makes explicit the maternal aura that had come to surround the piece, emphasizing as well the tone of intimacy that alternates throughout with public solemnity.

The combination of the intimate and the solemn reveals the work's confessional character as decisively Protestant. The label "German" is thus to be understood as "north German"—referring to the Protestant nativism of Luther and Bach. Indeed, one astute listener—the surgeon Theodor Billroth—diagnosed cultural difference as the root of the failure of the first three movements to please the Viennese: "I like Brahms better every time I meet him," he wrote to a friend; "his Requiem is so nobly spiritual and so Protestant-Bachish that it was difficult to make it go down here."[23]

None of the traditional liturgical texts of the Catholic requiem mass is used. The Roman Catholic requiem mass prayed for the salvation of the dead from the terror of damnation by intoning the power of Christ and the dogma of

---

[23] Malcolm MacDonald, *Brahms* (New York: Schirmer Books, 1990), p. 134.

the Resurrection. Brahms chose his texts from Luther's Bible—texts used previously by Heinrich Schütz in his *Cantiones sacrae* of 1625 and his *Geistliche Chormusik* of 1648—interspersing selections from the Hebrew Bible (Psalms, Isaiah, Solomon, Ecclesiastes, Hebrews) and the Christian (Matthew, Peter, James, John, Corinthians, Revelation). Christ and Resurrection are unmentioned. Rather, the focus is on death, survival, mourning, and renewal. As the musical enactment of a ritual of mourning, the German Requiem follows the Protestant duality of privacy and community. Choral writing symbolizes community. At the same time, the music's dependence on long, arched phrases gives the solitary listener—whether the solitude is experienced in a cathedral or, in the company of a sound system, in a living room—the sense that the immense musical edifice rises and subsides with his or her own every breath.

The central message of consolation is stated in the first section's opening phrase (Matt. 5:4): "Blessed are they that mourn; for they shall be comforted." It is repeated often, most clearly in the final section, which structurally echoes the first and carries the line (Rev. 14:13): "Blessed are the dead which die in the Lord from henceforth."

It is in the fifth section that the theological and musical discourse of consolation is evinced most subtly and also most simply. The soprano, intoning the maternal voice, says "I will see you again, and your heart will rejoice," while the choral line states "I will comfort you as one is comforted by his mother." There is little doubt that the first-person voice of the soprano represents the mother—specifically, Brahms's own mother. The choral voice here would seem to represent music itself, which claims the capacity to console *as* a mother would. In that word "as" lies all the difference: between the return of the dead and the memory of the dead; between magic and memory; between grace and consolation; between dependence and autonomy. Brahms might thus be understood to offer here a modern or rather a modernist successor to the *Stabat Mater*.[24]

The sensuality of musical sound marks it as a substitute carrier of maternal consolation. However, musical texture signifies the memory of maternal con-

---

[24] In an essay called "Stabat Mater," Julia Kristeva adds the following comment to her appreciation of Pergolesi's setting of Jacopone da Todi's thirteenth-century text: "Man overcomes the unthinkable of death by postulating material love in its place—in the place and stead of death and thought. This love, of which divine love is merely a not always convincing derivation, psychologically is perhaps a recall, on the near side of early identifications, of the primal shelter that insured the survival of the newborn. Such a love is in fact, logically speaking, a surge of anguish at the very moment when the identity of thought and living body collapses." See Kristeva, *Tales of Love*, trans. Leon S. Roudiez (New York: Columbia University Press, 1987), p. 252 and 234–63. The representation of the lamenting mother in the text and multiple settings by Catholic composers (Palestrina, Pergolesi, Haydn, Rossini, and Dvořák) seems to receive a commentary in this musical gesture of the Protestant Brahms. Rather than a representation of the Virgin Mother, we have a representation of the longing for maternal consolation. (See the discussion of Dvořák's *Stabat Mater* below.)

solation rather than a fantasmatic repetition or return of the real thing. The consolation no longer available from the mother resides now in music alone, and musical understanding and pleasure derive from a functioning subjectivity that knows the difference between memory and delusion. This point in the *German Requiem* traces the passage from the real presence of the dead mother to her displacement into the consoling agency of aesthetic experience. That new language of aesthetic consolation becomes, at this moment, the language of "music alone," without words or program. Thus the Requiem becomes itself a work of transition to Brahms's later symphonic work.

There is also a paternal voice in the Requiem. It is personified most explicitly in the baritone solos. This manly voice doesn't console; it calls to action. In the Requiem's sixth section, the baritone solo repeats the call made musically famous by Handel's *Messiah*: "Behold, I tell you a mystery; we shall not all sleep, but we shall all be changed, in a moment, in the twinkling of an eye, at the last trumpet." Like its maternal counterpart in the music of consolation, this voice of paternal militancy is sublimated into a purely musical presence. Its musical inheritor is that aspect of the Requiem's music that is militant and even dogmatic, as in the consistently resurgent tympani in places such as in the Requiem's second section ("For all flesh is as grass"), at the conclusion of the third section ("The souls of the righteous are in the hand of God"), and in other works, such as the opening bars of the First Symphony, where the kettledrum resounds with so dogmatic a fervor as to suggest that it is being pounded directly by Martin Luther's fists.

By the time the largest structural arc of the Requiem has been traversed—in the seventh section's repetition of the first one's message of consolation—a reconciliation of these maternal and paternal voices has been achieved. Invoked at some level here is the reconciliation of his parents that Brahms could not literally achieve; they had separated in 1864 and he had vainly tried to reunite them.

Mourning involves recovery—particularly the recovery from the self held hostage to the dead. "When the work of mourning is completed," Sigmund Freud writes in "Mourning and Melancholia," "the ego becomes free and uninhibited again."[25] Thus, the lost person is retained in the psyche of the mourner as an instance of memory, but without the libidinal attachment that impedes the functioning of the ego. The mourning for a parent is particularly significant psychic work in this regard, as the self has in any case to be molded in an act of separation from the parent. There are at least two parents commemorated in the *German Requiem*: a natural mother and, in Schumann, a musical father. Indeed, Brahms would never lose the sense of himself as the son of at least four parents, including Robert and Clara Schumann, and the son of a

---

[25] Sigmund Freud, "Mourning and Melancholia," in *General Psychological Theory*, ed. Philip Rieff (New York: Macmillan, 1963), p. 166.

north German tradition stretching back to Bach and Schütz. Robert Schumann thus stands as the most immediate musical father in Brahms's vividly present pantheon, intoning the contradictory paternal command at once to create and to obey.

The Requiem sets a musical agenda of reconciliation that will inform Brahms's music from this moment on. I would suggest that over a century of Brahms listeners have understood, perhaps unconsciously, the meaning and success of this musical discourse of reconciliation. This is the reconciliation of the maternal and the paternal, of the masculine and feminine, and of the north and the south. It is a cultural achievement as well as a musical one.

The central European fin de siècle redounds with analogous, if less successful, discourses of reconciliation. Max Weber, a generation younger than Brahms, suffered keenly between the draw of the inward religiosity of his southern German mother and the imperative of rationality and power he absorbed from his Prussian father. With the metaphor of modernity's iron cage with which he concluded *The Protestant Ethic and the Spirit of Capitalism*, he declared his, and social theory's, inability to reconcile the polarity. Weber thus abandoned the hope for consolation.

Freud confronted similar issues as he pioneered the psychoanalytic theory of the personality in the late 1890s. The mature personality, he began to argue, accrues as childhood desire is necessarily organized into socially functional behavior. With a male bias that remains controversial, Freud suggested that the mother was the first object of desire and the father the first countervailing, disciplining presence. Maturation subsequently involves the internalization—in correct dosages—of the disciplining presence of the father and the appropriate replacement of the mother with another object of desire. What Freud could never work out, in his evolving understanding of human development, was a model for the internalization of the mother. Psychoanalysis thus duplicated the Protestant narrative of the internalization of law and conscience. In the century since Freud developed his argument, psychoanalysis has struggled with great difficulty to develop a discourse of consolation that would be compatible with its central discourse of discovery and truth, rather than one that would in fact constitute a new crime of seduction.

From the foundation of the Requiem, Brahms did begin to work through, inarticulately, in music alone, the knotty problem of the co-internalization of law and consolation, of truth and comfort. The deepening harmony of militancy and consolation in his developing musical oeuvre points to a notion of the self as an integrator of maternal and paternal resonance. Brahms's musical itinerary points indeed to a resolution—however fleeting or inarticulate—of the cultural codes and anxieties of masculinity and femininity. As listeners—however inarticulate—to this music, a century later, do we not also want to draw from it a similar power of reconciliation? The popularity and significance of Brahms's music resides in its combination of intransigence and lyricism, in how it makes us feel at once inspired and consoled. We have perhaps underestimated both what we want from Brahms and what his music is able to give us. More than making us feel at times inspired and at times consoled, Brahms is able to weave both these rhetorics together. It is the harmonization of militancy and consolation that is unique in Brahms's music, making it as much a music for our fin de siècle as for his own.

Verdi, 1874

Giuseppe Verdi, no friend of the Church and acclaimed as a hero of the anticlerical Risorgimento, composed his Requiem Mass (1874) in commemoration of Alessandro Manzoni. Author, most famously, of the novel I Promessi Sposi, Manzoni was Verdi's literary analog and fellow national patriarch. Manzoni's devotion to the Risorgimento, however, is much clearer than Verdi's. Recent scholarship has attempted to redraw the boundaries between the myths and realities surrounding Verdi's relationship to Italian politics and nation-building. Although there is general agreement that Verdi was not the musical Garibaldi—or indeed the musical Manzoni—there is no consensus as to the historical truth of Verdi's political commitments. Personally conservative and a monarchist, he paid little attention to political events. The pressing debate remains at the level of the works.

In a recent essay on the chorus "Va pensiero" from Nabucco (1842), Roger Parker brings a series of questions to this piece's exceptional status and aura as the de facto Italian national anthem, and the marker of Verdi as the central voice of liberation and unification. Parker's analysis is musical and contextual. Musically, he argues for the nonexceptionality of the chorus in comparison with other choruses of the period. Contextually, he joins several other scholars, notably Frank Walker and John Rosselli, in questioning the received accounts of the chorus's original reception at the La Scala premiere of Nabucco (in Austrian-occupied Milan) in March 1842. It turns out that the standard account of the audience demanding an encore of the chorus in defiance of an Austrian prohibition on such "public enthusiasms" may be unfounded. I am less certain than Parker on this point, as Parker's certainty relies on the lack of evidence in contemporary press reviews. It remains possible, however, that the lack of commentary was produced by press censorship rather than by the nonexistence of the event itself. More bluntly, however, one is left with the question of what the cry "O mia patria" refers to in the first place: what kind of Italy, and what kind of emotion.[26] Verdi's work may not be so easily separa-

---

[26] Roger Parker, " 'Va Pensiero' and the Insidious Mastery of Song," in Leonora's Last Act: Essays in Verdian Discourse (Princeton: Princeton University Press, 1997), pp. 20–41; here at pp. 33–34.

ble from Risorgimento energies as Verdi's extraoperatic actions. Furthermore, mythmaking is itself a historical event, and the association of Verdi, man and work, with Italian politics is itself a historical fact.

There has never been much controversy in designating the *Messa da Requiem* as both a sacred and an anticlerical work. This paradox is usually fulfilled with reference to the national: the work's sacredness lies in its sacralization of the new nation produced by the Risorgimento. Moreover, the work's general rhetorical and musical militancy can be understood to express the unfinished work of the Risorgimento in the context of the new nation. I think this last claim is correct; its correctness points to a problem, however, in the association of the work with the new Italy. The Requiem's general rhetorical militancy makes it more difficult to distinguish the popular from the national, and to argue, as I intend to, that this work of the Risorgimento marks and insists on that very distinction.

Relevant as well is the broader historical and historiographical issue of Italian nationalism's "good press" in comparison with the German case. German unification in 1870 and the declaration of the German Empire in 1871 produced the strongest and most aggressive nation in Europe, transforming German nationalism, one might argue, from an expressive movement to an oppressive one. As we have seen, both the power and the anxiety inherent in German nationalism at the moment of unification lodge in the problematic remainder of religious difference. Whether this remainder was dissolved via transcendence or repression remains a subject for historical investigation. In any case, post-1870 German culture is largely triumphalist. Post-1870 Italian culture remains surprisingly melancholic, in this respect closer in tone to the culture of the French Third Republic, born out of necessity from the humiliation of the Franco-Prussian War of September 1870. A religious question emerges here as well. Although Italy, like France, remained overwhelmingly Catholic, the Risorgimento and the Church remained solid enemies through the first seventy years following the initial unification of 1860. This enmity, as is well known, was relaxed only by the Concordat between Italy and the Vatican signed by Mussolini in October 1929. For the generations of the Risorgimento and the early Italian nation, then, being Catholic required an agonizing choice between nation and church. In this regard, the combination of militancy and anxiety in the Verdi Requiem should not surprise.

The militancy of the soprano voice in the Requiem's *Libera me* recalls the writing for Amneris, three years earlier, in the Judgment Scene of *Aida*, where fury against the priests functions as a translucent allegory of an assault on the Church. Moreover, the geopolitics of *Aida*, with its multiple articulations of north-south conflict, was potentially interpretable to its original listeners in 1871 as an allegory of Italian unification and its tensions. Here, the intra-Italian north-south axis would function as a compatible overlay above the more obvious Orientalist, European-African axis.[27] Ethiopia might thus signify both "unredeemed" Italy in multiple ways: the peninsula before unification, and the impoverished south thereafter. The thrust of the intra-Italian allegory must be considered in the absence of Italian colonial involvement in Africa, a situation that would change in the 1880s and render, for example, the questions of race and Africa in *Otello* much more immediately relevant. (*Otello*'s February 1887 premiere followed within days of a massacre of five hundred Italian troops at Dog-Ali in Eritrea.) *Aida*, as Jeremy Tambling has accurately asserted, does not belittle Ethiopia. *Aida*'s third-act aria "O patria mia" produces the same words and the same complicated sentiment, at once nostalgic and militant, evident in "Va pensiero," thirty years earlier. Amonasro's words to Aida—again Tambling—echo old Risorgimento values: "Pensa che un popolo, vinto, straziato, per te soltanto risorger può [Think that a people, conquered, tormented, can rise again through you alone]."[28]

The rhetorical militancy of Verdi's Requiem is achieved first by its unanimity of voice. The four solo voices are rhetorically indistinguishable from the utterances of the chorus. In this rhetorical posture they resemble more the solo voices of Beethoven's choral writing than they do Verdi's other, operatic, solo voices. Where in Brahms's case the two solo voices invoke maternal consolation and paternal authority, I would assert that the distribution of Verdi's four solo voices supplies lines of sound that are undifferentiated both from the chorus and from each other. Consequently, they are ungendered. Entirely distinct from his operatic voices, these four voices are orchestral instruments; they are not singing people. This quality is evident from the moment of the soloists' first entrance in the Kyrie, in which they all four sing the same musical and textual material, exuding an emotional uniformity that David Rosen, in his study of the Verdi Requiem, characterizes as Verdi's insistence on a nonoperatic rhetoric.[29] (This quality seems to emerge in the visual rhetoric of performances. Singers seem instinctively to understand the work's rhetoric of nonpersonification and to abet it by matching their faces and bodies to the music they are singing and hearing, as if to depersonify themselves and become blank-faced instruments—incremental representatives of the massive collective subjectivity emanating from all around them.)

Rosen suspends his designation of non-operatic rhetoric in his discussion of the mezzo-soprano solo in the *Liber scriptus*. This passage is the first ex-

[27] On *Aida*'s orientalism, see Edward Said's chapter "The Empire at Work: Verdi's *Aida*," in *Culture and Imperialism* (New York: Alfred A. Knopf, 1993), pp. 111–31. See also Paul Robinson, "Is *Aida* an Orientalist Opera?" *Cambridge Opera Journal* 5:2 (1993): 133–40, and Fabrizio Della Seta, " 'O cieli azzurri': Exoticism and Dramatic Discourse in *Aida*," *Cambridge Opera Journal* 3:1 (1991): 49–62. My thanks to Graham Green for this last reference.

[28] Jeremy Tambling, *Opera and the Culture of Fascism* (Oxford: Oxford University Press, 1996), p. 77.

[29] See David Rosen, *Verdi: Requiem* (Cambridge: Cambridge University Press, 1995), pp. 20–22.

tended solo passage in the work; it was added after the first performances. (It thus carries a status similar to the soprano solo movement in the Brahms Requiem.) At the repetition of the second stanza ("Judex ergo cum sedebit, Quidquid latet apparebit, Nil inultrum remanebit [When the judge, therefore, shall preside, anything concealed shall appear, nothing shall remain unpunished]"), the mezzo, Rosen suggests, "stammers the final line." He adds the following observation:

> When music imitates a speaker who stammers because of the burden of emotion, weeps with stylized sobs, or prays in an imitation of plainchant, it can be said to accomplish a "performative act" and can force the reading that, despite the literal sense of the text, the singer is—or might as well be—a character, rather than an abstract, narrative voice. That is the case here, where, although the text remains in the third person, the mezzo-soprano speaks as a character.[30]

The problem facing this assertion is the relation between the performative act and the vagueness of its agency; it is a big step from the singing voice to the singing character. The distinction between voice and character, crucial to Verdi's Requiem for precisely the antioperatic rhetoric that Rosen has already emphasized, is not suspended here. In this deeply human and heartfelt passage, the mezzo maintains her voice as a voice of the people. She is voice; she is not a character.

An alternate hearing of the solo voices, which I think is wrong, would interpret them according to a kind of gender inversion, where femininity (in both the soprano and alto voices) is associated with militancy, and where masculinity (in both the tenor and bass parts, but especially the tenor's) is matched with supplication. Verdi seems scrupulous in the gender-neutral distribution of emotion, from the supplicant and terrified to the militant. Gender neutrality is set by the initial entrance of the four voices in the Kyrie, and is reinforced time and again by the echoing of solo melodies, as for example in the Lacrymosa, where the melody is first sung by the mezzo-soprano and is then echoed by the bass.

This gender neutrality is profoundly non-operatic—indeed non-Verdian, if we identify the composer according to his operatic style. Whose voice speaks through the Requiem's massive collective subjectivity? It seems to me that there are two answers: a blunt one and one that pays attention to modern Italian history and political theory. The blunt answer says: the nation, with the Italian nation taking its place in the 1870s among the new nations and nationalisms. After all, the agnostic Verdi first set out to write a requiem movement to honor Rossini, who had died in 1868. Accounts of the Requiem's genesis consistently begin with his proposition to Tito Ricordi that a

[30] Ibid., pp. 28–30.

requiem mass be composed by "the most distinguished Italian composers."[31] Verdi contributed the *Libera me* to this collective enterprise. The *Messa per Rossini* was not performed, and when Verdi set out to write his own Requiem, he used the 1869 *Libera me*. This decision came in 1873 on the death of Manzoni.

Already in 1869, Verdi identified Rossini and Manzoni as the two surviving voices of authentic Italy. (Manzoni was credited for having forged a national vernacular for Italy and thus filled the same role in the making of the nation that Goethe had done for Germany and Pushkin had for Russia.) This is crucial for two reasons. First, he marked them as surviving voices, implying that the soul and subjectivity of irredentism and unification were dying out, rather than coming into fruition with the impending unification of the nation. Second, he explicitly contrasted these musical and literary voices with the professional politicians at the helm of Italy's domestic and foreign politics: "There's no hope for us," he wrote in August 1868, "when our statesmen are vain gossips."[32]

Italian nationalism's "good press," as mentioned above, has been sustained by belief in its expressive rather than oppressive character. Second, Italian nationalism has been argued to have maintained itself as a popular movement, rather than becoming the ideology of a powerful state that could subjugate its own people just as easily as it could subjugate others. It is with a benevolent eye toward Italian nationalism that Antonio Gramsci coined the important term "the national popular." Thus, the second frame through which the voice of the Verdi Requiem can be heard is as a constitutive voice of the specifically Italian "national popular." Gramsci's notion of the "national popular," alluded to sporadically in the *Prison Notebooks* (and a founding principle of post– Second World War Italian Communism) refers to a historically specific collaboration between national and popular agendas, which can be mediated by "the intellectuals"—that last term itself carrying a specifically Gramscian investment.[33] This energy had, for Gramsci, precisely failed to ignite in the Risorgimento, of which his opinion was low, and whose impotence he described with an operatic metaphor. For Gramsci, the Risorgimento and Italian unification were imprisoned within "the operatic conception of life," in which posture is taken for politics (and performance, we might add, for performativity). Thus, Gramsci:

> Verdi's music, or rather the libretti and plots of the plays set to music by Verdi, are responsible for a whole range of "artificial" poses in the life of people, for ways of thinking, for a "style." "Artificial" is perhaps not the right word because among the popular classes this artificiality assumes naïve and moving forms. To many com-

---

[31] See ibid., p. 2.

[32] Ibid., p. 1.

[33] See Antonio Gramsci, *Selections from the Prison Notebooks* (London: Lawrence and Wishart, 1971), pp. 20, 130–33, 421, and 421n.

mon people the baroque and the operatic appear as an extraordinarily fascinating way of feeling and acting, a means of escaping what they consider low, mean and contemptible in their lives and education in order to enter a more select sphere of great feelings and noble passions. Serial novels and below-stairs reading . . . provide the heroes and heroines. But opera is the most pestiferous because words set to music are more easily recalled, and they become matrices in which thought takes shape out of flux.[34]

The harmony between the national and the popular depends on the legitimation of that process Louis Althusser named "interpellation." Interpellation identifies the process by which the modern subject is formed by power, specifically, by the power of the state. Althusser appropriates the term from its first usage in the work of Lacan, where interpellation functions as the founding instance of subjectivity, in other words, the marking of the potential subject as a participant in the symbolic order. Both Lacan and Althusser use the metaphor of "hailing" to describe this instance, as in the hailing of an individual by a policeman. Thus, the making of the modern subject is understood in terms of its inclusion into a symbolic order that is also an order of power. Subjectivization and subjection are simultaneous and, in fact, indistinguishable. Becoming a subject thus incorporates the terminological ambiguity of the word itself, which refers both to subjection (as in "the king's subject") and empowerment (becoming a self and agent). This is the paradigm subsequently adopted by Michel Foucault, with the expansion of the locus of power from the state to discursive formations and systems.[35]

Does every model of subject formation depend on interpellation, and is interpellation at least neutral and potentially normative? The normative notion of a national popular depends on a normative model of interpellation. Thus, the subject can be "hailed" as belonging to the nation in a way that is beneficial and indeed liberating to him or her. This possibility would separate, presumably, good nationalism from bad nationalism. According to this separation, to be blunt about the matter, Italian nationalism, emerging from the Risorgimento, has been judged good by most European historians; German nationalism has a decidedly more mixed reputation through the nineteenth century, partly because of the teleology that keeps National Socialism in mind as its ultimate outcome. Italian nationalism is thus expressive in that it fulfills the desire for individuality on the level of the personal as well as the collective.

---

[34] Antonio Gramsci, "The Operatic Conception of Life," in *Selections from the Cultural Writings*, trans. W. Boelhower, ed. David Forgacs and Geoffrey Nowell-Smith (Cambridge: Harvard University Press, 1985), pp. 377–78.

[35] For a lucid summary of the problem and discursive history of *assujetissement*, see Judith Butler, *The Psychic Life of Power: Theories in Subjection* (Stanford: Stanford University Press, 1997), especially the introduction, pp. 1–30, and the essay " 'Conscience Doth Make Subjects of Us All': Althusser's Subjection," pp. 106–31.

Another way to understand the potential of "good interpellation" or indeed "good nationalism" would be according to the allowances it makes for the nurturing of subjectivity. Here as always the crucial issue is the boundary between self and world. The category of subjectivity immediately complicates that boundary, as opposed to the alleged clarity brought by the category of the autonomous subject. Subjectivity, individual or collective, is a function of history, culture, and world, and therefore cannot posit an autonomous self or subject. Subjectivity must thus be measured according to its participation in the world from which it can draw no clear lines of separation. At the same time, its function and integrity derive from a freedom from or resistance to ideology and coercion.

It is possible to understand the vox populi of the Verdi Requiem as the voice of the national popular in a way that exemplifies and fulfills the Gramscian paradigm. Yet it is this very incorporation of the voice of the Requiem into the voice of the nation that I want to resist. The collective subjectivity of the Requiem explores a labyrinth between the two subject positions of conventional religiosity (as signaled by the form and text of the requiem mass) and post-Risorgimento nationalism (a position powerfully associated with Verdi and his followers). Similar to the way the German Requiem insists on privacy and intimacy and thus resists the appropriation, à la *Meistersinger*, into nationalist chauvinism, the Verdi Requiem resists nationalist interpellation, no matter how much more palatable we might judge the Italian version to have been. It does offer—as I want to argue that only music can offer—a call to collectivity that does not undermine freedom.

How and where can we *hear* this self-production of the Requiem's popular voice? I will draw what I hear to be the strongest example: the "Hostias"—the tenor solo passage that forms the third part of the Offertory. The text is as follows:

> Hostias et preces tibi, Domine,
> laudis offerimus; tu suscipe pro
> animabus illis, quarum hodie
> memoriam facimus; fac eas,
> Domine, de morte transire ad vitam.

> Our offerings and prayers we render
> to thee, O Lord, with praise.
> Do thou receive them for those souls
> which we commemorate today. Make them,
> O Lord, pass from death unto life.

Rosen describes the melody as "calm, but not motionless or without purposeful direction." In Verdi's idiom the melody clearly fits into a religious trope, as used in *Aida* and mocked in the final scene of *Falstaff*.[36] The musical rhetoric of the tenor voice—in continuing indifferentiation, as discussed above, from the other solo or choral voices—corresponds to the text in the energy of self-production as a form of self-offering. The passage lasts under three minutes and forms the core of the Offertory written around it. It is thus staged as a minimalist and decisive moment. I will risk an awkward use of a Freudian metaphor and suggest that the "Hostias" is the navel of the Requiem: its point of origin, its marking of a secret source. As the heart of the Offertory, its embodies a subjectivity understood as something offered. This rhetorical power, I want to assert, is the key and core of the popular that produces itself in resistance to national interpellation. What moves us, ultimately, in this passage, is thus the voice of the authentic popular and its existence in music alone.

I would illustrate this claim with reference to a recent cinematic setting for this music that I consider instructive precisely for its accuracy on these issues: Paolo and Vittorio Taviani's 1982 film *Night of the Shooting Stars* [*La notte di San Lorenzo*]. The film is about the persistence of fascism during the period of political vacuum between the fall of Mussolini in 1943 and the end of the war in 1945. The film is thus about the possibility of popular survival and renewal independent of the nation and its interpellative agents. The Verdi Requiem, the "Hostias" in particular, sounds as the leitmotiv—to echo Rosen's gloss on its melody—of the people's "purposeful direction." The difference between purpose and ideology is analogous to the difference between people and nation.

The setting is a Tuscan town called San Martino in August 1944, in that liminal moment when the German occupation and fascist authority are both disintegrating with convulsive violence and the Americans are overdue to arrive. The town has been targeted for destruction by the Germans in retaliation for the killing of a German. The bishop has negotiated (collaborated?) with the Germans for the safe harbor of the remaining townspeople in the cathedral. As they prepare to abandon their homes and enter the church, one citizen declares that he has "thought through" the situation and has decided to leave the village for the dangerous blackshirt-infested countryside to "find the Americans."

The "Hostias" is heard at the moments of the story's most absolute moments of violence and renewal. It is heard first as the camera scans the abandoned piazza and the facade of the harboring cathedral. The lyrical calm—with its visual as well as auditory sacred referents—is shattered by the explosion from within the cathedral that kills or maims those collected inside in a horrific acting out of German treachery and Italian cuckolding. It is heard for the second time as the surviving townspeople in the woods decide to take on self-chosen pseudonyms as an act of both strategic disguise (they are joining the partisans and need codenames) and symbolic rebirth. The young man who

---

[36] See Rosen, *Verdi: Requiem*, pp. 45, 47.

had sung the "Hostias" in the cathedral—as we now see and hear in a flashback (possibly the same soundtrack that provided the first rendition above)—chooses for himself the name "Requiem." This stunning moment exemplifies, I would argue, the moment of renewal and subjectivization of voice—the voice of the people—in a way that resists interpellation.

The ritual act of self-naming is certainly not undertaken in the name of the nation or indeed of religion. It proceeds in the name of the act of naming and offering. In the requiem liturgy, the "Hostias" is a part of the Offertory, a ritual context consistent with the act of naming. The naming of the self—the moment of subjectivization—is also an offering of the self. In this model of subjectivity, the offering of the self to another—a lover or a political cause—is posited as necessary for the retention of the self.

Dvořák, 1890

In a well-known pair of anecdotes, the conductor Hans von Bülow attacked Verdi's Requiem in the *Allgemeine Musikalische Zeitung* as "an opera in church costume [eine Oper im Kirchengewande]." To which Brahms countered: "Bülow has made an almighty fool of himself. Only a genius could have written such a work."[37] Now, in the Brahms-Wagner divide, as in the Mendelssohn-Meyerbeer divide discussed in chapter 3, genius signified authenticity and interiority and opposed itself to theatricality and costuming of all kinds. So Bülow's remark was, for Brahms, culturally and ideologically correct but monumentally misplaced.

The authenticity and power of the Verdi Requiem, as Brahms heard them, derived from its combination of monumentality and antitheatricality, with theatricality—as argued in chapter 1—signifying a representation in the name of some higher authority. Antonín Dvořák, Brahms's friend and admirer, had the same reaction. When he wrote his own Requiem in 1890, it was Verdi's he sought to match.

At the same time, the fact that Dvořák wrote this massive work for Birmingham, where it was premiered in October 1891, brought him squarely into the Mendelssohnian tradition of that city's musical and choral history. (Dvořák had been introduced to Mendelssohn's music at the age of seventeen in 1858, when he began studies with Josef Krejci in Prague.) The Protestant inflections of both Birmingham and Mendelssohn may be related to the invocations of Bach, specifically of the Kyrie of the B-minor Mass, that travel through the work. The Protestant rhetorical inflections of Dvořák's Requiem mark its difference from the *Stabat Mater* of a decade before, in which the iconographic depiction of the mourning mother relates to a Catholic aesthetic

---

[37] See Julian Budden, *Verdi* (London: J. M. Dent, 1985), p. 115.

of visuality. The stylistic passage from the *Stabat Mater* (1880) to the *Requiem* (1890) suggests a shift from a music of mimetic sensuality (vis-à-vis the narrative of the lamenting mother and its visual icons) to a narratological music capable of relating to the past in terms of internalized memory. Here again we have two models of history that correspond to the Catholic-Protestant divide in European culture: the past as materially present in ritual versus the past as commemorated through ritual.[38]

Confessionally as well as nationally, Dvořák's Requiem is the most complicated, and indeed the most cosmopolitan, of the three works under discussion in this chapter. Dvořák was not often received as a cosmopolitan, however. When he brought his Requiem to London in 1898, he might have preferred a reception from Bülow instead of the one he got from John Runciman, music critic for the *Saturday Review*:

> And then, as if not content with nearly ruining his reputation by that deadly blow, he must needs follow up "Saint Ludmila" with the dreariest, dullest, most poverty-stricken Requiem ever written by a musician with any gift of genuine invention. These mistakes might indicate mere want of tact did not the qualities of Dvořák's music show them to be the result of sheer want of intellect; and if the defects of his music are held by some to be intentional beauties, no such claim can be set up for the opinions on music which he has on various occasions confided to the ubiquitous interviewer. The Slav is an interesting creature, and his music is interesting, not because he is higher than the Western man, but because he is different, and, if anything, lower, with a considerable touch of the savage.[39]

Dvořák the Slav, Dvořák the primitive: whether as a curse, as above, or as a blessing, as in his American reception in the same decade of the 1890s, these twin stereotypes are constantly at his back. The same problem affects the assumption that the composer was throughout his life a "simple, devout Catholic": even if accurate with regard to his personal faith—a hard call to make, in any case—such a judgment of simplicity is not credible as a gloss on the music.[40]

Dvořák's identification with Verdi is articulated in a shared musical irredentism. German music, specifically the Viennese Parnassus, is the authority

---

[38] The Reformation era disputes over the ritual of Holy Communion form the locus classicus for these divergent senses and practices of history. The Catholic doctrine of transubstantiation holds that the wafer and wine are literally, magically transformed into the body and blood of Christ. The evolution of Protestant thought and ritual practice from Luther to Zwingli arrives at a doctrine of commemoration, in which no physical transformation takes place but where body and blood are symbolically invoked and commemorated by wafer and wine.

[39] John F. Runciman, "Anton Dvořák," in *Old Scores and New Readings: Discussions on Musical Subjects* (London, 1899), p. 253.

[40] See John Clapham, "Dvořák, Antonín," *New Grove Dictionary of Music and Musicians*, ed. Stanley Sadie (New York, 1980) 5:777.

against which a new popular voice is to be raised. Verdi is a much more compelling model than Brahms for this purpose, despite the friendship and mutual
respect that existed between Brahms and Dvořák. Indeed, the friendship was
part of the problem. As guardian of the Viennese Parnassus Brahms claimed
considerable authority, and Dvořák's deep esteem for him took the case of
courtly obsequiousness, matched in the musical world perhaps only by Bruckner's toward Wagner.[41]

The most obvious point of similarity between the Dvořák Requiem and the
Verdi is in fact too obvious: the use of the liturgical form and the Latin text.
The Latin signifies differently here. For Verdi, the Latin text is the official
language of sacred commemoration. Verdi's setting of the Latin liturgy allows
him to appropriate sacred words from their clerical contexts; the very use of
the text contributes to the work's anticlericalism. For Dvořák, the Latin is
also an irredentist gesture in its autonomy from two sites of Catholic power:
the ecclesiastical power of Rome and the imperial power of Vienna. Of the
two referents, the latter is politically more urgent. At the same time, the Latin
text prevents the double resistance to the hegemonies of Rome and Vienna
to redound into a gesture of nationalism—Bohemian, Czech, or other.

How and what does the national signify for Dvořák? Michael Beckerman
has convincingly suggested that the nationality question for Dvořák is tied
both to Bohemia and to America. In order to explore "the way Dvořák constructed himself as a national composer," Beckerman writes, one must trace
his travels in America in the 1890s.[42] It follows that Dvořák's self-construction
as a national composer relates closely to his popular designation as one, and
that perhaps more so in the United States than in central Europe. Dvořák was
brought to the United States in September 1892 by Jeanette Thurber, director
of the National Conservatory, in order to create an authentic American music.
Several ingredients contributed to this bizarre recipe: Dvořák's fundamental
status as a composer, second at the time only to that of Brahms; the suitability
of his style and temperament for integration into his classical idiom of American popular traditions, in particular Native and African American themes.
As is well known, Thurber gave the composer a copy of Longfellow's The Song
of Hiawatha, hoping he would find an operatic subject in it; it turned out that
he had known the work for decades, as its Czech translator was a close friend.
Dvořák played the nativist card, it seems, in his most cosmopolitan and indeed
most multicultural moments. "There is such a thing as nationality in music
in the sense that it *may take on* [emphasis mine] the character of its locality,"
he wrote to the editor of the *New York Herald* on 28 May 1893. Commenting
on his own Czech style, he observed: "I myself have gone to the simple, half-

[41] See David Beveridge, "Dvořák and Brahms: A Chronicle, An Interpretation," in *Dvořák and
His World*, ed. Michael Beckerman (Princeton: Princeton University Press, 1993), pp. 56–91.

[42] See Michael Beckerman, "The Master's Little Joke: Antonín Dvořák and the Mask of Nation," in Beckerman, *Dvořák and His World*, p. 135 and 134–54.

forgotten tunes of the Bohemian peasants for hints in my most serious work." Before hailing this alleged confession of primitive authenticity, Beckerman cautions, "there is no evidence that he was in any way part of a folk culture, nor did he even know a great deal about Czech folk music."[43] The nativist authenticities of Dvořák are thoroughly composed. The drive to make Dvořák "simple"—whether motivated by Runciman's hostility or Thurber's sympathy—reduces him to the status of a cultural commodity. The quality and intricacy of the music resists such a move.

The American "locality" of Dvořák's music involves multiple contexts. Curiously, the most underexplored cultural context is that of American religious culture and difference, specifically the differences between the urban (New York) and the rural (Iowa), the Protestant and the Catholic. The same model would suggest that the city and culture (religious and musical) of Birmingham informed both the text and contexts of the Requiem, premiered there in 1890. Birmingham's civic and choral tradition produced together the Birmingham Festival, which originated in the 1750s and 1760s under the auspices of Saint Martin's Church and the General Hospital. Handel's oratorios provided the musical fulcrum until Mendelssohn displaced him, conducting his oratorio *Paulus* there in 1837 and the premiere of *Elijah* in 1846. Fulfilling his own commission in 1890, Dvořák engaged a host culture with a decidedly Protestant aesthetic.[44]

Such multiple contexts would suggest that the Czech nation, whatever that might suggest, does not speak in Dvořák's Requiem. What does speak, however, is an authentic, musically conceived popular collectivity, in which a complicated, fluid subjectivity comes freely into being. The popular and the personal are reconciled through the work's consistent combination of militancy and introversion. In this practice the Requiems of both Brahms and Verdi find echoes. As does Verdi, Dvořák combines the opening Kyrie with the initial *Requiem aeternam*, and he gives the opening solo line to the tenor. But where Verdi moves outward to a massive proclamation, Dvořák continually returns to the private and the solitary. At times he seems, perhaps coyly, to be choosing the opposite effect. Wherin, for example, Verdi uses a full orchestral blast to announce the *Dies irae*, Dvořák uses the cellos. Most explicitly, he follows the opening *Requiem aeternam* with a Graduale, a soprano solo to the following text:

---

[43] Ibid., p. 141. Judit Frigyesi has made a similar argument about Béla Bartók. See Judit Frigyesi, *Béla Bartók and Turn-of-the-Century Budapest* (Berkeley and Los Angeles: University of California Press, 1998).

[44] Birmingham also signifies as a venue for English Catholicism. John Cardinal Newman lived there for the last thirty years of his life. Ten years after the premiere of Dvořák's Requiem, in October 1900, Edward Elgar's *Dream of Gerontius* premiered at the Birmingham Festival. Elgar became closely associated with the city, writing two oratorios for subsequent festivals and accepting an appointment as the first professor of music at the university in 1905.

In memoria aeterna erit justus,
ab auditione mala, non timebit.

The just man will live in eternal memory,
He will not fear the evil spoken of him.

As with Brahms, a lyrical, feminine voice offers consolation, but consolation in the form of justice rather than comfort. This is, moreover, the justice of private, personal vindication. It seems to advocate an ethic of personal dignity that provides, in a Kantian manner, its own reward: the consolation of Florestan in the dungeon. A similar rhetoric of contradiction seems to inform the Sanctus, which answers Verdi's choral seeting with a solo opening for the baritone. There is no *Libera me*.

Now, in harmony with this private, solitary discourse, there is also a discourse of proclamation, which I would rather call a musical discourse of interpellation. This is an ideal instance of interpellation, where the subjectivization demanded by external power, in this case, faith, is identical to the subjectivization produced by inner desire. At this juncture, the subject is told to be precisely what he or she wants to be. This most overpowering moment in the Requiem occurs at the end of the *Tuba mirum*, and is accompanied by church bells. At the same time, however, it marks the recapitulation of the movement's opening melody (sung by the contralto and chorus) and then repeated by low winds to the choral repetition of the phrase "Mors stupebit." The movement proceeds, then, at two levels of musical and textual narrative. On the surface level, the mortified solitary believer is swept up on the day of judgment. As a narrative of interpellation, the solitary voice is integrated into a subjectivizing totality. It is, I would argue, at this level of desire that the modern listener is moved by this most insistent moment of the Requiem. That Dvořák himself heard both of these narratives is suggested by the movement's conclusion: the full blast with church bells is succeeded by a short coda that seems both to reinforce and to undermine the preceding massive statement. Textually, it repeats; rhetorically, it questions the closure and therefore the authority claimed by the massive finale. Dvořák returns here to a music of introversion, as if to suggest that modern forms of solidarity are not to be given into fully.

Compare Dvořák's *Stabat Mater* (composed 1876–77) with the fifth movement, "Ihr habt nun Traurigkeit," of Brahms's *German Requiem* (1868–69), which has the quality of a virtual or displaced *Stabat Mater*. Their chronology notwithstanding, the Brahms movement can be construed as a modern commentary on Dvořák's neotraditional setting. In Dvořák's exquisite work, a satisfying, consoling music accompanies the depiction, via the traditional Jacapone da Todi text, of the lamenting Virgin Mother. The mother laments; the music consoles. In Brahms's movement, that gap is rhetorically recognized. In other words, the combination of music and words explicitly posits the desire for the consolation provided by the absent mother. The music's subject position is one of self-aware loss and mourning, or more accurately the work of mourning that results in the repair of the self. The return of the lost past is not conjured as a fantasmatic presence, but rather remembered with that measure of distance that in turn provides the space and foundation required for the possibility of a future.

According to this dynamic of memory—that agency of distance between present and past through which the future is grounded—the Requiems of Brahms, Verdi, and Dvořák engage the past and its loss as a foundation for a viable future. Hence the simultaneity of memory and forwardminded rededication. Dedication in the name of what or whom? In the name only of that self-referential popular collectivity materially embodied in choral singing, whose ethical and aesthetic coherence is contingent precisely on its indeterminacy.

I would like to end this chapter with some brief observations on a contemporary political moment defined by the performative "envoicing" of the people. The moment involves the popular movement that led in large measure to the collapse of the German Democratic Republic in the fall of 1989. The weeks prior to "the fall of the wall" in early November were punctuated by massive demonstrations in East German cities, most notably in Leipzig. During several of these demonstrations, the crowds began to chant "Wir sind das Volk [We are the People]." As a political gesture, the chant demanded that the regime recognize the gap between the voice of the people as authentically, subjectively expressed and the alleged "voice" of "the people" in whose name the regime had putatively operated. The chant's demand was a double one: to be heard as an authentic collective voice and to be recognized not only as citizens with rights but as a collective unit.

Eric Santner has recently analyzed this political moment, with reference to the work of Jacques Rancière.[45] Both observe that the demonstrators' demand not to be absorbed into the political will of the state was in fact followed by another, newer dynamic of reabsorption, as the chant "Wir sind das Volk" mutated into "Wir sind ein Volk [We are One People]." This is a change from a negative utterance to a positive one, from the marking of authentic envoicing as a refusal to be absorbed into an ideological system of power (the "state apparatus" of the German Democratic Republic) to a demand for inclusion (into a unified Germany governed by the state of the Federal Republic). In this change, the performed demand for the envoicing of the actual persons participating in the chant loses its momentum. The chanters' voices merge

---

[45] See Eric L. Santner, *On the Psychotheology of Everyday Life: Reflections on Freud and Rosenzweig* (Chicago: University of Chicago Press, 2001), pp. 126–27, and Jacques Rancière, *Disagreement: Politics and Philosophy*, trans. Julie Rose (Minneapolis: University of Minnesota Press, 1999), p. 123.

into the symbolic voice of the nation. At this point, as Santner suggests, "politics became reabsorbed into the police order, the arithmetic labor of apportioning parts and roles according to the perceived necessities of the global market system."[46]

How then to characterize that brief moment of subjectivity—the demand for subjectivity—that resides in the chant? The argument of this chapter as applied to the example from 1989 would assert that the act of envoicing, of subjectification, involved here is defined by the act of chanting itself and limited to the gesture of the chant. Only in and as chant does the statement "We are the people" make sense as a performative without an inherent contradiction. When those actual voices become symbolized in the service of something else—the nation, global capitalism—they lose the authenticity at once demanded and performed by their combined voices.

---

[46] The German nation-state since the unification of 1870 has produced an ambivalent relationship with the rhetoric of the people. Thus, the state claims to serve "the people," but the latter category is interpellated to signify a unified mass that in fact depends on the state for an articulation of that unity. A prime site for the performance of that unity is the inscription "Dem Deutschen Volke [To the German People]" on the pediment of the Reichstag (Parliament) in Berlin. The inscription was placed there in 1916 and has remained there through all subsequent regimes. The current, post-reunification parliament (the Bundestag) moved back into the building in 1999, when the federal government relocated to Berlin from Bonn. In a gesture interrogating the inscription, Hans Haacke produced an installation for one of the building's courtyards, consisting of the inscription "Der Bevölkerung [To the Population]." His chosen term questions the validity of the term "Volk" and its exclusionary implications, both in the Nazi period and in the current politics of German citizenship. For an account of the installation, see Hans Haacke, "Der Bevölkerung," in the *Oxford Art Journal* 24:2 (2001): 127–43. On its reception, see Roger Cohen, "Berlin Journal," *New York Times*, 31 March 2000, and my letter to the editor in the same newspaper, 4 April 2000, p. A22.

Chapter Six

MINOR MODERNISMS

> I sat at night in violent pain on a bench. Opposite me
> on another two girls sat down. They seemed to want to
> discuss something in confidence and began to whisper.
> Nobody except me was nearby and I should not have un-
> derstood their Italian however loud it had been. But now
> I could not resist the feeling, in face of this unmotivated
> whispering in a language inaccessible to me, that a cool
> dressing was being applied to the painful place.[1]

Music Trauma, or, Is There Life after Wagner?

In the introduction I suggested that the mutuality of form and ideology in Wagner produced a crisis of musical integrity. For Wagner, musical purity equals cultural purity. Music drama becomes the guarantor of the German absolute, of that style of German national assertion at once triumphalist and anxious in the years around 1870. Through the subtlety of his aesthetic and psychological inventions, Wagner may himself undermine the strength and consistency of his own doctrinal claims. The claims, however, remain intact. Moreover, they remain intact simultaneously as aesthetic and political claims. For this reason it strikes me as counterhistorical to separate Wagner's aesthetic and political tenets and practices.[2]

In this chapter, I will chart efforts to recover operatic integrity after Wagner. These efforts, and my analysis of them, both respect and adhere to the

[1] Walter Benjamin, "One-Way Street," in *"One-Way Street" and Other Writings*, trans. Edmund Jephcott and Kingsley Shorter (London: Verso, 1979), pp. 94–95.

[2] This position reflects my disagreement with Lydia Goehr's treatment of Wagner in her interesting study *The Quest for Voice: Music, Politics, and the Limits of Philosophy* (Berkeley and Los Angeles: University of California Press, 1998). For example, in a passage that represents her general position well, Goehr suggests that Wagner "went profoundly wrong whenever he filled in the ideal of the purely human with, say, substantively anti-Jewish content. But . . . the same formal view could also have been filled in differently" (p. 130). I would argue that the assertion of purity—whether posited by Wagner or by his interpreters in his name or in his defense—places into jeopardy any specific representation through which it is "filled in." In other words, the fact that Wagner's separation of the human and the Jewish was conflicted and often contradictory, as I argued in the preceding chapter, does not mitigate the basic violence of the separation.

Wagnerian principle of the primacy of music in opera. So my focus is indeed the problem of musical integrity, though I want to make it clear that I will be restricting discussion to opera and therefore not deal, in this chapter, with the more obvious, non-operatic succession to Wagner in, say, Brahms, Mahler, and Schoenberg. (I will address a similar recovery from within the symphonic or so-called absolute tradition in the final chapter.) The agenda under analysis here includes at once the survival and overcoming of Wagnerism on its own aesthetic terms: in the theater, in a location that is not only a key public arena in its own right but that has become in a literal way the theater of the nation. This recovery is simultaneous, I will argue, with the recovery of subjectivity, specifically a mode of subjectivity that resists the magnetism of identity and its ideologies.

As we have seen, Wagnerism relies on a deft reconciliation of apparent opposites: the ideology of absolute music on the one hand and the intensification of music's claim to signify on the other. In the music dramas, musical symbols achieve articulation as musical signs. I rely here on Carl Jung's distinction between a sign as "an analogous or abbreviated expression of a known thing" and a symbol as the expression of an unknown fact.[3] Post-Wagnerian musical subjectivity reverses the slippage from symbol to sign, engaging symbolism to distance itself from an idiom of signs, a repertory of signifiers. Signs produce, allegedly, identities. Codification, analogously, produces ideologies. Music (the sign) identifies, and thus asserts its identity with the nation. In Wagner's aesthetic, the optimal music, and its optimal carriers—genres (the symphony, music drama) and voice types (the *Heldentenor*)—identify national ideal types.[4] Post-Wagnerian musical symbolism, like the literary symbolism to which it relates closely and occasionally—as in the Debussy/Maeterlinck partnership, explicitly—practices a disarticulation of the musical sign.

In what voices, bodies, and languages does such political recovery and epistemological disarticulation take place? The modes and tropes of recovery involve an alliance of voice and symbol, of femininity and non-Germanness. Avoiding the trap of repetition by other means—opera replacing music drama, Czech nationalism replacing German nationalism—the challenge is to restore music as a discourse of subjectivity rather than as one of identity. Music *from* rather than *of*: music from the nation rather than of the nation. Like the Requiems engaged in the previous chapter, the operas discussed in this one develop as national operas in the sense that they accrue with specific referential coordinates in culture. They are local. But the fact that they are local does

---

[3] Carl Jung, *Psychological Types* (London: Routledge & Kegan Paul, 1949), cited by Victor Turner, *The Forest of Symbols: Aspects of Ndembu Ritual* (Ithaca: Cornell University Press, 1967), p. 26.

[4] For an analysis of the ideology of voice types and timbres in Wagner, see Marc A. Weiner, *Richard Wagner and the Anti-Semitic Imagination* (Lincoln: University of Nebraska Press, 1995).

not imply that they are isolated or, indeed, secondary. Through locality, the cosmopolitan is engaged. Accordingly, subjectivity is marked as fundamentally subversive when it claims the center from the vantage point of the periphery.

The claims of subjectivity are nationally and regionally inflected insofar as they are linguistically constituted. They move away from the center, from central Europe—that is, from *Mitteleuropa* and the term's nationalistic, Germanicizing inflection—to the east, west, and south. They buttress Nietzsche's claim that the recovery from Wagnerism requires the life and lightness of the south, which for him included both Bizet and Mozart. Indeed, we might ask whether post-Wagnerian recovery is not interpellated as a kind of neo-Mozarteanism, achieving distance from Wagner as Mozart did from opera seria. Counterintuitively, Wagnerian music drama as a modern opera seria is a proposition worth thinking about.

The claims of subjectivity are also gendered. "Assume," Nietzsche proposes at the opening of *Beyond Good and Evil*, "that truth is a woman. What then?" Nietzsche's taunt echoes Wagner's prior doctrine: "Music," Wagner had written in the essay "Opera and Drama" in 1850, "is a woman." Nietzsche subcutaneously implies here that once Wagner's music had declared itself a man—once it had been absorbed into the totalizing ideology of music drama—it had begun to lie.

Assume, now, that opera is a woman. What then? What does such a framing do to and for opera? What does it do to the category of "music drama"? Is music drama a man? Music drama, as we know, speaks German. Does opera, opera-as-woman, speak German? Does she want to speak German? When she must speak German, can she still sing in Italian? Or must she also speak Italian, or French, or Czech, or Hungarian? And what of the opposite scenario: what happens when Opera declines to speak German? What happens, after 1870, when she retains her right to speak Italian or French, and insists on her right to speak Czech and Hungarian? The ascendancy of German opera to 1870 produces a different result from the ascendancy of Italian opera a century earlier; its nationalist agenda produces resistance more than compliance. The trope of cultural resistance to German hegemony revives the operatic trope of heroic femininity.

The archive—acoustic and affective—of operatic heroic femininity is Italian. This is a deliberate and adopted Italianness, not a natural or circumstantial one. The association of the fiction of pure voice with Italy and femininity is a cultural artifact, not a natural fact. The operatic, Italian Handel is the rule here, not the exception. Thus, if the *New Groves Dictionary* describes Handel as an English composer of German birth, he is just as much an Italian composer. Similarly, Rousseau's desire to rescue melody from harmony as the priority of musical form coincided with his judgment that Italian was more musical than French. Rousseau was invoking a discursive tradition rather than a natural resource. Otherwise, he would have been contradicting another position, namely that a language feels authentic and indeed therapeutic to its own speakers: "One is affected only by accents that are familiar. . . . Bernier's cantatas are said to have cured a French musician of the fever; they would have given one to a musician of any other nation."[5] In Rousseau's parable, the national becomes synonymous with the local.

From Handel to Rousseau to the heyday of the bel canto tradition to Wagner's rejection of it (with the telling exception of Bellini), Italian vocal style is associated with the reference to pure voice. The singing voice is culture's reference to nature. Pure voice is a fictional projection that resides prior to culture, signification, and ideology. The art of the singing voice supplies the irony that both confirms and denies the material existence of pure voice. The singing voice is a product of art and therefore a province of culture, as are of course the words into which vocal sound is poured.

The mythic association of the voice of nature with the female voice (Odysseus's sirens, or the nymph Echo, for example) belongs to the association, long dismantled by feminist theory, of femininity with nature and masculinity with culture. The feminine in Italian opera is a complicated trope; it does not necessarily refer to woman or to women. The most common operatic ending involves the death of a woman but the triumph of the feminine. Opera can indeed, therefore, inscribe the undoing of women, in Catherine Clément's phrase, and at the same time rejoice in the victory of a transcendent femininity.[6]

Pure voice can neither speak nor sound. This understanding provides the historical grounding for operatic aesthetics. Opera develops by and into the understanding that pure voice is an externality to both vocal production and cognitive understanding. Pure voice is the angel's cry, in Michel Poizat's Lacanian formulation. As a phenomenological impossibility, pure voice is opera's foundational fiction. The operatic sublime results from the recognition of these boundaries, in those sequences abundant in Handel and Mozart where pure voice is engaged but not appropriated, where the convention articulates that pure voice is beyond singing just as pure feeling is beyond human experience.

In a typical irony, Wagner the enslaver of voice produces the character—Hans Sachs—who best expresses its ungraspability:

Ich fühl's und kann's nicht verstehen,—
kann's nicht behalten,—doch auch nicht vergessen:
und fass ich es ganz, kann ich's nicht messen!—

---

[5] J. J. Rousseau, *Essay on the Origin of Languages*, in V. Gourevitch, *Rousseau: The Discourses and Other Early Political Writings* (Cambridge: Cambridge University Press, 1997), pp. xv, 3. Cited by Goehr, *The Quest for Voice*, p. 105.

[6] Carolyn Abbate opens her book *Unsung Voices* with this duality of operatic femininity, in which, in her words, "this undefeated voice speaks across the crushing plot." See *Unsung Voices*, p. ix. See also Catherine Clément, *Opera, or the Undoing of Women*, trans. B. Wing (Minneapolis: University of Minnesota Press, 1988).

I feel it and can't understand it,—
can't grasp it, yet cannot forget it:
the more I try to hold on, the more I can't fathom it.

Wagner's didactic voice approximates less the Hans Sachs of the two soliloquies than the demagogue of his final oration. By the end of Sachs's operatic life he is himself swallowed by Wagner to become, through Wagner's voice, the agent of national ideology. The Faustian nineteenth century claims to colonize nature in the names of nation, capital, and modes of social reproduction. In the conundrums of later nineteenth-century nationalism and gender ideologies, pure voice becomes steadily impurer as its colonization is claimed. Now as before the trope of pure voice is feminine, but as an object of appropriation rather than an energy of ungraspability.

Assisted by his agent, music drama, Wagner traumatizes voice—first by marking its femininity, then by silencing it. In his final revision of the conclusion to the *Ring of the Nibelung*, Brünnhilde's voice is not allowed rhetorically to conclude the story her actions bring to an end. In silencing voice and femininity, music drama silences music. Music drama becomes music trauma. In act 2 of *Götterdämmerung*, Brünnhilde had briefly become an Italian opera heroine when she arrested the aesthetic of the opera in which she is a character. This means that she undermines the aesthetic of music drama, which is performatively and constatively German, antioperatic, and masculinist. Wagner's antioperaticism—his explicit anti-Italianism—is coincidental with his antifeminism. No wonder he decided finally to refuse to give the final say to his redemptive heroine Brünnhilde at the end of her operatic life. In death, she is again punished by the confiscation of her voice. Brünnhilde sings, but the orchestra plays, absorbing her voice as the fire and water absorb her body. Music drama in its full ideological pomp claims the summational voice.

Brünnhilde is precisely that kind of Italian operatic heroine who gets lost in this debate. Hers is the voice of heroic femininity. Operatic heroic femininity is an Italian trope, which in its own era of nationalism, irredentism, and unification offers the late nineteenth century a counter-German operatic voice: that of heroic femininity. To the decay of the North, symbolized by the Hall of the Gibichungs, she brings the geocultural mark of the East and the South. The mark of the East is her act of suttee, the Orientalist conceit of *Götterdämmerung* that has been rightly mocked from Nietzsche onward. But the mark of the South is her Italianate voice, which begins to flow from her diaphragm as soon as her armor has been cut. Pace Anna Russell, the problem is not that "love has taken all the ginger out of her," but rather that a twenty-year sleep has transformed her expressive style from a German one to an Italian one. In the second act of *Götterdämmerung*, Brünnhilde voices a plausible emulation of Norma; in her invectives against Siegfried she echoes quite credibly Norma's complaints against Pollione. The two couples are reunited, finally, in similar immolations except that Brünnhilde and her composer are clever enough to place her "Casta Diva" at the end of the opera.

Two planes of feminist enterprise are in play. First, the Italianate operatic heroine reenchants and restores moral and political codes rendered routine and stale by dominant masculinity, usually (not necessarily) associated with men. This work starts early in the century and motivates a good deal of opera buffa. This is, so to speak, Rosina's job. It's a long way from Rosina's 1816 restoration-comedy confidence in "Una voce poco fa" to Norma's 1831 post-revolutionary warning against "sediziose voci." The first advocates role playing; the second, the necessity to transcend conventional modes of representation and performativity altogether.

But after the mid-century mark, the operatic heroic feminine asserts a subversive responsibility, if not an achieved social and political power. This subversion attempts to restore the subjectivity both enabled and disabled by bourgeois ideology. Assume, then, that the second act of *Götterdämmerung* is the greatest Italian opera scene of the 1870s, and that it is defeated by music drama, the ideological form adequate to the German Empire.

Recall *Parsifal*: Kundry, before she is "allowed" to die, loses her voice literally and entirely. *Parsifal* as an ideology makes clear that communal regeneration requires the silencing of woman. Bayreuth, legislated as the only site capable of realizing *Parsifal* and its rituals of theatrical, communal, and national consecration, is par excellence the theater of 1870, of German unification and the moment of transition in the political and cultural meaning of European nationalism. In Germany, it is the moment of the transition from what can be called expressive nationalism to what can be called oppressive nationalism. Bayreuth brought the baroque ideology of the *teatrum mundi*—the theater of the world—into Protestant modernity, as a gift to the *Gründerzeit*.

Bayreuth assumed its role as the summer headquarters of this new coalition of Protestant-Catholic teatrum mundi. Bayreuth in the summer and the party of Wagner in Vienna in the winter: these are the upholders of what we can call music trauma. Wagnerian music trauma involves the reimposition of mimesis as an aesthetic ideology, with the corollary that aesthetic ideology have political power. This formulation includes the varieties of nationalism, racism, and misogyny inherent in Wagnerism. It speaks through the commands of identity formation that say "Be THIS, be THIS way, be LIKE THIS." And the referent is an image: a certain kind of body, demeanor, style—the national sign of an alleged national essence.

Music trauma has been hard to recover from. Even its most rigorous analysts have fallen under its spell. Nietzsche was the first. In his later work, his freedom from Wagner's hold grew as he admitted his continuing attraction. In a recent example, Philippe Lacoue-Labarthe has traced Wagnerism (through its transmission in Baudelaire, Mallarmé, Heidegger, and Adorno) in his book *Musica Ficta: Figures of Wagner*. Like his protagonists, Lacoue-Labarthe himself assumes the validity of a degree of mimesis that itself feeds the very trauma that shocks nineteenth-century subjectivity and music alike. Mimetic logic appears twice in his title. As he explains, "The Latin *fingere*, to which *musica ficta* refers, is the equivalent of the Greek *plassein/plattein*: to fashion, to model, to sculpt—thus, to figure."[7]

"It was Wagner," he writes, "in the last century, who seized this promise of opera with both the greatest lucidity and instinctive force." This is the mimetic promise. If, I would argue, this was the promise of opera—and this assertion is debatable—then it was decidedly not the promise of music. Nineteenth-century music emancipates itself precisely from mimesis. Wagner is the restorer of mimetic ideology to music, the inventor of a new musical language of pictures. Lacoue-Labarthe correctly observes that Baudelaire saw [*saw*] in Wagner a music of revelation ("I imagine a vast extent of red spreading before my eyes," he wrote to the composer); but then he takes the additional, fateful step of accepting the attachment of revelation to music: "what is happening here is that, for someone who had constructed his whole aesthetic on painting and poetry . . . this is the revelation of music itself."[8] Quickly, Lacoue-Labarthe accepts the Wagnerian understanding of mimetic logic, and the theater as the organ of mimesis, as the sole mode through which subjective and objective worlds can interact. It is Wagner himself whom Lacoue-Labarthe follows in conjoining music with figuration: "Musica Ficta."

If post-Wagnerian opera is posttraumatic opera, it must be understood according to the regeneration of voice. Subjectivity, in opera, coincides with voice. It exists, here as elsewhere, beyond the subject. It is therefore also beyond identity positions, including gendered and national positions. Giving voice means giving movement, elasticity, and resonance to its subject, granting it subjectivity. Thus, nation and gender are fused tropes in the operatic world: the posttraumatic regeneration of voice, post-Wagner, equals the regeneration of non-Germanness and a certain kind of subversive femininity.

I will proceed with three short allegorical readings from French, Hungarian, and Czech opera: Debussy's *Pelléas et Mélisande*, Bartók's *Bluebeard's Castle*, and Janáček's *Makropoulos Case*. I will close with a brief return to German-language Austrian opera in the examples of Schoenberg's *Moses and Aaron* and Berg's *Lulu*. (I should distinguish these last examples more carefully. Schoenberg and Berg were both born in Austria. In converting to Protestantism in 1898 and moving to Berlin in 1911, Schoenberg rejected an Austrian cultural and musical aesthetic. Using his own dichotomy of "style and idea," we can place Austria as the upholder of style and [northern] Germany as the upholder of idea. *Moses und Aron* postdates and reflects his reconversion to

---

[7] Philippe Lacoue-Labarthe, *Musica Ficta: Figures of Wagner*, trans. F. McCarren (Stanford: Stanford University Press, 1994), p. xvii.

[8] Ibid., pp. xix, 4–5.

Judaism in 1933, but it reflects as well his continuing rejection of the Austrian aesthetic.)

I want to be militant in refusing the assumption that these examples, works, or composers "represent" French, Hungarian, Czech, or Austrian (Austro-German, German) opera. I want to argue for a reconfiguration of *voice*, constituted (with the exception of *Moses und Aron*) in terms of a subversive femininity, which constitutes what I am calling posttraumatic opera. The prefix "post" always indicates, it seems to me, the dynamic of repetition with difference, in other words the friction between retention and transcendence. Thus, it would seem counterproductive of these works to reinstate Wagnerism with a mirror-Wagnerism—to reinstate nationalist opera in other languages, to replace the operatic hegemony of Bayreuth and Vienna with that of Paris or Prague. I don't believe that these works want to constitute national operatic voices. I believe they want to reconstitute subjectivity from within the trauma of mimetic identity, including nationalism and the other oppressive discourses of the late nineteenth century. In other words, they want to be Italian operas, insofar as Italian opera defines for the long nineteenth century the ability to refer to—never to become or imitate—pure voice. Since there can never be an embodiment of pure voice, it can only be a fiction: not produced by a body, and outside the symbolic order. It is the key fiction of Italian opera, the key to the trope of subversive femininity at the core of Italian opera. After Wagner, opera wants to be Italian, especially if it has to speak French, Hungarian, or Czech in order to become so.

The post-Wagnerian return to voice, to its sirenic pull to immediacy, is complicated by its enclosure within symbolism, within the thicket that several writers have named the forest of symbols.[9] The European fin de siècle was multiply invested in symbols and in thinking through them, in languages of art and scholarship. Poetics, psychoanalysis, and anthropology were transformed if not founded in the modernist engagement with culture, the latter understood in terms of symbolic systems. Maurice Maeterlinck's *Pelléas et Mélisande* emerges from the center of symbolist poetics. Fin de siècle symbolisms and their disciplinary epistemologies can be understood according to their interest in restoring authenticity to culture and cultural experience through the critique of the dominant historical, teleological concepts of culture. The critique of history, or rather the distinction between culture and history, can produce either (or both) the drive to the obscure, as in much symbolist and modernist poetic and literary practice (Mallarmé, Joyce) or the romance of the primitive. In the development of fin de siècle European anthropology, however, "primitive cultures" are quickly redefined not as cultures attached to or enslaved by nature but rather as cultures with alternative symbolic organiza-

---

[9] For example, Victor Turner, *The Forest of Symbols: Aspects of Ndembu Ritual*, cited above and discussed below.

tions of time and history.[10] The post-Wagnerian modernisms of *Pelléas*, *Blue-beard*, and *Makropoulos* move knowingly through the forest of symbols in the wish to rediscover voice. As the central object of desire, voice becomes a material impossibility for its contradictory constitution as absolutely concrete and absolutely abstract. Voice becomes the symbol of cultural renewal.

Why "minor modernisms"? The adjective contains a claim rather than a qualification. It suggests not that the three works or their composers are in any way secondary in historical or aesthetic importance. Rather, it seeks to engage what may be a core aspect of modernism's legitimacy, which is a critical, indeed subversive energy that redefines and reclaims the center from an allegedly peripheral position. This subversive periphery-to-center move may involve one or many cultural categories, among them region and language; the metropolitan in relation to the provincial, cultural/religious majority and minority relations; and sexual cultures and differences (especially hetero/homosexual difference).

This articulation of the "minor" refers to Gilles Deleuze and Felix Guattari's 1975 study *Kafka: Toward a Minor Literature*. As a German Jewish author writing in Prague, Kafka exemplifies the trope: "A minor literature doesn't come from a minor language; it is rather that which a minority constructs within a major language." Deleuze and Guattari propose three characteristics of minor literature: "the deterritorialization of language, the connection of the individual to a political immediacy, and the collective assemblage of enunciation." The last category refers to the principle that "literature is the people's concern."[11] "Language" here signifies a discrete spoken language: Kafka's German. Kafka's German is closely analogous to Maeterlinck's French and Balázs's Hungarian. (Maeterlinck was born in Ghent to a Flemish-speaking family; Béla Balázs, né Herbert Bauer, came from a German family in Budapest.) Beyond the languages of speech and their political and national constitutions, however, the model clearly allows for categories of language such as music and modernism. The application of the "minor" to music invokes an element of musical grammar—the minor as mode or key—that fits into the general argument precisely not as a pun or a metaphor but as a parallel dimension. Minor modes and keys can thus be heard as the idioms of "minor music," that is, music claiming the central, "major" position from a peripheral, subversive, or (at least apparently) melancholic position. The substitution of music for literature—or perhaps rather the inclusion of music as a category of literature—complies strongly with the completing sentence of Deleuze and Guat-

---

[10] See Elazar Barkan and Ronald Bush, eds., *Prehistories of the Future: The Primitivist Project and the Culture of Modernism* (Stanford: Stanford University Press, 1995).

[11] Gilles Deleuze and Felix Guattari, *Kafka: Toward a Minor Literature*, trans. D. Polan (Minneapolis: University of Minnesota Press, 1986), pp. 16, 18. The principle of literature as the people's concern recalls the discussion of the previous chapter.

tari's definition of the "minor": "We might as well say that minor no longer designates specific literatures but the revolutionary conditions for every literature within the heart of what is called great (or established) literature."

Three Fins de Siècle

The politics of Frenchness dominated the cultural politics of French music at the fin de siècle, as Jane Fulcher has recently demonstrated.[12] French identity was contested over at least two boundaries: an international one, in which the principal antagonist was Germany, and a domestic one, where the crucial divide lodged between the Dreyfusards and the anti-Dreyfusards. The common irritant across these boundaries was anti-Semitism. Moreover, the aesthetic and cultural—national—context of Debussy's music converge in the enduring debates over its relation to Wagner and Wagnerism.

Claude Debussy's engagement with the vexed politics of fin de siècle France remains inchoate. In January 1899 he signed a public petition in favor of reconciliation of the Dreyfusard and anti-Dreyfusard cultural, musical camps. Defenders of Dreyfus were also defenders of the Republic and of the legacy of the Revolution of 1789. Their most vocal champion in the musical world was the composer Alfred Bruneau, composer of operas with libretti by Emile Zola. The anti-Dreyfusards sought a definition of Frenchness that would remain pure of foreign (German and Jewish) influence. The composer Vincent d'Indy was most active here, creatively as well as institutionally. He was the founding director of the Schola Cantorum, chartered to promote both authentic French and sacred music in opposition to the history and cultural place of the National Conservatory (Conservatoire National de Musique), which had been founded in 1792 and had retained its symbolic association with the Revolution and the Republic. Before d'Indy, French musical nationalism, as personified by Camille Saint-Saëns, had valorized "French content," as epitomized by the values of "clarity, formal ingenuity, and grace."[13] D'Indy's ideological and aesthetic legerdemain consisted in his integration of Wagnerism, its discourses of myth, cultural mystification, and redemption, into a French vocabulary. The appropriation's key enabler was anti-Semitism. Debussy had no coherent investment in anti-Semitism but no sense of responsibility in avoiding its rhetorical temptations, either. As a signatory to the petition of 1899, he expressed a desire more for a release from political choices than for a political solution to France's

---

[12] Jane F. Fulcher, *French Cultural Politics and Music: From the Dreyfus Affair to the First World War* (Oxford: Oxford University Press, 1999).

[13] Ibid., p. 23; also pp. 6, 18. (The same values appear in characterizations of one side of the Cartesian tradition in French philosophy, its other side being Catholicism.)

ideological rifts. Debussy's political personality, in its apparently deliberate inconsequentiality, is most akin perhaps to that of Richard Strauss.

For Debussy, *Pelléas*, and its reception, the quality of Frenchness signifies in subtle ways across the spectra of tradition and innovation, left and right, popular and elite. The two "others" to French nationalist self-conception at the fin de siècle were the Germans and the Jews. During the long decade of the Dreyfus Affair (1894–1906), Germans and Jews were conveniently linked in opprobity: the Jewish artillery captain had allegedy divulged secrets to the Germans. The case for Dreyfus was also the case for the Republic; such alliances may have served to keep anti-Semitism in check among cadres of Dreyfusards, a profile that may apply to Debussy. Dreyfus's exoneration in 1906 released anti-Semitism as a more inchoate and indeed more useful ally of nationalism. Despite his marriage to a Jewish woman, Emma Bardac, Debussy in his public and private writing after 1904 indulges in a nationalism that slips into the anti-Semitism of the French right, specifically the *Action Française*. In a letter of 1906 he contrast's Rameau's perfect taste [*gout parfait*] and strict elegance [*élégance stricte*] with the tendencies of *cette mélasse cosmopolite*: this cosmopolitan muck.[14]

The astonishment of *Pelléas et Mélisande* is its resolution, in musical-dramatic terms, of the ideological issues that eluded Debussy in other discursive contexts. The plot of Maeterlinck's play of 1892 is easily absorbed in terms of a simple riff on that of *Tristan und Isolde*. Mélisande is wed to Golaud, but in love with his brother Pelléas. Golaud kills Pelléas; Mélisande dies. But Maeterlinck's symbolist aesthetic moves his work's center away from the plot, as music drama does. Thus, the relationship between Maeterlinck's work and Debussy's remains both essential and inscrutable. The same holds for the general place of Wagner in Debussy's composition and the national distinctions implied by their juxtaposition. Is *Pelléas* a second *Tristan*? A meta-*Tristan*? An anti-*Tristan*? A rewriting of *Tristan* in the less purposive musical idiom of *Parsifal*? Debussy's preoccupation with Wagner is clear. In Lydia Goehr's recent summary of its ramifications: "Throughout the decade-long composition of *Pelléas*, [Debussy] tormented himself over Wagner's legacy. He was as passionately against his influence (tearing up an early version of the score on the grounds that it was already all in Wagner), as he passionately embraced it, '*plus ardent*' and '*plus combatif*' as Maurice Emmanuel remarked. Debussy often distinguished himself from Wagner by speaking of an aesthetic 'purified' of German metaphysics, a purely French return to the simplicity of feelings."[15] *Pelléas* is an anti-*Tristan*,

[14] See ibid., pp. 185–86.

[15] Lydia Goehr, "Beauty and the Beast of Criticism: On Maeterlinck-Debussy's *Pelléas et Mélisande*," revised as "Radical Modernism and the Failure of Style: Philosophical Reflections on Maeterlinck-Debussy's *Pelléas et Mélisande*," *Representations* 74 (spring 2001): 55–82. See also Carolyn Abbate, "*Tristan* in the Composition of *Pelléas*," *Nineteenth-Century Music* 5 (1981): 117–41; R. Holloway, *Debussy and Wagner* (London: Eulenberg Books, 1979).

Goehr argues, insofar as it is an antiopera. Hence its status as a masterpiece has consistently blurred with its status as a failure. What concerns me here is Debussy's articulation of the problem in national terms.

Golaud finds Mélisande in the forest. He says: "Why are you crying? Don't be afraid [Pourquoi pleures-tu? N'ayez pa peur]." The initial question is stated in the second-person familiar; the second phrase makes a sudden transition into formal address. With this linguistic gesture Golaud wrests Mélisande from a context of unsocial nature into that of culture and sociability. This will be the first of many performative/transformative and violent gestures for which Golaud is responsible but at the same time unwitting. Mélisande calls him a giant, offering a precise exemplification of an argument of Rousseau's in the *Essay on the Origin of Languages*: "A savage meeting others will at first have been frightened. His fright will have made him see these men as larger and stronger than himself; he will have called them *Giants*."[16] (The critic Raymond Bouyer, questioning Debussy's originality, called him a more refined version of Wagner, the "German giant.")[17]

Assume an allegorical distribution of the protagonists, whereby Mélisande might be understood as an allegory of music, specifically as an allegory of a clarity of voice: an aesthetic ideal. Goehr suggests a compatible hypothesis, namely, that Mélisande might be understood as pure beauty. Both suggestions, indeed their interchangeability, are supported by Pelléas's association of Mélisande with beauty: "I looked everywhere and I did not find beauty; now I have found you; I have found it! [Je cherchais partout. . . . Et je ne trouvais pas la beauté; Et maintenant je t'ai trouvé; je l'ai trouvée!]" The central political gesture of the opera *Pelléas* is that purity exists only as a projection of an idealized natural state—Mélisande before her discovery by Golaud, before language, music, and culture. This noumenal ideal cannot exist in culture—hence Mélisande's death. In this political rejection of the harmony of purity and culture, *Pelléas* is in a profound way an anti-*Parsifal*. In the same allegorical grid, Golaud might be understood as Mélisande's antipode, as some codified system of culture, language, or, indeed, music. He might therefore be understood in terms of such a dominant musical aesthetic as Wagnerism. He removes her from nature as Alberich removes the Rhinegold; an orchestral citation to that effect sounds at the moment Mélisande's crown is spotted in the water. Golaud identifies himself to Mélisande as the prince of "Allemonde," which divides etymologically into Greek and French syllables signifying "other world" but which to French listeners will also sound like "Allemagne": Germany.

Mélisande knows nothing except her own name. This knowledge marks her difference from Parsifal, also a creature of the forest. By knowing and speaking

---

[16] Rousseau, *Essay on the Origin of Languages*, p. 254. Cavell (see below) makes the same point.

[17] Raymond Bouyer, "Le Debussysme et l'evolution musicale," *Revue musicale* (October 1902), cited by Fulcher, *French Cultural Politics and Music*, pp. 177–78.

her name, Mélisande brackets the topic of her own origins; she has no further interest in them and solicits no information. This gesture of acknowledging a topic in order to foreclose it establishes the opera's pattern of linguistic and communicative exchange. When Golaud insists that Mélisande cannot remain alone in the forest, he in fact marks her essential solitude. His statement "You will be afraid, all alone [Vous aurez peur, toute seule]" imposes the very sentence he wants to prevent. Having established her solitude, he will never, as her husband, lift that performative spell. Mélisande follows Golaud out of the forest, to his castle (from nature into culture) to music reminiscent first of the forest murmurs in *Siegfried* and then, more explicitly, to *Parsifal*'s first-act transformation music. Golaud, locked in gestures of Wagnerian repetition (he will shortly be slightly wounded, giving him an Amfortas-like moment, supported by musical quotations) is contradicted by the opera *Pelléas*, which delivers these gestures and citations as if consciously, working through them, in effect "uncomposing" them.

Golaud marries Mélisande, but then she meets the liberating and erotically fascinating Pelléas. While dallying with Pelléas, Mélisande loses her wedding ring into a well in the castle gardens. (Should this opera be called *Losing the Ring?*) The waters of the grotto are deep. Pelléas calls the grotto the fountain of the blind: "la fontaine des aveugles." Mélisande asks him how to account to Golaud for the loss of the ring, and Pelléas answers with a call for "the truth": "La verité! La verité!" Here again we have an echo of *Tristan* on the question of what "the truth" represents. In both operas, the truth is innocent at the level of circumstantial event. Thus, Tristan and Isolde fell in love through the effects of a love potion and cannot therefore be held responsible for their actions. Similarly, Mélisande lost her wedding ring innocently. But circumstantial innocence belies problematic depths: depths of desire with Isolde, of anomie as well as desire with Mélisande. The truth also represents, more inscrutably, the foundational aesthetic for which the opera *Pelléas* and it characters are in search. When Golaud sends Mélisande to find the ring, she sets off again in the company of Pelléas. The result is the grotto scene at the end of the opera's second act (the last act in Debussy's order of composition), in which opera is rededicated according to a new aesthetic.

Mélisande has told Golaud that she lost the ring in a grotto by the sea, while collecting seashells for his son Yniold. She must therefore explore the grotto to refine her alibi. There, Pelléas and Mélisande do not recover the ring, but they do recover (or rediscover) music. They look into the water as if into a mirror, and Pelléas exclaims: "Oh! Voici la clarté!" We know that the water is opaque. Pelléas's rhetoric advances from the demand for truth to the discovery of clarity. Clarity, one might assume, becomes the catchword for the desired aesthetic of Pelléas and *Pelléas*. What does "clarity" mean here? Answers combine psychoanalytic, musical, and political values.

As in Rousseau and Mozart, clarity here does not mean transparence. The water of the grotto is deep and dark. It is thus different from the water of the first scene in the forest, in which Mélisande had lost her crown. That water, as Golaud insisted, was shallow and transparent. The progress from the demand for truth to the discovery of clarity is one of psychoanalytic work, and indeed work that the opera actually adumbrates. The opera's forest of symbols guides the discovery of the world of darkness and clarity. The psychoanalytic texture is historically new; the idea of clarity as a critique of visuality we have seen in the fourth act of *Le nozze di Figaro*.

First, we have the obvious but not uncomplicated symbol of the well: the source, the vagina, the birth canal. The wedding ring is the symbol of that source, and, lost in the well, returns to the source. But humanity cannot return to the source, to the womb. Nature cannot return to origins, and neither can music. Mélisande, herself an allegory of music, has no origins. The loss of the wedding ring is certainly a displaced allegory of the loss of virginity, but also the loss of innocence and the loss of origins. The truth-value that Pelléas advocates, at the end of the scene at the well, is the psychoanalytic truth that forswears the recovery of origins, of the source. Here the opera struggles with a question that has tormented psychoanalytic thinking: that of the relation of origins to history. The service of much nineteenth-century historical practice to the agenda of nation-building linked historical understanding to the establishment of origins: origins of the nation, origins of individuals and groups within the nation. Origins conferred legitimacy. Thus, the release from the bonds of origins coincided with the release from ideologies of identity, especially on the part of those marginalized by such ideologies. The question then becomes the effect of the critique and disavowal of origins on history and on the materiality of the past.

As is well known, Freud's development of psychoanalysis involved the reconstruction of the historical past according to the dominant metaphor of archaeology. The repressed past, its events and its desires, return under the careful supervision of the analyst to achieve a new stability for itself and for the subject who carries it into a more ordered and bearable future. Psychoanalysis as historical understanding offers not the emancipation from the past but the possibility of peacemaking with the past. Revisions of the Freudian model have posed tough questions to its historical and historicizing foundations. Specifically, they have urged the distinction, in Donald Spence's formulation, between narrative truth and historical truth. Spence's hypothesis is "that the historical truth of an interpretation is less important than is usually assumed; that it may have no necessary relation to the actual past; and that Freud's well-known temptation to compare psychoanalysis with archeology may be a substantially misleading analogy." The analysand's progress, according to this revision, impinges on the internal coherence and the aesthetic satisfaction of a narrative rather than the discovery of historical fact or truth.[18]

The fin de siècle interest in symbols and symbolizations is closely related to its desire to reorganize the relation between present and past. The ambiguous referent and referential world of the symbol articulates the suspension in the relation between present and past, surface and depth, symptom and cause. Freud's own intellectual development incorporates this tendency. The historical/archaeological model that informs and controls the first edition of *The Interpretation of Dreams* (1900) is incrementally revised in subsequent editions to accommodate his increasing focus on the work of symbols and symbolization. (Freud's revisionary and counterrevisionary processes are obscured by James Strachey's variorum Standard Edition, which includes all cumulative later additions.) As John Forrester has shown, the largest additions to the post-1900 editions concern symbolism. Freud's interest in symbols swells between 1900 and 1914 and shows his interest, during these years, in the work of Jung.[19] Here as elsewhere, the poets preceded them. As Jung's work on symbols led him into a neo-Romantic, indeed neo-Schopenhauerian understanding of the symbol as, in Forrester's words, "the derivative, the earthly representative of the Noumenon," Freud refused this mystical path and repossessed the world of symbols into the functions of language, culture, and history.[20] For Freud in 1914, symbols function as "a relic and a mark of former identity."[21] The conflict with Jung over the symbol amounted, Forrester suggests, to a "fundamental difference of attitude towards the ineffable. Freud, in absorbing the ineffable into the inexpressible, and in his verbal rationalism, distrusted the symbol insofar as it became pure Image, and was detached from the Word. . . . Freud took the silence of the symbol, just as he took the silence of the transference, as creating a practical exigency: the necessity of connection."[22]

Pelléas moves its symbols through darkness in the search for clarity. The question remains whether clarity as an aesthetic involves historical as well as narrative truth. In the grotto scene, we have the realization of an aesthetic of clarity. Mélisande and Pelléas confirm their bond by developing together a story of their union, which means the exclusion of Golaud via a story about the loss of the ring that does not correspond to historical reality. Pelléas shows Mélisande how to see her reflection in the water. Does she see herself as object

[18] Donald P. Spence, *Narrative Truth and Historical Truth: Meaning and Interpretation in Psychoanalysis* (New York: W. W. Norton & Company, 1982), pp. 34–35 and passim.

[19] John Forrester, *Language and the Origins of Psychoanalysis* (New York: Columbia University Press, 1980), pp. 63, 70, and 63–130.

[20] Ibid., p. 111 and 102–22.

[21] Freud, *On Dreams* (1900), Standard Edition 5:352, cited by Forrester, *Language and the Origins of Psychoanalysis*, p. 97.

[22] Forrester, *Language and the Origins of Psychoanalysis*, p. 111.

(the narcissistic gaze) or as subject? Does the opera find "French music" in the depths of the grotto and its correlative Debussian sonic idiom? The music Debussy writes and advocates here is one of femininity, clarity and reason. At stake is a form of style-building—"Schule-machen"—perhaps even, in these profoundly altered terms, nation-building. But its musical, aesthetic terms do not recall the programmatic nation-building of *Lohengrin* or *Parsifal*. Debussy does not keep a nationalist discourse and merely substitute his own nation. The new music is indeed identified with France, as is the form of the drama: the five-act form recalls Racinian tragedy. But it is a nationalism of rationality and clarity rather than of mystification and darkness. It is a nationalism of negativity: the nation (France) and its music reconstituted against the countermodels (Germany and Wagner)—now models of what the nation should *not* be. It is a return of the Rousseauian and Mozartean principle of clarity without transparence, without visuality and its mimetic temptations. There is a kind of musical republicanism at work here that eluded Debussy in his nonmusical utterances.

If the figure of Mélisande functions as an allegory of music—without origin, hovering between nature and culture, desiring silence, that is, its own end— she may also be understood as an allegory of French music. If the opera *Pelléas* unfolds according to her—French music's—rededicated aesthetic, then this music desires its end and certainly its noninstitutionalization. This paradox represents an intensification of the one, identified by Goehr, that requires *Pelléas* qua antiopera also to be a failure as an opera. Here, the music must die if it is to avoid ideology. The work's intense sadness, commented on by the characters themselves, especially by the blind and clairvoyant King Arkel, involves the mortality of the music itself. Mortality and truth are linked; Golaud, who doesn't understand his own resonances, harasses the dying Mélisande with the admonition "Il faut dire la vérité à quelqu'un qui va mourir [One must tell the truth to someone who is going to die]." The "influence" of Debussy's music is tied to his sense of its mortality, to his disavowal of the need to be influential. This is in itself a substantial political gesture, tied perhaps to melancholy and anomie but also to a strong sense of aesthetic freedom. Performatively, it disavows school-building as well as nation-building.

This predicament of musical mortality as the context for musical, aesthetic truth creates interesting dramaturgical possibilities for the representation of Mélisande. Mélisande's presence as a quality rather than as a person opens the dramaturgical alternative of her not appearing onstage as a character at all. This alternative might either appear as a misogynist gesture itself or indeed as a critique of the male (patriarchal and fraternal) narcissism of the surrounding story. It is consistent with the Lacanian insight (which can in turn be understood either as misogynist or as a critique of misogyny) to the effect that "woman is a symptom of man," that is, that man's erotic encounter with woman remains narcissistic. (This option was realized in the final scene of

Jean Pierre Ponnelle's production of *Tristan* for Bayreuth in the 1980s, in which Isolde never arrives at Tristan's deathbed but appears to him as a hallucination, before his death in the arms of his companion, Kurwenal.)[23] In a cruel paradox, the character Pelléas may therefore be understood, despite himself, as both *frère* and *semblable* of his fratricidal brother, Golaud. That is, if Pelléas "represents" or, rather, articulates the Debussian aesthetic of clarity, he unavoidably and performatively becomes a voice of ideology. In the scenes with Mélisande, he becomes so in contrast to her own increasing propensity to silence. Pelléas becomes the Wagnerian presence to Mélisande's pure Debussy, but Mélisande is silent and Debussy's choice is therefore to Wagnerize or to disappear.[24]

Short of this paradox, when understood as an allegory of the music of *Pelléas et Mélisande*, the figure of Mélisande allows for a reading of the opera itself as an almost embarrassingly accurate allegory of the patricidal and fratricidal disputes—over music—in France between 1892 and 1902. Two discourses of clarity meet here, revisiting a powerful eighteenth-century opposition in French musical aesthetics. *Pelléas*'s discourse of clarity is Rousseauian; Debussy's is explicitly Rameauean. The worry in *Pelléas* over the boundaries of (lost) nature and (corrupt) culture is Rousseauian. During the decade of work on *Pelléas*, Debussy turned explicitly to Rameau as the "last master of French musical parody" of language, and thus the model composer in the service of the authentic cadences of the language. Debussy set Rameau against Gluck, whom he accused, in the second person: "You turn French into an accented language when it is really a language of nuances. (Yes, I know you are German.)"[25]

The convergence of *Pelléas*'s psychoanalytic and political arguments holds the center of Stanley Cavell's description of the opera in terms of its "enjambment of . . . the sublime and the ordinary."[26] Maeterlinck was an admirer of Ralph Waldo Emerson, describing him as "the sage of commonplace days, and commonplace days are in sum the substance of our being." Cavell describes this view as "congenial to my sense of Emerson as underwriting ordinary language philosophy."[27] I understand the ordinary, in Cavell's description of *Pel-*

---

[23] See Slavoj Žižek, "Why Is Woman a Symptom of Man," in *Enjoy Your Symptom! Jacques Lacan in Hollywood and Out* (New York: Routledge, 1992), pp. 31–67. Žižek also cites the example of Ponnelle's *Tristan* in a paper called "Run, Isolde, Run," given at the conference "Die Zukunft der Oper," Kulturwissenschaftliches Institut, Essen, May 2000.

[24] I owe the suggestion of the Pelléas/Wagner versus Mélisande/Debussy chiasmus to Lydia Goehr, in a conversation following a panel on the opera at the Bard Music Festival in August 2001.

[25] Fulcher, *French Cultural Politics and Music*, pp. 176, 180.

[26] Stanley Cavell, *A Pitch of Philosophy: Autobiographical Exercises* (Cambridge: Harvard University Press, 1994), p. 161.

[27] Ibid., p. 168.

léas, to refer to the world beyond aesthetic incorporation—an understanding I take to be compatible with the politics of ordinary language philosophy. Cavell describes Mélisande as knowing that she is "immured [a reference to Edgar Allan Poe's story, a favorite of Maeterlinck's], but within the world."[28] This insistence on immanence corresponds to a secular ethic of political responsibility. Freud affirms it in *Civilization and Its Discontents* with the citation from Grabbe: "We cannot fall out of this world [Wir können aus dieser Welt nicht fallen]." Pelléas's exclamation in the grotto, "Oh! Voici la clarté!" is accompanied by an orchestral swell depicting the rise of the moon, reminiscent of the erotically charged flash of moonlight in the first act of *Die Walküre*. But the light reveals, to Mélisande's horror, emblems of the extra-aesthetic world, of the Otherness assimilable by political responsibility: three sleeping poor people, the result, as Pelléas explains, of a famine in the land.[29]

Picture, in contrast, Tristan, newly arrived in Cornwall, circa 1860, commenting to Isolde in act 2 of their opera on the condition of the working class in England. The night that disavows the day, the love that obliterates the social world stands also for the aesthetic of music drama, which cancels all externality, everything outside of itself and its own formal and symbolic universe, and thus all social and political responsibility. Pelléas remains aware of an external, social dimension. Moreover, the vocal and musical silence of the three sleeping poor people signifies counterintuitively. The point, it seems to me, is not that they are condemned by music drama to silence but, rather, that their concerns are declared unincorporable by the surrounding musical-dramatic aesthetic and operation. Pelléas understands these boundaries. His death, at the hand of Golaud, is thus articulated as a political tragedy as well as a personal one.

Mélisande has a distant cousin in Judith, in Béla Bartók and Béla Balázs's *Bluebeard's Castle* of 1911. Mélisande and Judith inherit from Beethoven's Leonore the rhetorical burden of starring in a great composer's only opera. They share a parlando rubato vocal style that Bartók later stated had owed a debt to Debussy.[30] Both women are strangers in their husbands' mysterious realms; both infuse new and spare sonorities into the dense and dark textures of their adopted venues. Bartók's score is thicker than Debussy's, and herein we must face the validity of a cliché: blood (a central symbol of *Bluebeard*) is thicker than water, a central symbol of *Pelléas*.

---

[28] Ibid., p. 166.

[29] Sigmund Freud, *Civilization and Its Discontents*, trans. J. Strachey (New York: Norton, 1961), p. 12.

[30] See Carl Leafstedt, "*Bluebeard* as Theater: The Influence of Maeterlinck and Hebbel on Balázs's Bluebeard Drama," in *Bartók and His World*, ed. Peter Laki (Princeton: Princeton University Press, 1995), p. 120.

Bartók and Balázs's version of *Bluebeard's Castle* premiered in Budapest in 1918, seven years after its completion. No doubt it is a successful moment in international high modernism and symbolism. But it has also a specific cultural and allegorical significance as a Hungarian commentary on the themes of cultural fragmentation and communicative breakdown, themes that characterize the Habsburg fin de siècle in general. These themes generate the two contrasting energies: modernism and nationalism. Whether at the center of imperial geopolitical endeavors or at its increasingly vexed peripheries (in other words, whether coming from fin de siècle Vienna, Budapest, or Prague), the modernist explosion negotiated painstakingly with nationalist agendas. Jewish thinkers and artists were perhaps more accustomed to negotiating this dialectic, and they also paid for that proclivity by a resulting rise in anti-Semitism. The era of the Austro-Hungarian dual monarchy, following the compromise of 1867 and stretching until the collapse of the empire in 1918, encouraged nationalist and cosmopolitan agendas alike.

As Judit Frigyesi has shown, the twenty-two-year-old Bartók had shown his hand in a 1903 letter to his mother, in which he declared, "For my own part, all my life, in every sphere, always and in every way, I shall have one objective: the good of Hungary and the Hungarian nation." Frigyesi takes issue with the tendency of Bartók scholars to reconcile this attitude with the "broader humanism" of his later statements, most famously that of 1931: "My own idea . . . —of which I have been fully conscious since I found myself as a composer—is the brotherhood of peoples. . . . I try—to the best of my ability—to serve this idea in music."[31] Bartók in this period was also prone to conventional anti-Semitic attitudes, which Frygyesi credibly understands as one element in the cosmopolitan overstimulation of the largely German and Jewish city of Budapest.[32] For Frigyesi, Bartók's early nationalism carries its musical analogue in the *Kossuth Symphony* of 1903 (a celebration of Lajos Kossuth, hero of the Hungarian War of Independence of 1848) in ways unrepeated in later years. And in a perhaps predictable irony, Bartók found his principal model for the *Kossuth Symphony* in Richard Strauss's tone poem *Ein Heldenleben*.[33]

In 1911, Bartók was adjusting his direction from a conventional nationalist one to a more modernist and international one. This new articulation was generated in part by the watershed publication of Endre Ady's *New Poems* in 1906.[34] Ady had mounted a campaign against Hungarian "backwardness" with

---

[31] Judit Frigyesi, "Béla Bartók and the Concept of Nation and *Volk* in Modern Hungary," *Musical Quarterly* 78:2 (summer 1994): 255–87; 255. See also Frigyesi, "Béla Bartók and Hungarian Nationalism: The Development of Bartók's Social and Political Ideas at the Turn of the Century (1899–1903)" (diss., University of Pennsylvania, 1989), and Frigyesi, *Béla Bartók and Turn-of-the-Century Budapest* (Berkeley and Los Angeles: University of California Press, 1998).

[32] Frigyesi, "Béla Bartók and Hungarian Nationalism," pp. 49–63.

[33] Frigyesi, Ibid., p. 118.

[34] Ibid., p. 222.

respect to Europe and had thus severed nationalism (which he supported) from chauvinism and national sentimentality. For this position his collection of poems was denounced by the Hungarian prime minister, István Tisza.[35] Bartók and Kodaly's collection of *Hungarian Folksongs* was also published in 1906. Frigyesi's analysis provides an importrant correction to the conventional narrative of the "emergence" of Bartók as a Hungarian national composer, which is in fact commonly dated to around 1906. The revised picture divides a conventional, chauvinist youthful nationalism of the *Kossuth Symphony* with a cosmopolitan agenda into which folk culture and music are to be integrated.

For Balázs, author of *Bluebeard*'s text, no metaphor is more central than that of home and its elusiveness to modern consciousness. The question of "home" and its elusiveness connects psychology with politics, the self (the home of the ego) and the homeland. The symbiosis of modernity and anomie cannot be compromised by nationalism, which according to this view is at least partly motivated to do just that. Balázs found a principal aesthetic source for his position in symbolist poetry and drama, especially the work of Maeterlinck. (The importance of Maeterlinck for Balázs stands symmetrically with that of Debussy for Bartók.) Balázs labored the theme of home and homelessness in the company of the so-called Sunday Circle, in which he played a central part along with such figures as Georg Lukács, Arnold Hauser, Karl Mannheim, Oscar Jászi, and Jászi's wife Anna Lesznai.[36] Balázs and Lesznai together successfully wrote fairy tales and produced new classics in Hungarian children's literature. At the same time, they speculated in diaries and essays about the philosophical significance of the fairy tale. In their analysis, the fairy tale arrogates too much success in the resolution of the problems it raises. In Mary Gluck's summary: "All fairy tales, they seemed to agree, have in common with mysticism and erotic love the impulse to overcome man's imprisonment within the self. . . . In a fairy tale there can be no tragedy, no irreducible conflict between the self and empirical reality, because the genre does not recognize the world as foreign from the self, having laws of its own. The fairy tale is a 'happy art,' wrote Lesznai, in which 'everyone has a mission . . . and everyone can return home.' "[37] In *Bluebeard*, neither homeland nor self provides the sense of home. The removal of the work from fairy tale to the more apposite category of myth is achieved by Bartók's music.

Communicative breakdown is a leitmotiv of fin de siècle culture. In Vienna in the decade 1900–1910, the most heralded spokesman of these anxieties is Hugo von Hofmannsthal. Bluebeard's baroque castle would seem to combine the style and concerns of the "Letter of Lord Chandos" with the tragic and

---

[35] Ibid., p. 246.

[36] See Mary Gluck, *Georg Lukács and His Generation, 1900–1918* (Cambridge: Harvard University Press, 1985).

[37] Ibid., pp. 155–56.

mythic stakes of *Elektra*. The extended and aggravated dialogue between Judith and Bluebeard is in an important sense related to the so-called Recognition Scene in Richard Strauss's scoring of Hofmannsthal's *Elektra*, first performed two years before *Bluebeard* in 1909. (Bartók had unkind words to say about *Elektra* in general, but his comments do not impinge upon this particular point.) Elektra and Orest are long separated siblings; when Orest enters the decayed palace courtyard of their murdered father and finds his abused sister, neither recognizes the other. Their interview proceeds in the ironic agony of mutual dismissal. In talking past each other, they instantiate the collapse of family bonds, of emotional connection through rational self-presentation and exchange. Bluebeard and Judith are similarly opaque to each other on the level of rational self-presentation and mutual understanding as agents. In the first poem of his 1911 collection *The Wanderer Sings*, Balázs asserts that the bond between men overrides that between a man and a woman.[38] The position recalls the structure of Maeterlinck's *Pelléas et Mélisande*, where the bond of brotherhood (and its fratricidal inversion) seems to override the bond of the lovers. But Bartók's music argues for the intensity of the subliminal intimacy between Bluebeard and Judith. On a sublime and subliminal level, theirs is a dialogue of total intimacy and understanding. Theirs is a sexual bond, a bond deeper and more terrifying than a linguistic one. To be conceptually and historically specific, theirs is a bond of masochism.

The symptoms and the clinical discourse of masochism belong to the Central European fin de siècle, a context well known to Bartók and Balázs. The clinical term "masochism" was coined in 1886 by the psychiatrist Richard Krafft-Ebing (in his work called *Psychopathia Sexualis*) and taken up, as "sadomasochism," by Freud in his 1905 *Three Essays on Sexuality*. Krafft-Ebing named the syndrome after Leopold von Sacher-Masoch, whose 1870 novel *Venus in Furs* had exposed in fictionalized form his own predilections. Krafft-Ebing defined masochism as the derivation of pleasure from pain, either physical or psychic. Psychic pain included humiliation, and indeed the fantasy of humiliation and the desire for it. Masochism is, crucially, a male, heterosexual syndrome, the consensual delivery of power and punishment by a male body and mind to a female agent.

It seems clear enough that Bluebeard and Judith are locked inside a masochistic contract. The contract is masochistic and not really sadomasochistic, as the personal and cultural crisis signified is Bluebeard's and not, significantly, Judith's. For Bartók and Balázs, Bluebeard is modernity; Bluebeard is, we have the right to assume, Hungary. In their story, it is Judith who possesses agency, but that agency has been given to her by Duke Bluebeard. Why did you come here? Bluebeard asks her, placing, if retroactively, her arrival into her own

---

[38] See Paul Banks, "*Bluebeard's Castle*: Images of the Self," liner notes for *Bluebeard's Castle*, dir. Pierre Boulez, Chicago Symphony Orchestra, Deutsche Grammophon, 1998.

hands. Unlike Mélisande, she was not whisked up from an anonymous oasis in nature; she chose, desired to be Bluebeard's wife. This motivation established, Bluebeard and Judith proceed to invert the signs of the gender status: he becomes feminized, according to the cultural rules of fin de siècle decadence, and she, according to the same rules, becomes masculinized. Bluebeard's body and soul are of course symbolized by his castle; the opening of its seven doors becomes an act of multiple penetration.

The doors are opened with keys given by Bluebeard to Judith; the key is the phallus, given up by the man to the woman. The phallic woman must be complemented by the invaginated man; this inversion occurs at the opening of the first door. The first opened door reveals "a blood-red rectangle in the wall like an open wound." As the image appears, Bluebeard asks Judith "What do you see?"—making it clear that what she sees he has never seen. She has a power of the gaze—the power to see inside him—that he has never had. Bluebeard's "wound" is a cousin of Amfortas's in its signification of feminization and decadence, but it is more explicitly vaginal. Now, the room behind the first door reveals itself as the torture chamber. But the first and sole relevant instrument of torture has already been exposed: the key, the penetrating phallus requisitioned seven times by Judith. The blood motive reappears at every door. Everything is covered in blood, and this is menstrual blood more than battle blood: the blood, according to a well-known mythical trope, of the feminized man rather than of the hero. The second door reveals an armory, the third reveals precious jewels, and the fourth reveals flowers.

The opening of the fifth door is the musical and dramatic hinge of the work as well as its most explicitly political moment. The orchestra at full throttle and the soprano on a high C greet the display, behind the door, of Bluebeard's entire kingdom. Like Wotan displaying the completed Valhalla to Fricka, Bluebeard declaims: "Now behold my spacious kingdom. Gaze down the dwindling vistas. Is it not a noble country?" As he did with the *Kossuth Symphony*, Bartók here combines an allusion to Hungarian land with an orchestral rhetoric reminiscent of Richard Strauss. Notwithstanding the Wagnerian foundation of Bluebeard's gesture, the music of the fifth door recalls not *Das Rheingold* but rather the loudest cadences of Strauss's *Thus Spoke Zarathustra*. The citation's effect is powerful but its logic is obscure. The bombast is unashamed, possibly suggesting an irony that would combine Bluebeard and Strauss's hero. Consistent with such a reading, Judith's reaction is the rhetorical opposite of Fricka's: rather than bathing in her man's musical rhetoric as a way of sharing his dominion, she reacts tersely, to absolute silence from the orchestra. This happens twice, and both instances shock. Judith's reaction is at the very least ironic, and indeed perhaps dismissive. In 1911, the glorious Hungarian plains show themselves to be emasculated.

The sixth and the seventh doors do not open easily. The sixth reveals a lake of tears; the seventh reveals the three living prior wives of Bluebeard.

The parade of jeweled wives reveals Judith to be the last wife. The first wife, Bluebeard says, was found at dawn, the second at noon, the third at dusk, and Judith at midnight. The cycle is complete, and at the opera's end Judith takes her place among the living entombed, as Bluebeard laments "Henceforth all shall be darkness." Bluebeard's castle is the masochistic iron cage.

And yet, the masochistic bond itself is broken by the seventh door. Entombed, Judith loses her agency as Bluebeard tragically regains his. But this is the grim agency of patriarchy and possession, the bonds of history and conventional masculinity, reasserting themselves after the grim inversion of the masochistic experiment. The enslavement to patriarchy is an accurate comment on the status of the Austro-Hungarian Empire in its final decade. Literary modernism and literary criticism in early-twentieth-century Central Europe revalorized allegory as a trope more adequate than symbol to the task of confronting history through art.

Symbol, wrote Walter Benjamin, conjures myths and universals; allegory, history, and particulars. Benjamin's intervention—proallegory and antisymbol—sought to reinsert history, materiality, and secularity into a system of cultural metaphors that from Romanticism to symbolism had privileged the mystical, the universal, and the neoreligious. At the same time, tropes specific and internal to a work may function ambiguously as both symbol and allegory. In this vein, it is accurate to suggest that Bluebeard himself might be understood as an allegory of Hungary, and Judith as one of Austria. From the complicated nationalistic perspective of Bartók and Balázs, the Austro-Hungarian bond is understandable as one of masochism. What does Austria want?—they may be understood to be asking. What does the empire of Maria Theresa, of Catholicism, of the baroque, of a politics legitimized by grace and form, want with Hungary? The political hint suggested by the fifth door is made manifest by the seventh. The bonds of masochism are overlaid with the bonds of history, which reveal themselves in turn as a higher level of masochism itself. Such are the stakes of masochism as a cultural as well as a clinical predicament. For Bartók, Balázs, and Bluebeard, Austria, like opera, is a woman; Hungary is a man, a masochist, a self-enslaver. It is of course finally Bluebeard who kills Judith: masochism ends indeed, as in John Noyes's recent formulation, in the mastery of submission, in the staging of self-subjection in the service of a new domination.[39] There is no way out of Bluebeard's castle.

Written from the other side of the Habsburg debacle of 1918, Leoš Janáček's *Makropoulos Case* of 1926, unlike *Bluebeard*, is precisely about the conditions of escape from a masochistic bond—in this case from the bonds of empire,

---

[39] See John Noyes, *The Mastery of Submission* (Ithaca: Cornell University Press, 1997). See also Suzanne R. Stewart, *Sublime Surrender: Male Masochism at the Fin de siècle* (Ithaca: Cornell University Press, 1998), in which the staged, theatrical context of the masochistic bond is emphasized.

history, and the tyranny of repetition. How clearly the imprint of the Habsburg *longue durée* is inscribed in this work!

Janáček fashioned his libretto from Karel Capek's successful play of 1922. At its center is a diva—in other words, the operatic voice. She is Emilia Marty. She is 337 years old. Once she was Elena Makropoulos, daughter of Hieronymos Makropoulos, court physician to Emperor Rudolf II (1576–1612), the last Holy Roman Emperor to have his seat and court in Prague. Rudolf's court culture is famously rich for its prolixity not only of painters and musicians but of astronomers (including Tycho Brahe and Johannes Kepler) and alchemists. Alchemy is of the greatest interest to the invocation at work here. By imperial command, Hieronymos Makropoulos developed a potion for eternal life and by imperial command again, tested it on his own daughter. When the girl fell into a coma, the emperor executed his doctor. The girl eventually awoke to the condition of immortality and escaped. The potion must be remixed every three hundred years, and those three hundred years are now up.

For Habsburg-dominated Bohemia, the span of three hundred years carries a numerological aura. It marks the years separating 1618 from 1918: the first date marking the start of the Thirty Years' War in Prague (the result largely of Rudolf's incompetence), the second date marking the end of the Habsburg Empire, in Bohemia and everywhere else. The span marks the repetition of historical trauma.

Between Elena Makropoulos and Emilia Marty there have been other identities: Elsa Müller, Elian MacGregor, Ekaterina Myshkin, Eugenia Montez . All have been singers. The lives of the accumulated "E. M."s coincide with the history of opera and the history of the baroque and neobaroque worlds. But these personal identities and their attached life experiences and historical contexts are not continuous. The diva Emilia Marty is exhausted not from longevity alone but from fragmentation and historical rupture. Her history, like the modernist literary, scenic, and indeed musical structure of this opera, is one of montage. Only short lives, she explains in her death scene, can make sense.

Emilia's memory structure is fragmented and neurotic, this partly attributable to the exhaustion that is her main symptom. Like Janáček's music, she produces melody always interrupted by an oversupply of texture. Janáček's orchestral idiom is at once exhilarating and exhausting to the listener for this confrontation of temporality, memory structures, and melody on the one hand, and its textural and sonic density and nervousness on the other. Counterintuitively, density and nervousness coincide as sonic analogues to bureaucratic modernity.

The diva Emilia Marty who enters the lawyer's office in the first act engages two competing worlds. Identified with the past are her own person, the diva as type, seduction, enchantment, reenchantment, and the illusion of immortality and its conceits: beauty and power. Identified with the present are legal bureaucracy and the rule of the document—legal and scientific. The main legal document is the contested will of the Baron Prus. The will has been in litigation for close to a century, as Prus had bequeathed his estate to the illegitimate son he fathered with Elian MacGregor, an alias, of course, of Emilia Marty. Attached to the disputed will is the scientific document in question: the immortality formula concocted by Hieronymos Makropoulos, given to Prus by his lover Elian MacGregor at a time when its renewal was a remote consideration.

Emilia's motives are conflicted. On the one side, her purpose is to recover the formula and renew her longevity for another three hundred years. On the other side, she seems increasingly ready to give up the renewal of the potion and to die. What she requires is a death scene adequate to her operatic heritage. How can this be produced? There are two choices: a death scene by staging or by subjective inhabitation. This sequence, and its two agendas of affective and cultural reenchantment, inform the settings of the opera's three acts. The first is a Kafkaesque lawyer's office, one of modernity's most disenchanted places. Here, the legal case that involves the document containing the Makropoulos potion is being haggled over. Emilia infiltrates and supplies the bureaucrats with details about the life histories of the long-dead originators of the case in question. The following two acts follow Emilia's reverse road to reenchantment from bureaucracy to theater to magic. The second act takes place backstage in a Prague theater following a Marty performance; the third takes place in a hotel room after she has arranged to purchase, in exchange for sex, the Makropoulos document from its present owner. In the end, she exchanges reenchantment for death. Moreover, the death she chooses and enacts is not an operatic one but an inarticulate disappearance. It is also a legitimation of that aspect of legal bureaucracy that orders filial succession.

Immortality requires infanticide. Emilia Marty—at the time Elian MacGregor—was not sufficiently concerned with her own son to safeguard his inheritance. In the last act's penultimate scene, she shows hostile indifference to the news of the suicide of Janek Prus, son of Jaroslav Prus, with whom she has just slept in exchange for the Makropoulos formula. She is now exposed by a trail of documents, containing signatures in her various guises, that prompt the lawyer in the Prus-Gregor case to accuse her of forgery and threaten her with arrest.

She confesses the condition of her imposed immortality—call it music trauma—as follows:

> What hideous solitude!
> It's all in vain, Krista,
> whether you sing or keep silent—
> no pleasure in being good,
> no pleasure in being bad.
> No pleasure on earth,

no pleasure in heaven.
And one comes to learn
that the soul has died inside one.

Ta hrozná samota!
Je to, Kristinko, stejně marné,
zpívat či mlčet—
Omrzí být dobrý,
omrzí být spatný.
Omrzí země,
omrzí nebe!
A pozná,
že v něm umřela duše.

Emilia's renunciation of immortality is accompanied by a second reversal, namely her recognition of the order of generational succession and its legal safeguards. The text to Capek's play contains a lament for the bereaved father Jaroslav Prus that was excised in the condensation that produced the libretto: "So, you see, eternal life! If we only thought of birth—rather than of death. Life is not short, as long as we can be the cause of life—."[40]

What does Emilia now achieve, other than death? This is another way of asking the question: what does opera want? There are two answers: knowledge and pleasure (*Wissen* and *jouissance*), the one troped by European modernity as German and masculine, involving mastery, and the other as French and feminine, involving submission. The gender inversion active in *Bluebeard* comes from Judith's desire to know and Bluebeard's desire to submit. In *The Makropoulos Case*, Emilia attempts to pass on the forbidden knowledge of immortality to a guileless successor. Her refusal of mimetic continuity for herself does not extend to a moratorium on mimetic repetition for another. But the men she has seduced attempt to block the transmission; finally, the young beneficiary refuses the bequest and burns the document containing the formula. She has learned from the dying Emilia's laments that only opera can provide what history cannot: the synthesis of knowledge and pleasure—and that in the form of an illusion, in the theater, for a fee. The diva Emilia Marty has provided that illusion for others for three hundred years. Now she does it one last time as the character in her own opera, at the moment she gives up the privilege of living operatically in real life—living real life as an imitation opera. Emilia dies in confusion, "crumpling up," having become interchangeable with the Makropoulos document itself.

The opera's final moments sound out the death of Emilia and the liberation of the orchestra, that is, of music alone. This may appear reminiscent of Brünnhilde's immolation scene: fire, death, and orchestra. What Janáček gives us is

[40] Karel Capek, *The Makropoulos Secret* (Boston: John W. Luce and Company, 1925), p. 164.

precisely the emancipation from that Wagnerian contract whereby voice is subsumed by orchestral master-narrative. Janáček's orchestra forges a way out of music drama and music trauma. Recall that Emilia Marty does not achieve Brünnhildian wisdom or humaneness. She renounces immortality but wishes, in her last moments, supported by Liebestodian surges in the orchestra, to transfer it to an ingenue-in-waiting. It is the ingenue—who carries the re-demptive name "Krista"—who refuses the legacy. She burns the document containing the immortality formula.

The stage directions for the opera's finale and Emilia Marty's death read: "She crumples up. The document is consumed in flames." What happens is that the woman and the paper switch the demises that operatic tradition would supply them. The paper receives an immolation; the woman crumples. Imagine Brünnhilde refusing to enact the apocalypse and burning the recipe instead; imagine her, rather than setting the Rhineland on fire, handing Gu-trune a piece of paper containing the legal invalidation of Wotan's lease on Valhalla. In this regard, Emilia Marty's death and the end of The Makropoulos Case suggest a profound post-Wagnerian correction, in operatic as well as cultural-historical terms. In 1926, the romance of apocalypse had lost the naiveté it may still have had in 1876. The mass death of 1914–1918 enacted a kind of continental infanticide. Emilia Marty's immolation—or perhaps, rather, anti-immolation—elects to burn not the world but the formula that may be responsible for the burning of the world.

Emilia Marty's embrace of mortality produces the freedom to narrate her history. The row of "E. M." identities are placed into order. Subjectivity, in the guise of organized temporality, emerges. This performative subjectivity characterizes Janáček's orchestra at the moment of the opera's denouement. Its idiom achieves the union of texture and melody that has so far eluded it. There is some reminiscence of some of the great passages from Richard Strauss of this period. This orchestra, unlike Wagner's, retains, even insists on, a femi-nine self-gendering. It doesn't silence the voice of the heroine; it confers that very heroic status by absorbing her voice into heroic proportions. It is because of this rhetorical continuity with the heroine, and her achievement of an ordered mortality rather than one of apocalpyse and redemption, that Janá-ček's orchestra tells the truth where Wagner's lies.

Emilia Marty's death and its orchestral correlative combine mortality with secularity; there is no operatic redemption—Erlösungsoper—at work here. Death at the end of The Makropoulos Case signifies the choice of mortality rather than the fall into victimhood. In this way, the nonredemptive momen-tum corresponds to a victory over repetition. The string of "E. M."s that Emi-lia Marty has deployed to regenerate her temporal identities corresponds in part to Judith's predecessors in Bluebeard's cabinet. Emilia's choice of mortal-ity releases her from the tyranny of repetition to which Judith and Bluebeard succumb.

The Road into the Open

"Here is a remarkable fact, as yet unnoticed," wrote Arnold Schoenberg in February 1931, in a short fragment called "National Music" ["Zu nationalen Musik"]. "Debussy's summons to the Latin and Slav peoples, to do battle against Wagner, was indeed successful; but to free himself from Wagner—that was beyond him. His most interesting discoveries can still only be used within the form and the way of giving shape to music that Wagner created. Here it must not be overlooked that much of his harmony was also discovered independently of him, in Germany. No wonder; after all, there were logical consequences of Wagner's harmony, further steps along the path the latter had pointed out."[41]

Schoenberg's apparent point is not that Debussy should have succeeded in stepping out from Wagner's shadow but rather that he ought not to have tried. Universal musical progress, he implies, has a German itinerary, which he goes on to map via an account of his own formative models: Bach, Mozart, Beethoven, Wagner, and Brahms, supported by Schubert, Mahler, Strauss, and Reger. Schoenberg's declared compositional genealogy amounts as well to his own personal (and Wagnerian!) family romance in the descent of German music.

I conclude this chapter with some brief comparative remarks on Schoenberg's *Moses und Aron* and Berg's *Lulu*, wary of implying that this chapter's discussion of post-Wagnerian opera must necessarily return to German opera. That is not my implication. The anomic radicality of these two operas' musical idiom alone would render implausible such a nationally, linguistically based classification. This radicality of idiom would immediately problematize any claim or rhetoric of return. Rather, their idioms place the works within the rhetoric of the "minor" under examination here, notwithstanding the canonic place they hold in standard histories of modern and/or twentieth-century music.

My purpose is more limited but also more polemical. I want to draw a sharp distinction between these two works on the question of how they confront German and Wagnerian tradition and the attendant conundrum of subjectivity, nationality, and gender. I want to suggest that Berg achieves a critical remove from that tradition in ways that Schoenberg, contrary to a more standard view, does not. With this assertion I would question the received duality of Schoenberg and Berg as prophet and priest of the new music. Or perhaps not: I am interested in interpreting—through the work—Schoenberg's self-understanding as prophet, as Moses. And I am interested in understanding Berg's lack of aesthetically evident interest in such an investiture. More, then, than Schoenberg, Berg accomplishes that break through a sustained engage-

[41] Arnold Schoenberg, "National Music (2)," in *Style and Idea: Selected Writings of Arnold Schoenberg*, ed. Leonard Stein, trans. L. Black (Berkeley and Los Angeles: University of California Press, 1975), pp. 175–76.

ment, in *Lulu*, with the fiction of pure voice. This engagement is a highly self-conscious one, armed with the hyperrationality of twelve-tone composition. Berg's musical language does not totalize; it stands back from dominating the characters as it stands back from systematizing the orchestral idiom.[42] Schoenberg, on the other hand, remains locked within the paradigm of the signifying voice and the coordination of the signifying voice (Moses's truth, Aaron's art) with the management of orchestral rhetoric. Schoenberg's Moses is the transmitter of law and the word, the font of idea as the antidote to style.

German opera and operatic aesthetics in the nineteenth century, after and distinct from Mozart, had not attached themselves to a fiction of pure voice, but to one of a signifying voice. With Wagner, the female/feminine voice can occasionally burst through in transgressive referentiality to Italian style, but, as the singing trajectory of the *Götterdämmerung* Brünnhilde shows, it is trumped by the signifying authority of the orchestra and its musical-dramatic system. The German operatic voice signifies as the national voice. The ability of opera after Wagner to offer a degree of emancipation to voice and to voice-bearing characters relates to the ways their musical aesthetics decline to assert the authority of the orchestra. Opera after Wagner has the latter's long shadow to contend with but it also has the ability to refer to Wagnerian paradigms and thus take distance from them. What we may still call French, Hungarian, or Czech opera, with reference to *Pelléas*, *Bluebeard*, and *Makropoulos*, can anchor itself in a linguistic and national subject-position and immediately mark its distance from the German and Wagnerian example. (To disavow the presence of the Wagnerian example for these works amounts to a denial of historical fact.) But German-language opera after Wagner may be in the same predicament. For Richard Strauss and Hans Pfitzner the need to mark distance from Wagner is not an issue. For Brahms and Mahler it is, and the response is to stay away from opera altogether.

---

[42] I take the phrase "musical language" and the assertion that the twelve-tone set does not dominate it from George Perle, *The Operas of Alban Berg, Volume Two/Lulu* (Berkeley and Los Angeles: University of California Press, 1985), ch. 4 (pp. 85–236; here p. 85). The first three of five principles through which Perle describes the musical language of *Lulu* are as follows:

1. *Lulu* is based not on one twelve-tone set but on many, in violation of Schoenberg's stated principle that a single twelve-tone set ought to govern all the tone relations of a given work.

2. Some of these sets are, like the characteristic Schoenbergian "tone row," defined by the order of the notes, but others ("tropes") are exclusively or primarily defined by their segmental content.

3. Even where Berg uses a Schoenbergian type of set, that is, a series, he exploits this in a manner that is basically different from Schoenberg. The Schoenbergian series is an invariant intervallic structure that is assumed to retain its identity regardless of its direction (prime, inversion, retrograde, retrograde-inversion) and that remains independent of the explicit linear contour of any given compositional statement of the series. In *Lulu*, however, a characteristic melodic contour is a dominant attribute of the series.

What post-Wagnerian German opera does do with the fiction of pure voice is to mark the operatic zone beyond voice with a kind of meta-aesthetic of opera based on two possibiities: silence and scream. Specifically, Moses's silence and Lulu's scream, the two paradigmatic meta-musical gestures of second-Vienna-school opera.

Silence inhabits most famously Schoenberg's *Moses und Aron*. How self-consciously did Schoenberg float his opera's unanswerable question: does silence mark emptiness or fullness, nonrepresentation or representation, fragment or totality? Though not empirically silent, Moses's *Sprechstimme* carries a silence-effect in its disavowal of song. Moses's silence is echoed by Schoenberg's decision not to compose the third act, despite a letter of 26 May 1933 specifying that he would complete the opera "in six to eight weeks." (The date is of course politically charged.) Commenting on Moses's final lament "O Wort du Wort das mir fehlt [Oh Word thou Word that I lack]," Michel Poizat observes as follows:

> The long F-sharp pedal on the strings is perhaps the most perfect musicalization of silence that imposes its absolute presence when all words fail. It is the pendant, in a way, of the E-flat that begins *Das Rheingold*.

An astonishing comment, considering the fact that the opening of *Das Rheingold* articulates the intent to tone-paint the history of the universe.

> It speaks the truth that Moses unknowingly has just discovered: this lack, this gap—which gapes at the very heart of language and which humankind has tried to overcome through such figures as God-the-Word—this gap is silence: God is silence. From here on nothing more can be said: opera can go no further.[43]

Whose or what authority informs this rhetoric of finitude? To what extent does the silence of *Moses und Aron*, its disavowal of representation, fold into its opposite, the silence of totalization? Is this opera an anti-*Parsifal* or a neo-*Parsifal*? Adorno and Lacoue-Labarthe ask this question as well. "It is as if," writes Lacoue-Labarthe, "in the end, *Moses and Aaron* were nothing other than the negative (in the photographic sense) of *Parsifal*, thus accomplishing, in a paradoxical manner, the project of the total work."[44] Schoenberg never stops signifying according to the dominant aesthetic of nineteenth-century German opera, which is finally a Wagnerian aesthetic. The anti-*Parsifal* becomes a neo-*Parsifal*.

---

[43] Michel Poizat, *The Angel's Cry: Beyond the Pleasure Principle in Opera*, trans. Arthur Denner (Ithaca: Cornell University Press, 1992), p. 109. See also my introductory note, "Music, Language, and Culture," *Musical Quarterly* 77:3 (Fall 1993): 397–400.

[44] Lacoue-Labarthe, *Musica Ficta*, p. 121.

The paradoxical alliance of *Moses und Aron* and *Parsifal* brings another irony into relief. Biographically and politically, Schoenberg's attention to Moses accompanies his return to Judaism. But, as the fragment "National Music" shows, it accompanies as well his reinstantiation of the aesthetic and historical canon of German music. Schoenberg's Moses, bearer of the word and idea, carries the cultural style of north German Protestantism (a style in part identified by the very disavowal of style itself). More than the archetypal Jew, Moses is the archetypal German. Moses may resolve this dialectic by instantiating the Protestant-Jewish fusion and the irony of their shared articulation as both aesthetic and antiaesthetic, style and antistyle. Schoenberg and his Moses both embrace a modernist understanding of culture that separates history from origin. Culture—here, German-Jewish culture—is understood according to creative fusion rather than originary determination. The fact that Moses loses and lacks the word may point to the power of the moment, in 1933, of that culture's dissolution.[45]

The same moment informs *Lulu*, left incomplete on Berg's death in 1935. If Lulu's scream can be understood to function as the hypermodernist analogue to Moses's silence, is it ideologically compromised in a similar way? I would argue that it isn't. Many people have suggested what Mitchell Morris adeptly writes in his article "Admiring the Countess Geschwitz": namely, that Lulu's *Todesschrei* is a picture cluster, that it is "accompanied by a tremendous fortissimo (*fff*) chord containing all twelve pitch-classes—the basic material of the opera's musical universe."[46] Lulu's death-scream is a sound cluster that breaks sound as it is a picture that shatters pictures. Recall that the opera audience's first view of Lulu is of the portrait of her being painted, an instant metonymy for the opera itself. Lulu's only adequate interlocutor in the opera, the Countess Geschwitz, is excluded from the scene of the picture of Lulu. (Her first lines are the opera's first words: "Darf ich eintreten [May I come in]," the words of the outsider, here a sexual outsider. The stage provides a spatial metaphor for the social and political scene, as it did in *Le nozze di Figaro* in 1786. Understood on its own, the moment of Lulu's death is Wagnerian: the orchestra draws on and totalizes its accumulated vocabulary to mark and control the existential moment. But this apparent echo of the end of *Götterdämmerung*, with an orchestral apotheosis and the silencing of the heroine, moves quickly

---

[45] In his last work, *Moses and Monotheism*, Freud also separated history from origin with his infamous argument that Moses was an Egyptian who created Hebrew monotheism by grafting an earlier form of Egyptian monotheism. The polarities that Freud and Schoenberg bring to their modernist Moseses (Egyptian-Hebrew in the one case and German-Jewish in the other) both point to an understanding of culture in terms of creative fusion rather than originary determination. See Freud, *Moses and Monotheism*, trans. K. Jones (New York: Vintage Books, 1939).

[46] Mitchell Morris, "Admiring the Countess Geschwitz," in *Queering the Pitch: The New Gay and Lesbian Musicololgy*, ed. P. Brett (New York: Routledge, 1994) pp. 359–60.

from a repetition through a quotation to a rejection. It is broken by Lulu's scream, an extramusical counterpoint to the totally musical "scream" of the orchestra, and secondly by the continuation of the final scene and the envoicing of the (momentarily) surviving Countess Geschwitz. Lulu's death, the shattering of the picture-Lulu by the scream, open the opera musically for Geschwitz, who is able to offer an elegy to music that rests outside the appropriate ideologies of musical representation. Whereas Moses's silence claims to disavow music, Lulu's scream and its orchestral analog incorporate all music, approximating, to repeat Lacou-Labarthe's metaphor, a photographic negative of Mélisande's silence.

I would support Morris's designation of Geschwitz as "queer to the end": an attribute understood through her final lament as residing outside, both dramatically and musically, the opera itself.

> And when Jack murders Lulu and mortally wounds the Countess, the opera is essentially over. Lulu's *Todesschrei*, as I have mentioned, encompasses the musical universe of the opera in its total chromatic saturation; what occurs after it is in some sense outside the opera. First, there is a view from the world of men in the form of a brutal postscript by Jack, himself only barely a man even though he is the essence of the opera's masculinity: "That was a piece of work!"

(I would interrupt Morris here to suggest that he misses a level of corroboration. The world of men here includes the composer Berg, musical son of the cluster Schoenberg–Dr. Schön–Jack the Ripper. "That was a piece of work" becomes a black-humored comment on the opera that has just ended, if Morris's sense of the ending is correct.)

> And then the Countess speaks, outside time and the opera's end where she seems to persist, outside the humanity that has been explicitly denied her as a being of the third sex. She doesn't die as the Schopenhauerian Schön and Lulu do—it may be that she doesn't exactly die at all, but remains even after the end of the opera, hovering. Queer to the end, her detachment from the sordid rounds of heterosexual exploitation makes her a noble ghost.

This passage allows itself a conflation of the homosexual and the queer, conferring the mantle of subversion on sexual identity alone. That conferral may result in an insufficient exploration of the richness and overdetermination of the queer (that is, the multiply subversive) quality of Geschwitz and of her stunning final moment. The first principle of the character Geschwitz is the differentiation, rather than duplication, of her love for Lulu vis-à-vis that of Lulu's male attachments. Geschwitz's sexual and moral queerness thus parallels the national queerness I have been stressing in this chapter. The point is therefore not, pace Morris, that Geschwitz's love is not heterosexual (qua ideological) in the same way that the point is not that *Pelléas*, *Bluebeard*, and *Makropoulos* are not German. The point is rather how lesbian love along with, in these examples, French, Hungarian, and Czech language and style do not attempt to substitute, impersonate, and duplicate the authority of heterosexuality and Germanness.

In a unique recovery of the Italian aesthetic of the fiction of pure voice that at the same time avoids its recolonization through the ideology of signification, Geschwitz represents that voice of subversive femininity that retains the right to speak German. But the finality and ultimately sexual as well as ethical subversion of her queer voice must be understood, I would argue, to reside in her literal assumption of center stage and center music at the conclusion of the opera. The opera *Lulu* does not end with Lulu's death, but with the apotheosis of a certain kind of extra-*Lulu* musical subjectivity in a world beyond Lulu but not, precisely, beyond the Countess Geschwitz. The violence of Lulu's murder is corroborated by her decidedly extramusical scream. This moment and its treatment by the composer fall perforce both within and outside the mainstay of the operatic convention of the deaths of heroines. It is typical and unique. Its uniqueness—its categorical difference from the death of Carmen, for example—involves the refusal of death on Lulu's part. Her person and her musical configuration both refuse to participate in the operatic convention that involves "the undoing of women." This stance of refusal, rather than any essential formal quality, takes her scream out of the bounds of music. The expiring Geschwitz's lament for Lulu—"Ich bin dir nah! bleibe dir nah, in Ewigkeit! [I am beside you, remain beside you, forever!]"—becomes, on the other hand, a Mahlerian lament for music, at once within and outside music, embodied and disembodied. It recalls the song "Ich bin der Welt abhanden gekommen [I have come unhinged from the world]" and its final declaration of a kind of love-death "in my song"—"in meinem Lied." There is still music here. The lament for music and subjectivity reveals the persistence of both.

Sound clusters transcend musical images. If Berg's musical style is personified in the character of Geschwitz, it takes form in a confrontation with a music of mnemonic devices and images; in other words, against the memory and picture systems that Wagner had provided his listeners. The musical idiom of *Lulu* does not confound either memory or subjectivity, but it does confound the mnemonic habits of its listeners—certainly its first-generation listeners but just as likely its later ones as well.

Lulu is subsumed by her image. Geschwitz's lament outlives even herself. The end of opera, the end of representation, does not and cannot mean the end of music, just as the end of subjectivity and voice is impossible, even— especially—in 1933. Or, summarize this chapter in the following way. In 1831, Norma proposes, from within her initial admonition against seduction by voice: "Assume that subjectivity is a woman. What then?" In 1933, Geschwitz laments: "Assume that subjectivity is a woman. What now?"

Chapter Seven

THE MUSICAL UNCONSCIOUS

The imaginary arc rendered by Gustav Mahler's late, completed symphonies, numbers five through nine, composed between 1901 and 1909, suggests the formal sequence of a gigantic classical symphony in four movements. According to this map—tendentious as it might seem, the Fifth Symphony would offer a sustained orchestral statement and narrative, corresponding to a self-assured, expository initial movement: a new beginning, a rededication of Mahler's symphonic exploration with a difference. The difference involves the resolution of the problem of representation. The dramatic logic of the first four symphonies might be described as the path of the subject and outsider through a maze and regime of representation. Variously, this subject obeys, resists, and transcends this regime. In the later works, the musical subject can be heard to argue both within and about the world, with representation amounting to one element of the world and therefore one object of reference.

"Mahler," Schoenberg wrote in 1912, "was no friend of program music."[1] The observation is incisive. Nonetheless, in his first four symphonies Mahler had oscillated, with evident agony, between an abstract musical discourse and the inclusion of words and representational narratives. The First Symphony (1884–88), the so-called Titan Symphony, told the story of a hero, its proximity to program music reinforced by its use of themes from the *Songs of a Wayfarer* cycle in the second movement and its invocations of Moravian and Jewish melodies in the third. The Second Symphony, the so-called Resurrection symphony, offered a parable of the inclusion and redemption of an outsider. Biographically, it accompanied and commented on Mahler's 1897 conversion from Judaism to Catholicism. In formal terms, this is much more a work of "program music" than the First Symphony. It adds a text belatedly, out of a sense of teleological necessity, much in the style of Beethoven's Ninth.[2] In a formal correlative to the work's message of the inclusion and redemption of the outsider, music itself is redeemed by text. Mahler appears to have been embarrassed by this resolution and, at least occasionally, dis-

---

[1] Arnold Schoenberg, "Gustav Mahler: In Memoriam," in *Style and Idea* (Berkeley and Los Angeles: University of California Press, 1975), p. 467.

[2] See my discussion of the Second Symphony in chapter 6, "The Catholic Culture of the Austrian Jews," of *Austria as Theater and Ideology: The Meaning of the Salzburg Festival* (Ithaca: Cornell University Press, 2000). See also Carl E. Schorske, *Eine österreichische Identität: Gustav Mahler* (Vienna: Picus Verlag, 1996).

avowed the program; at a performance of the work in Munich in 1900, he withheld the printed text from the audience, stating that "the music must speak for itself."[3] For Adorno, the program of the Second Symphony overcomes the first-person musical voice that opposes it from within the work: "The prototypical Scherzo of the Second Symphony, based on the *Wunderhorn* song of St. Anthony's sermon to the fishes, culminates in the instrumental outcry of one in despair. The musical self, the 'we' that sounds from the symphony, breaks down."[4]

From this point on in Mahler's symphonic work, the juxtaposition of music with and without texts, of "program" and "absolute" music, remained a key issue. Its resolution was not at hand. The gigantic Third Symphony added texts briefly in the middle of the work and then rhetorically disavowed their inclusion, choosing to end in the domain of absolute music, or music alone. In Adorno's terms, the Third Symphony engages the world and then leaves it behind to conclude in a mode of intense and protracted contemplation. The magisterial, contemplative final movement anticipated the mood and scale of the Ninth Symphony as perhaps no other moment in the Mahlerian canon does. The pattern of representation revealed and disavowed appears to be reversed in the Fourth Symphony (1900), which again adds text and voice in the final movement. This song-finale, "Das himmlische Leben," had in fact been composed in 1892. Max Graf's negative review of the Fourth Symphony in 1902 included the remark: "This symphony has to be read from back to front like a Hebrew Bible." Donald Mitchell observes that "it may have been that Mahler was not offended by what may have been intended or at least understood as a good Jewish joke. In any event, wittingly or unwittingly, Graf's perception matched Mahler's own."[5]

It might be worth interrogating the effect that Mahler's compositional dialectic on the issue of representation might have had on his dramaturgical and conducting style during his years at the helm of the Vienna Court Opera (1897–1907). What, for example, was the logic of his most enduring "invented tradition," which placed the Leonore Overture no. 3 after the emancipation scene in the second act of *Fidelio?* Was it the wish to reabsorb into music alone the dramatic action that has just unfolded onstage, and thus to validate it with a sterner idiom, achieving, in Guido Adler's phrase, "that clarity which was to him the highest principle of reproduction"?[6]

[3] Henry-Louis de la Grange, *Mahler* (Garden City: Doubleday, 1973), 1:596.

[4] Theodor Adorno, *Mahler: A Musical Physiognomy*, trans. E. Jephcott (Chicago: University of Chicago Press, 1992), p. 7.

[5] See Donald Mitchell, "Swallowing the Programme: Mahler's Fourth Symphony," in *The Mahler Companion*, ed. D. Mitchell and A. Nicholson (Oxford: Oxford University Press, 1999), pp. 187–216; p. 200. Mitchell draws his title from Adorno.

[6] Guido Adler, *Gustav Mahler*, trans. Edward Reilly (Cambridge: Cambridge University Press, 1982), p. 31.

The opening trumpet call and funeral music of the Fifth Symphony seem to recapitulate the life of the hero from the First Symphony. In the shadow of the expository confidence of the Fifth, the Sixth and Seventh Symphonies would together constitute a lengthy, indeed exaggerated, adagio movement, at least functionally calling into doubt the logic and solidity of the initial exposition. The Eighth provides the sequence with a titanic, carnivalesque scherzo, charting a musical odyssey from the baroque to the contemporary that duplicates the agenda of the great literary work it latches onto in its second half: Goethe's *Faust*, Part Two. The earlier agony of representation is replayed here as an immense and generous joke. In its final phrases, it lets *Faust*'s last verses do the theoretical work: "Alles vergängliche ist nur ein Gleichnis [Everything transitory is but a likeness]." You are not in the theater, it reminds the audience; you have not seen an opera, you are moving around inside Mahler's mind as well as your own. Finally, the magisterial Ninth, capable, as Adorno suggested, of understanding its own death through its incorporation of managed silences and its references to larger and unrepresentable silence, integrates exposition and self-doubt, achievement and defeat, into a metaphor of a generous and coherent life that can be honored for an integrity that courts neither representation nor resolution.

The conceit that a large-scale musical form, or series of works, might duplicate a smaller one—musical phylogeny duplicating musical ontogeny, as it were—is not without explicit historical precedent. In *Die Meistersinger von Nürnberg*, Wagner clearly duplicated at the level of the full, three-act opera the internal sequence of the three-part art song that lodges at the center of the plot. The point of the unified life lesson and music lesson taught by the old hero Hans Sachs to the young hero Walther von Stolzing (two sides of Richard Wagner) promotes the normative harmonization of order and innovation. Thus, the discipline of the three-part song can be compatible with great length and most specifically with the relative swell of the third part. Accordingly, the opera's third act is twice the length of each of the first two acts. The five-hour opera becomes the perfect song.

In Mahler's case, a four-part sequence with the adagio as second part and the scherzo as third duplicates the sequence of the classical symphony as no single symphony of his does on its own. At the same time, however, the tone of melancholic austerity that predominates in most of the individual symphonies (the obvious exceptions being the Second and Eighth), as well as in *Das Lied von der Erde*, dominates in these middle works as well. The long adagio movement in this fictional sequence corresponds to the Sixth and Seventh Symphonies, which together form the darkest, most difficult, and most opaque of Mahler's music. The Sixth is often described as tragic, in which case it is often observed that the narrative of the "life of the hero" conventionally assumed to be the default narrative of the Mahlerian symphony here finds a final and tragic denouement. It contains stretches of nostalgia, sentimentality, and even kitsch.

The Seventh Symphony resists such mnemonic vignettes. In its disavowal of ideology, it is Mahler's most fully skeptical work. What has often been remarked is that its three middle movements consist of a "shadowy, spectral Scherzo" surrounded by two slow movements, each of which carries the title *Nachtmusik*: night music.[7] The two *Nachtmusik* movements were composed first.

A circumstantial clue has both helped and impeded interpretation of this work, which Mahler talked about little. Mahler worked on this symphony in 1904 and 1905 (it was premiered only in September 1908). In the fall of 1903 he had visited Amsterdam; he later told Dutch friends that the first of the two "night music" movements had been inspired by Rembrandt's painting *The Night Watch*, which he had seen in the Rijksmuseum. Mahler's friend Alphons Diepenbrock commented that Mahler had not wanted to describe Rembrandt's *Night Watch* in music but had rather wanted to offer a "point of comparison." A stronger statement was offered by the conductor Willem Mengelberg, who affirmed that Mahler had been overwhelmed by Rembrandt's painting.

Rembrandt's *Night Watch* (1640–42) was commissioned by a militia of Amsterdam, specifically the company of Frans Banning Cocq. It depicts Banning Cocq, his splendidly costumed lieutenant Willem van Ruytenburgh, and "a gathering," in Simon Schama's words, "of scattered and diverse figures marching as a single body out from the obscure depths of a great arched gateway, past our viewpoint, and specifically a little way off to our left."[8] Rather than painting these two civic patricians in positions associated with formal portraiture, Rembrandt paints them in imaginary action—a theatrical gesture in service of an ideology of action and hence of the untheatrical. The painting celebrates the modernist, civic values of Calvinist Amsterdam, as exemplified by the citizen soldier. The two highlighted officers walk in animated conversation; Banning Cocq holds out his left hand in emphatic gesture while van Ruytenburgh looks him in the eye with intense but possibly not uncritical interest. Around them throng militia members (sixteen of whom had paid Rembrandt to have their portraits included), pikemen, musketeers, standard bearers, a hired drummer, and a powder monkey; its human ensemble, in Schama's words, "a microcosm not just of the militia but of the whole teeming city." Here is a part of Schama's summary of the painting and its effect, which I would ask the reader to absorb as if it were also about the work inspired by the painting, namely Mahler's symphony:

---

[7] The phrase "shadowy, spectral Scherzo" is from Donald Mitchell, "Mahler, Gustav," in *The New Grove Dictionary of Music and Musicians*, ed. Stanley Sadie (New York: Macmillan, 1980), 11:521.

[8] Simon Schama, *Rembrandt's Eyes* (New York: Alfred A. Knopf, 1999), p. 488.

Classicist critics were right to be appalled by *The Night Watch* because, despite its fine calculations of color, tonal values, composition, and form, it pays such scant attention to the rules of decorum. It was the most immodest thing Rembrandt ever did, not in self-advertisement but in terms of what he thought he could achieve in a single work. It is the acme of Baroque painting because it does so much, because it *is* so much. . . . It is a noise, a brag, a street play.[9]

The first movement of the Seventh Symphony, marked *Langsam (Adagio)*, develops a march through a melody sustained by horns and trumpets, supported by strings and drums. The first of the two *Nachtmusik* movements also depicts a patrol. Musical references abound to similar motives in *Des Knaben Wunderhorn*. Mahler himself said that he had imagined a " 'patrol' advancing though a 'fantastic *chiaroscuro*.' "[10] The term *chiaroscuro* would indicate a reference to Rembrandt's painting, which is governed by the same technique. At regular intervals, bowing is attacked *col legno*—with the stick side rather than the hair side of the bow—as if Rembrandt's pikes were being invoked. More than that, however, Mahler's own remark would seem to imply an interpretation of the deep plot of Rembrandt's painting. Mahler is associating a patrol with a presence of light within darkness. The light delivered is artificial; dawn is not at hand. Night music signifies a sustained condition of darkness rather than an interlude before the return of day and light. The desire for night over day is a standard device of love stories, from Shakespeare's *Romeo and Juliet* to, perhaps most relevantly here, Wagner's *Tristan und Isolde*. Removed, however, from the dynamics of hidden love, the recognition of obscurity and night as a prosaic existential reality has a particular austerity, and nowhere more so than in this work of Mahler's.

The movement decisively reverses the historical musical iconography of the night watch. In the nineteenth century, the tone is established resolutely by Mendelssohn's *Lobgesang* [Hymn of Praise] Symphony, the so-called Second Symphony of 1840. Its sixth number is a piece for tenor, soprano, and chorus in which the passing of night is delivered as an act of direct and complete redemption. God is quoted with the statement "Ich will dich erleuchten [I will enlighten thee]" followed by the following lines:

> TENOR:
> Wir riefen in der Finsternis:
> Hüter, ist die Nacht bald hin?
> [TENOR:
> We called in the darkness:
> Watchman, will the night soon pass?]

---

[9] Ibid., p. 495.

[10] Henry-Louis de la Grange, "Mahler: Symphony No. 7," liner notes, dir. Pierre Boulez, The Cleveland Orchestra, Deutsche Grammophon, 1996.

CHOR:
Die Nacht ist vergangen,
Der Tag aber herbeigekommen.
[CHORUS:
The night has passed,
The day is at hand.]

The chorus arrives to a thundering resolution that offers no more room for doubt than a Haydn oratorio.

The confidence of the Nightwatchman is rendered ironic but not really undermined in the lovely cameo in act 2 of Wagner's *Meistersinger*. He appears twice, first to announce that the clock has struck ten and to remind the Nurembergers to "guard your fires and your light" and second to announce that the clock has struck eleven. At his second appearance he is unaware that a riot has taken place between his two passages.

Mahler's music suggests the energy of thinking in the night rather than through it. That energy does suggest the presence and viability of a viable subjectivity. It cannot claim the rhetorical or contextual position whereby a heroic subjectivity is possible, but it does have the option of presenting its very achievement of subjectivity as heroic, accompanied as it is by the refusal to attach itself to a rosy or otherwise ideological picture of the world. In this context, we might recharacterize Mahler's leading narrative trope as that not of the hero but of subjectivity itself.

Mahler's musical discourse of subjectivity and its survival into the twentieth century parallels Freud's project of psychoanalysis, whose goal can also be glossed, I would argue, as the survival of subjectivity in a world of multiply and increasingly alienated subjects. Running throughout Freud's work is the principle that the secular, immanent, and political world cannot be escaped or transcended. As early as 1893 he concluded his *Studies on Hysteria* with the statement that the goal of therapeutic intervention is to "succeed in transforming . . . hysterical misery into common unhappiness"; in *Civilization and Its Discontents* (1930) he repeated that "we cannot fall out of this world."[11] Adorno's corollary, with reference to Mahler: "What the immanence of society blocks cannot be achieved by an immanence of form derived from it."[12]

Freud redefined subjectivity for the twentieth century in a manner consistent with the metaphor of the night watch. Like Rousseau, he divided the legacy of the Enlightenment between the values of reason, whose retention he prized, and of transparence, which he viewed skeptically as an agent of ideology, or instrumental reason. The relationship of reason with nontranspar-

---

[11] Josef Breuer and Sigmund Freud, *Studies on Hysteria*, trans. J. Strachey (New York: Basic Books, n.d.), p. 305; *Civilization and Its Discontents* (New York: W. W. Norton and Co., 1961), p. 12.
[12] Adorno, *Mahler*, p. 6.

ence generated Freud's theory of the unconscious. The unconscious, which Freud later renamed the id, grounds the human person in desire, unsociable desire that must be managed if civilization is to exist. Mental health (a term Freud uses in *Studies on Hysteria*) is built on measured contact between consciousness and the unconscious, between ego and id. This contact proceeds explicitly in the guise of a night watch, as it is in dreams that patterns of desire find their richest and most efficient medium for portage to the surfaces of consciousness. It is thus in *The Interpretation of Dreams* (1900) that Freud's theory of the mind and the method of psychoanalysis is first worked out. The night watch that characterizes the human mind operates through the delicate balance of reason and censorship, a balance present in both dreaming and interpreting. Since dreaming is posited to be universal, Freud accords a kind of radical egalitarianism to his model of the mind. Minds and lives are understood as intricate webs of desire, narrativity, obfuscation, and revision. Everyone is neurotic, but everyone is also Tolstoy. Having taken transparency away from the Enlightenment, Freud compensates for its loss with an enhanced promise of equality and creativity.

Mahler's symphonic work (in both senses of the word) strikes me as an uncanny combination of dreaming and interpreting. His false cadences work like dream structures, disappearing as they seem about to resolve. They resemble symphonic cadences of Brahms in the way they seem ethically to cut off narrative and rhetorical postures that cannot be fulfilled truthfully. But where Brahms's cadences form lines of argument and thereby correspond to activities of the conscious mind, of the ego, Mahler's engage patterns of desire in which the ego traffics, to the extent that it can, with the id.

In a discussion of *Moses und Aron*, Adorno cites Schoenberg on Mahler as follows:

> In this [the ninth] symphony the author hardly speaks any longer as a subject [*als Subjekt*]. . . . This work no longer speaks in the first person [*im Ich-Ton*]. What it offers is what might be called objective, almost dispassionate statements of a beauty which is only perceptible to those who can dispense with animal warmth, and feel at home in an atmosphere of cool intellectuality.[13]

---

[13] Theodor Adorno, "Sacred Fragment:" Schoenberg's *Moses und Aron*," in *Quasi Una Fantasia*, trans. R. Livingstone (New York: Verso, 1992), p. 231. I have supplied a few original German terms to underscore the accuracy of Livingstone's translation, which is important for my general argument. Adorno's source is Schoenberg, "Gedenkrede über Gustav Mahler" (Prague, 1913): the publication of a 25 March 1912 address in Prague. See Arnold Schoenberg, *Mahler: Rede am 25. März 1912 in Prag, mit einem Essay von Werner Hofmann* (Hamburg: Europäsche Verlaganstalt, 1993), pp. 47–48. This is the same essay as the one cited above, in translation, as "Gustav Mahler: In Memoriam," in *Style and Idea*. The translation of the same passage in *Style and Idea*, however, is inaccurate.

Adorno's purpose here is to invoke the vicarious function of Schoenberg's understanding of Mahler for the musical aesthetic of *Moses und Aron*. What remains unarticulated is the gap between Schoenberg's remarks and Adorno's own treatment of the Mahler Ninth. Adorno concludes his study *Mahler: A Musical Physiognomy* with a lyrical and melancholic chapter called "The Long Gaze," an appreciation of the Ninth Symphony and *Das Lied von der Erde* as melancholic reviews of lost pasts. From this point of view, in which Mahler's last works are asked to function vicariously for Adorno, the Mahler symphonies become "ballads of the defeated," of those "cast from the ranks, tramped underfoot."[14] Mahler's truth, in Adorno's summation and, indeed, totalization, lodges in his severing of the subject from the world: "Ich bin der Welt abhanden gekommen." At the same time, Adorno is not consistent in his melancholic totalization of Mahler. The same chapter contains a crucial observation on the linkages of analytical subjectivity and Jewishness in Mahler's music:

> What is Jewish in Mahler does not participate directly in the folk element, but speaks through all its mediations as an intellectual voice, something non-sensuous yet perceptible in the totality. This, admittedly, abolishes the distinction between the recognition of this aspect of Mahler and the philosophical interpretation of music in general.[15]

Here, Mahlerian (like Freudian) subjectivity is understood to be mediated and analytical. Adorno again: "Mahler's vigilant music is unromantically aware that mediation is universal."[16] Jewishness works as both a mode and a metaphor of subjectivity, where analytical distance can become indistinguishable from alienation. Adorno shares with Mahler the association of Jewishness with alienation, an association that is in both cases powerfully circumstantial and contextual but not, it must be emphasized, essential or essentializing. In important moments, the Jewish subject-position combines with the position of the refugee, which Adorno of course experienced literally: "Every intellectual in emigration is, without exception, mutilated."[17]

Mahler and Freud met only once, in an externally undocumented encounter that is conventionally reported as a clinical exchange. If it is fair to suggest that the survival of subjectivity forms their shared agenda for the twentieth century, then one would like to think that the topic came up during their four-hour walk through the streets of Leiden in August 1910.[18] A perceived

[14] Adorno, *Mahler*, pp. 166–67.

[15] Ibid., p. 149.

[16] Ibid., p. 15.

[17] Theodor Adorno, *Minima Moralia*, trans. E. Jephcott (London: New Left Books, 1974), p. 33. This thought dates from 1944.

[18] De la Grange, *Mahler*, 3: 769, Ernest Jones, *The Life of Sigmund Freud* (New York: Doubleday, 1955), p. 272.

crisis in his marriage had led Mahler to request the meeting, which Freud described many years later as follows:

> I analyzed Mahler for an afternoon in the year 1912 (or 1913?) in Leiden. If I may believe reports, I achieved much with him at that time. This visit appeared necessary to him, because his wife at the time rebelled against the fact that he withdrew his libido from her. In highly interesting expeditions though his life history, we discovered his personal conditions for love, especially his Holy Mary complex (mother fixation). I had plenty of opportunity to admire the capability for psychological understanding of his man of genius.[19]

It is impossible to know whether Freud's impression of Mahler's analytical gifts included a judgment on or indeed an interest in his music. Here is Adorno again (who had such an interest):

> Mahler's symphonies plead anew against the world's course. They imitate it in order to accuse; the moments when they breach it are also moments of protest. Nowhere do they patch over the rift between subject and object; they would rather be shattered themselves than counterfeit an achieved reconciliation.[20]

The Ninth Symphony clarifies the change in Mahler's musical rhetoric from the early focus on representation and its discontents to the late elucidation, as Adorno suggests, of musical subject and musical world. The irreconcilability between them results from the articulation of musical subjectivity as divided consciousness. Adorno's observation, cited just above, is essential and can be understood to have made possible the post-1960 understanding and valorization of Mahler. At the same time, however, Adorno's own sentimentalization of Mahler, as the hero of the very austerity and political integrity he demands, compromises at least functionally that very judgment. Put another way, Adorno resists that combination of analysis and symptomaticity that Mahler's musical discourse fearlessly combines; as a result, the symptomaticity of his own discourse increases.

The massive opening andante movement, I would suggest, addresses the same thing as the effect it produces on the listener: overstimulation. In this sense, the music includes the idea of death as one of the many stimuli of life that amount to the overabundance of the world. Composed of the present and the past, of everyday life and history, the world is too big and demands too much. For Freud, this excess of worldly pressure is what creates the unconscious, the residue of experience that consciousness can ignore for the sake of

---

[19] Sigmund Freud, letter to Theodor Reik, 4 January 1935, cited in Reik, *The Haunting Melody: Psychoanalytic Experiences in Life and Music* (New York: Grove Press, 1953), pp. 342–43. See also de la Grange, *Mahler*, 3:769; Ernest Jones, *The Life of Sigmund Freud* (New York: Doubleday, 1955), p. 272.

[20] Adorno, *Mahler*, p. 7.

its ability to function and to survive. When consciousness cannot control overstimulation, the result can be trauma.[21] In this opening movement, Mahler incorporates a world of overstimulation and produces a kind of musical trauma-effect.

In this case, it remains the task of the ensuing three movements to work through (to use a Freudian term) the trauma-effect of the first movement. The second movement scherzo is marked "in the tempo of a *Ländler*": the Austrian dance that is the predecessor to the waltz. It is not a parody, Adorno suggests, but a dance of death, a movement of "irreconcilable and obtrusive negativity."[22] The third movement is a rondo burlesque. The middle movements function as comic interludes but very dark ones. Paradoxically, they relieve the heaviness of the outside movement but wind up offering a more sinister sense of the world than either the opening andante or the closing adagio.

Overstimulation or analytical organization? Latent or manifest content? Dream or dream analysis? The import of Mahler's work for the succeeding century rests in the irresolvability of these alternatives. Mahler's musical idiom, here unlike Freud's interpretive/scientific one, is neither formally inclined nor ethically obligated to separate them. Mahler's listener does not occupy a contracted therapeutic venue, despite the therapeutic experience many might claim to have through the act of listening. This emotional and intellectual investment, which concert listeners have increased exponentially since the 1960s, recognizes instinctively and implicitly (if not often analytically) the work of subjectivity inherent in Mahler's late symphonic discourse. The music's distinction between subjectivity and subject resides in the recognition that subject and world cannot be separated. In play here is thus the Winnicottian principle that holds that the origins of subjectivity cannot be isolated to either the self or the world, and that the choice is not to be enacted.[23] Similarly, the Mahlerian blurring of self and world has nothing to do with a sentimentalizing assertion of a oneness between them. Rather, the boundary itself is always in mind and in question, giving the music its motivation and its urgency.

For this reason, I would call the Ninth Symphony the Song of the World. The pun in the epithet is obviously motivated by the work's compositional as well as emotional proximity to *Das Lied von der Erde*, the Song of the Earth. The genitive construction confuses deliberately: is this is a song about the earth or the earth's own song? The proposition that the earth, that nature, is speaking amounts to a neo-Romantic conceit that Mahler had used before:

---

[21] For a discussion of trauma as a quantitative disorder of pressure, see Eric L. Santner, *On the Psychotheology of Everyday Life* (Chicago: University of Chicago Press, 2001), pp. 31–32 and passim.

[22] Adorno, *Mahler*, p. 161.

[23] See the references to Winnicott on pp. 8 and 154 above.

the movements of the Third Symphony carry such titles as "What the earth tells me," "What love tells me," etcetera. But the earnestness, scale, and artifice of the work itself swiftly dispatch this precious scaffolding. The same holds for *Das Lied von der Erde*. Its final movement, *Der Abschied* [the departure] offers a sustained contemplation of death, its lyrics armed, to be sure, with archetypal Romantic metaphors: "Ich wandre in die Berge und suche Ruh' [I wander into the mountains and search for peace]." Spared of—and from— such lyrical correlatives, the Ninth Symphony is limited to music alone in the construction of a similar discourse, which adds the boundary of life and death to that of self and world. As Adorno asserts, Mahler's idiom offers no reconciliation between subject and object-world; contra Adorno, it draws no clear boundary between them.

The Ninth Symphony's final adagio movement corresponds to *Der Abschied* and indeed to the final movements of the Third and Fifth Symphonies in its intensification of rhetorical scale and analytical insurgency, accompanied by the disavowal of representation, a *Bilderverbot*. In this context Paul Bekker claimed perhaps more than he intended to with his (untranslatable) observation that all Mahler's symphonies are finale-driven: "alle Sinfonien Mahlers sind Finalsinfonien."[24] The adagio's perhaps most arresting effect lodges in the driving repetitions of its opening two-measure phrase and the a tempo first full thematic statement that immediately follows in measure 3. These statements repeat without signifying, indeed while apparently refusing to signify, marking death and the unconscious as two aspects of self and world (self-as-other and nonself). These gestures of refusal are allied with numerous and occasionally shocking silences. Mahler's silences work as membranes, shoring up at once the integrity and the self-imposed limitations of the music's first-person effusions. The music stops to take stock of itself, to question radically its relation to the world. In the silences lodges the profound locutionary and, I would argue, the ethical difference between Mahler's valedictory music and the similarly conceived rhetoric of Richard Strauss, for example in the *Metamorphosen*. Strauss's phrases, effecting wisdom and melancholy, suppress and repress silences, thus doing the same to subjectivity and its musicalized rhetoric of self-awareness.[25] Paralleling a baroque principle produced by anxiety, Strauss's music wants to fill a void, so that the void will not be filled by the overstimulatory energies of the world and the unconscious. Mahlerian subjectivity wants the unconscious and the analytical to traffic with one another, so that the resulting music might think about the world with heightened conviction.

---

[24] Paul Bekker, *Gustav Mahlers Sinfonien* (Berlin: Schuster & Loeffler, 1921), p. 20.

[25] For a longer discussion of the *Metamorphosen* and the comparison with Mahler, see my essay "Richard Strauss and the Question," in *Richard Strauss and His World*, ed. Bryan Gilliam (Princeton: Princeton University Press, 1992), pp. 164–89.

Index

Page numbers in italics refer to illustrations.